The Class Structure
of Pakistan

T0345803

The Class Structure of Pakistan

Taimur Rahman

OXFORD
UNIVERSITY PRESS

OXFORD
UNIVERSITY PRESS

Oxford University Press is a department of the University of Oxford.
It furthers the University's objective of excellence in research, scholarship,
and education by publishing worldwide. Oxford is a registered trade mark of
Oxford University Press in the UK and in certain other countries

Published in Pakistan by
Oxford University Press
No. 38, Sector 15, Korangi Industrial Area,
PO Box 8214, Karachi-74900, Pakistan

ISBN 978-0-19-940012-6

Second Impression 2021

Typeset in Adobe Garamond Pro
Printed on 55gsm Book Paper

Printed by Kagzi Printers, Karachi

for

Mahvash, Ama, Ba, and Jamal

Contents

List of Tables

Appendix

List of Figures

Introduction

One of Hegel's most significant contributions to modern thought was the notion that the development of history is the result of internal contradictions. Materialist epistemology infers these internal contradictions as class contradictions. The starting points of a materialist study of the dynamics of any given society, therefore, are the mode of production and class structure of that society. By the same token, the aims of this thesis are to examine the dominant mode of production and class structure of Pakistan.

The study looks at the pre-colonial and pre-capitalist[1] class structure of the period of the Mughal Empire, the specific colonial path of transition to capitalism, and the class structure of contemporary Pakistan. The objectives of this analysis are limited to the economic aspects of the question; hence, it is not a historiography nor does it delve into political, cultural, or ideological spheres in any depth.

In India, since the 1970s, there has been a rich debate on the question of the mode of production of that country (see for instance Byres, 1985; McFarlane, Cooper, and Jaksic, 2005; Patnaik, 1990). However, such a detailed discussion on the mode of production has yet to take place in Pakistan. While there has been much research on agrarian relations in the wake of the Green Revolution, this debate has mainly focused on whether agriculture could be characterised as feudal or capitalist (see for instance Khan, 1981; Zaidi, 2005). In this research on the Green Revolution it was, and still is, taken for granted that pre-capitalist relations were feudal.

The first proposition of this study is that the term 'feudalism' is inapplicable to the pre-colonial and pre-capitalist mode of production of South Asia. In contrast, Marx's notion of the Asiatic mode of production (AMP) is arguably more consistent with the historical evidence of the Mughal jagirdari system.[2]

Feudalism was a medieval European phenomenon based on serfdom, private ownership of land, and rent as the principal form of surplus extraction. Pre-colonial South Asia, however, was without serfdom, private ownership of land, or rent as the dominant form of surplus extraction. The pre-colonial mode of production of South Asia was based on the village community organised along the lines of a caste system. The jagirdar, a representative of the state, appropriated land revenue from village communities. However, neither the jagirdars nor the muzaras[3] were property owners.

In sum, the relations of production, forms of property, and dominant forms of surplus extraction that characterised Mughal South Asia were qualitatively different from those of medieval Europe. The historical evidence from the region seems to be more compatible with the concept of the AMP.

The second proposition is that the specific paths of capitalist transition of South Asia and Europe were distinct from each other. Whereas the European transition towards capitalism occurred through the republican and/or the Junkers path (Lenin, 1899: Preface; Moore, 1966), the transition of South Asia occurred under the influence of colonialism. This colonial path included three distinct features: foreign domination, siphoning of surplus, and capitalism planted on the AMP. The planting of capitalism on the AMP has produced a combination of European capitalism and the AMP in South Asia, that this study terms 'Asiatic capitalism'.

This book examines this concept of Asiatic capitalism through an empirical study of the dominant agrarian relations in contemporary Pakistan. Evidence suggests that wage labour is present, but not dominant, in agriculture. Instead, various forms of Asiatic labour relations remain dominant. At the same time, there has been an increase in land inequality over the last sixty years indicating continuing differentiation of the peasantry. There is also a trend away from tenant farming and towards owner farming. These patterns seem to indicate that pre-capitalist relations continue to exist within the overall framework of a capitalist economy.

Lastly, the study empirically demonstrates the dramatic structural transformation of the economy that has occurred in the last century. The small and isolated village communities made up the economic foundation of the AMP. The enormous increase in the population, together with the development of massive urban centres, since Independence demonstrates how the ancient mode of production is being superseded by a new mode of production. In relation to the history of South Asia, this transformation is historically unprecedented and can be seen to accelerate in the second half of the last century.

However, the AMP is not being replaced by large-scale capitalism; rather, mainly by petty commodity production and small-scale capitalism. The vast majority of the agricultural workforce is not engaged in wage labour. Similarly, the majority of the non-agricultural working population is engaged in handicraft and manufacturing. In sum, the class structure of contemporary Pakistan is dominated by Asiatic capitalism in agriculture, and petty commodity production and small-scale capitalism in manufacture.

Given that this book examines the class structure of Pakistan at a grand historical level—spanning the pre-colonial, colonial, and post-colonial periods—the regional or historical specialist may legitimately object that it fails to do justice to the complexity of the region, period, or debate among scholars. And, this would be a fair objection if the purpose of the thesis was indeed to present a detailed analysis of these periods or regions.

However, this is not the case. Instead, the purpose of examining these different regions and periods is only to counter-pose the principal and extremely general features of their class structures to our subject of interest: that is, the class structure of contemporary Pakistan. For instance, the Mughal Empire is examined only to the extent that the principal features of its class structure can be contrasted with those of feudal Europe in order to argue that the former is not feudal but Asiatic. Hence, any scholar looking for a detailed examination of the class structure of the Mughal Empire or of feudal Europe in this book is bound to be disappointed. Similarly, the colonial path of transformation is examined only to the extent of identifying the principal and most general features of this transition in relation to European transitions. Hence, any scholar looking for a detailed examination of colonialism or European transitions will equally be disappointed.

Given then, that this book only examines these regions at a very broad level, is it perhaps not prudent to leave out these grand historical discussions and just focus on contemporary Pakistan? Moreover, post-modernist scepticism of grand historical narratives equally comes to mind in this regard.

The disadvantage of an approach without recourse to comparative history, even if it is at a very broad level, is that it can only offer us a snapshot frozen in time. It cannot offer an understanding of either the historical context or of the movement and trajectory of the class structure of Pakistan. Hence, it argues that to understand the historical movement and trajectory of the class structure of contemporary Pakistan, it is necessary to examine the nature of pre-capitalist relations and the colonial transformation.

Critics may legitimately argue that there are very many exceptions to the general features identified in this study. These criticisms would be entirely valid if this study at any point asserted that these general features were uniform or universal. However, it only contrasts certain dominant features of Mughal India, Colonial India, and Medieval Europe. Last but certainly not least, this study readily acknowledges, in the detailed literature reviews on the subjects, that these dominant features make sense only within a certain framework of scholarship.

With all these limitations of grand historical generalisations, made within a Marxist framework, it is only fair to ask whether this book advances our understanding of the specifics of the class structure of contemporary Pakistan or whether it makes a meaningful contribution to social sciences. One would argue that it makes an original contribution in two ways.

Firstly, class analyses have largely been neglected in the literature on South Asia in recent years (Chibber, 2006). While there have been studies about agrarian relations (Akram-Lodhi, 1993; Khan, 1981), the post-colonial state (Alavi, Burns, Knight, Mayer, and McEachern, 1982), and the class structures of Pakistani villages (Ahmed, 1977) or labour movements (Ali, 2005; Shaheed, 2007), most of this work is either out of date or focuses only on specific localities. There have been few published studies on the class structure of Pakistan in recent times. This study, therefore, fills a gap in our knowledge by examining the class and mode of production of Pakistan as a whole, and in contemporary times.

Secondly, this study also makes an original contribution by advancing three hypotheses:

1) By utilising the concept of the AMP, it raises concerns about the unilinear interpretations of history.
2) It makes the case for multiple paths of capitalist transformation. In the context of South Asia, it argues that the transition to capitalism

does not occur through the republican or Junkers path, but through a colonial path.

3) It argues that the socio-economic formation of contemporary Pakistan is a transitory form that combines features of the Asiatic and capitalist modes of production, termed 'Asiatic capitalism'.

PREMISES OF THE STUDY: MODE OF PRODUCTION AND CLASS

This work on the class structure of Pakistan is based on the framework of historical materialism. The starting point of a materialist analysis of society is the investigation of the material conditions of the existence of that society (Marx and Engels, 1968: 61).

One of the most significant insights of historical materialism is that the social, political, cultural, and ideological conceptions of humans are dialectically connected to the economic foundations of a given society. Marx expressed these findings succinctly in an oft-quoted passage in the *Preface to a Contribution to the Critique of Political Economy* (Marx, 1998d: 8):

> In the social production of their life, men enter into definite relations that are indispensable and independent of their will, relations of production which correspond to a definite stage of development of their material productive forces. The sum total of these relations of production constitutes the economic structure of society, the real foundations, on which rises a legal and political superstructure and to which correspond definite forms of social consciousness. The mode of production of material life conditions the social, political and intellectual life process in general. It is not the consciousness of men that determines their being, but, on the contrary, their social being that determines their consciousness.

In this passage, Marx suggests that the mode of production is the sum total of relations of production that correspond to a given productive force of society. However, there are, of course, other definitions of the mode of production. Hindess and Hirst argue that a mode of production is 'an articulated combination of relations and forces of production' (1975: 9). The term 'articulated' implies that only one set of relations of production can correspond to one set of forces of production. Chris Wickham argues that the definition offered by Hindees and Hirst is overly 'restrictive' (Wickham 1985: 185). Hamza Alavi argues that the mode of production should also incorporate the superstructure (Alavi et al., 1982).

This study utilises the definition developed by G.E.M. de Ste. Croix who argues that the defining feature of any mode of production is the mode of surplus extraction (Ste. Croix, 1981: 133). This criteria is derived directly from Marx's following observation (1956: 790–791):

> The specific economic form in which surplus-labour is pumped out of direct producers determines the relationship of the owners of means of production and direct producers. . . . It is always the direct relationship of the owners of the conditions of production to the direct producers, which reveals the innermost secret, the hidden basis of the entire social structure, and with it the corresponding specific form of the state.

It is the mode of surplus extraction that determines the size and utilisation of surplus, distribution of the products, direction and pace of growth, and the nature and degree of power of the ruling class and the state (Ste. Croix, 1981: 173).

Moreover, since the mode of surplus extraction is directly tied to the relations and forces of production, it is not in contradiction with Marx's definition in the *Preface to a Contribution to the Critique of Political Economy*. Ste. Croix's definition offers a relatively succinct concept that sums up Marx's notion of a mode of production being the "sum total of relations of production that correspond to a given productive force of society' (Marx, 1998d: 8).

For instance, Marx and Engels also concluded that the modes of surplus extraction for ancient society, feudalism, and capitalism were based on slavery, serfdom, and wage labour, respectively. In their writings, they frequently equated the mode of surplus extraction, labour relations, and the mode of production. For instance, Engels (1891: 216) wrote:

> Slavery is the first form of exploitation, the form peculiar to the ancient world; it is succeeded by serfdom in the middle ages, and wage-labor in the more recent period. These are the three great forms of servitude, characteristic of the three great epochs of civilization; open, and in recent times disguised, slavery always accompanies them.

A criticism may be levelled that societies rarely exist in pure forms and that actual existing societies combine several modes of production (see Wolpe, 1980). The identification of the dominant mode has been a matter of significant academic debate from the late 1960s (Balibar, 1970; Laclau, 1977; Poulantzas, 1973). How does one define the dominant mode of production within a complexity of social relations? Does one define the dominant mode of production in terms of surplus extraction, labour relation, reproduction of economic relations, or political power? This study is of the view that the dominant mode of production cannot be identified by a priori definition, but only by investigation of the dynamics of specific social formation.

On the one hand, one needs to avoid the error of 'over-schematic' arguments (Wickham, 1985: 166). That is, as Mukhia explains, 'to argue against the notion of an Indian feudalism need not lead one to the acceptance of the Asiatic mode of production' (Mukhia, 1981: 293). On the other hand, in the words of Wickham (1985: 166), one also needs to avoid the error of formulating:

> new modes or categories of analysis that are, in effect, nothing more than claims in traditional historical fashion for the historical uniqueness of specific areas: 'I study Byzantium, or some part of Africa, or India, or the Mediterranean; it is empirically different from the medieval West or the Roman Empire; therefore I can establish a new mode'—Byzantine, or African, or Indian mode.

Wickham argues that Habib, Lewin, Mukhia, and Anderson give in to this 'defeatist' method (ibid.). The extreme of such 'defeatist' methodology would be Maxime Rodinson who argues that 'if one were to try and classify the modes of production thus observed, the result would be an infinite variety' (Rodinson, 1977: 74).

Avoiding such over-schematic and defeatist arguments, the study does not attempt to fit the mode of production into any pre-conceived schematic of history. Instead, it attempts to proceed from the facts rather than from any ideal forms.

Class

There is a rich debate on what constitutes a 'class'. Some define 'class' in terms of hierarchy, income, or class-consciousness (Habermas, 2006:

281–294; Roberts, 1975: 13–31; Turner, 1990: 169–196). For the purposes of this study, however, class is defined as a historically constituted relationship of a stratum of society to the means of production. The study uses Lenin's definition of class (1919):

> Classes are large groups of people differing from each other by the place they occupy in a historically determined system of social production, by their relation (in most cases fixed and formulated in law) to the means of production, by their role in the social organisation of labour, and, consequently, by the dimensions of the share of social wealth of which they dispose and the mode of acquiring it. Classes are groups of people one of which can appropriate the labour of another owing to the different places they occupy in a definite system of social economy.

For instance, the capitalist class is defined as 'the class of modern capitalists, owners of the means of social production and employers of wage labour' (Marx and Engels, 1998: 8). The proletariat is defined as 'the class of modern wage labourers who, having no means of production of their own, are reduced to selling their labour power in order to live' (ibid.).

This definition makes it very clear that the defining properties of a class are not subjective but, in fact, objective relations to the means of production. In other words, classes may or may not be conscious of their interests and their members need not be aware of their material relationship. However, the degree of self-consciousness about their objective economic relationship to the means of production plays no determining role in their social existence.

Property is the juridical expression of a class-based division of labour that, in turn, is the economic foundation of surplus extraction. On this basis, Marx argued that the various modes of production based on surplus extraction can also be identified by the different forms of ownership. He broadly identified four forms of society that have been the subject of controversy since then (Marx, 1998d):

> In broad outlines Asiatic, ancient, feudal, and modern bourgeois modes of production can be designated as progressive epochs in the economic formation of society.

The study takes these definitions as a starting point. These concepts are re-examined in greater detail in the relevant chapters.

FORMAT OF THE ARGUMENT

Given the absence of a substantial body of work on the AMP in Pakistan, it is imperative to examine how others have addressed this question in their contexts. Hence, Chapter 1 reviews the academic literature on the concept of the AMP.

Chapter 2 examines the historical data and the principal critiques of the AMP in South Asia. It argues that jagirdari is not feudalism and also examines the path of capitalist development of South Asia. It argues that South Asia's path of transition to capitalism was different from European transitions to capitalism. This path is termed 'the colonial path of transition to capitalism'. It examines some of the features of this path of transition and argues that colonialism resulted in a transitory form which was a mixture of the Asiatic and capitalist modes of production. This transitory form is termed 'Asiatic capitalism'. In Asiatic capitalism, commodity production and private ownership of the means of production are combined with pre-capitalist forms of unfree labour (Asiatic labour relations).

Chapter 3 examines the agrarian relations of contemporary Pakistan in relation to the concept of Asiatic capitalism. It demonstrates, on the one hand, the growing differentiation of the peasantry and the gradual erosion of traditional tenant farming. And, on the other, the relatively slow development of wage labour. It concludes that the available data does not contradict the notion of Asiatic capitalism.

Chapter 4 examines the development of industry in Pakistan in relation to the concept of Asiatic capitalism. It argues that the non-agricultural sector is dominated by petty commodity production and small-scale capitalism. Large-scale industry is mainly the product of market structures created by the state and that industrial labour is a small percentage of the Pakistani working classes. The available data suggest that Asiatic labour relations continue to exist within the context of petty commodity production and small-scale capitalism.

In conclusion, this study argues that the mode of production of contemporary Pakistan is best described as Asiatic capitalism. This conclusion points towards avenues for future research, linking these findings regarding class structure to politics, society, and culture.

NOTES

1. Since capitalism was introduced through colonialism, pre-colonial and pre-capitalist refers to one and the same period in this context.
2. 'Jagirdari' were pre-capitalist relations under the Mughal Empire.
3. 'Muzara' is an Indian peasant working under the jagirdar.

1

Feudalism or the Asiatic Mode of Production

He [Shukobsky] feels himself obliged to metamorphose my historical sketch of the genesis of capitalism in Western Europe into an historico-philosophic theory of the general path imposed by fate upon every people, whatever the historic circumstances in which it finds itself, in order that it may ultimately arrive at the form of economy which will ensure, together with the greatest expansion of the productive powers of social labour, the most complete development of man. But I beg his pardon. (He is both honouring and shaming me too much.)

Marx (1877)

Academic literature on the AMP spans three periods. The first is of the writings between the seventeenth and nineteenth centuries. The development of the materialist interpretation of history and the concept of the AMP by Marx and Engels constitutes another period. During this period, the concept of the AMP was accepted largely without controversy by the Marxist intelligentsia. In the third period, the development of the anti-colonial movement led to debates that resulted in the rejection of the AMP. Thereafter, the concept has largely disappeared from the lexicon of the communist parties and Marxist intellectuals. It has, occasionally, aroused interest after the Second World War, either as a result of Karl Wittfogel's anti-communist interpretation or of the writings of certain French and Soviet Marxists.

Given the incredibly broad sweep of Western academic literature on the AMP, it is impossible to do justice to these works within one chapter. This section provides only a brief overview of some of the most influential writings on the subject. It begins with the orientalist literature of the seventeenth century. Then, it re-examines Marx's and Engels' writings on the AMP. Given that Marxists around the world continue to appeal to the authority of these figures, it was important, for the purposes of this study, to explain their views in some detail. Lastly, it briefly revisits the debates that led to the decline of the AMP within the Marxist movement.

WHAT IS THE ORIENT?

The earliest Western conception of the Orient can be found in the writings of Herodotus and Aristotle in Ancient Greece (Aristotle, 1988: VII. vi.327b; Herodotus, 1942). Later, in the medieval period, Western writings were mostly in the form of travelogues. Of these, the earliest surviving text was written by Marco Polo in the thirteenth century, entitled *Il Milione*[1] (Polo, 1958). With the development of better techniques of navigation and the gradual emergence of a world market in the sixteenth century, the number of European explorers travelling the globe searching for new markets and opportunities increased. Their writings, about their travels, gave rise to what has subsequently been called 'orientalist literature' (Said, 1978). During this period, the term 'Orient' was mainly used for China, South Asia, and Persia. Later, the Turkish Empire, the Arab lands, and North Africa were also included; at times, Central Asia (Khiva and Bukhara) was considered to be an extension of South Asia and Persia (Krader, 1975: 5).

ORIENTALIST WRITINGS

TRAVELOGUES

From the travelogues of the seventeenth century, two important concepts about the Orient were assimilated into European thought: first, that Asia was without private property in land; second, that Asiatic states were despotic (Krader, 1975: 28).

Orientalist literature during this period was closely linked to Western commercial interests in South Asia. Anglo-Indian literature begins with Father Thomas Stephens' letters[2] and Ralph Fitch's travel journal (Edwardes, 1972; Southwood, 1924). Facing hostilities with the Dutch and Portuguese traders in the Indian Ocean,[3] the British East India Company was convinced of the absolute need to obtain a guarantee, from the Mughal Emperor, for the safeguard of their trade. Consequently, at the request of the British East India Company, the British Crown established a diplomatic mission in India under Sir Thomas Roe. His journal, about this diplomatic mission to the court of the Mughal

Emperor Jehangir in Agra from 1615–1618, and Edward Terry's account of the same mission entitled *Relation of a Voyage to the Easterne India* were closely tied up with British interests in India (Roe, 1926; Terry, 1655).

Similarly, William Methold's *Relations of the Kingdome of Golconda* (narrating the author's experiences in South India in 1618), William Bruton's *Newes from the East Indies* (a narrative about how the British gained a foothold in Orissa in 1632), and John Fryer's *New Account of East India and Persia* (dealing with contemporary politics of western India during the reign of Aurengzeb), all belong to the milieu in which the British East India Company expanded its interests in South Asia (Methold, 1931; Ward & Trent, 1907–21: Ch. X § 1).

Similar efforts were made by France under Louis XIV who, in order to develop trade with India, formed the French East India Company in 1664 under his finance minister Jean Colbert. Colbert gave Francois Bernier the task of providing information on India in order to assist the further establishment of the Company. Bernier sailed for Surat in 1658 and, in March 1659, became the personal physician of Dara Shikoh. In addition to providing an account of the war of succession for the throne between Dara Shikoh and Aurengzeb, Bernier's collection of letters, published as *Travels in the Mughal Empire*, contains detailed information about the economic, religious, and social conditions of Mughal India (Bernier, 1934). Even greater detail is contained in Jean Chardin's ten-volume book entitled *The Travels of Sir John Chardin* (Chardin, 1996). Similarly, Jean Tavernier's *Travels in India* and Jean de Thevenot's *Voyages* have also been cited extensively (Tavernier, 1925).

Aside from these British and French writers, Italian writer Niccolao Manucci's descriptions of the Mughal court in *Storia do Mogor* is equally regarded as one of the most exhaustive accounts of that period (Manucci, 1996).

ENLIGHTENMENT VIEWS OF THE ORIENT

The eighteenth century, also known as the *Age of Enlightenment*, witnessed a dramatic transformation in all spheres of human life in Europe: in science the development of Newtonian physics, in philosophy the challenge of continental rationalism and British empiricism, in the arts the re-emergence of neoclassicism, and in politics the growth of republicanism are considered some of the hallmarks of this period. Marxist historians view this century as a period of the increasing political dominance of the bourgeoisie over feudalism in Europe.

During this period of political struggle between feudalism and a newly emerging bourgeoisie, the attention of European thinkers was turned to questions of state power. Oriental politics was of interest to Enlightenment thinkers, principally to make a point about European politics (Krader, 1975: 43). One of the main theoretical contributions in this century, with respect to the Orient, was the theory of 'oriental despotism' (O'Leary, 1989: 59).

Montesquieu, considered to be the foremost representative of the doctrine of oriental despotism, divided the governments of the world into three categories: republic—a state in which sovereignty belongs to the people; monarchy—a state in which one person governs 'by fixed and established laws', and the nobility checks the power of the monarch; and despotism—a state where 'a single person directs everything by his own will and caprice' (Montesquieu, 1977, Book II). Montesquieu based this distinction between oriental despotism and European monarchies on the writings of seventeenth century European travelogues. He argued that whereas the power of the European monarchs was constrained by the rule of law enforced by the autonomous nobility, Asiatic rulers had despotic (absolute) power over their courtiers. In other words, oriental despotism described the relations between Asiatic rulers and their courtiers and carried no necessary implications about the power of the Asiatic ruler over peasants. In his book *The Spirit of the Laws*, Montesquieu ascribed oriental despotism to the absence of a temperate climate (Montesquieu, 1977). Montesquieu argued that people living in warm countries were 'hot-tempered', whereas those living in cold countries were 'icy' and 'stiff'. In contrast, the climate of middle Europe, especially France, was optimal for the development of republican governments. This explanation, for obvious reasons, is no longer accepted. However, the theory of the three forms of state power was so influential that, whether in opposition or agreement, nearly all the political thinkers of that period defined their views in relation to it (Sawer, 1977: 13).

For instance, Immanuel Kant described the government of China as paternalistic and despotic (Kant, 1983). Herder likened China to an 'embalmed Egyptian mummy' and stated that 'in China and India . . .

there is no true historical progress but only a static unchanging civilization' (Fogel, 1984: 3–5; Rose, 1951: 58). Baudeau claimed that the arbitrary will of the Asiatic despot extended not only over the property of the subject but even over his person (Krader, 1975: 33). Anne-Robert-Jacques Turgot maintained that although civilisation in Asia had developed before Europe, this advantage of early development had turned into its greatest disadvantage because, as a result, the East was not sufficiently ripe for the task of moral and political development (Krader, 1975: 42).

However, it would be incorrect to conclude from this characterisation that the European appraisal of the East was entirely negative. This negative appraisal is often drawn from the use of the term 'despotic'. But the term 'despot' has itself undergone a change in connotation. The word despot is etymologically traced to the Greek term 'despotes', which means 'master' or 'absolute ruler'. Through Medieval Latin it was transferred to sixteenth century French vocabulary as 'despote'. During the Byzantine Empire the term was, in fact, a formal title that the emperor accorded to provincial rulers in the realm. After the Turkish conquest of Constantinople, the term merely denoted a minor Christian ruler under the Turkish Empire. Thus, the term did not take on a strongly pejorative meaning until relatively recently.

Moreover, most European writers drew a distinction between 'despotism' and 'tyranny'. For instance, Voltaire, who greatly admired China, wrote that Montesquieu's distinction between European monarchies and Asiatic empires was put to use only by 'obscurantist, obstinate, and egotistic magistrates' (Koebner, 1951). He made a distinction between despotism and tyranny and argued that although China's empire was despotic, it was not tyrannical (O'Leary, 1989: 66). In his *Essay on Customs*, Voltaire argued that in China 'good' was rewarded and 'evil' punished (Voltaire, 2001). On this basis he opined that a meritocracy and sage-rulers governed China. This view, shared by F. de la Mothe le Vayer and Christian Wolff, gave rise to the theory of the philosopher-king.

This distinction between despotism and tyranny is also found in the Physiocrats. For example, Quesnay had a very positive appraisal of China's government in his memoirs. He reasoned, in direct contrast to Montesquieu, that although the government was despotic, it was 'legitimate' because it conformed to a universal system of natural laws

(Krader, 1975: 34). In much the same way, Alexander Dow drew a distinction between 'arbitrary' and 'legitimate despotism' (Krader, 1975: 35). Marquis de Condorcet's theory of the ten stages of progress also accepted the distinction between arbitrary and legitimate despotism (Condorcet, 1995; Krader, 1975: 43). Paul-Henry Thiry Holbach, too, utilised the distinction between despotism and tyranny.[4] F. de la Mothe le Vayer, Christian Wolff, G.W. Leibniz, and Matthew Tindal made an even more positive appraisal of Chinese society (Krader, 1975: 29–43). Abbé Raynal, writing against the British East India Company, said that in Bengal 'a methodical tyranny had succeeded to an arbitrary authority' (Krader, 1975: 36). Thus, while Raynal considered the Mughal Empire to be despotic, he associated tyranny only with British rule in India. J.G. von Justi and Adam Ferguson denied, altogether, that governments of the East could be characterised as despotic (Kalyvas and Katznelson, 1998; Menzel, 1956;). For example, Justi stated that the 'chief characteristic of despotism is not found in China, where the most respectable servants of the State are bound precisely to the laws' (Krader, 1975: 32). Adam Ferguson argued that despotism was the product of the degeneration of government and, therefore, not associated necessarily with the Orient (Ferguson, 1966).

So, we note that, for eighteenth century European thinkers, despotism was not the equivalent of tyranny. Moreover, some thinkers altogether denied the legitimacy of the use of the term exclusively for Asia.

POLITICAL ECONOMY AND THE ORIENT

Before the nineteenth century, explanations for the real or alleged differences between European and Asiatic medieval states were principally sought in religious, climatic, racial, and moral theories. The emergence of classical political economy, at the end of the eighteenth century, opened the door to explanations that examined the connection between politics and the economy. Ownership of land, the land revenue tribute extracted from the village community by the State, and the social division of labour now became central to understanding Asian society.

Adam Smith and Richard Jones are credited with having developed the point of view of classical political economy on Asia (Krader, 1975: 55). Smith introduced the notion that, in Asia, there was an identification of land tax and land rent, and asserted that the oriental state paid particular attention to public works (Smith, 1976: 204, 251–3). Jones posited that there were four types of rent: serf rent (labour rent), rent in kind, ryot rent (rent as tax), and cottier rent; and reasoned that the absence of private property in Asia formed the economic basis for oriental despotism (Jones, 1956: 7–8, 138: 141–2).

This notion, that the absence of private property was the economic basis of oriental despotism, was widely held by the thinkers of that period. James Mill and John Stuart Mill held that the Mughal emperor was the owner of land (Krader, 1975: 67–8; Mill, 1821: 138–9, 145, 213, 224). John Stuart Mill opined that, as result of the lack of development of private property, Asiatic society was stagnant. He argued that it developed extremes of riches and poverty and, on the whole, remained less developed economically than Ancient Roman society (Krader, 1975: 56–7; Mill, 1848: 30, Book II, ch. 9, section 1 & 4). Alexander Dalrymple, Sir J.B. Phear, Henry Maine, Sir William Hunter, and M.M. Kovalevsky were all of the opinion that there was no private property (in land) in India (Hunter, 1882: 517; Krader, 1975: 65–7; Maine, 1907). Similarly, Abbé Guyon and Olcarious held the view that, given the despotic nature of the Asiatic state, all rights of people as private owners were simply overridden (Krader, 1975: 68–9).

Hegel was scathingly critical of the lack of development of individual property and, especially, of the Indian caste system. He argued that this system gave scope for unlimited tyranny by destroying all feelings of self, moral consciousness, and rebellion. He also noted that India had no recorded history and that its ideological life was dominated by religion (Hegel, 1837).

However, there were some European thinkers who upheld that private property existed in Asia. Mark Wilks wrote that private ownership of land was an ancient right in India (Wilks, 1930: vol. 1, 117). He argued that the village was the repository of the sum of rights to the land and adjudged any dispute between private owners (Krader, 1975: 62). Similarly, Krishna, Anquetil-Duperron, Baden-Powell, Pohlmann, and Cambell argued that community property did not exist in India (O'Leary, 1989: 66–7; Krader, 1975: 65–7). Mountstuart Elphinstone, though indecisive, also weighed in on the side of individual proprietorship of land (Elphinstone, 1841: 71; Krader, 1975).

MARX AND ENGELS ON THE ASIATIC MODE OF PRODUCTION IN INDIA

Nineteenth century political economy had a profound impact on Karl Marx and Frederick Engels who developed the concept of the AMP based on the writings of these predecessors of theirs. Since the concept of AMP is principally attributed to them, it makes sense to look at their writings on the subject in some detail. The first reference in their writings to oriental despotism can be found in *Critique of Hegel's Philosophy of Right*. Marx (1843a: Remark to § 279) wrote:

> Either, as in Greece, the *res publica* was the real private concern, the real content of the citizens and the private man was slave, that is, the political state as political was the true and sole content of the citizen's life and will; or, as in Asiatic despotism, the political state was nothing but the private will of a single individual, and the political state, like the material state, was slave. What distinguishes the modern state from these states in which a substantial unity between people and state obtained is not that the various moments of the constitution are formed into particular actuality, as Hegel would have it, but rather that the constitution itself has been formed into a particular actuality alongside the real life of the people, the political state has become the constitution of the rest of the state.

The thrust of the above passage is that while the bourgeois state is very different from the ancient states of Greece and Asia, Hegel's view that the bourgeois state has resolved the conflict between private interests and the general interest is incorrect. This passage lends the impression that the young Marx subscribed to the conventional eighteenth century notion of oriental despotism. However, in a letter written to Arnold Ruge in the same year, Marx (1843b) rejected Montesquieu's distinction between European monarchies and Asiatic despotism:

> The monarchical principle in general is the despised, the despicable, *the dehumanised man;* and Montesquieu was quite wrong to allege that it is honour [Montesquieu, *De l'esprit des lois*]. He gets out of the difficulty by distinguishing between monarchy, despotism and tyranny. But those are names for *one and the same* concept, and at most they denote differences in customs though the principle remains the same.

In the 1840s, Marx did not write or publish any major pieces on Asia. At this stage, he was principally occupied with the development of historical materialism. During his exile in London and after the failure of the 1848 revolutions, Marx began to study Asia more deeply. Influenced mainly by Hegel, he began by pondering the question of why the history of the East appeared as the history of religions. Upon reading François Bernier, Marx (1853a) felt he had arrived at the answer and wrote to Engels:

> Bernier rightly sees all the manifestations of the East—he mentions Turkey, Persia and Hindustan—as having a common basis, namely the *absence of private landed property*. This is the real key, even to the eastern heaven.

Engels (1853) replied:

> The absence of landed property is indeed the key to the whole of the East. Therein lies its political and religious history. But how to explain the fact that orientals never reached the stage of landed property, not even the feudal kind? This is, I think, largely due to the climate, combined with the nature of the land, more especially the great stretches of desert extending from the Sahara right across Arabia, Persia, India and Tartary to the highest of the Asiatic uplands. Here artificial irrigation is the first prerequisite for agriculture, and this is the responsibility either of the communes, the provinces or the central government.

Taking into consideration Engels' comments, Marx (1853b) summarised their findings:

> The stationary nature of this part of Asia, despite all the aimless activity on the political surface, can be completely explained by two mutually supporting circumstances: 1. The **public works** system of the central government and, 2. Alongside this, the entire Empire which, apart from a few large cities, is an agglomeration of **villages**, each with its own distinct organisation and each forming its own small world.

These two mutually supportive ideas, namely public works and the village community, formed the basis of a series of articles written on the impact of British imperialism on India and China, for the *New York Daily Tribune*, between 1852 and 1858. The most widely quoted of these articles, with respect to India, are 'The British Rule in India' and 'The Future Results of British Rule in India' (Marx, 1853: 1853b).

Scathing in his criticism of British colonialism, Marx wrote that England had broken the entire framework of Indian society and uprooted that society from all its ancient traditions and past history. The handloom, spinning wheel, and union between agriculture and manufacture were destroyed by British steam and science. Further, the great irrigation works were utterly neglected by the colonial government, resulting in famine and the destruction of Indian cities.

On the other hand, he cautioned against any kind of romanticism of the Asiatic system. He said that the AMP had made man the unresisting tool of superstition, enslaved society beneath traditional rules, and deprived it of all grandeur and historical energies. The result was an undignified, stagnate, and vegetative life. He maintained that the AMP had been the solid foundation of 'oriental despotism' and had 'restrained the human mind within the smallest possible compass' based on 'class and slavery' (ibid.).

These remarks may be interpreted as a justification for colonialism. However, Marx's position on the 1857 War of Independence clearly demonstrated that he supported the struggle for freedom from colonialism (see Anderson, 2010). At the same time, he felt that the destruction of the AMP and the introduction of capitalism was nonetheless a step forward in history. For Marx, the development of productive forces through capitalism was necessary for the final end of class exploitation. Thus, he argued that the British, though motivated by the vilest interests, had inadvertently initiated a social revolution in India. He contended that steam and science were the 'laying of the material foundations of Western society in Asia' (Marx, 1853).

In his notebooks, published as *Grundrisse*, Marx explored the central features of the Asiatic system and introduced the notion that the particular manner of the breakdown of ancient communes gave rise to different pre-capitalist modes of production; namely, Asiatic, Ancient, and Germanic modes of production.[5] In relation to the Asiatic form, Marx (1858a) wrote:

> In the Asiatic form (at least, predominantly), the individual has no property but only possession; the real proprietor, proper, is the commune—hence property only as *communal property* in land

Similarly (1858a):

> Amidst oriental despotism and the propertylessness which seems legally to exist there, this clan or communal property exists in fact as the foundation, created mostly by a combination of manufactures and agriculture within the small commune, which thus becomes altogether self-sustaining, and contains all the conditions of production and reproduction within itself. A part of their surplus labour belongs to the higher community, which exists ultimately as a *person* and this surplus labour takes the form of tribute

Regarding public works in Asia, Marx (1858a) said:

> The communal conditions of real appropriation through labour, *aqueducts*, very important among the Asiatic peoples; means of communication etc. then appear as the work of the higher unity—of the despotic regime hovering over the little communes

In 1858, Marx became more interested in the agrarian relations of India as a result of the controversy stirred up by Lord Canning's proclamation, after the annexation of Oudh, that the British Government had confiscated proprietary rights in the soil. This stirred up a debate in Britain about the nature of the claims to landed property made by the zamindars, talukdars, or sardars of India. One side maintained that these were real private property holders, while the other maintained that they should be considered mere tax-gatherers. Marx agreed with the latter view and stated that it was not only based on a 'more thorough study of the institutions of Hindostan' but was also confirmed by the results of the Bengal settlement (Marx, 1858b). He considered the entire controversy to be the result of 'English prejudices or sentiments, applied to a state of society and a condition of things to which they have in fact very little real pertinency' (Marx, 1858b).

Finally, in his famous preface to *A Contribution to the Critique of Political Economy* (1859), Marx introduced the term Asiatic Mode of Production:[6]

> In broad outline, the Asiatic, ancient, feudal and modern bourgeois modes of production may be designated as epochs marking progress in the economic development of society.

The AMP was also utilised in *Capital* without any substantial alteration. For example, in Volume 1 Marx used the phrase, 'In the ancient Asiatic and other ancient modes of production' (Marx, 1998a: 114). Similarly, in a footnote he wrote, 'A more exhaustive study of Asiatic, and especially of Indian forms of common property, would show . . .' (Marx, 1998a: 112). The most significant and detailed passage, however, is contained in a lengthy passage from chapter sixteen titled 'Division of Labour in Manufacture, and Division of Labour in Society' (1954, 513–5):

> Those small and extremely ancient Indian communities, some of which have continued down to this day, are based on possession in common of the land, on the blending of agriculture and handicrafts, and on an unalterable division of labour, which serves, whenever a new community is started, as a plan and scheme ready cut and dried. Occupying areas of from 100 up to several thousand acres, each forms a compact whole producing all it requires. The chief part of the products is destined for direct use by the community itself, and does not take the form of a commodity. Hence, production here is independent of that division of labour brought about, in Indian society as a whole, by means of the exchange of commodities. It is the surplus alone that becomes a commodity, and a portion of even that, not until it has reached the hands of the State, into whose hands from time immemorial a certain quantity of these products has found its way in the shape of rent in kind. The constitution of these communities varies in different parts of India. In those of the simplest form, the land is tilled in common, and the produce divided among the members

It is clear, from this passage, that Marx continued to regard pre-colonial India as a society based on the common property of the village community, where the state appropriated surplus as a tribute.

One may object that Marx seems to have dropped any reference to public works in the above passage. This apparent negligence exists only because Marx's focus was the division of labour in manufacture and society. The passage, therefore, describes the division of labour in the village community in India, in order to contrast it with the capitalist division of labour. Public works receive attention in chapter 16, where Marx (1954: 736–7) wrote:

> It is the necessity of bringing a natural force under the control of society, of economising, of appropriating or subduing it on a large scale by the work

of man's hand, that first plays the decisive part in the history of industry. Examples are, the irrigation works in Egypt, Lombardy, Holland, or in India and Persia where irrigation by means of artificial canals, not only supplies the soil with the water indispensable to it, but also carries down to it, in the shape of sediment from the hills, mineral fertilisers. The secret of the flourishing state of industry in Spain and Sicily under the dominion of the Arabs lay in their irrigation works.

In *Capital Volume Three*, published posthumously by Engels, Marx's (1894: Ch. 20) comments on India and China were:

> The broad basis of the mode of production here is formed by the unity of small-scale agriculture and home industry, to which in India we should add the form of village communities built upon the common ownership of land, which, incidentally, was the original form in China as well.

Similarly, in his discussion of ground rent in part six of the same volume, Marx clearly distinguished three sets of pre-capitalist landed property relations: Asiatic, slave, and serf-based forms. The analysis of the 'The Genesis of Ground-Rent' in chapter 47 was based on the same distinction between Asiatic, slave, and serf-based landed property relations. In this context, Marx (1894: Ch. 47) wrote:

> Should the direct producers not be confronted by a private landowner, but rather, as in Asia, under direct subordination to a state which stands over them as their landlord and simultaneously as sovereign, then rent and taxes coincide, or rather, there exists no tax which differs from this form of ground-rent. Under such circumstances, there need exist no stronger political or economic pressure than that common to all subjection to that state. The state is then the supreme lord. Sovereignty here consists in the ownership of land concentrated on a national scale. But, on the other hand, no private ownership of land exists, although there is both private and common possession and use of land.

Thus, Marx continued to develop the idea of the AMP from his early journalistic writings in 1853 to the writing of his most celebrated work, *Capital*. The essential features, which were elaborated on in his journalistic articles on the impact of British rule in India and form the basis of his various comments in *Capital* on India, are:

1) Natural economy
2) Absence of private property in land
3) Public works as the basis of the state
4) Surplus extraction by the state

There is a common misconception that Marx abandoned or developed reservations about the theory of the AMP in later life (Asiatic Mode of Production on Marxist Internet Archive, 2009; Habib, 2002: 5). After *Capital*, Marx returned to the subject of pre-colonial society in India and took detailed notes on Elphinstone's *History of India*, Sewell's *Analytical History of India*, and M.M. Kovalevsky's *Communal Landholding: The Causes, Course, and Consequences of its Disintegration*. These notes were published by the Institute of Marxism-Leninism under the title *Notes on Indian History* (1959).

Marx's comments on Kovalevsky clearly refute the notion that the latter dropped the concept of the AMP in his later life. Kovalevsky had argued that India had become feudal under Mughal rule (O'Leary, 1989: 127):

> Of all the four factors usually, though unjustly, acknowledged by medieval historians to be the sole aspects of German-Roman feudalism, three—the beneficial systems, farming out and commendation—may be said to exist in India conquered by the Muslims. Only of patrimonial justice, at least, so far as the civil code is concerned, it is possible to say that it was absent in the empire of the Great Mughal

Marx's comments on this passage were as follows (O'Leary, 1989: 127):

> On the grounds that the 'beneficial system', 'farming out' (the latter, though, is by no means purely feudal—the proof—Rome) and commendation occur in India, Kovalevsky sees here feudalism in the West European sense. But Kovalevsky forgets about serfdom which is absent in India and which is of the greatest importance. As to the individual role of protection (cf. Palgrave) not only of the bonded but also of the free peasants by the feudals (who functioned as *vogts*), this was in India of little importance, with the exception of the *wakufs*. The idealization of the Land (*Boden-Poesie*) characteristic of Germano-Roman feudalism (see Maurer) is as of little interest to India as it is to Rome. In India land is nowhere so noble in the sense of being, for instance, inalienable for the benefit of those outside the nobility. However,

Kovalevsky himself sees the basic difference—the absence of patrimonial justice where civil law is concerned in the Empire of the Grand Mughal.

Thus, Marx systematically rejected Kovalevsky's attempt to categorise India as feudal, stating that the latter failed to prove the most important feature of feudalism, namely serfdom. As for the other features, (1) the beneficial system existed in Rome and was not an essential feature of feudalism; (2) land was not considered a prized or noble object in India, as it was in Europe where it could not be alienated to commoners; and (3) patrimonial justice, by Kovalevsky's own admission, was absent in India (L.S. Gamayunov & R.A. Ulyanovsky in Krader, 1975). Marx also refuted Kovalevsky's argument that the Muslim land tax (*kharaj*) on the peasantry had transformed land into feudal ownership (O'Leary, 1989: 127).

Similarly, Marx's notes on Lewis H. Morgan's *Ancient Society* (1877), Sir John Budd Phear's *The Aryan Village in India and Ceylon* (1880), Sir Henry Maine's *Lectures on the Early History of Institutions*, and John Lubbock's *The Origins of Civilization* (1870)—all published posthumously in one collection as the *Ethnological Notebooks*—also demonstrate that he continued to reject the theory that India was feudal. Commenting sarcastically on John Phear, he wrote, 'That ass Phear describes the organisation of the [Indian] rural community as feudal' (O'Leary, 1989: 128).

The same ideas can be found in the works of Engels. In *Anti-Duhring*, Engels (1934: 224) asserted that the state and village community own the land in the East:

> In the whole of the Orient, where the village community or the state owns the land, the very term landlord is not to be found in the various languages, a point on which Herr Dühring can consult the English jurists, whose efforts in India to solve the question: who is the owner of the land?—were [in] vain.

In the same book, Engels explained that state power begins with the gradual separation from society of people vested with a 'social function' in primitive societies. Further, in the specific case of Asia, that social function included the maintenance of irrigation. Engels (1934: 228–9) wrote:

there were from the beginning certain common interests the safeguarding of which had to be handed over to individuals, true, under the control of the community as a whole: adjudication of disputes; repression of abuse of authority by individuals; control of water supplies, especially in hot countries; and finally when conditions were still absolutely primitive, religious functions. Such offices are found in aboriginal communities of every period—in the oldest German marks and even today in India. They are naturally endowed with a certain measure of authority and are the beginnings of state power. . . . It is not necessary for us to examine here how this independence of social functions in relation to society increased with time until it developed into domination over society; how he who was originally the servant, where conditions were favourable, changed gradually into the lord; how this lord, depending on the conditions, emerged as an Oriental despot or satrap, the dynast of a Greek tribe, chieftain of a Celtic clan, and so on; to what extent he subsequently had recourse to force in the course of this transformation; and how finally the individual rulers united into a ruling class. Here we are only concerned with establishing the fact that the exercise of a social function was everywhere the basis of political supremacy; and further that political supremacy has existed for any length of time only when it discharged its social functions. However great the number of despotisms which rose and fell in Persia and India, each was fully aware that above all it was the entrepreneur responsible for the collective maintenance of irrigation throughout the river valleys, without which no agriculture was possible there.

Thus, Engels contended that *oriental despotism* was based on the village community, common ownership, and artificial irrigation (1934: 231):

Where the ancient communities have continued to exist, they have for thousands of years formed the basis of the cruellest form of state, Oriental despotism, from India to Russia.

That is why, when Russian populists advanced the argument that the Russian commune (obshchina) could be the foundation of a socialist society, Engels was scathing in criticism (1874):

Such a complete isolation of individual communities from one another, which creates throughout the country similar, but the very opposite of common, interests, is the natural basis for *oriental despotism*; and from India to Russia this form of society, wherever it has prevailed, has always produced it and always found its complement in it.

The evidence indicates that Marx and Engels described the pre-capitalist mode of production of India not as feudal but as the AMP. Even in the last years of their lives, Marx and Engels continued to regard India as an Asiatic society.

THE AMP SINCE THE TWENTIETH CENTURY

This section revisits twentieth century debates on the AMP. The first part presents Lenin's views on the AMP; the second is an examination of the debates and circumstances under which the Soviet Communist Party rejected the concept of the AMP; and the last part reviews the writings of Western Marxists after the 1960s.

The AMP was central to the early Marxists' ethnological studies of Asia. Karl Kautsky, Paul Lafargue, and Rosa Luxemburg studied pre-capitalist societies and 'employed concepts of primitive communism, agrarian communism, oriental society, oriental despotism, and the Asiatic mode of production' (Bailey and Llobera, 1981: 50). Bailey and Llobera concluded that '[in] these ethnological works neither oriental society nor oriental despotism was particularly controversial' (Bailey and Llobera, 1981: 51).

Similarly, Russian Marxists considered their country to be on the crossroads between Asia and Europe (Engels, 1874; Marx, 1857, 1867, 1881, 1982). The founder of the Russian Marxist movement, Georgi Plekhanov, wrote: 'Hegel generally held that the Slav world constituted an entity midway between Europe and Asia' (Plekhanov, 1897). In 'Our Differences' (1881), a polemical article against the Norodniks, Georgi Plekhanov argued that the Russian commune had been the economic basis of Russian absolutism (Bailey and Llobera, 1981). Similarly, in his article 'Socialism and the Political Struggle' (1883), he asserted that:

[peasants] 'rebelled' not for a redistribution of the land, but against oppression by the administration, against the excessive burdens of the taxation system, against the Asiatic way in which arrears were collected, and so on and so forth.

In his pamphlet *A New Champion of Autocracy* (1889), Plekhanov explained how Asiatic Russia was in the process of Europeanization:

The old Muscovite Russia was noted for her completely Asiatic character. This strikes one in the economic life of the country, in all its usages and the whole system of state administration. Muscovy was a kind of China in Europe instead of in Asia. Hence the essential distinction that whereas the real China did all she could to wall herself in from Europe, our Muscovite China tried by every means in her power from the time of Ivan the Terrible to open at least a small window on Europe. Peter succeeded in accomplishing this great task. He effected an enormous change which saved Russia from ossifying. But Tsar Peter could do no more than was within the power of a tsar. He introduced a permanent army with European equipment and Europeanized the system of state administration. In a word, to the Asiatic trunk of Muscovite Russia the 'carpenter tsar' attached European arms. . . . The fact was that the European arms were little by little exerting enormous influence on the trunk of our social organism. It started gradually to change from Asiatic into European. . . . In our country the formation of this class [bourgeoisie] is of still greater significance. With its appearance the very character of Russian culture is changing: our old *Asiatic* economic life disappearing, giving place to a new, *European* one. It is the working class in our country that is destined to finish the greatest work of Peter—to complete the *Europeanization of Russia*.

In his book *Fundamental Problems of Marxism*, Plekhanov maintained that primitive community could break up and evolve into one of two lines of social development: the Asiatic or slave (Plekhanov, 1969). His view was that while primitive communism had been succeeded by slave society in the West, in the East it had given rise to a distinctive 'oriental' line of historical development (Baron, 1974: 392). He stated (1969: 117):

In states like China or ancient Egypt, where civilized life was impossible without highly complex and extensive works for the regulation of the flow and overflow of big rivers and for irrigation purposes, the rise of the state may be explained largely by the direct influence of the needs of the social productive process . . . the above must not be lost sight of if an incorrect and one-sided idea of the historical role of the state is to be avoided.

In his book *History of Russian Social Thought (1914–17)*, Plekhanov wrote (Baron, 1974: 390):

Peculiarities of the [Moscovy Russian] historical process very noticeably set it apart from the historical process of all the countries of the European West and recall [instead] the developmental process of the great oriental despotisms.

Hence, for Kautsky, Lafargue, Luxemburg, and Plekhanov, the concept of the AMP did not arouse any serious controversy.

LENIN ON THE AMP

There is contention about whether Lenin accepted the notion of the AMP and/or its appropriateness to Russia. Since the 1930s, Soviet scholars have upheld that references to the 'Asiatic' mode by Marx, Engels, or Lenin merely emphasised variations within the slave or feudal modes of production. For instance, the Soviet scholar Miff wrote (Sawer, 1977: 85):

> by the 'Asiatic' mode of production Marx understood one of the varieties of feudalism. . . . This is the way that this question has been understood by us up to now and this is the way that Comrade Lenin understood it.

Writers in the West have often agreed with this notion. Sawer writes that Lenin's theory of imperialism 'tended to suggest that colonial areas such as Asia had enjoyed the normal (i.e. Western) pattern of historical development until being subjected to the effects of Western imperialism' (Sawer, 1977: 75).[7] O'Leary states that Lenin 'rejected the empirical appropriateness of Plekhanov's application of the [AMP] to Tzarist Russia' (O'Leary, 1989: 151).

In fact, Lenin did not disagree either with the concept of an AMP or with the characterisation of ancient Russia as Asiatic (McFarlane et al., 2005: 285). To begin with, Lenin frequently referred to Marx's *Preface to the Critique of Political Economy*, reproducing, in full, the passage containing the reference to the AMP. For example, Lenin quotes the *Preface* as early as 1894 in *What the 'Friends of the People' Are . . .* and also in his 1914 biography and exposition of Marx's work entitled *Karl Marx* (Lenin, 1914a, 1894b). Lenin's *Conspectus of the Correspondence of K. Marx and F. Engels 1844–1883*, published in 1959 (Moscow), clearly demonstrates that Lenin studied the concept of the AMP. In these notes, Lenin wrote (Sawer, 1977: 92):

The 'key' to Oriental systems is the absence of private property in land. All land = the property of the head of state. . . . The Asiatic villages, self-enclosed and self-sufficient (natural economy) form the basis of Asiatic systems + public works of the central government.

Like Plekhanov, Lenin considered Tsarist Russia to be a country that lay at the crossroads of the European and Asiatic civilisations. This was not merely a reference to the geographical fact that Russia spanned the Eurasian continent but, more importantly, a reference to the socio-economic formation of Tsarist Russia that was a combination of European feudalism and the AMP. On the social structure of Russia, he wrote (Lenin, 1894a):

the feudal exploitation of the peasantry in the grossest, *Asiatic forms*, when not only did the means of production not belong to the producer but the producers themselves differed very little from 'means of production'.

While criticising the bureaucracy, he described Russia as 'semi-Asiatic' and said, '[we] see this institution [bureaucracy] everywhere, from autocratic and semi-Asiatic Russia to cultured, free and civilised England, as an essential organ of bourgeois society' (Lenin, 1897b). Similarly, criticising the Stolpyn reforms,[8] he wrote, 'The monarchy had to defend itself against the revolution, and the semi-Asiatic, feudal Russian monarchy of the Romanovs could only defend itself by the most infamous, most disgusting, vile and cruel means' (Lenin, 1911c). In the same article he continues (ibid.):

Stolypin the pogrom-monger groomed himself for a ministerial post in the only way in which a tsarist governor could; by torturing the peasants, by organising pogroms and by showing an ability to conceal these Asiatic 'practices' behind glib phrases, external appearances, poses and gestures made to look 'European'.

Lenin described Russian reaction as a combination of 'unmitigated Asiatic backwardness with all the loathsome features of the refined methods used to exploit and stultify those that are most downtrodden and tormented by the civilisation of the capitalist cities' (Lenin, 1905b). Declaring the Bolsheviks' opposition to the ruling class, he wrote, 'We whole-heartedly support to the very end the peasants' struggle against semi-feudal landlordism and against the Asiatic political system in Russia' (Lenin, 1906d).

Further evidence can be found in Lenin's repeated references to the struggle between European [bourgeois-democratic] culture and Asiatic backwardness. He wrote that capitalism in Russia was converting 'Asiatic forms of labour, with their infinitely developed bondage and diverse forms of personal dependence, into European forms of labour' (Lenin, 1897a). In this context, he argued that Narodnism[9] played 'into the hands of stagnation and Asiatic backwardness' (ibid.). He wrote that the Asiatic political system in Russia was giving way to European capitalism (1903b):

> What is surprising, rather, is that Russia's development along European capitalist lines should already, despite her Asiatic political system, have made so strong a mark on the political grouping of society.

At other times, he pointed out how the transformation of Russian institutions remained skin-deep and how they were still Asiatic in nature. For example, he stated, 'The Provisional Regulations of 1899 tear off the pharisaical mask and expose the real Asiatic nature even of those of [Russia's] institutions which most resemble European institutions' (Lenin, 1901b). He claimed that (1905f):

> in Russia purely capitalist antagonisms are very very much overshadowed by the antagonisms between 'culture' and Asiatic barbarism, Europeanism and Tartarism, capitalism and feudalism; in other words, the demands that are being put first today are those the satisfaction of which will develop capitalism, cleanse it of the slag of feudalism and improve the conditions of life and struggle both for the proletariat and for the bourgeoisie.

Similarly, making the case for 'democratic reforms', he stated (1905h):

> the democratic reforms . . . will, for the first time, really clear the ground for a wide and rapid, European, and not Asiatic, development of capitalism. . . . [The democratic dictatorship] may bring about a radical redistribution of landed property in favour of the peasantry, establish consistent and full democracy including the formation of a republic, eradicate all the oppressive features of Asiatic bondage, not only in village but also in factory life . . . [the Bolsheviks] . . . want the people, i.e., the proletariat and the peasantry, to settle accounts with the monarchy and the

aristocracy in the 'plebeian way,' ruthlessly destroying the enemies of liberty, crushing their resistance by force, making no concessions whatever to the accursed heritage of serfdom, of Asiatic barbarism and human degradation.

In a follow-up article, Lenin argued the case that conditions in Russia were conducive to a 1789-type revolution, instead of an 1848-type one of a slow transition, because the contradictions between autocracy and political freedom had no intermediate stages. He concluded that '[In Russia] despotism is Asiatically virginal' (Lenin, 1905a).

In his seminal work *The Development of Capitalism in Russia* (1899), while discussing the rise of the peasant bourgeoisie in the context of the AMP, Lenin wrote:

the threads both of merchant's capital . . . and of industrial capital . . . merge in the hands of the peasant bourgeoisie. It depends on surrounding circumstances, on the greater or lesser degree to which the Asiatic way of life is eliminated and culture is widespread in our countryside as to which of these forms of capital will develop at the expense of the other.

This reference, to the 'Asiatic way of life', was repeated when Lenin compared the systems that prevailed in landlord farming and pre-industrial textile manufacture (1899):

In both cases, the old system merely implies stagnation in the forms of production (and, consequently, in all social relations), and the domination of the Asiatic way of life. In both cases, the new, capitalist forms of economy constitute enormous progress, despite all the contradictions inherent in them.

Lenin pointed out characteristics of Russia's socio-economic formation, which were derived from the AMP, in innumerable passages. For example, he referred to:

[The] Asiatic abuse of human dignity that is constantly encountered in the countryside (Lenin, 1894b).

The Chinese people suffer from the same evils as those from which the Russian people suffer—they suffer from an Asiatic government that squeezes taxes from the starving peasantry and that suppresses every aspiration towards liberty by military force (Lenin, 1900).

[The] hopeless poverty, ignorance, lack of rights, and degradation, from which the peasants suffer, lay an imprint of Asiatic backwardness upon the entire social system of our country (Lenin, 1901c).

[T]here neither is nor can be any other means of combating unemployment and crises, as well as the Asiatic-barbarian and cruel forms the expropriation of the small producers has assumed in Russia, than the class struggle of the revolutionary proletariat against the entire capitalist system (Lenin, 1901a).

numerous remnants of the pre-capitalist, serf-owning social system, . . . are responsible for the Asiatically barbarous forms of exploitation and the agonising extinction of the many-million-strong peasantry (Lenin, 1902a).

The entire working class and the entire country are suffering from this absence of rights; it is on this that all the Asiatic backwardness in Russian life rests (Lenin, 1903a).

The whole colonisation policy of the autocracy is permeated with the Asiatic interference of a hide-bound bureaucracy (Lenin, 1907b).

Features of Asiatic primitiveness, governmental graft, the schemes of financiers who share their monopoly incomes with highly-placed officials, are still boundlessly strong in Russian capitalism (Lenin, 1913c).

As a matter of fact, this progress, perpetuating as it does appalling poverty and bondage among the masses of the peasants, only worsens their conditions, makes crises more inevitable, and intensifies the contradiction between the requirements of modern capitalism and barbarous, medieval and Asiatic 'winter hiring' (Lenin, 1914b).

A bourgeois revolution for the purpose of preserving landed proprietorship is being carried out . . . by Stolypin in the crudest Asiatic forms (Lenin, 1907c).

[the Russian ruling autocracy] . . . surpasses even the barbarism and uncivilised behaviour of the Asiatic governments (Lenin, 1911e).

only a victorious revolution, can make lasting changes in the life of peoples and seriously undermine medieval rule and semi-Asiatic forms of capitalism (Lenin, 1910a).

In his scathing condemnation of Tsarist Russia, Lenin frequently used terms such as 'Asiatic police tyranny',[10] 'Asiatic censorship',[11] 'Asiatic conservatism of the autocracy',[12] 'autocracy's Asiatic savagery',[13] 'Asiatic barbarity',[14] 'Asiatic philistinism',[15] 'slave, Asiatic, tsarist Russia',[16]

'Asiatic barbarism',[17] 'Asiatically corrupt Russian officials',[18] 'the accursed canker of Asiatic tyranny',[19] and 'Asiatic despotism'.[20]

Godes, a vitriolic opponent of the AMP, wrote (Ulmen, 1972: 439):

> in Lenin's works the term 'Asiatic' always serves as a synonym for an extreme form of feudalism and backwardness. No one will claim that Lenin classified Russia among countries with an Asiatic mode of production, but it was to Russia that he very frequently applied the term 'Asiatic'.

However, this claim is contradicted by Lenin's unambiguous statement that the term feudalism is not applicable to Russia. When Plekhanov wrote the expression 'the feudal-handicraft period,' Lenin replied (1902b):

> 'The feudal-handicraft period'. . . . Here, an expression seems to have been chosen, as though deliberately, which is least applicable in Russia, for it is questionable whether the term 'feudalism' is applicable to our Middle Ages.

Lenin made it very clear that the term 'feudalism' could only be used, inexactly, in the context of Russia. He wrote, 'The feudal (let us use this not very exact, general European expression) landowners . . .' (Lenin, 1911d).

Lenin's debate with Plekhanov, at the Stockholm Congress in 1906, regarding the Bolshevik program of the nationalisation of land is sometimes misconstrued as an attack on the AMP. For instance, the historian A.G. Prigozhin wrote (Sawer, 1977: 89):

> At the Fourth (Unity) Congress in Stockholm, Lenin raised precisely the objection that Plekhanov was attempting to construct the Menshevik conception of the Russian revolution out of his analysis of the 'Asiatic character of Russian despotism' and of the Russian commune. If Marx and Engels really took the viewpoint of acknowledging an 'Asiatic' mode of production in Russia, then it was not Lenin who was right as we have thought and believed up till now, but Plekhanov: it was Menshevism that was right, and not Bolshevism.

Firstly, it is dogmatic to argue that the AMP cannot exist because otherwise Lenin would be incorrect. Secondly, Plekhanov had insisted that since nationalisation of land was the economic basis of Muscovy before the reign of Peter, the program of nationalisation of land by the

Bolsheviks would result in the restoration of the AMP. Lenin pointed out that this view was historically inaccurate: 'it is absurd to talk about the land being nationalised before the reign of Peter I' (Lenin, 1906c) and contended (ibid.):

> Insofar as (or if) the land was nationalised in Muscovy, the economic basis of this nationalisation was the *Asiatic mode of production*. But it is the *capitalist mode of production* that became established in Russia in the second half of the nineteenth century, and is absolutely predominant in the twentieth century. What, then, remains of Plekhanov's argument? He confused nationalisation based on the Asiatic mode of production with nationalisation based on the capitalist mode of production.

It is quite clear from this passage that Lenin is not arguing against the concept of the AMP; rather, he is pointing out that Plekhanov had mistakenly equated nationalisation under the *AMP* with nationalisation under *capitalism*.

In the article 'The Agrarian Programme of Social-Democracy in the First Russian Revolution, 1905–1907', Lenin further clarified his position. He argued that the Mensheviks did not understand that the bourgeois revolution in Russia could be of two types: the landlord-bourgeois revolution or the peasant-bourgeois revolution. Lenin asserted that 'without a "clearing" of the medieval agrarian relationships and regulations, partly feudal and partly Asiatic, *there can be no* bourgeois-revolution in agriculture' (Lenin, 1907b). He stated that the old distribution of land was based on the will of the landlords' bailiffs or 'the officials of Asiatic despotism', and not on the needs of free commercial agriculture (Lenin, 1907b). He also stated that nationalisation of the land could thoroughly sweep away the survivals of medievalism and Asiatic semi-decay (ibid.):

> The Minutes of the Stockholm Congress fully confirm the statement made in my Report that Plekhanov impermissibly confuses the restoration which took place in France on the basis of capitalism with the restoration of 'our old, semi-Asiatic order'.

Mocking the view that nationalisation on the basis of capitalism would restore the AMP, Lenin continued (1907b):

What is this? A historico-materialistic analysis, or a purely rationalistic 'wordplay'? Is it the *word* 'nationalisation' or certain *economic changes* that facilitate the restoration of the semi-Asiatic conditions? Had Plekhanov thought this matter over he would have realised that municipalisation and division eliminate *one* basis of the Asiatic order, i.e., medieval landlord ownership, but leave another, i.e., medieval allotment ownership. Consequently, in *essence*, in the *economic essence* of the revolution (and not in virtue of the term by which one might designate it), it is nationalisation that *far more radically* eliminates the *economic* basis of Asiatic despotism.

This detailed analysis of the agrarian debate, by Lenin himself, clearly demonstrates that Prigozhin misconstrues the debate between Plekhanov and Lenin as one over 'acknowledging an 'Asiatic' mode of production in Russia.' In fact, the debate was over the question of whether municipalisation or nationalisation would be the best course of action for sweeping away the AMP. The existence of the AMP in Russia was, in fact, never a subject of debate between Lenin and Plekhanov.

Lenin's comments on Intellectuals are also instructive with respect to the AMP. In Lenin's view, intellectuals in pre-capitalist Russia were divided into two big camps: 'those who made up to the government, and those who were independent; by the former were meant hired hacks and those who wrote to order. This crude division, which corresponded to pre-capitalist, semi-Asiatic relations, is undoubtedly now obsolete.' But he was happy to note that this distinction was now obsolete because ' . . . . Russia [was] rapidly becoming Europeanised' (Lenin, 1914c). In this context, although Lenin greatly admired Lev Tolstoi, he considered the latter's portrayal of pre-capitalist Russia as romanticism and wrote, 'Tolstoi-ism, in its real historical content, is an ideology of an Oriental, an Asiatic order' (Lenin, 1911a).

It may be objected that Lenin changed his views after 1913, when he wrote *Backward Europe and Advanced Asia* (Lenin, 1913a). The title certainly suggests that Lenin no longer associated 'backwardness' with Asia. How then is this to be reconciled with the fact that as late as 1923, several years after the socialist revolution, Lenin still contrasted 'Asiatic ignorance' with European culture? For example, he wrote (1923):

Let those Russians, or peasants, who imagine that since they trade they are good traders, get that well into their heads. This does not follow that all. They do trade, but that is far from being cultured traders. They now trade in an Asiatic manner, but to be a good trader one must trade in the European manner. They are a whole epoch behind in that.

Similarly, with respect to the domain of education and culture, he stated, 'We must bear in mind the semi-Asiatic ignorance from which we have not yet extricated ourselves' (Lenin, 1922).

Lenin felt that the term 'AMP' might unintentionally strike Asian people as insulting. Describing the ruling class of Russia as 'un-European and anti-European', he wrote, 'we would say Asiatic if this did not sound undeservedly slighting to the Japanese and Chinese' (Lenin, 1914d). In fact, Lenin frequently used the word 'patriarchal' as a substitute for the word 'Asiatic'. For instance, he stated (1908):

> Once the latifundia are retained, this inevitably means also the retention of the bonded peasant, of métayer, of the renting of small plots by the year, the cultivation of the 'squire's' land with the implements of the peasants, i.e., the retention of the most backward farming methods and of all that *Asiatic barbarism* which is called patriarchal rural life.

For this reason, the word 'patriarchal' is used where one would expect to find the word 'Asiatic' in the 'Thesis on the National and Colonial Question' of the influential Second Congress of the Communist International. Lenin says, 'With regard to the more backward states and nations, in which feudal or patriarchal and patriarchal-peasant relations predominate . . .' (Lenin, 1920).

Thus, the evidence suggests that Lenin had studied the concept of the AMP; he considered Russia's socio-economic formation to be a combination of the Asiatic and European modes of production; his disagreements with Plekhanov were never over the characterisation of Russia as Asiatic but over the question of the appropriate agrarian policy to destroy Asiatic relations; and, he frequently substituted the word 'patriarchal' for 'Asiatic'. In sum, the evidence seems to weigh in favour of the view that Lenin accepted the concept of the AMP.

AMP AND THE COMMUNIST PARTIES

Despite the fact that early Marxists upheld the concept of the AMP, the communist parties of Asia do not uphold this analysis. Take, for example, the (year 2000) programme of the Communist Party of India (Marxist):

> 6.6   The Adivasi and tribal people who constitute seven crores of the population, are victims of brutal capitalist and *semi-feudal exploitation*

> 2.2   Communist Party of India (Marxist) . . . places before the people as the immediate objective, the establishment of people's democracy based on the coalition of all genuine *anti-feudal*, anti-monopoly and anti-imperialist forces led by the working class on the basis of a firm worker-peasant alliance

> 2.2   The nature of our revolution in the present stage of its development is essentially *anti-feudal*, anti-imperialist, anti-monopoly and democratic

> 2.3   The first and foremost task of the people's democratic revolution is to carry out radical agrarian reform in the interests of the peasantry so as to sweep away all the remnants of *feudal and semi-feudal fetters* on our productive forces of agriculture as well as industries

(Programme of the Communist Party of India (Marxist), 2000, emphases added)

The Communist Party of India and the Indian Maoists maintain the same views. The Communist Party of India (Marxist-Leninist) argues that the two 'basic contradictions' in the present circumstances are:

1.   The contradiction between imperialism and Indian people, and
2.   The contradiction between *feudalism* and broad masses of the people

(Programme of the Communist Party of India (Marxist-Leninist), 2005, emphasis added)

Hence, the communist parties of India do not uphold the concept of the AMP and, instead, maintain that India is semi-feudal.[21] Similar references to feudalism can also be seen in the programmes and statements of the Communist Party of China after the 1930s.

How was it that the model of Marxism-Leninism, adopted by the Communist Parties in Asia, rejected Marx's analysis of the AMP? Most importantly, what were the theoretical objections to the AMP?

The 1920s was a period of the rise of the communist movements in the colonial world. The Communist Party of China (CPC) was formed in 1921, the Communist Party of Indonesia (PKI) was formed in 1924, the Communist Party of India (CPI) was formed in 1925, and the Communist Party of Indochina came together in 1930. As a result, the question of the nature of pre-colonial Asiatic society was no longer a purely academic question but became one of immediate practical politics. For the Soviet party, the communist movement in China became the immediate focal point of the debate on the AMP.

In 1925, Eugene Varga began the debate on the AMP by publishing an article entitled 'Economic Problems of the Revolution in China' (1925). Explaining the Asiatic basis of state power in China, he wrote (Sawer, 1977: 81–82):

> [State power] arose in China out of the necessity to regulate the water supply, to provide protection, from floods, and to ensure the irrigation of land. Hence a ruling class was formed of a special type unknown in the sphere of European culture—namely a class of literati.

In the same year, David Riazanov, the director of the newly founded Marx-Engels Institute, wrote two articles in which he brought attention to the validity of the AMP as a Marxist concept—the first was an explanatory preface to Marx's article 'Revolution in China and in Europe', and the second was entitled 'Karl Marx on China and India' (Riazanov, 1925a, 1925b).

Following Riazanov, John Pepper used the term in an analysis of pre-colonial China in the article 'Europo-American Imperialism and the Revolution in China', published in Pravda in May 1927 (Sawer, 1977: 84). Similarly, a young British Marxist named Paul Fox, who was studying at the Marxism-Leninism Institute at the time, also wrote an article that was strongly supportive of the notion of the AMP, entitled 'The Views of Marx and Engels on the Asiatic Mode of Production and their Sources' (Sawer, 1977: 94).

However, arguably the most prolific and influential Soviet advocate of the AMP during this period was Liudvig I. Mad'iar. Mad'iar was in China in 1926–27, when he played a leading role in the defence of the

Soviet consulate in Shanghai against a White Russian attack. From 1928 to 1934, he worked in the Eastern Secretariat of the Comintern where his ideas had a wide impact. His books—*The Economics of Agriculture in China* (1928), *Essays on the Economy of China* (1930), and his lengthy introduction 'The Legitimacy of the AMP' to the work of M.D. Kokin and G. Papaian—are considered the main theoretical statements within the Communist Party of the Soviet Union (CPSU) of that period, in support of the AMP (Bailey and Llobera, 1981: 76–94; Fogel, 1988: 59).

Following Mad'iar, M.D. Kokin and G. Papaian's book *Ching t'ien; The Agricultural Structure of Ancient China* claimed that the AMP was a valid Marxist concept with respect to China. However, Kokin and Papaian did not regard the AMP as absolutely stagnant, and attempted to demonstrate the social and economic development that had occurred within this mode of production (Sawer, 1977: 94).

Other writers supporting the AMP included A.I. Kantorovich, S.A. Dalin, A.I. Lomakin, and A.V. Efimov. Kantorovich introduced the notion that peasant revolts in China should be considered 'as the necessary means for maintaining equilibrium in [the Asiatic] system' (Sawer, 1977: 82). Dalin, while at the University of Workers in China in 1926, based his analysis of the Taiping rebellion of 1928 on Kantorovich's notion of revolts as a means of maintaining equilibrium in the AMP (Sawer, 1977: 90–91). After the Second World War, Dalin was responsible for reopening the debate in 1964 in the Soviet Union (Sawer, 1977: 90). Lomakin also based his arguments on Kantorovich's views on Asiatic rebellions (Sawer, 1977: 91). Efimov's *Concepts of Economic Formations in the Work of Marx and Engels and their Use in Clarifying the Structure of Eastern Societies* analysed textual evidence from the writings of Marx and Engels to support the AMP (Efimov, 1930; McFarlane et al., 2005).

The Communist International also acknowledged the validity of the AMP in the 1920s. For instance, the programme adopted by the Sixth Congress in 1928 referred to 'countries . . . with a predominance of medieval/feudal relations or of the 'Asiatic Mode of Production'' (Sawer, 1977: 86). Similarly, communist parties under the influence of the Comintern reflected this thinking in their own discussions. For example, the Draft Agrarian Program discussed at the plenum of the Central

Committee of the CPC in 1927 asserted that the AMP had dominated China from the third century BC (Sawer, 1977: 84).[22]

The CPSU itself debated the concept of the AMP in the Fifteenth Congress in 1928, and V.V. Lominadze argued the case for the AMP (Bailey and Llobera, 1981: 100).

> I consider that the types of social relationships which are found in the Chinese countryside can only very conditionally be considered to be feudal, and then only with the qualification that they resemble very little the European Middle Ages. Survivals of the unique Chinese feudalism, which it would be better to call the Asiatic mode of production, as Marx did, are the reason for the continued and extremely sharp class struggles in the Chinese countryside.

At this Party Congress, Lominadze was challenged by Miff, who stated (Sawer, 1977: 85):

> If you, Comrade Lominadze, read the letters of Engels and Marx on this question you will be convinced that by the 'Asiatic' mode of production Marx understood one of the varieties of feudalism; to be specific, that there are secondary differences in essence from the usual form of feudalism but that there are secondary differences of a more external kind, in the sphere of the juridical and historical system. This is the way that this question has been understood by us up to now and this is the way that Comrade Lenin understood it.

In the late 1920s, the debate reached such intensity that a series of conferences were organised on the issue. In 1929, at the Society of Marxist Historians, S. Shmonin reasoned that the AMP dominated precapitalist Russia. However, he did not consider the AMP as a separate mode of production, but as a condition of stagnation that could occur in any pre-capitalist mode of production (Sawer, 1977: 89).

Another debate was aroused by Sergei M. Dubrovsky's report for the Scientific Association of Oriental Studies entitled 'On the Question of the Nature of the "Asiatic" Mode of Production, Feudalism, Serfdom and Trading Capital' (1929) (Sawer, 1977: 92). Dubrovsky denied the validity of the AMP, and argued for the existence of no less than ten modes of production (Fogel, 1988: 60). This view was opposed by both the supporters and the opponents of the AMP and, in May 1929, a conference was organised by the Sociological Section of the Society of

Marxist Historians to discuss Dubrovsky's report (Sawer, 1977: 92). Dubrovsky and Mad'iar presented two separate dissenting reports to the Eastern Section of the All Union Conference of Marxist Agriculturists in January 1930 (Sawer, 1977: 93). Dubrovsky's view was largely rejected.

Another conference was held in Kharkov, followed by two others in Baku and Tbilisi in 1930 (Sawer, 1977: 93). The Tbilisi discussion revolved around T.D. Berin's unpublished book *Feudalism and the Asiatic Mode of Production*, in which he demonstrated the existence of the AMP in Marx's work (Sawer, 1977: 93). However, the opposing views of Mikhail Godes and Sergei Dubrovsky prevailed (Fogel, 1988: 60).

Specialists studying India also debated the notion of the AMP. For instance, A.I. Shtusser's *Marx and Engels on India* confirmed the existence of the AMP (Sawer, 1977: 94). Similarly, I.M. Riesner's study of Mughal India led him to accept that the system would be better described as Asiatic rather than feudal. Riesner asserted that (Sawer, 1977: 93):

> it is necessary for us to turn back directly to Marx. The charge against us 'Aziatophiles'[23] of Eastern chauvinism is quite groundless. Our task, despite the Indian nationalists who blanket Indian history with the fog of mysticism, consists in discovering in this history the laws of class struggle.

On the other hand, A.A. Bolotnikov, M.P. Zhakov and Alagardian accepted that the AMP was upheld by Marx, but denied that there was empirical evidence in Mughal India to support it (Sawer, 1977: 93).

In sum, there was no dearth of discussion or published material on the AMP in the 1920s. In fact, as L.V. Danilova correctly claimed, 'the question of the Asiatic mode of production was never off the agenda' (Sawer, 1977: 84).

Marian Sawer argued, in *Marxism and the Question of the Asiatic Mode of Production*, that the 'Aziatchiki', as their opponents dubbed supporters of the AMP, began to lose influence when the AMP came to be identified with the view that China did not require a democratic revolution and, therefore, that the alliance between the communist and nationalist parties was a mistake (Sawer, 1977: 95). Varga and Lominadze had indeed, earlier, maintained that since feudalism was absent in China the national bourgeoisie of China was purely a product of imperialism and could not carry out a bourgeois-democratic revolution (Sawer, 1977: 85, 95). The Aziatchiki were, therefore, perceived to be closer to the Trotskyite position on China, even though Trotsky himself made no mention of the AMP (Sawer, 1977: 95). The suppression of the Communist Party of China in 1927 resulted in even stronger criticism against the supporters of the AMP (McFarlane et al., 2005: 295). However, this view is contested by Stephen P. Dunn in his book *The Fall and Rise of the Asiatic Mode of Production* (Dunn, 1982). Dunn considers that the removal of the AMP from Soviet Marxism was not due to these political reasons but due to the weakness of the theory.

Despite this continuing controversy, it is clear that the debate on the AMP came to a decisive head at a conference organised in Leningrad in 1931 (McFarlane et al., 2005: 295). In the background of this conference was the continuing ideological struggle within the Bolshevik party against Trotskyism. Stalin, Miff, and Bukharin defended the Comintern line of an alliance with the Chinese Nationalist party against sharp criticism from Trotkyists (Sawer, 1977: 85). At the Leningrad conference, Kokin and Papaian defended the AMP but they were apparently defeated and the position of Godes and Evgenii Iolk was upheld (Fogel, 1988: 61).

At this debate, Kokin argued that Asiatic rulers should be considered a ruling class, whom he termed 'bureaucrats' (1931: 95):

> The surplus labour or product was extracted by the bureaucrats from the direct producer. I cannot call this group of people other than bureaucrats, although it would be possible to find another name for them. But this is not important. The term is not important. Marx and Engels did not give a name to this class. When mention is made of the ruling class in Asiatic society, Marx speaks of the state. This is why I chose the word bureaucrat as, in my opinion, it is the most appropriate name. . . . This is more or less what I wanted to say about the process of class formation and the creation of the state in oriental society. It is perfectly clear that the classics of Marxism speak clearly of the specific characteristics of oriental society and in particular, of the oriental state; it is perfectly clear that these propositions do not contradict the teachings of Marx or Lenin on the state.

In response, Godes asserted 'the reaffirmation of unilinearism' (Godes, 1981). In his article, entitled by the same name, he insisted that supporters of the AMP could not explain how class struggle in the AMP led to the next stage of social development, that they could not explain what occurred after the Chou period in China, that the AMP could not be taken as a separate mode of production, and that the AMP would play into the hands of nationalists or imperialists in colonial countries (Godes, 1981: 99–104). He wrote (1935: 104):

> The theory of the Asiatic mode of production, which emphasises the exclusive specificities of oriental history, can easily play into the hands of nationalist elements in the Orient. They could hide under the veil of this exclusive nature and insist that the teachings of Marx and Lenin are inapplicable to the Orient. At the same time, this theory of exclusivity completely satisfies imperialism, since it is associated with the view that the oriental society was stagnant and therefore that European capitalism played a messianic role.

In much the same way, Iolk combined the objections that had been raised in past discussions and concluded that the AMP would only cause confusion among the proletarian vanguard in colonial countries. He stated (1931: 97):

> . . . it is perfectly clear that the interpretation of individual statements by Marx and Engels on the Orient, presented to us in the guise of a superficially perfected theory about a particular Asiatic mode of production, is absolutely unacceptable from a political point of view. . . . When, for example, the Chinese comrades are presented with a theory that the gentry are not an example, a survival, of the feudal order, that in China there were certain peculiar 'Asiatic' relations, and so on, this of course can disorient and confuse the ideology of the proletarian avant-garde.

It seems reasonable to assume that, among other things, one strong factor in this debate was the perception that the AMP might lead to charges of Eurocentric prejudice from the anti-colonial nationalist movement. Given that the AMP could easily be confused for eighteenth century racist notions of *oriental despotism*, critics argued that its use by the Comintern could play into the hands of imperialists. Soviet scholars were eager to prove, to these rising anti-colonial movements, that their approach to the colonised people was fundamentally different from that of the West. For example, take the following statement Secretary of the Soviet Academy of Sciences S. Ol'denburg's (Sawer, 1977: 76):

For us there exists no division of peoples and countries into an Orient and an Occident, which are opposed to one another and which it would be appropriate to study in a different manner. In our Union, the Orient has the same rights as the Occident, and we study it with the same Marxist methodology as the Occident. There has been, and there is, class struggle in the East, just as much as in the West. The history of the Orient knows the same formations as those of the West. Such are the fundamental principles which govern our study of the Orient.

The above statement, addressed to the anti-colonial intellectuals of the Third World, is indicative of the urgent need felt by Soviet scholars to distinguish Soviet Eastern studies from the Orientalist tradition of the colonial powers, in order to attract intellectuals from the anti-colonial movement to the communist movement as represented by the USSR. Godes even went to the extent of arguing that China and India were in the first stages of capitalism when these societies were colonised. He wrote (Sawer, 1977: 77),

The misfortune of Asia, and of the two greatest of its peoples—the Indians and Chinese—consists in the fact that the period of the completion of the process of primitive accumulation in Europe found China and India in the first stage of this process.

Thus, the Soviet party seems to have concluded that all references to the AMP in the works of Marx, Engels, or Lenin were to be understood not as references to a distinct mode of production but to an Asiatic variation of slave or feudal society. By the mid-1930s, this view came to dominate the CPSU. This view of 'Asiatic variants' of slave and feudal society acknowledged the peculiarities of Asia, including the existence of rural communities and public works, but did not consider these sufficiently significant to warrant their categorisation as a distinct mode of production. For instance, V.V. Struve contended that whether the producer is owned by the state or by an individual makes no difference to the slave mode of production (Sawer, 1977: 191–2). As a result of the influence of these Soviet debates, the majority of communist parties in Asia officially adopted the argument that the pre-colonial mode of production was feudal and that its specific features were merely 'Asiatic variants' of feudalism.

Interest in the AMP continued among Marxist scholars in China and Japan (Fogel, 1988: 61). In the 1920s and 1930s, the works of supporters of the AMP—including Varga, Wittfogel, Mad'iar,[24] Kokin, and Papaian—were translated into Chinese and Japanese. In China, Kuo Mo-jo opened the debate in 1930 with the publication of his work *A Study of Ancient Chinese Society* (Fogel, 1988: 62). Another scholar, Li Chi, held opinions close to Mad'iar's and argued that Marx had clearly identified the AMP as a distinct stage of social development (Fogel, 1988: 63).

However, after the mid-1930s, Chinese scholars no longer supported the AMP (Fogel, 1988: 67). From that point on, the commonly-held position was that the AMP was a variant of slave or feudal society. For instance, Lu Chen-yu, Hu Ch'iu-yuan, Wang I-Ch'ang, Liu Hsing-t'ang, Ho Kan-chih, and Hou Wai-lu all discussed the AMP at length and took several ideas from it. However, they continued to plead that the pre-colonial relations in China were a variant of European ancient or feudal relations (Fogel, 1988: 61–7).

The first serious attempt to apply the AMP to the history of Japan was made by Hattori Shiso in his influential book *A History of the Meiji Restoration* (1928). Similarly, Hirata Yoshie held that Karl Marx had considered China 'Asiatic'. Debate on the AMP flourished in 1933 and 1934 and, during this period, Terajima Kazuo's journal *Proletarian Science* published several articles on the AMP. Moritani Katsumi, Ozaki Hotsumi, and Watanabe Yoshimichi supported the notion of an AMP. On the other hand, Noro Eitaro, Hani Goro, and Hayakawa Jiro thought of the AMP as a form of 'state feudalism' or a variant of slavery or serfdom (Fogel, 1988: 67–77).

Thus, communist parties in the East gradually came to accept the Soviet view that developed after the 1931 Leningrad conference, and the concepts of *Asiatic slavery* or *Asiatic feudalism* came to substitute the AMP.

POST-SECOND WORLD WAR DEBATES

After the Second World War, the AMP, ironically, became part of the anti-communist arsenal of the Cold War. A view emerged that the Soviet Union did not represent socialism but a modern form of the AMP. The main proponent of this argument was Karl A. Wittfogel, a former member of the German communist party associated with the Frankfurt School of Social Research.

When Wittfogel was part of the communist movement, he had argued in the article 'The Stages of Development in Chinese Economic and Social History' that classical feudalism and, later, capitalism failed to develop in China because of an overgrown Asiatic bureaucratic state (Wittfogel, 1935: 110). Similarly, in the article 'The Theory of Oriental Society', he contended that the centralised forms of Asiatic governments were essentially 'stationary' (Wittfogel, 1938: 157).

However, after the war he immigrated to the USA, renounced his ties to communism, and became a zealous anti-communist.[25] In his most famous book, *Oriental Despotism* (1957), he opined that pre-colonial Asia and the Soviet Union were essentially ancient and modern forms of oriental despotism (Wittfogel, 1963: 438–43). In Wittfogel's view, these non-Western societies were totalitarian. They crushed all opposition, individuality, creativity, and freedom. In contrast, the capitalist West stood for freedom and individuality (Wittfogel, 1963: Ch. 4, 5, pp. 447–9). He warned newly independent countries, such as India, against the despotism of planned economy and argued that the greatest threat to freedom came not from capitalism but from Soviet socialism (Wittfogel, 1963: 443–6).

Wittfogel's *Oriental Despotism* became a tool in the Cold War, and invited both support and criticism.[26] It is difficult to find anyone in Western academia writing on the subject of pre colonial China who has not in one way or another commented on Wittfogel's work (Nureev, 1990: 53–4). R. Garaudy, F. Heichelheim, I. Shafarevich, and G.L. Ulman agreed with Wittfogel's views equating the USSR or China with the AMP (Nureev, 1990: 53). Other anthropologists, such as Julian H. Steward and Barbara Price, restricted Wittfogel's analysis to the role of irrigation in pre-capitalist societies (Bailey and Llobera, 1981: 195–207, 216–33). Still other respondents engaged in the Wittfogel debate included M. Belov, G. Niemeyer, C. Friedrich, and L. Schapiro.

The eminent China scholar Joseph Needham criticised Wittfogel's work in the following terms (1959: 58–9):

instead of a mature and deeply-thought out contribution to scholarship, we now find in our hands a political tract which later generations will only be able to understand in the context of the 'cold war' period . . . the book may be said to constitute the greatest disservice which has yet been done to the objective study of the history of China.

Needham was not alone in this negative evaluation. Wolfram Eberhard concluded that 'as Wittfogel's theory stands today, it may perhaps be used by somebody as a political weapon, but I can hardly believe that it will be used as a tool in sociological analysis' (Eberhard, 1958: 181). Arnold Toynbee denounced it as 'lies' and 'heinous offences against the human race' (Toynbee, 1958, 197). Soviet scholar I.A. Levada was equally scathing (1962: 184):

> Having disavowed a class analysis of social structure, Wittfogel progressed down the inclined plane of reactionary sociology, which eventually led him into the role of a scholar-apologist of capital and colonialism.

Similarly, Lawrence Krader wrote (1981: 238):

> [Wittfogel's] major weakness is that he could not or refused to grasp the totality of the social relations of production—which quite naturally includes not only the managers but the class of direct producers who are bound by the necessities of surplus product/labour extraction, which goes to the state. It is wrong to make bureaucrats independent of the totality of production relations, as Wittfogel does.

Edmund Leach demonstrated in 'Hydraulic Society in Ceylon' that Wittfogel's concepts did not bear out the empirical reality of irrigation and government structure in Ceylon (Leach, 1959). Gunter Lewin pointed out that Wittfogel's theory ignored production and was a form of ecological or geographical determinism (Lewin, 1963).

In Asia, Wittfogel's views were either sharply rejected or made little impact. In India, eminent historian D.D. Kosambi mocked it as 'pseudo-scientific verbiage' (Shabad, 1959: 324). Irfan Habib also critiqued Wittfogel's views in more or less the same manner (Habib, 2002: 29). In China, debate on the AMP remained completely marginal during this period. After 1978, some authors began to utilise Wittfogel's interpretation of the AMP to characterise the Communist Party of China. Wu Dakun considered the People's Republic of China to be 'semi-Asiatic' (Brook, 1989: 14–19). In the same period, certain intellectuals within the Soviet Union also attempted to utilise Wittfogel's theory against Maoist China. L.S. Vasil'ev wrote (Sawer, 1977: 102):

Marx pointed out with marvellous historical insight that the patriarchal peasant commune which was the historical basis for various forms of despotic rule in the past could only become the foundation for 'barrack communism'. This deep insight can now be illustrated by the trend developments have taken in China caused by attempts to substitute a petty bourgeois theory and practice of Maoism for true Marxism.

Some of these debates on China are captured in Timothy Brook's book entitled *The Asiatic Mode of Production in China* (Brook, 1989).

POST-WAR WESTERN CONTRIBUTIONS

Post-war interest in the AMP kicked off after 1958 with the writings of Jean Surate-Canale. Surate-Canale, a member of the central committee of the Communist Party of France (PCF), was interested in understanding tropical Africa in terms of the AMP. Under his influence the programme of the Centre for Marxist Research (CERM), set up by PCF in 1960, included research on the AMP. Between 1962–64, the Marxist journal *La Pensée* became the centre of a revived interest in the AMP with contributions from P. Boiteau, Jean Suret-Canale, Jean Chesneaux, Maurice Godelier, Charles Parain, and others (Sawer, 1977: 193–194). In 1964, *La Pensée* took out a special edition exclusively on the AMP (*La Pensée*, 1964: No. 114). The most influential of these articles were later published in the book *Sur Le Mode de Production Asiatique* (CERM, 1969).

In addition to French Marxists, the Hungarian scholar Ferenc Tokai was also central to the development of a new scholarship on the AMP. In his book *The Asiatic Mode of Production* (1966), Tokai argued that AMP was the product of internal and external isolation. He defended the universal validity of the five-stage theory by arguing that tendencies towards slave and feudal society in China demonstrated the universal propensity of all societies to gravitate towards these modes of production (Sawer, 1977: 194).

There were certain significant departures in this new post-war scholarship. Firstly, it equated the AMP with primitive communist society. Hence, the AMP was considered a universal transitory stage between classless and class society. It followed, therefore, that it was not the Asian line of development that was exceptional. Instead, it was the

Western line of development that was distinct. For instance, Jean Chesneaux wrote in 1964 (Sawer, 1977: 194–195):

> The Asiatic mode of production, for the very reason that it has been the most general form of evolution of primitive communist society, has established itself in very diverse regions, in societies on which both history and geography have imposed very different rhythms of development. Brutally destroyed in the Mediterranean by the Dorian invasion at the beginning of the first millennium BC, liquidated by the Spanish conquest in America in the sixteenth century, it nevertheless continued slowly to evolve in countries such as China, Egypt, India, and in Black Africa.

The notion of the AMP as a transitory stage from a classless to class society was taken up by Soviet scholar M.A. Vitkin, who wrote, with reference to a discussion held at the Institute of the Peoples of Asia on the AMP in 1965, that (Sawer, 1977: 195):

> the emphasis on the fundamental particularity of Asiatic history characteristic of nineteenth-century historiography underwent a sharp about-turn at the close of the century, so that the history of the East was assimilated to that of Europe. The particularity of the East was discovered to be only relative . . . because, as the latest information indicates, ancient Europe (Mycenae etc.) also experienced a stage similar to that which Marx described as characterising the ancient East. The acceptable meaning of the Asiatic mode of production seems to be that it is the last stage of the primitive communal formation, the transition stage to class society.

Secondly, the new scholarship suggested that public works were not a necessary feature of the AMP. Godelier contended that there could be two different types of Asiatic formations: those with, and those without public works (Bailey and Llobera, 1981: 264–277). Since public works were excluded as a defining feature of the AMP, Surat-Canale argued that the concept could be employed to understand pastoral and other primitive communities.

Thirdly, the new scholarship attempted to demonstrate that the AMP was not economically or socially stagnant. The internal dynamic of the AMP was the tension between the efforts of the elite groups to transform their social position into private ownership of the means of production (especially land), and the resistance of the village community to this transformation. Surat-Canale wrote (Sawer, 1977: 196):

their internal contradiction (collective property—class property) may be resolved by the dissolution of collective property and the appearance of private property.

Similarly, L.A. Sedov remarked (Sawer, 1977: 196):

it is difficult to imagine that dialecticians such as Marx and Engels might be parties to the possibility of absolute stagnation in societies of the type under consideration.

At the same time, this new scholarship remained conspicuously distant from the concept of multiple paths of historical development. Instead, it asserted that each mode of production was principally embodied in one region in a given historical epoch. Moreover, the centre of human progress shifted from region to region over the course of human history. Maurice Cornforth wrote (Sawer, 1977):

Human society as a whole passes through the five stages we have listed [primitive communism, AMP, slave society, feudalism, capitalism], and the way is prepared for the appearance of a new system only as a result of the development of the previous system. But the new system does not necessarily appear first in that place where the old one has been most strongly entrenched and most fully developed. Indeed, in those communities where the old system has become most strongly entrenched it may be hardest to get rid of it, so that we know, this is what happened in the case of the first break-through of socialism, which was effected in Russia, 'the weakest link in the chain of imperialism', and not in the more advanced capitalist countries.

In conclusion, these new concepts of the AMP departed from Marx's original notions of the AMP as a class society based on village communities, public works, with states extracting surplus through a tribute. This was stated quite unambiguously by Soviet scholar L.V. Danilova while summarising the proceedings of the Seventh International Congress of Anthropology and Ethnography held in Moscow in 1964 (Sawer, 1977: 194):

The majority of the participants in the discussion, in its current stage, were of the opinion that by Marx's conception of the Asiatic mode of production one should understand not so much a specific particularity of the East (especially the particularity associated with the necessity for irrigation works) as those regularities characteristic of nearly all early class societies, and which were retained over a prolonged period in many of the societies of Africa, Asia and pre-Columbian America.

Although the AMP was at times used as a catch-all category for all societies that had avoided classification in the slave or feudal modes of production, nonetheless, it stimulated new research into tropical Africa, ancient America, and Pacific pre-capitalist communities. P. Boiteau wrote on Madagascar, De Santis on the Incas in Peru, H. Bibicou and Divitciogly re-interpreted Ottoman Turkey, K. Deme analysed pre-colonial Senegal, K. Mannivane looked at Laos, R. Gallisot brought his knowledge to bear on Algeria and North Africa, M.A. Chekova re-examined Vietnam, Saad wrote on Egypt, Coquery-Vidovitch researched pre-colonial Africa.

L. Sedov—a critic of AMP—wrote on Kampuchea, Dhoquois examined the theoretical domain of the AMP, and R. Garaudy's work 'The Chinese Question' (1969) re-interpreted socialist countries as Asiatic, much like Wittfogel (for details see McFarlane et al., 2005: 288–290). It also influenced Marxist scholars from Vietnam. Ngyyen Long Bich wrote two articles in the 1960s that appraised the concept of the AMP positively in relation to pre-colonial Vietnam, Khoi Le Thanh looked at ancient Vietnam from the prism of the AMP, and Tran Viet wrote on the epistemological obstacles to the AMP (McFarlane et al., 2005: 303; Thanh, 1973).

In the Soviet Union, L. Danilova's 'Discussion on Various Problems and Questions of Philosophy' was seen as a turning point after which scholars began to pay serious attention to the AMP (McFarlane et al., 2005: 299). A series of conferences and counter-conferences were similarly organised to discuss the AMP in 1966, 1968, and 1971 (Sawer, 1977: 193–197).

Ter-Akopian, Melekishvilli, and Kringer wrote in support of the AMP (McFarlane et al., 2005: 299). V.N. Nikiforov's *History of the Far East* did not endorse the AMP but underscored its importance as an analytical category (McFarlane et al., 2005). On the other hand, A.I. Pavlovskaya's 'Concerning the Opening of Discussion About the Asiatic Mode of Production', Garushchan's 'On the AMP', and Porsnev's 'Periodization and the Historical Project in Godelier and Marx' were seen as standing in the opposite camp (McFarlane et al., 2005: 299–300). Other scholars to comment on this debate included Dubrovsky, M.A. Korostova, K.Z. Ashrafyan, V.I. Krimov, I.A. Stuchevsky, Krilov, Sedov, Kim, I.V. Kachanovski,[27] Djakanov, I.L. Andreev, G.A. Bagaturia, L.S. Vasil'ev, G.S. Kiselev, R.I. Kosolapov, D.N. Platonov, and V.G. Popov (McFarlane et al., 2005; Nureev, 1990: 53–54). Also, dissidents from Eastern Europe and the Soviet Union, such as Rudolf Bahro, Zdeněk Mlynář, and Svetozar Stojanović, wrote polemics on the 'Asiatic' nature of Soviet socialism (Mlynář, 1990; Nove, 1979; Nureev, 1990: 53; Stojanovi'c, 1973).

A similar, but relatively independent development occurred in Britain. Since the 1930s, Vere Gordon Childe, one of the pioneers of modern archaeology, underscored the importance of productive forces in developing an understanding of ancient societies. In his celebrated book *Progress and Archaeology* (1971), and articles such as 'The Bronze Age' (1930), Childe emphasised the relationship between oriental and Western history. This research provided archaeological evidence in support of the Hegelian reading of Marx's progressive economic stages of historical development (Orenstein, 1954).

Similarly, Joseph Needham's meticulous study of scientific development in China, entitled *Science and Civilization in China*, argued that China was scientifically more advanced than the West till the 1600s. Its subsequent decline was a result of historical, economic, social, and cultural factors (Needham, 1969: 190–217). Needham's research provided evidence that the historical line of development of China was entirely distinct from the West and, as his research progressed, he became warmer to the concept of the AMP (McFarlane et al., 2005: 286–287).

However, it was, arguably, the publication of *Marx's Writings on Pre-Capitalist Economic Formations* (1964), and Eric Hobsbawm's support of the notion of the AMP in the introduction to this work, that provoked a debate on this question in British Marxist circles (Hobsbawm, 1964). The journal *Marxism Today* of the Communist Party of Great Britain became the locus of some of this debate in the 1960s. Among the numerous contributors were Griffiths, Simon, Lewin, Hoffman (who accused the AMP of being a Trojan horse aimed at subverting Marxism), Thorner (in India), and Kiernan (in Scotland) (McFarlane et al., 2005: 288). The debate led to greater acceptance of the view that the European path of development should not be assumed to be universal (McFarlane et al., 2005: 288–289).

Under the influence of Bronisław Malinowski, the London School of Economics also became a centre of new contributions to the debate. The social anthropological writings of Ernest Gellner, such as *Thought and Change* (1964) and *Soviet and Western Anthropology* (1980), raised an interest in the concepts of oriental society and oriental despotism (Gellner, 1964, 1980). One of Gellner's students, Brendan O'Leary, converted his doctoral dissertation into a book entitled *The Asiatic Mode of Production: Oriental Despotism, Historical Materialism, and Indian History* (O'Leary, 1989).

Other British contributions to the debate included Anne M. Bailey and Joseph R. Llobera's *The Asiatic Mode of Production: Science and Politics* (1981), which contains a well-chosen collection of excerpts from all the significant writers on this issue; Stephen Dunn's *The Fall and Rise of the Asiatic Mode of Production* (1982), which recaptured recent Soviet debates on the AMP; and Perry Anderson's *Lineages of an Absolutist State* (1979), which contended that Marx's view of India was primarily inspired by Hegel and rejected the AMP (Anderson, 1979; Bailey and Llobera, 1981; Dunn, 1982). Other British scholars involved in this debate included S.H. Barron, Edmund Leach, G. Lichteim, and Jonathan Friedman (McFarlane et al., 2005).

In Australia, Barry Hindess and Paul Q. Hirst's book *Pre-Capitalist Modes of Production* rejected the concept of the AMP on the basis that it was in contradiction to the laws of historical materialism (Hindess and Hirst, 1975). Other contributions from Australia included Marian Sawer's excellent work *Marxism and the Question of the Asiatic Mode of Production*, which helps to reconstruct the early Soviet debates that led to the rejection of the AMP by the communist parties (Sawer, 1977).

Lawrence Krader, director of the Institute of Ethnology at the Free University of Berlin, brought together Marx's scattered writings on the AMP in his book *The Asiatic Mode of Production: Sources, Development and Critique in the Writings of Karl Marx* (Krader, 1975). He argued that, for Marx, the AMP was the first form of class-divided exploitative society or 'political society'. As a result of Krader's influence, scholarship on the AMP is today divided between the primitivist interpretation (the view that the AMP is a universal transitory form between classless and class society), and the modernist interpretation (the view that the AMP was one of the first forms of class society) (Smith, 1979).

Studies of the Ottoman Empire have also utilised the concept of the AMP. Huri Islamoglu and Caglar Keyder analysed the Ottoman Empire by examining the articulation of the Asiatic and other modes of production (Bailey and Llobera, 1981: 301–334). Similarly, John Foran utilised an articulation of modes of production methodology to analyse seventeenth-century Iran (Foran, 1988).

Jurgen Golte and Heinz Dieterich have used the AMP to understand the state and economy of the Incan Empire (Bailey and Llobera, 1981; Dieterich, 1982). Fritjof Tichelman explained the social stagnation of pre-colonial Indonesia in his book *The Social Evolution of Indonesia* with the help of the concept of the AMP (Tichelman, 1980). Timothy Brook's *The Asiatic Mode of Production in China* brings together a collection of essays, written between the late 1970s and early 1980s, by Chinese scholars on the subject of the AMP (Brook, 1989). In addition, I. Wallerstein, J.A. Rapp, E.C. Welskopf, I. Banu, J. Taylor, D. Llanes, B. Turner, V. Ruben, R. Fox, C. Wickham, B. Stein, and F. Perlin have also commented on the AMP in various works (see McFarlane et al., 2005).

CONCLUSION

This chapter has traced the development of the concept of the AMP, from European sources of the seventeenth century to the twentieth century. European scholarship of Asia began with the travelogues of the seventeenth century. These writings underscored that Asia was without private property in land, and that Asiatic states were despotic. In the context of struggles for state power between the feudal and bourgeois classes during the eighteenth century in Europe, these views on Asia developed into the theory of oriental despotism. The emergence of political economy, by the end of that century, turned the scholars' attention towards ownership of land, land revenue tribute extracted from the village community by the state, and the social division of labour of Asian society. These notions of state public works and the village community crystallised into the theory of the AMP authored by Marx and Engels.

The AMP was central to any Marxist examination of Asian societies in the early twentieth century. For Kautsky, Luxemberg, Plekhanov, Lenin, and others, the AMP was not controversial. However, the AMP began to lose influence in the 1930s, and communist parties adopted the view that the AMP was not a distinct mode of production. All references to the AMP in the works of earlier Marxists were now understood as 'Asiatic variations' of slave or feudal society.

After the Second World War, interest in the AMP was revived first as a result of the work of Karl Wittfogel and later as the product of the research of French and British Marxists. However, the work of these French and British Marxists suggested that the AMP was a universal transitory stage between classless and class society, did not consider public works as central to the AMP, and did not consider the AMP to be exploitative or economically or socially stagnant. Hence, it was a departure from Marx's view that the AMP was a stagnant exploitative class society.

Why communist parties dropped the AMP remains an open question. Leszek Kolakowski has stated that AMP contradicted certain basic tenets of Soviet Marxism: the AMP appeared to stress geographic factors over the primacy of productive forces; it emphasised the social stagnation of Asia; it contradicted the notion of the inevitability of social progress, and implied that social development was exclusively a European phenomenon (Kolakowski, 1978, Vol. 1, 350). Marian Sawer has contended that the AMP was dropped because of political imperatives; mainly, that it was associated with an anti-Comintern line on China (Sawer, 1977, 75–95). Stephen P. Dunn has challenged the notion that strictly political reasons explain the removal of the AMP from Soviet Marxism. He has argued that the AMP was challenged on the grounds of empirical evidence (see for instance Dunn, 1982; Kelly, 1984, 198; Stillman, 1984, 767). Karl Wittfogel asserted that the AMP implied that an exploitative state could exist without private property, and this was an uncomfortable conclusion for the rulers of an Asiatic USSR (Wittfogel, 1963). Some of the principle criticisms of the AMP in relation to India are examined in the next chapter.

NOTES

1. This book is now simply known as *The Travels of Marco Polo*. Despite the widespread success of his book, the sceptical audience in his hometown of Venice

considered his portrayal of immense Eastern wealth to be greatly exaggerated. It is thought that Christopher Columbus, who discovered the American continent in 1492 while attempting to find a western route to the Far East, was also influenced by Marco Polo's travels.

2. Father Thomas Stephens lived in Goa in 1579.

3. The British East India Company established a trade transit point in Surat in 1608, but hostilities with Dutch and Portuguese traders in the Indian Ocean continued. The Battle of Swally in 1612, against the Portuguese, convinced the Company of the need for a diplomatic mission.

4. Although Holbach thought that China was 'governed by an arbitrary and capricious monarch', he did not hold this judgement about the East as a whole. For example, he praised the Sikhs as a 'republican people' (Krader, 1975, 42).

5. This concept of the path of the breakup of the commune has remained largely unexplored in comparative literature on medieval Asia and Europe because it deals with a period about which there is scarce reliable data (Krader, 1975).

6. Marx, however, made an exception for Japan, about which he stated: 'Japan, with its purely feudal organisation of landed property and its developed *petite culture*, gives a much truer picture of the European middle ages than all our history books, dictated as they are, for the most part, by bourgeois prejudices' (Marx, 1998a: 1025).

7. In fact, Lenin explicitly stated that the export of capital 'greatly accelerates the development of capitalism' in the colonial world (Lenin, 1917: 707). Further, Lenin quoted Hilferding with approval, 'The old social relations become completely revolutionised, the age-long agrarian isolation of "nations without history" is destroyed and they are drawn into the capitalist whirlpool. Capitalism itself gradually provides the subjugated with the means and resources for their emancipation and they set out to achieve the goal which once seemed highest to the European nations: the creation of a united national state as a means to economic and cultural freedom' (Lenin, 1917; 745). This implies that capitalist-imperialism altered, and accelerated, the line of social development of Asia *towards* the European line of social development.

8. Stolypin reforms were changes in the agrarian policies of Imperial Russia in 1906 by Pyotyr Stolypin who was Prime Minister from 1906 to 1911.

9. Narodnism was a social and political movement in late nineteenth century Russia for a socialist revolution on the basis of the peasantry.

10. Lenin (1902c).

11. Lenin (1905d).

12. Lenin (1905g).

13. Lenin (1905e).

14. Lenin (1905c; 1911b).

15. Lenin (1907a).

16. Lenin (1913d).

17. Lenin (1913b; 1908).

18. Lenin (1906a).

19. Lenin (1906b).

20. Lenin (1906e; 1906b; 1904; 1910b; and 1907b).

21. Communist parties maintain that India is semi-feudal and semi-capitalist—not semi-feudal and semi-Asiatic.

22. This assessment was disavowed at the Sixth Party Congress of the Communist Party of China in 1928.

23. Aziatophiles was a reference to those who supported the notion of the AMP.

24. Mad'iar was arguably the most extensively translated, published, and cited Soviet author on ancient China (Fogel, 1988: 64).

25. Wittfogel actively helped Joseph McCarthy in his witch-hunt against communists and progressives in the USA. The infamous Senate Internal Security Subcommittee (SISS) initiated a hearing in 1951–52 against the Institute of Pacific Relations (IPR): prominent China specialist Professor Owen Lattimore was charged with being a 'subversive' and misdirecting the Roosevelt and Truman Administrations' China policy, bringing about the 'loss' of China and the 'betrayal' of the Chinese Nationalist Party (Newman, 1992: 334). Eager to prove his new US patriotism, Karl Wittfogel joined the crusade against his former friend and became the first scholar to testify against Lattimore (Newman, 1992: 335).

26. Wittfogel's work was allegedly promoted through publications, scholarships, seminars, and organisations that were making a conscious effort to promote research directed at fighting the Cold War. For instance, in the late 1950s, the Ford Foundation, through the Social Science Research Council, 'poured hundreds of millions of dollars' to finance area studies (Lewis and Wigen, 1999). The committee created to research China included John King Fairbank, George Taylor, and Karl Wittfogel. Similarly, the CIA provided funds through the Paris-based Congress for Cultural Freedom for the journal *China Quarterly* that inaugurated with a debate on Wittfogel's book *Oriental Despotism* (MacFarquhar, 1995).

27. I.V. Kachanovski's book *Slave Owning, Feudalism or the Asiatic Mode of Production?* (Moscow 1971) was considered a serious assault on the Western promoters of the concept of the AMP.

2

AMP, Colonial Path, and Asiatic Capitalism in South Asia

Infinitely diverse combinations and elements of this or that type of capitalist evolution are possible

V.I. Lenin (1899: 33)

This chapter makes two propositions. Firstly, it proposes that the mode of production of pre-colonial South Asia was AMP rather than feudal. It examines various criticisms relating to the principal characteristics of the AMP: that is, natural economy, absence of private property in land, state and public works, and surplus extraction by the state. Divergences, in characterising the dominant mode of production of South Asia, do not principally revolve around the empirical facts. Historians generally agree that the dominant economic system of the Mughal state was jagirdari, where surplus extraction was carried out in the form of land revenue (divan) collected from village communities by representatives of the state. Hence, the debate in Indian historiography is mainly centred on how one can categorise land revenue as a mode of surplus extraction. This chapter proposes that surplus extraction through land revenue from village communities should be considered to be qualitatively different from feudal rent. The Indian feudalism hypothesis obscures the distinguishing features of Mughal India and feudal Europe. Moreover, the Indian feudalism thesis broadens the definition of feudalism so that the term loses specificity and explanatory power. In sum, the chapter argues that South Asia travelled a path of historical development that was distinct from Europe.

Secondly, the chapter revisits the debate on the paths of transition to capitalism. How does one mode of production change into another? What are the mechanisms and dynamics of transition? The capitalist transitions of Europe can be divided into two general categories: the republican, and the Junkers path (see Lenin, 1899: Preface; Moore, 1966). This chapter proposes that India's transition to capitalism occurred through a third path that was altogether distinct from Europe: the colonial path of transition to capitalism. It identifies three key features of India's colonial path: foreign domination, the siphoning of surplus, and capitalism planted upon the AMP. Moreover, this colonial path of capitalist transformation resulted in the metamorphosis of the AMP into capitalism, giving rise to a transitory form that the study terms 'Asiatic capitalism'. Alavi and Bagchi have argued that colonial capitalism is itself a mode of production (Alavi, 1980; Bagchi, 1982). However, this chapter argues that colonialism did not give rise to a distinct mode of production but to a distinct path of capitalist transition.

WORKABLE GENERALISATIONS?

At the outset of any socio-economic analysis of South Asia, one is confronted with the question of whether workable or analytically useful generalisations about such a vast region are even possible. In this instance, given the diversity and complexity of South Asia's socio-economic formation, is it even possible to talk about a single mode of production? Kosambi argued that (1956: 50):

> India is not a mathematical point but a very large country, a sub-continent with the utmost diversity of natural environment, language, historical course of development. Neither in the means of production nor in the stages of social development was there overall homogeneity in the oldest times. Centuries must be allowed to pass before comparable stages of productive and social relationships may be established between the Indus valley, Bengal and Malabar. Even then important differences remain which makes periodisation for India as a whole almost impossible, except with the broadest margins.

The received wisdom from European orientalist historians was that the socio-economic formation of South Asia was quite distinct from that of Europe. British historians, such as W.H. Moreland and James Mill, had opined that the political economy of pre-colonial South Asia was not based on private property of land or feudal rent. Instead, it was based on village communities and a tax collected in the name of the ruler (Mill, 1821; Moreland, 1929). Marx, as shown earlier, adopted these views in his theory of the AMP.

Leading Indian historians have generally regarded Marx's charac-terisation of India as 'orientalist'. Indian nationalist historians, such as R.P. Tripathi, Ibne Hasan, and P. Saran, have considered Mughal institutions to be feudal (Hasan, 1970; Saran, 1941; Tripathi, 1956). Bipan Chandra asserted that historical research, over the last century, has demonstrated that Marx's basic notions regarding Indian society were 'essentially incorrect' (O'Leary, 1989: 262).

Indian Marxists, such as M. Athar Ali, Satish Chandra, Irfan Habib, S. Nurul Hasan, and D.D. Kosambi, brought questions regarding the division of labour and state formation to the fore (Ali, 1993; Chandra, 1959; Habib, 1963; Hasan, 1973; Kosambi, 1956). Nonetheless, the framework of 'feudalism with Asiatic features' dominated the writings of early twentieth century Indian Marxist intellectuals. For instance, S.A. Dange's *India: From Primitive Communism to Slavery* (written while he was in prison in the 1940s) described pre-colonial India as a society based on slavery and feudalism with Asiatic features (Dange, 1955). D.D. Kosambi's *An Introduction to the Study of Indian History*, considered a Marxist classic in India, also utilised the concept of feudalism for India (Kosambi, 1956). Both Kosambi and R.S. Sharma asserted that India did not pass through a stage of slavery, but had been feudal since the middle of the first millennium (Sharma, 1965). The eminent Indian Marxist historian Irfan Habib rejected the concept of the AMP and claimed that Marx himself developed reservations about the AMP after 1867 (Habib, 2002: 5). In Habib's view, pre colonial India was not stagnant or without history, and he regarded such views as a product of the colonial project (Habib, 2002: 234). Nonetheless, Habib also rejected the notion that Mughal India could be regarded as feudal and preferred to use the term 'medieval political economy' to describe pre-colonial India (Habib, 1985: 49).

However, in more recent times there has also been a growing recognition among historians, such as Sarvepalli Gopal, Romila Thapar, Radhakamal Mukherjee, Harbans Mukhia, Brij Narain, and Ravinder Kumar, that ancient India's mode of production was distinct from Europe's. The collection of essays in the book *Feudalism and Non-European Societies*, edited by Terry Byres and Harbans Mukhia, have brought together some of the most significant contributions in this regard (Byres and Mukhia, 1985). On the one hand, influential scholars such as Shiva Chandra Jha, D.D. Kosambi, Ram Sharan Sharma, and

B.N.S. Yadav argued that pre-colonial South Asia was feudal (Jha, 1963; Kosambi, 1956; Sharma, 1965; Yadav, 1973). On the other hand, A.R. Desai, N. Ram, Anupam Sen, and Shelvankar considered the AMP to be an appropriate characterisation of pre-colonial South Asia (Desai, 1966; Ram, 1972; Sen, 1982; Shelvankar, 1943). Samir Amin, Kate Currie, John Haldon, and Chris Wickham have also upheld a similar concept to the AMP, preferring to use the term 'tributary mode of production' (Amin, 1976; Currie, 1980, 1984; Haldon, 1993; Wickham 1985). This debate is supplemented by the debates on the mode of production of contemporary South Asia and the colonial mode of production (Alavi, 1982; Banaji, 1972; Patnaik, 1990).

Of late, 'revisionist' historians, such as Muzaffar Alam, C.A. Bayly, Gerard Fussman, Frank Perlin, Chetan Singh, Burton Stein, and Andre Wink, have emphasised the study of regional elites and the 'segmentary' nature of state-power, challenging the view that the Mughal state was centralised (Alam, 1986; Bayly, 1983; Fussman, 1982; Perlin, 1985; Singh, 1988; Stein, 1980; Wink, 1986). Since the 1980s, the perspective of 'history from below', associated with Subaltern Studies and inspired by the writings of Ranajit Guha and Eric Stokes among others, moved the focus away from questions of political economy altogether (Guha, 2000; Stokes, 1978). Although there is an ever-increasing amount of literature on ancient and contemporary South Asia, research on the mode or production declined as a result of the ideological impact of the collapse of the Soviet Union (Chibber, 2006).

Given this complex body of literature, it is necessary to define the limits of the analysis of this chapter. The chapter is not concerned with the socio-economic formation of pre-colonial South Asia in its entirety. Firstly, that would require an analysis of several periods, such as the Harrapan, Mauryan, Gupta, Vijayanagar, Delhi Sultanate, and so on. Secondly, it would require an analysis at several levels: social, cultural, political, economic, and ideological. It is neither the intention of this section to contest the empirical evidence on pre-colonial India, nor to present new evidence to supplement the existing literature. Instead, the study is limited to only investigating the dominant mode of production of Mughal India.

AMP in South Asia

This section examines the empirical evidence and criticisms relating to the four distinctive features (as identified in Chapter 1) of the AMP in Mughal India: natural economy, absence of private property in land, public works as the basis of the state, and surplus extraction by the state. It endeavours to show that if one is consistent with the criterion that the mode of surplus extraction is the defining feature of a mode of production, the logical conclusion seems to be that a society where land revenue is the dominant mode of surplus extraction must be distinct from slavery, feudalism, and capitalism.

Natural Economy

Certain authors have rejected the concept of the AMP on the grounds that whereas Marx characterised India as a natural economy, one can demonstrate the existence of a cash nexus in pre-colonial India. For instance, Habib (1995: 26) wrote:

> In Capital III, the 'Indian community', like the society of European antiquity and the middle ages, is said to possess, through the union of agriculture and handicraft, a 'mode of production' able to sustain a *natural economy*—*or an economy without exchange.* [Emphasis added]

He (1995: 234) continued:

> the moment one goes to the actual evidence, it becomes apparent that Marx's description contains grave errors of fact—such as *his assumption that the cash nexus did not exist*, or that there was no or little artisan production for the market. [Emphasis added]

Similarly, Chaudhuri and Raychaudhuri and Habib have also contended that Marx significantly underestimated the degree of monetisation in pre-colonial India (Chaudhuri, 1985; Raychaudhuri and Habib, 1982). Opponents of the AMP are likely to conclude, much like O'Leary, that 'the scale, range and penetration of exchange relations in urban and rural Mughal India were so extensive that they violate certain necessary conditions of the AMP [i.e. an economy without exchange]' (O'Leary, 1989: 292). This line of criticism is premised on the faulty logic that a natural economy is an economy entirely devoid of exchange.

For classical political economy, all pre-capitalist modes of production—including the AMP, slavery, and feudalism—were considered to be 'natural economies'. For instance, in *Capital*, Marx repeatedly used the term 'natural economy' in relation to slave and feudal societies (Marx, 1998b: 79, 336; 1998c: 537, 542, 608, 613). Similarly, Engels used the term 'natural economy' to characterise ancient and feudal societies in *Anti-Duhring*, *The Peasant Question in France and Germany*, and *The Early History of Christianity* (Engels, 1934: 105, 116, 1894–95, 1894). The term 'natural economy' does not refer to an economy without exchange, but to an economy where the division of labour is not determined by exchange.

Marx never asserted that the cash-nexus did not exist in India. His assertion was limited to the view that exchange did not determine the division of labour in ancient India. Marx explicitly wrote, 'production here [in pre-colonial India] is independent of that division of labour brought about, in Indian society as a whole, by means of the exchange of commodities' (Marx, 1998a: 513).

This observation by Marx is supported by most modern scholarship on ancient India. Empirical evidence suggests that the division of labour in Mughal India was based on customs and traditions, particularly around the caste system (Stevenson, 1954). The general consensus, among scholars, is that 'much of India's agricultural and artisan product even in this century was disposed of through "marketless trade" related to patterns of marriage, clientage and religious activity' (Bayly, 1985). Market forces played little role in determining the overall social division of labour. Although there was a cash-nexus—Habib estimated that about 250 million rupees were in circulation even at the time of Emperor Akbar—the producers within the village communities did not, generally, procure the basic necessities of life from the market (Raychaudhuri and Habib, 1982: 360–381).

Marx and Engels stated that, in the AMP, handicraft was carried on as a secondary occupation of agriculture (Marx, 1998a: 512). Eric Hobsbawn elevated handicrafts into the distinctive feature of the AMP. He wrote (1964: 33):

> The fundamental characteristic of this system [AMP] was 'the self sustaining unit of manufacture and agriculture', which thus contains all the conditions for reproduction and surplus production within itself.

However, Marx never claimed that handicraft as a secondary occupation of agriculture was exclusive to the AMP. On the contrary, he explicitly stated the opposite and argued that handicraft was carried out as a secondary occupation of agriculture in all pre-capitalist modes of production. He wrote (1954a: 700):

> Domestic handicrafts and manufacturing labour, as secondary occupations of agriculture, which forms the basis, are the prerequisites of that mode of production upon which natural economy rests—in European antiquity and the Middle Ages as well as in the present day Indian community.

Similarly, Chris Wickham's detailed study argued that handicraft was carried out as a secondary occupation of agriculture in the Roman empire (Wickham, 2005: ch. 8). Thus, Hobsbawm's understanding of the AMP is quite obviously a departure from Marx's (Singh, 1983).

One of the pitfalls of reading Marx on the AMP is to read passages concerning India in isolation from the context of the overall discussion. In nearly all the passages where Marx mentions the AMP, his chief objective is 'to throw particular aspects or characteristics of capitalism and of the development of capitalism into relief' (Kitching, 1985). The object of these passages is not to elucidate the features of the AMP but to elucidate the features of capitalism.

For instance, in the section that contains the oft-quoted passage on India in *Capital I* (1954b, 513–5), Marx observed that in pre-capitalist modes of production the social division of labour was carried out in accordance with an authoritative plan, while there was little or no division of labour within the workshop. In contrast, under capitalism, there was anarchy in the social division of labour and a strict plan in the workshop. To illustrate this observation, Marx repeated what he believed were well-established facts about India. He stated that in pre-capitalist India there was a 'blending of handicraft and agriculture' (that is, little or no division of labour in manufacture) while Indian society as a whole was organised in accordance with a rigid caste system (social division of labour is organised in accordance with a plan). In contrast, in capitalism, anarchic market forces organised the social division of labour, while the division of labour in the workshop was organised in accordance with a strict plan. Marx (1954a: 513) concluded:

While division of labour in society at large, whether such division is brought about or not by exchange of commodities, is common to economic formations of society the most diverse, division of labour in the workshop, as practised by manufacture, is a special creation of the capitalist mode of production alone.

In summary, the central purpose of this passage was to argue that the division of labour in manufacture was a distinctive feature of capitalism. Hence, it should come as no surprise that the characteristics of the AMP emphasised in this passage from *Capital* are not exclusive to Asia, because Marx's objective was not to emphasise the distinctive characteristics of the AMP but to emphasise the distinctive characteristics of capitalism.

In conclusion, Marx never argued that Mughal India was entirely devoid of exchange. His argument was that the division of labour was not based on exchange. Secondly, Marx held the view that handicraft was carried out as a secondary occupation to agriculture in all pre-capitalist modes of production.

ABSENCE OF PRIVATE PROPERTY IN LAND

There are two major criticisms relating to the view that Mughal India was characterised by the absence of private property. The first contests the empirical evidence, and the second argues that the absence of private property contradicts Marx's view that the AMP was based on class exploitation.

As discussed in Chapter 1, nearly all early European orientalists—including François Bernier, Mountstuart Elphinstone, Sir William Hunter, W.H. Moreland, Henry Maine, James Mill, John Stuart Mill, and Sir J.B. Phear—maintained that pre-colonial India was characterised by the absence of private property in land (Bernier, 1934; Elphinstone, 1841; Hunter, 1882; Maine, 1907, 1880; Mill, 1821; Mill, 1848; Moreland, 1929; Phear, 1880). Marx and Engels also argued that the absence of private landed property was a distinct feature of the AMP (Engels, 1853; Marx, 1853a, 1853b). Even among modern historians, the view prevails that the Mughal system existed without private property in land (Habib, 2002: 107). According to historian Burton Stein (1985: 82), between the tenth and seventeenth centuries:

the basic system of agrarian production and property continued to be communal in the sense that productive resources vested in corporate peasant groups. Mastery over productive means was not individual: productive resources were pooled and distributed customarily by headsmen, benefits were allocated by shares.

Historians generally agree that the Mughal system was organised along the lines of the Iqta system. The jagirs (area of land) allotted by the Mughal kings were not hereditary and jagirdars were re-transferred every three or four years (Habib, 2002: 95). One of the leading historians of Mughal India, Irfan Habib, has opined that private property, in the form of saleable individual right to specific fields, simply did not arise in [Mughal] India (Habib, 2002: 134). Historians agree that private property in land was introduced by the British colonial government through the Permanent Settlement Act of 1793 (Gopal, 1949; Habib, 2002: 192). For these reasons, the Indian feudalism hypothesis has been inviting increasing criticism for drawing too close a parallel between European and Indian social formations (see for instance Wink, 1990).

However, certain historians point to ancient texts, or carvings on the walls of temples, to argue that private property in land existed. For instance, Ram Sharan Sharma and B.N.S. Yadav argued, on the basis of ancient texts, that private property in land developed in South Asia from the fourth to the seventh and eighth centuries (Sharma, 1965: 263–272; Yadav). Dharma Kumar made a case for the existence of private property in land with respect to the Kindgom of the Cholas of Tanjore, based on carvings on the walls of temples (Kumar, 1985). However, there are three unresolved counter-arguments to these views.

Firstly, Marx and Engels drew a distinction between possession and ownership and argued that, despite the absence of private property, there was individual and collective possession of land in pre-colonial India (Krader, 1975: 100; Marx, 1973: 471). Given this distinction, it is uncertain whether these ancient texts are referring to the alienation of property or alienation of possession.

Secondly, the well-acknowledged fact that land revenue was the dominant form of surplus extraction contradicts the notion of private property in land. By definition, private ownership of land gives the landlord complete control over the land and its produce. On this basis, when the land is leased to a tenant, the landowner receives some form of rent. In other words, when land is private property, one can expect surplus to take some form of rent. However, land revenue was appropriated by the state from the village community as a whole. Hence, the very existence of land revenue as the principle form of surplus extraction indicates that the form of ownership of land was substantially different from landed private property. According to Anderson, even in China where private property in land had developed further than in Islamic civilisations, 'it still fell short of European property concepts' (Anderson, 1979: 543).[1]

Thirdly, to refute the existence of the AMP, it is not sufficient to prove the mere existence of private property. It is necessary to prove that private property existed as the dominant form of property. The existence of private property in a specific period or region certainly underscores the complexity of India's social formation. However, it does not undermine the view that the absence of private property in land was the dominant feature of the mode of production of pre-colonial South Asia.

Certain critics of the AMP argue that class exploitation is only possible in the context of private property. In their opinion, the absence of private property in land and exploitation are incompatible and contradictory (see for instance O'Leary, 1989).

However, this criticism fails to recognise that property can take different concrete forms, and that private property is merely one of the many forms of property. For instance, Marx and Engels frequently used the terms 'ancient property', 'feudal property', and 'bourgeois property' (Marx, 1998c, 1846, 1844, 1968). In the Communist Manifesto, Marx stated, 'The French Revolution . . . abolished feudal property in favour of bourgeois property' (Marx and Engels, 1998: 28). Ancient property includes private ownership of the producer (slave), but land may or may not be private property. For instance, in Rome, land could be owned either as private property or state property (*ager publicus*). Similarly, under manorial feudal property, legal and economic power over the fief—including land and serfs—belonged to the lord. In this system, the serfs were tied to the land and to their lord through a system of vassalage. Hence, the producer had direct access to land, and only the expropriation of the serf laid the foundation for capitalist private property.[2] Hence, for Marx and Engels, modern private property was the highest stage of development of property. In the Communist Manifesto, they wrote (1848: 28):

modern bourgeois private property is the final and most complete expression of the system of producing and appropriating products, that is based on class antagonisms, on the exploitation of the many by the few.

Hence, if modern bourgeois private property is only 'the final and most complete expression' of exploitation, other forms of property and exploitation are not only possible but also implied in the above passage.

Lastly, not only can feudal exploitation exist without pure private property, but even capitalist exploitation can exist without private property in land. As long as labour power and all other means of production (aside from land) are private property, capitalism would continue to exist. In fact, Marx was an advocate of the nationalisation of land for the speedy development of capitalism (Marx, 1847: 173–187). If capitalist exploitation can exist without private property in land, it is arguably not a stretch to contend that other forms of exploitation can also exist without private property in land.

STATE AND PUBLIC WORKS

The Marxist theory of the state argues that the state emerged when primitive societies endowed a certain measure of authority in certain individuals to safeguard the common interests of the community and combat conflicting interests (Engels, 1934: part II, ch. 4). With the gradual historical development of productive forces, society began to produce a surplus, and class exploitation emerged on the basis of the extraction of this growing surplus. These authorities, based initially on the common interests of the community, increasingly separated themselves from society. Through a long historical process, 'he who was originally the servant [of the community], where conditions were favourable, changed gradually into the lord' and finally united into a ruling class (Engels, 1934: part II, ch. 4).

According to Marx and Engels, the formation of Asiatic states was conditioned by the material circumstances of those societies. In South Asia, 80 per cent of the annual precipitation occurs in the monsoon season (Bagla, 2006). Hence, the control of rain, river, and floodwater, through channels, dams, dykes, and so on, is vital for agriculture. This control of water requires the organisation of collective labour. It follows that the organisation of this collective labour gave rise to various unifying authorities that became the precursors of the Asiatic state.

In other words, the common interests of communities, that formed the beginning of state-power in all societies, included the control of water in Asia. The material necessity of collective labour for artificial irrigation evolved into a system of surplus extraction, by the state, from village communities (Engels, 1853; Marx, 1853a, 1853b). The land revenue collected by the Mughal state was not merely a tax but a claim on production itself. During the Mughal period, the 'state is held to have extracted between 40 and 45 per cent of gross agricultural produce, the value of which was accumulated in the hands of a very few imperial military nobles (mansabdars)' (Bayly, 1985).

Critics of the AMP have argued that the state was not as centralised as argued by Marx and Engels. For instance, Muzaffar Alam, C.A. Bayly, Gerard Fussman, Frank Perlin, Chetan Singh, N.A. Siddiqi, Burton Stein, and Andre Wink have emphasised the 'segmentary' nature of state-power (Alam, 1986; Bayly, 1983; Fussman, 1982: 74; Perlin, 1985: 74; Singh, 1988: 74; Siddiqi, 1970: 74; Stein, 1980: 74; Wink, 1986: 74). Other critics have pointed out that the irrigation system of Mughal India was not built by a central authority but often by local authorities. For instance, Edmund Leach demonstrated that the irrigation system in Ceylon was mostly on a small scale and locally organised (Leach, 1981: 207–215). Similarly, Burton Stein wrote (1985: 85):

> In most parts of south India, at least, 'mastery of the means and processes of production' was vested in local peasant communities under whose chiefs there was sustained and successful development of irrigation potentials in the southern peninsula.

Although there are many scholars in India who argue the case for a centralised Mughal state (see for instance the Aligarh School of Historians or Ali, 1993), what is more pertinent is that the observations about segmentary state power may be entirely accurate and yet in no way contradict the AMP. This is because the focus on the degree of state centralisation misunderstands the concept of the AMP. This misunderstanding may be based on the incorrect identity drawn between Marx's concept of oriental despotism and Wittfogel's concept of oriental despotism (Wittfogel, 1963).

Not only did Wittfogel make the 'hydraulic state' the centre of the AMP, but he also caricaturised it as a highly centralised, bureaucratised, and totalitarian instrument. In doing so, though Wittfogel once claimed to be a Marxist, he was closer to the European chauvinist views of Montesquieu than to Marx.

As shown earlier, Marx never considered the Asiatic state to be any more or less centralised, oppressive, or despotic than other ancient or medieval European states (Marx, 1843b). The crux of Marx's conception was that the organisation of collective labour for artificial irrigation (whether by the central state or localised authorities) resulted in a specific form of surplus extraction that Marx termed the AMP.

In summary, whereas Wittfogel attempted to prove that the Asiatic state was, by definition, more oppressive than the forms of state found in the West, Marx's concept of oriental despotism was an explanation of the material conditions that brought about a system in which the dominant form of surplus extraction was through state collection of land revenue.

A second line of criticism, with respect to the Asiatic state, is that the coterminous origins of the Asiatic ruling class and state violate the principles of historical materialism (O'Leary, 1989: 184–191). O'Leary wrote (1989: 189):

> [The] Marxist theory of the state is jeopardized by such a fusion precisely because there seems to be no pre-existent class which brings the state into being, and therefore the emergence of the state cannot be explained in the proper Marxist way—through the operation of class struggle.

Marx and Engels never understood the emergence of the ruling class and state as a spatially or temporally distinct phenomenon. It would be a mistake to assume that a ruling class emerges, rules for a period of time without a state, and at some future point after its formation organises a state. Just as social relations and legal expression develop together, the emergence of a ruling class and state should also be understood as coterminous, evolutionary, gradual, and a self-transformative phenomenon.

Lastly, O'Leary continued that the Asiatic state, traditionally understood to be part of the superstructure, was also endowed with a vital economic role (surplus extraction). He argued that the fact that the economic base and superstructure in the AMP could not be empirically and conceptually separated contradicts historical materialism (O'Leary, 1989: 182–184).

In fact, there is no evidence to suggest that Marx or Engels viewed the base-superstructure as empirically exclusive spheres. They viewed this distinction as theoretical abstractions of complex social relations. It does not follow that since the base and superstructure cannot be empirically separated, they can also not be conceptually separated. For instance, economic and political activities are very closely intertwined in the interventionist Keynsian state and may be difficult to empirically separate. However, the conceptual separation of the academic fields of economics and political science is unaffected by the existence of the interventionist state. Hence, the only thing that one can conclude from the fact that the Asiatic state also plays a vital economic role is that an interpretation of historical materialism that posits that the base-superstructure must be empirically exclusive (as opposed to theoretical abstractions of complex social relations) is simply untenable in light of the facts of history.

SURPLUS EXTRACTION AND CLASS FORMATION

As stated already, the dominant form of surplus extraction in Mughal India was land revenue collected from village communities by representatives of the state (Habib, 2002: 147). Armies for territorial conquest, luxuries for the ruling class, the great architectural achievements of this period—including forts, mosques, and monuments—and so on were all based predominantly on the extraction of land revenue. Moreover, this land revenue was not rent from the land but a claim on the crop (Habib, 2002: 186). It was estimated to be between a third and half of total produce, depending on the productivity of the land (Habib, 2002: 190). Stein (1985: 60) wrote:

> [Nobles and rajas alone] commanded 36 per cent of the total revenue of the empire and controlled about the same proportion of arable land in their jagirs; a mere 445 mansabdars (including the above elite) controlled 61 per cent of land revenues and probably one half of the lands of the empire.

Military leaders, called mansabdars, were ranked in accordance to the number of foot soldiers and horsemen under their control (Habib, 2002: 94). 'Mansabdar' literally means rank-holder (mansab means rank). It was the generic term for the grading of all military officials of the

Mughal Empire, with the Mughal Emperor determining their appointment, promotion, suspension, and dismissal.

Mansabdars of higher rank were awarded a personal iqta, called a jagir—land granted to army or state officials for limited periods in lieu of a regular wage (Cahen, 1968). Neither the offices, nor the estates that supported these jagirdars, were hereditary. Hence, the land allotted to them (jagir) was not owned as private property (Moreland, 1929: 217–219). In fact, these jagirdars were usually transferred from one jagir to another every three or four years (Habib, 2002: 95). The definition of 'jagirdar', provided by Soviet editors in a collection of articles by Marx and Engels entitled 'On Colonialism' (Marx and Engels, 1960, 356–7), is as follows:

> Jagirdars—representatives of the Moslem feudal gentry in the Great Mughal Empire who received, in temporary use, big estates (jagirs) for which they did military service and supplied contingents of troops.

Furthermore, the jagir cannot be considered a fief. Not only were these jagirs not hereditary but, unlike Europe, judicial powers over the jagir were not vested in the jagirdar. They were vested in another representative of the state, called the qazi. Thus, while jagirdars were certainly landlords (they enjoyed the right to lord over the peasants and village as a representative of the state), they were not landowners in the sense of owners of the land.

These jagirdars did not live on the rural jagirs, but lived in the cities (Habib, 2002: 212). The urban population of Mughal India was about 15 per cent of the total population (Raychaudhuri and Habib, 1982: 167–171). Trade between cities and the country mainly flowed in one direction: the country supplied the cities, and the cities sent little or nothing back. Habib (2002: 231) wrote:

> It is not to be forgotten that practically no rural market existed for urban crafts; rural monetization was thus almost entirely the result of the need to transfer surplus agriculture produce to the towns.

Handicraft production in the cities (karkhana production) did not supply tools or implements for villages, but were organised to produce luxury goods 'in order to meet the requirements of the aristocrats' (Habib, 2002: 211, 220). The surplus from jagirs was mostly used to retain the Mughal army and sustain the ruling class. Very little was used for the building of new tools or technology (Habib, 2002: 99, 204–212). Thus, the production of the means of production was diffuse and poorly developed.

Below the ruling class of jagirdars stood a class of zamindars, ta'allugdars, muqaddams, and patels. The zamindars were principally tax collectors and in northern India extracted in kind (and later in cash) on average about a tenth of the surplus product (Habib, 1969: 242, 1963: 162–167; Raychaudhuri and Habib, 1982). They had the right to collect land revenue from the village but were not landowners. Habib (1985: 48) wrote:

> the zamindar's own very limited claim upon rent belies any existence of landed property properly speaking; in part at least, it served as an instrument for the realisation of the claims of the higher authority, the state.

Thus, as Habib has pointed out above, the rajas, jagirdars, mansabdars, zamindars, ta'allugdars, muqaddams, patels, and so on all lived off the surplus appropriated from the village communities in the form of land revenue; yet, none of these classes owned land as private property.

At the lowest rung were the muzaras (peasants), differentiated by hereditary castes. The labour relations of muzaras were quite distinct from those of European serfs. Firstly, the muzaras were tied collectively to the village community through the caste system imposed by extra-economic coercion. Therefore, unlike European feudalism, peasants were not principally bound to the soil or to the fief, but rather to the community. Although there was 'great abundance of land' (Habib, 2002: 183), the individual was bound to the community because settled agriculture required collective labour, animal power, implements for clearing, watering, and fertilising the land. The technical necessity of collective labour was also a means of social domination. The individual had no alternative but to work with, and through, the community (Habib, 2002: 183). Thus, while in Europe unfreedom was individual because the serf or slave was tied to the lord or master as an individual, in South Asia the forms of unfreedom were collective because surplus was appropriated from the entire village. Hence, the village was not a sovereign body or a republic but a tributary body.

In summary, whereas in feudalism, the feudal lord owned the manor and the dominant economic form of surplus extraction was rent; by contrast, in Mughal India, jagirdars were not owners of land and the dominant economic form of surplus extraction was land revenue (mal) (Wickham, 1985: 183–184). Wickham and Amind termed the Mughal system the 'tributary mode of production' (Amin, 1976; Wickham, 1985: 183–184). However, in so far as land revenue is the form of surplus extraction of the tributary and the Asiatic mode of production, Byres and Mukhia have argued that there is no essential difference between the tributary and Asiatic mode of production (1985: 14).

Secondly, while European forms of pre-capitalist bondage—slavery and serfdom—were codified as law, in South Asia the forms of bondage were kept in place by oral traditions of religious practices, rites, and customs that together made up the caste system. Natural necessity, social necessities, and rituals all became interrelated and internalised in religion. Although caste is only justified in the Hindu religion, even 'Islam made almost no impact on the caste system' (Habib, 2002: 142). The practice of caste was prevalent all over the subcontinent during the Mughal period (and is present even today) (Desai, 1976; Singh, 1977). 'The Christians, the Muslims and the Sikhs all practiced caste even when their religion decried it' (Jodhka, 2002). The fact that surplus extraction occurred not through the institution of serfdom but through a different form of subjugation codified as the caste system is itself an indication that the mode of production of Mughal India was not feudalism.

Advocates of the Indian feudalism hypothesis either deny that serfdom is a central feature of feudalism, or argue that serfdom was a feature of Mughal India. L.A. Sedov defined feudalism in the following manner (Sawer, 1977, 77):

> given the cultivators work on their own land with the aid of their own implements, and that they alienate their surplus labour in the interest of a third persons, they are therefore subject to feudal exploitation.

This broad definition of feudalism encompasses only two features: 1) the cultivators possess land and implements; 2) they alienate surplus labour in the form of surplus produce or labour services to a third party. Hence, the mode of surplus extraction of serfdom was no longer considered central to the definition of feudalism.

Alternatively, Sharma has tried to prove the existence of serfdom by broadening its definition to include all forms of forced labour. Thus, we are offered Sharma's rather obscure definition: 'serfdom means giving more surplus labour than surplus product' (Sharma, 1985: 30). Similarly, quoting B.N.S. Yadava's study on forced labour mentioned in the ancient Hindu text of *Skanda Purana*, Sharma concluded that 'serfdom cannot be dismissed as an incidental feature [of pre-colonial India]' (Habib, 1985: 32; Sharma, 1985: 30).

However, most historians of South Asia are agreed upon the fact that pre-colonial South Asia was not dominated by serfdom. For instance, Habib has pointed out that the 'varied forms of subjection [in Mughal India] . . . have little in common with serfdom' (Habib, 1985: 47). Similarly, Mukhia has stated that there is 'the absence of serfdom in Indian history' (Mukhia, 1985b: 268).

Given the complete absence of serfdom, a class structure where jagirdars are not owners of land, the village community differentiation along caste lines, and land revenue as the principle form of surplus extraction, is it unreasonable to argue that the mode of production of Mughal India was substantially different from feudalism? In the words of Chris Wickham (1985: 170–171):

> a 'state class' based on a public institution, with political rights to extract surplus from a peasantry that it does not tenurially control is certainly common enough in Asia, and not only in Asia.

In conclusion, historians of South Asia are generally agreed that the dominant mode of surplus extraction during Mughal India was land revenue. Arguably, the necessity for collective labour to organise artificial irrigation for agriculture resulted in land revenue as the dominant form of surplus extraction. Land was not property. An intermediary class of zamindars acted as the collectors of the land revenue from the mass of peasants (muzareen) who were organised along the lines of a hereditary occupational division of labour known as the caste system. Hence, strictly speaking, there was no serfdom in South Asia.

This system of surplus extraction can neither be described as slavery nor as serfdom. In slavery, the producer was the private property of the master. Surplus was appropriated directly from the labour of the slave to the slave owner. While there certainly were slaves in South Asia, the peasants (muzareen) in the village communities were not the private property of the jagirdars.

Similarly, in feudal society the serf was tied to the land (fief) under the protection of the feudal lord. The feudal lord owned the land as property, and surplus was appropriated from the serf to the landowner as rent. While unfree or coerced labour was widespread in South Asia, the jagirdars were not owners of land, and the form of unfreedom of the muzareen did not occur through the institution of serfdom.

Jagirdars were not landowners, jagirs were not fiefs, muzareen were not serfs, and land revenue was not rent. In other words, the key economic relations of Mughal India were significantly distinct from European feudalism, and it seems a stretch to consider that the two constituted the same feudal mode of production. Lastly, given that land revenue was the main form of surplus extraction in Mughal India, the evidence seems to weigh in favour of concluding that the dominating mode of production of Mughal India was the AMP.

Colonial Path and Asiatic Capitalism

In order to understand the contemporary class structure of Pakistan, it is imperative not merely to explore the mode of production that preceded capitalism but also to examine the specific form or path of transition to capitalism. South Asia's transition was a product of colonialism. This colonial path had three distinctive features: foreign domination, the siphoning of surplus, and capitalism planted upon the AMP. Moreover, it resulted in a transitory form, termed 'Asiatic capitalism'. Let us briefly survey the literature on the transition to capitalism.

Review of Literature on Transitions

While analysing primitive accumulation in *Capital*, Marx made references to diverse forms of pre-capitalist agrarian relations (Asiatic, feudal, medieval, clanic community, communal, state, tribal, primitive squatter, peasant allotments, and holdings of bonded peasants) (Marx, 1998b: Part VIII). Marx demonstrated that capital, through a variety of ways and means, takes hold of diverse pre-capitalist relations and subordinates and remoulds them to itself. Similarly, in the discussion on the economic basis of capitalist ground rent in *Capital III* and *Theories of Surplus Value*, Marx also examined its historical forerunners— rent in kind, money-rent, quit-rent, labour service, corvée, and so on (Marx, 1856: Part VII, 1861). Additionally, Engels investigated how capitalism in agriculture led to the absorption of the peasantry into an urban economy or into rural capitalism (Engels, 1894, 1850).

Building on these views, Lenin developed the concept of paths of transition to capitalism in his work *The Development of Capitalism in Russia* (Lenin, 1899). Lenin thought that 'infinitely diverse combinations and elements' of capitalist evolution were possible (Lenin, 1899: 33). With respect to Europe, he identified two paths: the republican and the Junkers path (Lenin, 1899: Preface).

In the republican path, the landlord economy was broken up by revolution. Large landownership was expropriated by the peasantry by revolutionary means. Nearly all relics of serfdom were destroyed and labour-service was uprooted. Small peasant farming and commodity production received an enormous impetus. In summary, the republican path was the path of popular revolution that made a clean break with the past. Working people played a significant and active role in this transition. This revolutionary republican transition was epitomised by the French Revolution (LeFebvre, 2001; Lefebvre et al., 2005; Soboul, 1975).[3]

The distinctive feature of the Junkers path was that the feudal lords themselves slowly metamorphosed into capitalists. Prussian landlords (the Junkers) epitomised this transition, leading Lenin to term this transition the Junkers path. Napoleon's astounding military victories, following the French Revolution, demonstrated the organisational superiority of the new republican state. These victories led to the recognition within the defeated central European feudal empires of the need to modernise their armies. The modernisation of the army, in turn, led to the modernisation of the economy. The monarchist bourgeoisie and large landlords played a dominant role in this historical transition. The well-to-do peasants allied themselves with the landlords while the mass of the peasantry suffered degradation, enslavement, and expropriation on a vast scale. In Lenin's words (1899: Preface):

> The old landlord economy, bound as it is by thousands of threads to serfdom, is retained and turns slowly into purely capitalist, 'Junker' economy. The basis of the final transition from labour-service to capitalism is the internal metamorphosis of feudalist landlord economy. The entire agrarian system of the state becomes capitalist and for a long time retains feudalist features.

A number of scholars were influenced by the concept of paths of transition. Alexander Gerschenkron reasoned that the timing of industrialisation produced different paths of historical development (Gerschenkron, 1952). However, it was really Barrington Moore Jr's book *The Social Origins of Dictatorship and Democracy* that sparked widespread interest, especially in the 1960s and 1970s, on this question in Western academia (Moore, 1966).

Moore argued that the republican and Junkers path also explained the development of democracy (Byres, 1996; Moore, 1966). Societies of the republican path experienced the rapid development of productive forces and democracy. In contrast, societies of the Junkers path retained significant economic, political, and cultural aspects of the old order, which in turn gave birth to dictatorships and fascism. While Moore's argument was criticised as 'economic determinism' by writers such as Almond (1967), Lowenthal (1968), Rothman (1970), Wiener (1976), and Zagorin (1973), nonetheless, it also generated a new scholarship that utilised this comparative approach (see Bendix, 1967; Black, 1967; Gusfield, 1967; Harootunian, 1968; Hobsbawm, 1967; Link, 1967; Ness, 1967; Poggi, 1968; Shapiro, 1967).

Since then, historians have identified several paths of capitalist transition with respect to Europe. Jairus Banaji, Rodney Hilton, and Cristobal Kay examined the specific forms of feudal landed property in Europe that resulted in divergent historical paths (Banaji, 1976; Hilton, 1974, 1976, 1978, 1990; Kay, 1974). Similarly, Robert Brenner asserted that the transition to capitalism was the result of specific features of English feudalism (Aston and Philpin, 1985; Brenner, 1976). This specificity of the English transition has also been explored by Albritton (1993), Carter (1976, 1977), Cohen (1990), Gray (1993), Manning 1975), Russell (2000), Well (1979), Wrightson (1977), and Zmolek (2000). Similarly, Angelo (1995), Byres (1996), Mandle (1983), Mann (1987), McClelland (1997), and Post (1995) have examined the distinct paths of transitions of the North and South of the United States of America. Banaji has argued that these historically contingent paths of capitalist development may also lead to the articulation of forms of capitalism (Banaji, 2011). In summary, there is widespread acceptance of the notion that there is diversity in the paths of transition to capitalism.

REVIEW OF LITERATURE ON TRANSITION IN SOUTH ASIA

The view that colonial transitions are distinct from European transitions is even more widely acknowledged. In fact, the comparative method influenced the *Journal of Peasant Studies* and the *Journal of Agrarian Change* (see for instance Bernstein and Brass, 1996: 1–21; Chibber, 1998; Dinerman, 2001; Haj, 1994; Post, 1995). Dependency theory and world systems theory make a distinction between the metropole and the periphery. Samir Amin has talked about 'capitalism of the centre' and 'capitalism of the periphery' (Amin, 1974: 142). Alavi (1980) and Bagchi (1982) have argued the case for a colonial mode of production. Kathleen Gough has argued that South Asia was a a model of 'colonial style merchant capitalism' (Gough, 1969: 367).

Overall, the literature on the transition of South Asia can be divided along three lines: first, supporters of the British Empire and modernisation theorists; second, Indian nationalists; and third, a variety of Marxists and other leftists.

Arguably, in the case of India, there was a line of continuity between open apologists of imperialism and modernisation theorists. Both placed the principal responsibility of underdevelopment on traditional Indian institutions. Morrison (1911) and Anstey (1952) asserted that British rule set South Asia on the path of modernisation and progress. Myrdal's *Asian Drama* (1968) advocated modernisation, rationality, equality, planning, democracy, and cultural change through the state. Similarly, Krueger opined that 'rent seeking' and lack of competition characterised the Indian state and society. Lal (1984) maintained that the cultural aspects of Hindu society provided a circumstance in which the pre-colonial Indian economy came to rest at an equilibrium that was below optimum, resulting in stagnation. In more recent times, Ferguson's works *Colossus* and *Empire* (2004, 2005) have picked up on the same themes. Hence, for imperial apologists and modernisation theorists, the causes of underdevelopment are traditional Indian institutions, and the prescription is their replacement by 'modern' institutions.

Nationalist historiography is the mirror opposite of modernisation theory. The thrust of nationalist historiography is that not only did British colonialism prevent India from industrial prosperity but, rather, it deliberately de-industrialised the country. During the heyday of the nationalist movement, the political imperative to undermine the moral and ideological legitimacy of colonialism dominated the discourse of

Indian nationalist scholars. History was a terrain of struggle against colonialism. Nationalists such as Dadabhai Naoroji (1901) and R.C. Dutt (1906) asserted that colonialism de-industrialised India, drained society of its wealth, and condemned the people of South Asia to backwardness and poverty. Similarly, historians such as A.K. Coomaraswami (1977), K.P. Jayaswal (1988), R.C. Majumdar (1967), R.K. Mookerjee (1919), and H.C. Raychaudhuri (1953) engaged in what has been termed an 'unashamed glorification of the ancient Indian past' (Thapar 1968). Others, such as A.I. Chicherov, contended that pre-colonial South Asia was on the verge of a capitalist take-off before the arrival of the British (Chicherov, 1971; Raychaudhuri and Habib, 1982). Frank Perlin maintained that 'proto-capitalism' in South Asia had begun in the sixteenth century (Perlin, 1983), while Iqtidar Alam Khan reasoned that Indian feudalism had already created a bourgeois middle class that would have inevitably generated capitalism (Khan, 1976: 28, 29).

The Marxist position on colonialism is more complex. Although Marx considered capitalism to be an exploitative system, he also considered it a historical advance over feudalism. In the same way, he considered the victory of capitalism over the AMP to be a historical advance. On the one hand, Marx bitterly criticised the loot and plunder of colonialism in his writings (1887: 1078):

> The colonial system ripened, like a hot-house, trade and navigation. . . . The treasures captured outside Europe by undisguised looting, enslavement, and murder, floated back to the mother-country and were there turned into capital.

Marx opined that colonial loot laid bare the process of primitive accumulation of capital (1887: 1075–1075):

> The discovery of gold and silver in America, the extirpation, enslavement and entombment in mines of the aboriginal population, the beginning of the conquest and looting of the East Indies, the turning of Africa into a warren for the commercial hunting of black-skins, signalised the rosy dawn of the era of capitalist production. These idyllic proceedings are the chief moments of primitive accumulation.

Marx concluded that the people of India would only realise the benefits of modern science and industry when colonialism was overthrown. As a result, Marx and Engels wrote thirty-two articles in support of the revolt of 1857, dubbing it a 'national revolt' (Marx, 1857a). They also wrote nearly another dozen articles, and many letters, denouncing British rule in India and criticising various aspects of colonialism.

On the other hand, Marx argued that in the final analysis, capitalism provided the people of India with the very tools for their liberation. Marx termed this dialectic 'historical retribution' (1857b). Hence, to consider Marx an apologist for colonialism would be no less an injustice to his position than to consider him an apologist for capitalism.

Lenin argued that with the domination of finance capital, formation of cartels, export of capital to colonies, domination of the world economy by a few great powers, and the super-exploitation of the colonies, capitalism had reached the stage of imperialism (Lenin, 1917). This view became the basis for communist support for national liberation movements (Lenin, 1920). M.N. Roy and Rajani Palme Dutt developed the case for India's independence on the basis of Lenin's theory of imperialism (Dutt, 1940, 1957; Roy, 1987, first published in 1922).

Paul Baran's *Political Economy of Growth* (1957) contended that underdeveloped economies could not reach their growth potential because the core capitalist countries were exploiting them. This notion received further development in the writings of Cardoso (1979), Frank (1969), dos Santos (1970) and others, leading to the formation of dependency theory. Similarly, Wallerstein's world systems theory also posited that the development of the core was predicated upon the exploitation of the periphery (Wallerstein, 1974).

Colonialism has been the subject of a rich debate between dependency theory and Marxism (see Angotti, 1981). On the one hand, dependency and world systems theorists, such as Amin (1974, 1976), Barratt-Brown (1974), Emmanuel (1972), Sweezy (1946), and Wallerstein (1974), have departed from Marx's views on colonialism. On the other hand, orthodox Marxists, such as Avineri (1968), Desai (1971), Fernández and Ocampo (1974), and Kiernan (1974, 1981, 1995), have defended Marx's notion of historical retribution. Brenner (1977) and Weeks and Dore (1977) are equally critical of dependency theory. Others, such as

Bill Warren (1973), regarded the theory of imperialism as a reversal of Marxism. Warren asserted (1980: 47):

> Lenin's essay reversed Marxist doctrine on the progressive character of imperialist expansion and . . . erased from Marxism any trace of the view that capitalists could henceforth represent an instrument of social or economic advance, even in pre-capitalist societies. The historic mission of capitalism was declared ended.

Similarly, Geoffrey Kay contended that 'capitalism created under-development not because it exploited the underdeveloped world but because it did not exploit it enough' (Kay, 1975: 10). Foster-Carter (1978) and Szymanski (1977) challenged dependency theory and asserted that the accumulation of capital from the colonies was of only marginal importance to the development of capitalism.

Moreover, dependency theory confronts specific issues with respect to South Asia. For one, South Asia inherited a relatively well-developed industrial infrastructure from British colonial rule (Tomlinson, 1979: 44). Furthermore, private foreign capital is no longer as powerful as it once was in post-colonial South Asia (Cassen, 1978: 333). For these reasons, certain authors maintain that South Asia does not easily fit into the framework of dependency theory or world system analysis (Banaji, 1977: 14; Fox, 1984: 460; Petras, 1978: 31).

Some of the most vigorous Marxist scholarship on colonialism emerged from South Asian scholars. Scholars, such as Ahmad (1992), Bagchi (1972), Chandra (1979), Habib (1985), Patnaik (2006), and Sen (1982), have contended that colonialism represented an exploitative society where the development of productive forces simultaneously represented new forms of oppression for the vast majority. While they accepted that Mughal India represented an archaic system, they argued that colonialism was neither the best nor the most desirable path of development. Alavi (1980) and Bagchi (1982) reason that modern South Asia should be considered an example of a 'colonial mode of production'.

Coinciding with the emergence of neo-liberalism, subaltern studies inspired by scholars, such as Dipesh Chakrabarty (1989), Partha Chaterjee (1993), Ranajit Guha (2000), Gyan Prakash (1990), and Gayatri Spivak (1988), sought to write a narrative of the history of colonialism from below. Various Marxists, such as Aijaz Ahmad (1995),

Arif Dirlik (1997), San Juan (2002) and Neil Lazarus (1999), have subjected subaltern studies to criticism.

However, one historical fact that nearly all scholars are agreed upon is that the capitalist transition of South Asia did not occur through a popular revolution but as a consequence of British colonial rule. Superficially then, the general category of the Junkers path seems to bear many similarities to the transition under colonialism. In both cases, there was no popular revolution and these societies retained significant features of pre-capitalist modes of production. Both these transitions are forms of 'capitalism from above' (Byres, 1996). What, then, justifies the creation of another category distinct from the Junkers path?

By examining this literature on transitions and on India's colonial experience, this thesis identifies three distinctive features of India's transition: foreign domination, siphoning of surplus, and capitalism planted on the AMP. These features are by no means exhaustive of India's transition. But, they are points of divergence between the European paths and the path of transition of India. Arguably, the colonial path contained all the retrogressive features of 'capitalism from above', with the addition that the state, society, and the economy were structured for colonial, and later neo-colonial, exploitation.

The term 'colonial path' is not used in this study in the narrow political sense to merely denote the formal colonial empire. Large parts of India were controlled through indirect rule, and yet the impact of British rule was equally influential in such princely states. Conversely, certain parts of British India were formally occupied, but mainly as buffer regions against Tsarist expansion. Hence, the economic transition of these regions was far less pronounced. For instance, Balochistan and the North-West Frontier Province[4] were considered buffer provinces against Russia. Since the socio-economic impact of colonial domination is not restricted to the formal empire (Gallagher and Robinson, 1953), areas of India that were outside the formal colonial empire are, for the purposes of this study, included within the ambit of the colonial path of transition.

FOREIGN DOMINATION

The first distinguishing feature of South Asia's transition to capitalism is the domination of that society by the bourgeoisie of another country.

The British colonial state in India principally safeguarded the political, economic, and cultural interests of the British bourgeoisie. It was composed mainly of an army and a bureaucracy. Army officers made up the largest percentage of the British colonial elite, and the military had absolute priority in the allocation of resources in India (Gupta and Deshpande, 2002; Marshall, 1997: 102). These resources served to maintain an average annual troop strength of about 200,000 soldiers (mostly Indian) during the nineteenth century (Kaminsky, 1979: 78). About a quarter of the British army was kept in India during the first half of the nineteenth century (Marshall, 1997: 93). At the same time, only approximately 1,500 highly-trained bureaucrats, called the Indian Civil Service, provided the executive machinery of the colonial bureaucracy. They were instilled with the 'habit of authority', and were referred to as the 'steel frame' of British rule in India (Beaglehole, 1977: 249, 240; Marshall, 1997). Other princely states were controlled through a system of residents or political agents called 'indirect rule' (Fisher, 1984).

Colonial rule also required hegemony over indigenous culture (see Arnold, 1994; Chatterjee, 1993; Guha, 1988, 1997; Nandy, 1983; Washbook, 1988). The British enjoyed primary historical agency and, according to certain historians, there was little real interaction between the two cultures (Bayly, 1997: 179; Raj, 2000: 119). Albert Memmi wrote that the colonialist 'endeavors to falsify history, he rewrites laws, he would extinguish memories. Anything to succeed in transforming his usurpation into legitimacy' (Memmi, 1991: 52). A colonial intelligentsia was required to fulfil this task of cultural hegemony. This colonial elite lived in physical and ideological enclaves, separating themselves from ordinary people (Marshall, 1997: 101; Mason, 1973). In fact, the structure of colonial cities was predicated upon this segregation of the coloniser from the colonised (Kosambi and Brush, 1988: 33, 46). Just as there was segregation of living spaces, so was there one set of laws for the colonial elite and another for Indians. Racism and discrimination were written into law and colonial culture (Major, 1999; Memmi, 1991: 74).

British colonial rule led to the creation of a Westernised indigenous bourgeoisie. The British began introducing Western thought and culture in India from 1830 (Bellenoit, 2007). These measures principally included teaching three things: the English language, modern law, and modern administration. This process gathered pace after 1860, when the railway system was laid down and foreign trade increased (Stokes, 1973: 146). The purpose of these reforms was, in the famous words of Thomas Babington Macaulay, member of the Supreme Council of India (1835):

> to form a class who may be interpreters between us and the millions whom we govern,—a class of persons Indian in blood and colour, but English in tastes, in opinions, in morals and in intellect.

British reformers, such as Charles Grant, T.B. Macaulay, Lord Bentinck, Jeremy Bentham, James Mill, Thomas Munro, Charles Metcalfe, John Malcolm, Mountstuart Elphinstone, and many others, thought that British rule would lead to the modernisation of India (Whitehead, 2003). Therefore, Indian intellectuals who favoured the introduction of Western thought were promoted. For instance, the British promoted the modernist interpretations of religion by Ram Mohan Roy and Syed Ahmed Khan. This is not to imply that the European colonisers alone were responsible for introducing scientific knowledge or that the colonised were passive recipients or onlookers (Peabody, 2001: 820). But, generally, Western thought came to dominate the colonial intelligentsia of India.

This Westernisation, however, was limited to the elite. The ordinary people of India remained largely outside the Westernised educational system. Martin Carnoy estimated that overall literacy levels remained below 5 per cent between 1830 and the end of the nineteenth century (Carnoy, 1974: 108). Among the women and lower castes, illiteracy was as high as 99 per cent in the early twentieth century (Haggerty, 1969: 32).

With the help of the British, these Westernised elite became organised into political parties. Both the Indian National Congress and the Muslim League were created and promoted by Englishmen and encouraged by the Viceroy of the time (Pernau, 2006). These parties were created to improve relations between the British and the Indian people, in order to consolidate British rule in India. That is why the first four presidents of the Congress were Englishmen (Spear, 1958: 569).

Marx said, 'There is something in human history like retribution; and it is a rule of historical retribution that its instrument be forged not by the offended, but by the offender himself' (Marx, 1857b). It was this very class of Indians that acquired the tastes, opinions, morals, and intellect of the coloniser that played an instrumental role in the struggle against colonialism. The role of the Westernised bourgeoisie in the nationalist movement is, arguably, an example of Marx's historical retribution. Albert Memmi's classic work *The Colonizer and the Colonized* explored the contradictions and tensions within this social group (Memmi, 1991).

Certain British reformers, such as Thomas Munro and Mountstuart Elphinstone, anticipated the end of British rule and urged measures to train Indians in the art of self-government (Rajan, 1969: 90). Hence, in a certain sense, Macaulay's proclamation before the House of Commons in 1833 that the day the Indians demanded European institutions would be 'the proudest day in English history' is not without historical irony. One could say that Macaulay's wish was fulfilled, in some way, in the shape of the nationalist movement (Spear, 1958: 576). Both the success and the limitations of the nationalist movement were arguably connected to the contradiction of opposing British rule under the class hegemony of this indigenous bourgeoisie. Tomilson wrote (1982: 335):

> Gandhi was able to lead effectively so long as the British accepted him as an important constructive element in Indian political life, and treated him accordingly, and so long as he was able to instruct his followers to perform actions that fitted with their own perceived needs.

In summary, whether in the shape of colonialism or the nationalist struggle against it, in relation to European transitions the influence of British colonial domination is a distinguishing feature in South Asia's transition to capitalism.

SIPHONING THE SURPLUS

During the colonial era, South Asia integrated into the world market in a manner that was principally beneficial to Britain. Marx wrote eloquently that just as capital subjects the 'country to the rule of the towns', so 'nations of peasants [were subjected to] nations of bourgeois, the East on the West' (Marx and Engels, 1998). The structural logic of capitalism 'binds in a single interconnected process the development of capitalism in the metropolitan centre with the political control and economic exploitation of the colonies' (Mukherjee, 1985: 172–173). In other words, the colonised countries were subject to the rule of advanced capitalist countries.

Although there is no generally accepted Marxist theory of unequal exchange, Marx touched on this issue by reasoning that under capitalism the 'favoured country recovers more labour in exchange for less labour' (Marx, 1998c: 279). Marxian scholars have viewed unequal exchange as a facet of merchants' capital central to surplus extraction from economically backward societies (Agarwala, 1989; Amin, 1976; Barrientos, 1991; Floto, 1989; Joseph and Tomlinson, 1991; Nakajima and Izumi, 1995; Persky, 1992; Schweickart, 1991).

Contrary to the doctrines of free market, colonial India became a supplier of cotton for British textile mills not merely as a result of market forces but also state intervention. While new export commodities, such as tea and indigo, were developed by private British capital, the colonial state created the conditions for the ruin of Indian pre-capitalist manufacture and handicraft, and for the rise of capitalist industry (Marshall, 1997: 100). For instance, in *History of British India*, historian H.H. Wilson wrote (quoted in Dutt, 1940: 118):

> It was stated in evidence (in 1813) that the cotton and silk goods of India up to the period could be sold for a profit in the British market at a price from 50% to 60% lower than those necessary to protect the latter by duties of 70% and 80% on their value, or by positive prohibition. Had this not been the case, had not such prohibitory duties and decrees existed, the mills of Paisley and Manchester would have been stopped in their outset, and could scarcely have been again set in motion, even by the power of steam. They were created by the sacrifice of the Indian manufacture.

In relation to international trade, the Registry Act of 1815 imposed a 15 per cent duty on ships built in India. The Act stipulated that goods from the south and east of the Cape of Good Hope could only be traded in British ships, three-fourths of the crew or seven mariners per hundred tonnes of goods would have to be British, and only those ships would be allowed to port in London whose master was British (Sangwan, 1995: 138). From 1840 to 1886, India's foreign seaborne trade increased more than eight-fold but, because of these regulations, it was mainly lucrative for the British and played a vital role in their balance of payments (Seal, 1968: 34).

As a result of state and market forces, the total value of Indian exports kept falling while the total value for British imported goods kept rising. For instance, between 1815 and 1832, while the total value of exported Indian cotton goods fell from £1.3 million to below £100,000, the total value of English cotton goods imported into India rose from £26,000 to £400,000 (Dutt, 1940: 119). The proportionate value of Indian exports kept falling well into the twentieth century. In 1840–69, India's export-import ratio was 172.5 per cent; by 1870–1912, it had declined to 148 per cent; and by 1913–38, it had fallen to 133.4 per cent (Basu, 2006).

Consequently, India's share of world manufacturing output fell from 25 to 1.7 per cent between 1750 and 1900 (Davis, 2001: 293). India's share of world GDP declined from 22.6 per cent in 1700 to 3.8 per cent by 1952 (Table 2.1 and Figure 2.1). In 1914, although India was still the world's fourth largest manufacturer of cotton textiles, its population remained mired in poverty (Kiernan, 1967; Visualizing Economics, 2008).

Table 2.1: Shares of World GDP (%)

	1700	1820	1890	1952
China	23.1	32.4	13.2	5.2
India	22.6	15.7	11.0	3.8
Europe	23.3	26.6	40.3	29.7

Source: Davis, M. (2001: 293).

A comparison of the levels and growth of GDP per capita from 1500 to 1998 also demonstrates the growing differentiation between Britain and India, especially after the colonial period (Tables 2.2 and 2.3).

During the British colonial period, India's imperial commitments were three-fold: firstly, to provide a market for British goods; secondly, to financially sustain the British Empire's interests; and thirdly, to maintain a large number of British troops, raised from Indian revenue, to be used as an imperial fire-brigade (Tomlinson, 1982: 134). For these purposes, surplus from India was siphoned to Britain through a variety of avenues, ranging from remittances (whether in the shape of gifts or salaries), unequal exchange, trade surpluses, interest charges, capital repayments, and so on. Moreover, the process of surplus extraction was not restricted to the formal empire (Gallagher and Robinson, 1953: 5).

Figure 2.1: Percentage of World GDP: China, India, Japan, Latin America, Western Europe, and United States, 1500–2000

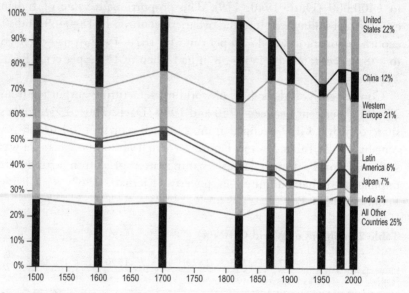

Source: Visualizing Economics (2008).

Table 2.2: Levels of GDP Per Capita in Britain and India, 1500–1998 (1990 international dollars)

	1500	1700	1820	1913	1950	1998
Britain	762	1405	2121	5150	6907	18,714
India	550	550	533	673	619	1746

Source: Maddison (2001: 90).

Table 2.3: Growth of Per Capita GDP in Britain and India, 1500–1998 (annual average compound growth rates)

	1500–1700	1700–1820	1820–1913	1913–1950	1950–1998
Britain	0.31	0.34	0.96	0.80	2.10
India	0.00	- 0.03	0.25	- 0.23	2.18

Source: Maddison, A. (2001: 90).

Owing to the variety of avenues, it is very difficult to estimate the surplus siphoned from India to Britain. The first estimates, made by nationalists such as Dadabhai Naoroji and R.C. Dutt, amounted to about Rs 1,355 million (in 1946–47 prices)—the central economic demand of the nationalist movement to halt the economic drain was based on these figures—which, according to a recent recalculation, would account for more than 4 per cent of the national income for that year (Habib, 1985: 375–376). More recent estimates are even higher. P.J. Marshall has estimated that some £3 million were sent home before 1757, and about £15 million between 1757 and 1784 (Marshall, 1976: 256)—that is, more than half a million pounds annually. Similarly, Alavi has calculated that between 1771 and 1779 military charges absorbed a third to half of government revenue, while civil charges were between one-fifteenth and one-seventh of revenue (Alavi, 1982: 57–58). Salaries of British employees accounted for a large portion of these civil charges, and were also remitted out of the country. The balance, of approximately £1.3 million a year, was used to buy Indian goods for export to England (Alavi, 1982: 57–58). In the decade from 1793–94 to 1802–03, this figure rose to about £1.5 million annually (Alavi, 1982: 62). Alavi has estimated that if one adds the transfer of goods by private individuals and through other European trading companies to the economic drain, about £2 million was being transferred a year (Alavi, 1982: 63). Up to 30 to 40 per cent of Britain's trade deficit with other industrial countries was met by this balance of trade surplus from India in the nineteenth century (Saul, 1960: ch. 8). Historians have estimated that the net transfer of capital from India to Britain averaged 1.5 per cent of GNP in the late nineteenth century (Basu, 2006). To sum it up, the second distinguishing feature of South Asia's transition is the siphoning of surplus as a result of the capitalist integration into the world economy.

CAPITALISM PLANTED UPON THE AMP

In the early colonial period, the principal source of income for the British colonial state was the collection of land revenue (Stokes, 1973: 144). Hence, the British, much like earlier conquerors of India, began the colonial period by feeding off the surplus generated from the social foundation of the AMP. Had the British persisted with the unaltered foundations of the AMP, their rule may not have been very different from that of the various conquerors that had preceded them, and the mode of production would have remained unchanged.

However, unlike their predecessors, the British belonged to a capitalist society. Hence, one of the features of British colonial rule was the capitalist imperative for the extraction of maximum surplus. These imperatives led the British to introduce mechanisms to increase surplus extraction that, in turn, brought about fundamental changes in the mode of production of South Asia.

After the death of Aurangzeb in 1707, the Mughal Empire began to weaken. The British East India Company filled this void and expanded its sphere of interest. The Company won a decisive victory over the Mughal Empire at the Battle of Plassey in 1757. This victory was further consolidated by another conquest in 1764, when the BEIC defeated the Mughal emperor, Shah Alam II, at the Battle of Buxar. As a consequence of these defeats, the Emperor granted the BEIC the right to collect land revenue (called Diwani) in Bengal, Bihar, and Orissa on behalf of the Mughal emperor (Baden-Powell, 1896; Brown, 1994; Peers, 2006). After 1764, while the Mughal emperor continued to rule in name, real power was now held by the BEIC. By 1827, this pretence at collecting land revenue on behalf of the Mughal emperor was done away with and the Mughal rulers, for much of the nineteenth century, lived off a pension from the BEIC. Once firmly in control, the British sought to increase land revenue collection. Dutt estimated that (1940: 106):

> In the last year of administration of the last Indian ruler of Bengal, in 1764–65, the land revenue realised was £817,000. In the first year of the Company's administration, in 1765–6, the land revenue realised in Bengal was £1,470,000. By 1771–2, it was £2,341,000, and by 1775–6 it was £2,818,000

A striking example of the sheer inhuman ruthlessness of land revenue collection by the colonial authorities was that even during the Bengal famine of 1769–70, when nearly a third of the population was wiped out from hunger, the Court of Directors of the BEIC specified no relief measures. Instead, land revenue was 'more rigorously collected than ever' (Dutt, 1906: 51–52). While a third of the population starved to death, colonial authorities increased collection to further fund the expansion of the British Empire. Through the system of land revenue collection,

India not only paid for its own conquest but also for the conquest of much of the East (Alavi, 1980: 43).

This plunder and poor management by the British is said to have exacerbated the Bengal famine (Davis, 2001; Gopal, 1949). Ironically, it also resulted in a fall in the collection of land revenue. It was not the destruction of millions of lives, but the fall in the collection of land revenue, that compelled the BEIC to introduce a new system of land revenue collection. It was hoped that this new system would be more efficient and rational, and would also increase agricultural output and land revenue through the introduction of market incentives.

In 1793, the British introduced the first Permanent Settlement Act. Successive Permanent Settlement and Land Alienation Acts followed, resulting in a fundamental change in the mode of production of South Asia (Barrier, 1967: 355). The Permanent Settlement Act brought about two fundamental changes: private property in land, and fixed land revenue. Marx dramatised the introduction of private property in land as 'the great desideratum of Asiatic society' (Marx, 1853).

Between 1794 and 1819, the buying and selling of land increased dramatically; the entirely new phenomenon of a commercial land market was established (Cohn, 1961; Islam, 1979). The Permanent Settlement Act also led to the emergence of numerous intermediaries and to the fragmentation of land holdings. Whereas before the Permanent Settlement Act there was no private property in land, and agriculture was organised by the village community, 'by the late nineteenth century 88.5 per cent of the 110,456 permanently settled estates of Bengal and Bihar were less than 500 acres in size' (Sarkar, 1983: 33).

With the registration of land as private property, jagirdars, zamindars, and ryots became landowners (Baden-Powell, 1896; Jha, 1980: 53). Hence, the commercialisation of land began the slow metamorphosis of classes from 'lineages and local chiefs' to capitalists, 'civil servants', 'merchants and bankers' (Cohn, 1960).

Stimulated by the development of markets and state intervention, agricultural production was increasingly directed towards cash cropping (Sen, 1992: ch. 2). New cash crops, such as sugarcane, opium, and indigo, were introduced. The increasing profitability of cash crops often led to appreciation of the price of the lands on which these crops were grown (Cohn, 1961: 621–622). From 1893 to 1945, there was a 7 per cent decline in the production of food crops while cash crops increased by over 80 per cent (Kedia and Sinha, 1987: 191, 198). To increase production of cash crops, the British expanded irrigation and created canal colonies (Gilmartin, 1994). By the 1920s, 10 million acres of land were irrigated by government canals (*Agricultural Statistics of the Punjab*, 1937). This commercialisation of agriculture has been well documented by historians (see for instance Bharadwaj, 1985; Mody, 1982; Raj et al., 1985; Washbrook, 1994).

Although the government was barred from enhancing its revenue demands on landowners—the Act fixed the land revenue at an annual collection of £3,400,000 (Mukherjee, 2004)—if the landowner failed to pay the land revenue (also called kist[5]) on the stipulated date, the government had the right to auction the whole or a portion of the land to clear arrears (see Permanent Settlement Act 1793, Section 1, Regulation 1). The colonial administrative machinery—including the executive, judiciary, and police—was geared for the collection of land revenue and for strict action in case of non-payment (Baden-Powell, 1896, 1895; Cohn, 1961; Wright, 1954). This threat of liquidation was real and the cause of significant resentment among the landowners. Baden-Powell admitted that (1896):

> even fourteen years after the Permanent Settlement the parties on whom so valuable a source of wealth had been conferred were totally unappreciative of its advantages; and this solely because there was a condition for punctual payments of the land revenue, and a stringent law of sale in case of default.

In fact, non-payment of land revenue resulted in the British Indian army's campaign against the powerful Hathwa and Betthia rajas in 1766–67 (Jha, 1980: 53–57). A first-hand view of the colonial administration's efforts to extract land revenue and seize land can be found in Baden-Powell's book *A Short Account of the Land Revenue and its Administration in British India* (1894).

In order to ensure that the landowner had all the necessary coercive means to extract surplus from the producers (whether tenants, bonded slaves, wage workers, or others) the British gave legal sanction for wide-ranging extra-economic despotic powers to the landowners. For instance, Regulation VII of 1799 (known as the Haftam) gave the zamindars the power to confiscate and sell the crops, cattle, or other properties—without any judicial intermediation—when recovering arrears from defaulting tenants. The zamindars could summon the defaulting tenants to their katcheris (self-made courts controlled by zamindars) and keep them confined in fetters until the arrears were paid. If tenants ran away with their family or property, the zamindar could impose community fines on the entire village or villages. Moreover, rent could be enhanced by the zamindar to any level, without any regard to previous customs. Regulation V in 1812 even gave zamindars the power to create their own permanent settlements by leasing out their land, for any period, to any number of intermediaries who would have the right to auction the land in case of non-payment of arrears.

In addition, various forms of pre-capitalist extra-economic extraction of surplus, such as abwab,[6] nazrana,[7] begar,[8] selami,[9] and so on, remained in place. A detailed exposition of these oppressive practices is contained in Adrienne Cooper's excellent study entitled *Sharecroppers and Landlords in Bengal, 1930–50* (Cooper, 1983: 226–255).

This system of oppressive traditions and customs, sanctioned by the colonial state, together with the capitalist imperative of surplus value extraction was vividly described by Marx as 'European despotism, placed upon Asiatic despotism', forming 'a more monstrous combination than any of the divine monsters startling us in the Temple of Salsette' (Marx, 1853, 1853b). Private property in land, introduced through the Permanent Settlement Act, was no doubt the 'great desideratum of Asiatic society' but, because this transition combined the oppressive features of the AMP with the oppressive features of capitalism, it was arguably even more destructive than European paths of transition (Marx, 1853).

According to Mike Davis, six million Indians died an unnecessary death at the hands of British colonialism in the years 1876 to 1878 (Davis, 2001). Davis wrote: '[i]f the history of British rule in India were to be condensed into a single fact, it is this, that there was no increase in India's per capita income from 1757 to 1947' (Davis, 2001: 311). The radical writer William Digby wrote, 'When the part played by the British Empire in the nineteenth century is regarded by the historian 50 years hence, the unnecessary deaths of millions of Indians would be its principal and most notorious monument' (Digby, 1901). Similarly, the classic study of agricultural growth in pre-independence India by George Blyn, *Agricultural Trends in India 1891–1947*, concluded that agricultural growth in food crops from 1891 to 1947 was no more than

0.1 per cent per annum, implying a per capita decline in the availability of food (Blyn, 1966).

These oppressive conditions led to a series of peasant revolts in the nineteenth century. These revolts included the Faraizi movement (1830–1857), Santal Pargana (1855), Indigo districts (1859–1861), Tuskhali (1872–1875), Pabna (1873), Chhagalnaiya (1874), Mymensing (1874–1882), and Munshiganj (1880–1881).

Peasant revolts, and the War of Independence in 1857, forced the British to take note of the plight of the peasantry, eventually leading to the legal recognition of some of their demands. For instance, the Rent Act of 1859 rolled back the haftam and introduced the 'patta system' whereby the annual rent was fixed (cash or kind) and the zamindar could not raise it. The Bengal Tenancy Act of 1885, the Amendment Act of 1928, and the Bengal Tenancy Act of 1938 successively acknowledged greater rights for tenants. Thus, legal recognition of the rights of the peasants was itself the product of a protracted class struggle against the colonial state and the zamindars.

In summary, the Permanent Settlement Act developed private property and commodity production within the AMP in India. This Act represents the process of primitive accumulation through the colonial state. Marx described the process of capitalist primitive accumulation (that is, the process of the formation of capital and wage labour) as 'the historical process of divorcing the producer from the means of production' (Marx, 1998a: 1021). While this transition, in different regions, reveals a great diversity in detail, some generalisations can be made. Firstly, that the colonial state played a vital role in this process of primitive accumulation in India. Secondly, while private property in land and commodity production came about at various stages and in different ways, wage labour took much longer to emerge. Hence, Asiatic relations continued to dominate economic relations. The colonial administration destroyed the rights based on custom and practice associated with the Asiatic village community and, in their place, provided legal sanction and wide-ranging despotic powers to the zamindars. This new form of oppression led to a series of revolts that resulted in the legal recognition of certain peasant demands by the state. In other words, the state-led colonial transition to commodity production and private property preceded the transition of Asiatic relations to wage labour.

One also observes that under colonial rule, not only were the seeds of capitalism introduced through the state but the principal instrument of increasing surplus was also the colonial state. In other words, while capitalism, in theory, primarily utilises economic means to increase surplus value extraction (that is, the threat of unemployment), the colonial system additionally utilised the coercive machinery of the state to extract land revenue.

As far as manufacturing was concerned, the unity of agriculture and handicrafts (a characteristic of the AMP) was undermined by British industrial production and state intervention (Gopal, 1949). Goods produced by the BEIC were sold in various domestic and international markets, leading to the commercialisation of all relations (see for instance Ludden, 1995; Sen, 1998; Siddiqi, 1995). Amiya Bagchi has estimated that craft employment in Bihar contracted from 18.6 per cent to 8.5 per cent of the total labour force between 1807 and 1814 (Bagchi, 1976). Craftsmen, thrown out of work, often returned to their villages. From 1824 to 1837, the population of Dacca decreased from 150,000 inhabitants to only 20,000 (Basu, 2006). As a result, between 1891 and 1921, the percentage of the population dependent on agriculture increased from 61.1 to 73.0 per cent (Dutt, 1940: 203). This destruction of the 'domestic industry of the peasant', to clear the way for inter-national capitalist production (see Engels, 1892; Marx, 1887: ch. 24, sec. 25), was termed 'deindustrialisation' by Indian nationalist historians.

There is no doubt that British colonial rule also introduced a number of new elements into the economic landscape of India. The British introduced railways that became the forerunner for modern industry and ended village isolation (Thorner, 1955, 1947). The steamship linked, or annexed, India to Europe, and the telegraph consolidated the political unity of India. The British set India along a path of rapid introduction of modern industry, resulting in the recruitment of an industrial labour force that began to dissolve the hereditary divisions of labour, upon which rested the Indian castes (Desai, 1966; Misra, 1961; Morris, 1960; Mukherjee, 1970). The British also introduced the printing press, modern science, education, and administration. However, the press was patronised by the East India Company, and European education was reserved exclusively for a small elite (Marshall, 1997: 105). Nonetheless, by introducing modern industrial production into the economic fabric of India, Britain inevitably introduced modern capitalist economic relations (Stokes, 1973: 141). Ironically, the principal financial source, for the introduction of nearly all these modern elements into the political life of India, was the surplus extracted from a system of land revenue collection that was a direct continuation of the AMP.

The destruction of the AMP was both the prerequisite, and the inevitable result, of the introduction of modern industry in India. But, the speed and form of this destruction and reconstruction of social relations was determined principally by the costs and benefits of such a transition to British capitalist interests. Since the driving forces behind this transition were the political and economic imperatives of empire (Stokes, 1973: 142–143), the colonial system could not generate the kind of capitalist modernisation seen in Europe. In other words, the economic development of the country was stimulated only in so far as it benefited the wealth of the English ruling class (Misra, 2000: 337).

Moreover, as mostly occurred in the rest of the world, this transition to capitalism incurred a frightful human cost. In the words of Ira Klein, 'millions suffered "death by development"' (Klein, 2000: 546). On the one hand, colonialism introduced capitalism; on the other, the peculiar path of this introduction was itself a fetter to the development of India (see for instance Banerjee and Iyer, 2005; Dutt, 1906; Kumar, 1965; Mukherjee, 1933; Nanavati and Anjaria, 1944). The paradox of colonialism was that it was simultaneously the impetus for the introduction of industrial production and, because it subjected the development of the colony to the interests of the coloniser, it was also a fetter on its full and free development. It was at once free trader and mercantilist, the 'fugleman of modernity' and the 'latest predatory conqueror of Asia' (Stokes, 1973: 160).

If one accepts that these three features are sufficient to distinguish India's transition to capitalism from European transitions, what do they imply about the mode of production of India during colonialism? Was the mode of production capitalist, given that the British were a capitalist society that dominated India? Or was it Asiatic, given that the colonial state relied on the extraction of land revenue? Or was it a combination of the two? Finally, if it was a combination, what was the specific form of this combination?

Asiatic Capitalism

It is not difficult to accept that the socio-economic formation of colonial India was the result of a violent collision of two distinct civilisations and their respective modes of production: capitalist Britain and Asiatic India. The previous section also revealed that under colonialism, private property in land and commodity production developed on the basis of labour relations that were characteristic of the AMP. In other words, certain features of capitalism (private property) developed before other features (wage labour). How can we explain this uneven development?

The literature on agrarian transitions suggests that this uneven development of certain elements of capitalism before others is not peculiar to colonial India. For instance, in Europe, private property in land was generally a hegemonic institute long before the development of capitalism. Similarly, merchants' and usurers' capital existed before the development of industrial capital. Commodity exchange and markets, although limited, also preceded the emergence of capitalism.

There are also instances of the combination of two modes of production. For example, in the slave-holding Southern states of USA, a system of commodity production and private property existed on the basis of the chattel slavery of Africans working on plantation colonies (Byres, 1996; Post, 2003). The capitalist transformation of Prussia occurred through a slow evolutionary process, whereby the feudal Junkers transformed into capitalists, giving rise to a combination of serfdom and capitalism (Moore, 1966).

This unevenness in transitions occurs, according to Lenin, because capital 'takes hold' of pre-capitalist relations, 'subordinates' them, and finally 'remoulds them after its own fashion'. Lenin (1917a: Part I) wrote:

> Capital finds the most diverse types of medieval and patriarchal landed property—feudal, 'peasant allotments' (i.e., the holdings of bonded peasants); clan, communal, state, and other forms of landownership. Capital takes hold of all these, employing a variety of ways and methods. . . . Capitalism subordinates to itself all these forms of landownership: communal-allotment holdings in Russia; squatter tracts or holdings regulated by free distribution in a democratic or a feudal state, as in Siberia or the American Far West; the slave-holding estates in the American South, and the semi-feudal landholdings of the 'purely Russian' gubernias. In all these cases, the development and victory of capitalism is similar, though not

identical in form. . . . Capital subordinates to itself all these varied forms of landownership [feudal, clan, communal (and primitive-squatter), state, etc] and remoulds them after its own fashion.

Hence, an 'infinitely diverse combinations of elements of this or that type of capitalist evolution are possible', wrote Lenin (1899: Preface). If capitalism can come about through infinitely diverse combinations, is it useful to conceptualise a specific combination as a definite 'transitory form'?

For instance, Marx considered the metayer (sharecropping) system of France to be a transitory form. In this regard he wrote (1894: 1074):

As a *transitory form* from the original form of rent to capitalist rent, we may consider the metayer system, or share-cropping, under which the manager (farmer) furnishes labour (his own or another's), and also a portion of working capital, and the landlord furnishes, aside from land, another portion of working capital (e.g., cattle), and the product is divided between tenant and landlord in definite proportions which vary from country to country. [Emphasis added].

Similarly, a number of contemporary authors have developed this notion of sharecropping as a transitory form of labour relations (for a detailed discussion, see Byres, 1983). Perhaps this notion can be extended to understanding capitalist transitions as a whole. What if one was to accept that capitalist transitions, whether though colonialism or other paths, invariably occur through a dialectical development that involves identifiable 'transitory forms'? Let us explore this notion.

A transitory form is defined, for this study, as relatively stable intermediate complex economic relations that come about during the transition from one mode of surplus extraction to the other. Given that transitions, in general, may occur through a wide variety of paths, for the purposes of this study, a transitory form may be any of the following: a structured articulation of two modes of production, a hybrid, or a combination of the elements of two modes of production, and so on. Hence, transitory forms are composed of a combination of two different forms of surplus extraction.

Hence, the difference between a transitory form and a mode of production is not so much their relative degrees of stability but that whereas a mode of production is defined by a single mode of surplus extraction, a transitory form is a combination of two (or more) modes of surplus extraction. The examination of history clearly demonstrates the distinct existence of the modes of surplus extraction that combine into a transitory form (in this instance, the distinct existence of the Asiatic and capitalist modes of production).

Conceptualising a transitory form does not imply that there is an a priori or teleological endpoint, nor that these forms cannot remain in place for long historical periods. Avoiding this supposition also steers clear of conceptualising modes of production as Weberian ideal types. Instead, the conception of transitory forms helps one understand the dialectical interpenetration between capitalist and pre-capitalist relations, and the tensions and contradictions between them. It is an attempt to address Balibar's contention that historical materialism also requires a theory, or theories, of transition (Balibar, 1970: 257–258; Wolpe, 1980: 7–9).

However, a general theory of transitions is beyond the scope of this thesis. What is relevant to this study is to analyse the specific form of transition of South Asia. Hence, this definition, though lacking in detail and arguably rigour, is sufficient for the purposes of this study.

In colonial India, capital took hold of, subordinated, and finally remoulded economic relations. This process gave rise to a system of private property and commodity production on the basis of Asiatic labour relations. The study terms this specific combination 'Asiatic capitalism'. In short, Asiatic capitalism is the transitory form where private property in land and commodity production occurs on the basis of Asiatic labour relations.

Hence, Asiatic capitalism is not a new mode of production—such as Banaji and Alavi's colonial mode of production (Alavi, 1975, 1981; Banaji, 1972). While a mode of production is defined by the mode of surplus extraction, Asiatic capitalism is the name offered to the economic forms emerging/arising from the colonial capitalist transformation of South Asia.

Furthermore, since all transitions from one mode of production to another are the subject of entire historical periods, transitory forms are quite capable of surviving for long historical periods, especially in the context of slowly-changing productive forces. The spread of markets, free labour power, secular government, foreign capital, commoditisation, consumerism, business culture, and so on—in short, the spread of the economic, political, and cultural values of capitalism—tends to slowly undercut the AMP. Thus, while there can be no doubt that Asiatic relations are gradually being replaced by capitalist relations (based on wage labour), this transition can be so gradual, especially in the context of the imperialist siphoning of surplus, that it can be said to constitute an entire historical period of its own.

We know, from history, that pre-capitalist classes and ideologies, even when defeated, may stubbornly resist capitalism. Marx gives the example of how even pre-capitalist 'association of agriculture with manufacture put up a stubborn resistance to the products of the big industries' (Marx, 1998c: 443). This is even more so in the AMP. Marx and Engels were of the opinion that Asiatic relations held out the longest because the nature of these relations enslaved the individual to the community. They wrote (1979):

> The Asiatic form (of community, as against the Roman and Germanic) necessarily survives longest and most stubbornly. This is due to the fundamental principle on which it is based, that is, that the individual does not become independent of the community, that the circle of production is self-sustaining, unity of agriculture and craft-manufacture, etc. If the individual changes his relation to the community, he modifies and undermines both the community and its economic premise; conversely, the modification of this economic premise—produced by its own dialectic, pauperization, etc.

This stubborn resistance of pre-capitalist relations has been the recurring subject of the mode of production debate among Marxists studying India. The debate began when a study by Ashok Rudra, A. Majid, and B.D. Talib reasoned that the Green Revolution had not resulted in the emergence of capitalist farmers in the Punjab (Rudra et al., 1990). The debate involved Utsa Patnaik, Paresh Chattopadhyay, R.S. Rao, Andre Gunder Frank, Ranjit Sau, Jairus Banaji, Hamza Alavi, Pradhan H. Prasad, and many others (see Patnaik, 1990c; Thorner, 1982). In this rich debate, the colonial mode of production, colonial capitalism, semi-feudalism, the extent and limitations of capitalist development, and many other questions were developed, reviewed, and critiqued. The study's analysis of Asiatic capitalism as a transitory form is a departure from this debate only in so far as (1) it argues that pre-capitalist relations were Asiatic rather than feudal; (2) in place of the semi-feudalism hypothesis, it posits the concept of Asiatic capitalism as a transitory form.

A critic could legitimately ask whether this concept of Asiatic capitalism, as a transitory form, is of any value in terms of explanatory power. Firstly, grasping the concepts of colonial path and Asiatic capitalism may help to shed light on India's capitalist transition in the context of world historical timing. For instance, in the revolutionary republican path, pre-capitalist society is broken up by a social revolution that destroys all the relics of serfdom and large landownership. In this path, small peasant farming and peasant differentiation is the basis for the development of capitalism. On the other hand, the colonial path of transformation retains significant aspects of the economic base and superstructure of Asiatic society. In that sense, the colonial path is similar but not identical to the Junkers path. In class terms, this implies the continuing dominance of the zamindar class in agrarian relations and the continuing patriarchal unfreedom of the peasant masses. Only when the surplus, extracted through Asiatic labour relations, is reinvested to purchase labour power for the accumulation of surplus value does capital come into being. This maelstrom of capitalist development, through the colonial path, frequently leads to uprisings, wars of national liberation, nationalist anti-colonial movements, and anti-imperialist struggles. Some classes fight to preserve their pre-capitalist way of life while others struggle to hasten the process of modernisation. Significant sections of the working population, disaffected by the destructive process of colonial capitalism and hoping to ameliorate their conditions of life, make up the mass base of such movements.

Secondly, the further theoretical implication of Asiatic capitalism, as a transitory form, is that the transition of economic relations in South Asia is through the metamorphosis of Asiatic relations into capitalist relations. In short, capitalist relations do not develop as a spatially distinct sector, especially within agriculture. Instead, the whole economy undergoes a slow metamorphosis from pre-capitalist to capitalist relations. Hence, research methodologies that set out to identify a purely capitalist sector, which can be compared to a pre-capitalist sector, will inevitably underestimate the development of capitalism. Moreover, there are some economic categories that make no sense outside capitalism (for example, profit rate) and can be systematically misreported or mis-represented in transitional agrarian holdings. It follows that any estimation of the development of capitalism should include the development of wage payments, utilisation of machines, market orientation, and so on, for the whole of the agrarian economy over a period of time. This insight is also in keeping with the objections that were raised by various authors engaged in the debate on the mode of production of India (see for instance Patnaik, 1990b, 1990a; Rao, 1990).

Can this metamorphosis of Asiatic relations into capitalism be empirically verified? If Asiatic relations are slowly metamorphosing into capitalist relations, one can expect to find the development of private property, commodity production, the growing economic differentiation of the peasantry, the gradual elimination of traditional tenant farming on the one hand (that is, all the results of capitalist development), together with the relative lack of development of wage labour on the other (considered the defining characteristic of capitalism). The next chapter examines the agrarian relations of contemporary Pakistan in relation to the concept of Asiatic capitalism.

NOTES

1. This is arguably also the reason why, despite the fact that although a weak form of landed property was present in China, Marx continued to regard it as an example of the AMP.
2. European feudal landed property is distinct from capitalist private property, just as serfdom is distinct from wage labour. The latter represents the complete divorce from the means of production and, hence, the final development of property into private property.
3. For an alternative understanding of the French Revolution, see *Rethinking the French Revolution: Marxism and the Revisionist Challenge* by George C. Comninel (2000).
4. The North-West Frontier Province (NWFP) is now officially called Khyber-Pakhtunkhwa.
5. 'Kist' is an individual payment made by the landlord, whereas 'diwani' is the right to collect land revenue from the empire.
6. 'Abwab' is derived from the Arabic word bab, which means door, section, chapter, or title. In the Mughal period, all temporary taxes over and above regular taxes were called abwabs (Banglapedia, 2009).
7. In any marriage ceremony, the panchayet (council of elders) of the mahalla (neighborhood) of the bride would receive a certain amount of money from the bridegroom as 'nazrana' (a present) (Banglapedia, 2009).
8. 'Begar' was a form of social labour without payment. It was justified as a pious act—to give free labour to the priestly classes. Such a free labour system is not to be confused with the use of slave and bonded labour (Banglapedia, 2009).
9. Payment made for the transfer of rights or ownership, possession, or use of land.

3

Agrarian Class Relations in Pakistan

We suffer not only from the living, but from the dead. Le mort saisit le vif![1]

Marx (1887: 22)

The previous chapter examined the notion of the colonial path and the transitory form of Asiatic capitalism. This chapter investigates the available data on agrarian class relations of contemporary Pakistan in relation to the cogency and validity/explanatory power of the concept of Asiatic capitalism. It is divided into two sections. The first briefly reviews the literature on the agrarian question. The second examines the empirical evidence with respect to the agrarian class structure of Pakistan. The results suggest that there is growing differentiation of the peasantry and the gradual erosion of traditional tenant farming, combined with only the slow development of wage labour. The theoretical implications of these results are discussed at the end of the chapter.

OVERVIEW OF LITERATURE ON AGRARIAN CHANGE

One of the most significant intellectual fault lines in agrarian political economy is between the Marxists and the populists. This section briefly overviews the Marxist and populist literature on the agrarian question, and also briefly examines the literature on Pakistan. This brief review of the literature is necessary in order to situate this analysis within the broader literature of agrarian change.

While analysing primitive accumulation in *Capital I*, Marx demonstrated that capital, through a variety of ways and means, takes hold of diverse pre-capitalist relations, and subordinates and remoulds them to itself (Marx, 1998b: Part VIII). Similarly, while discussing the economic basis of capitalist ground rent in *Capital III* and *Theories of*

Surplus Value, Marx also examined its historical forerunners—rent in kind, money-rent, quit-rent, labour service, corvée labour, and so on (Marx, 1998c: Part VII, 1861). Engels investigated how capitalism in agriculture resulted, on the one hand, in the peasantry being absorbed into an urban based economy and, on the other, a rural based capitalist agriculture replacing peasant production (Engels, 1894, 1850).

Lenin further elaborated the concept of peasant differentiation and asserted that increasing commercialisation of agriculture was leading to de-peasantisation in Russia (Lenin, 1899: Ch. 2). Similarly, Rosa Luxemburg's *Accumulation of Capital* and Karl Kautsky's *The Agrarian Question* analysed the process of primitive accumulation and the development of capitalist agriculture in pre-capitalist societies, while Mao Zedong's brief but influential essays provided the methodology for countless studies on categorising classes within the peasantry (Kautsky, 1988; Luxemburg, 1973; Mao Zedong, 1926, 1927, 1933). The ferment of of anti-colonial and national liberation struggles gave rise to contributions from thinkers who were simultaneously activists and revolutionaries, such as Amílcar Cabral (1969; 1980), William Hilton (1976), Solomon T. Plaatje (1975), M.N. Roy (1987), and others.

The question of the impact of differentiation, especially on the middle peasants, has been the subject of significant debate since the 1960s (see Alavi, 1965; Charlesworth, 1980; Wolf, 1966, 1969). This transition of rural labour to capitalist forms of labour,[2] and the forms and nature of extra-economic coercion and unfree labour as a serious impediment to the modernisation of agriculture,[3] have been some of the central concerns of these debates. Dobb underlined the centrality of the differentiation of the peasantry in the transition from feudalism to capitalism (Dobb, 1954, 1958, 1963). The Brenner debate, and later the contention between Brenner and Wood, also resulted in extensive research on similar questions (Aston and Philpin, 1985, Journal of Agrarian Change, Vols. 1–2). The work of Byres, Curwen, Shanin, Bernstein, and Brass, among others, resulted in the Peasants Seminar of the University of London 1972–1989, *Journal of Peasant Studies*, and *Journal of Agrarian Change*. Contributors to the debate included scholars such as Banaji (2003), Brass (1999), Breman (2007), Patnaik and Dingawey (1985), Prakash (1990), Rao (1999a; 1999d), Rudra (2000), and others.

The combination of capitalist and pre-capitalist labour relations in India is particularly relevant to this chapter. Mohan Rao reasoned that semi-feudal relations involved the fusion of political and economic power, such that the ruling classes exercise extra-economic coercion to enslave labourers in debt bondage and coercive relations (Rao, 1999, 1999d). Similarly, Jan Breman opined that colonial capitalism transformed pre-capitalist bondage into capitalist indentured labour (Breman, 1974, 1993). In his longitudinal study of the relations between the landowning Brahman Anavil caste and the bonded labourers of the Dubla caste in south Gujrat, Breman asserted that during most of the nineteenth century most Dublas preferred bondage to becoming landless labourers because pre-capitalist relations provided some degree of economic security (Breman, 2007). However, from the second half of the nineteenth century, the commercialisation of agriculture, among other factors, led to the erosion of paternalistic security and the worsening of exploitation through bondage (Lerche, 2007). Hence, Breman reached the conclusion that, in contemporary times, relations between bonded labourers and their masters were essentially economic and capitalist in nature. Tom Brass asserted that unfree labour was not merely compatible with, but an essential part of, modern capitalism (Brass, 1999: 12–14, 300). He argued that unfree labour relations are a means, available to capital, to discipline and cheapen labour. Furthermore, unfree labour relations, imposed by capital, serve to halt or destroy the development of proletarian class consciousness (Brass and van der Linden, 1997). Brass called this process de-proletarianisation (Brass, 1999). For Jairus Banaji (2003), however, the very distinction between free and unfree labour was fictitious. For Banaji, capital is defined in terms of the accumulation of surplus value (as opposed to wage labour). Hence, while capitalist accumulation could not be based on unfree labour at the level of social capital, at the individual level capital may work through a multiplicity of forms of exploitation including wage labour, peasant family labour, or bonded labour (Banaji, 2003: 80, 83).

Populists and neo-populists, on the other hand, made the case for an independent peasant economy. They argued that individual peasant production, undertaken by family labour, could not only hold out against the development of capitalism in agriculture but that such an outcome was non-exploitative and hence desirable. Populists, generally, are opposed to the Leninist notion of peasant differentiation. Taking inspiration from the writings of Chayanov, populists conceive of peasants as an independent class (Chayanov, 1966). They contend that the peasantry is characterised by certain 'core elements of peasant society—household, kin, community, locale—produce (or express) a distinctive *internal* logic or dynamic, whether cultural, sociological, economic, or in some combination' (Bernstein and Byres, 2001: 6–7). These concepts of 'peasant essentialism'[4] were reworked and renewed in the 1960s, to evolve into neo-populism in David Mitrany's work *Marx Against the Peasant* (1961).

The central concepts of neo-populism were further developed from a combination of two very apparently divergent sources. Neo-populism combined with certain notions of neo-classical economics to become, what has been termed by C.D. Scott, 'neo-classical populism' (Scott, 1977: 245). Keith Griffin's *The Political Economy of Agrarian Change* (1974) and Michael Lipton's *Why Poor People Stay Poor* (1977) influenced the central concepts of neo-classical populism—namely, landlord-bias, urban-bias, and the inverse relationship between landholding size and productivity. These arguments are the contemporary neo-classical populist defence of individual small peasant farming utilising family labour. Among the neo-populists, the work of Theodore Shanin, who extended these themes to issues of development in the 'under-developed' societies, also stands out (1971; 1972; 1973; 1974; 1983; 1985; 1986). As opposed to the Leninist capitalist differentiation, Shanin asserted the presence of a 'levelling mechanism', with respect to social mobility, within the peasantry (Shanin, 1972). Similarly, Lewin challenged Lenin's evidence regarding the differentiation of the peasantry in Russia (Lewin, 1968).

The focus of Marxists and populists was the extent to which capitalism had penetrated into the so–called Third World, peasant differentiation, and the economic viability of the peasantry as an independent class under capitalism (Bhattacharyya, 2001; Cowen and Shenton, 1998b, 1998a; Krishnaji, 1995; Nugent, 2002). With the growing influence of post-modernism, however, there was a shift in the kinds of questions that were raised in agrarian change in development studies. The emphasis shifted from questions of political economy to questions about culture, ethnicity, identity, ecology,[5] gender,[6] religion, and nationality.

On the one hand, arguably, this epistemological change has had the positive impact of focusing greater attention on previously neglected questions. On the other hand, it has replaced the peasant movements of a previous period with the nebulous notion of New Social Movements.[7] Thus, the emphasis on the need for a socialist revolution has been replaced, in the literature concerning New Social Movement, by a relatively undefined notion of 'resistance'.[8]

For instance, one of the more influential works that touches on this concept of resistance is James C. Scott's *Weapons of the Weak* (Scott, 1990). In an earlier work, Scott developed the idea that the fear of famine, and the central importance of household subsistence, shapes the moral economy of the peasant (Scott, 1976). Therefore, traditional traits associated with peasants, such as resistance to innovation or the desire to own land, were the result of the evolution of a rational peasant strategy to minimise the risks of starvation (Scott, 1976). In his more recent and famous work, *Weapons of the Weak*, Scott utilised the concept of the moral economy to help explain everyday forms of peasant resistance and why open revolts and rebellions remained rare (Scott, 1990). He argued that such everyday forms of resistance had a greater cumulative effect than organised collective action.[9]

Similarly, this method of analysis of everyday forms of resistance parallels the notion of a study of history from below, known as Subaltern Studies. Ranajit Guha's studies of peasant uprisings in India have been considered some of the founding texts of subaltern studies (Guha, 1974, 1983, 1988, 1997, 2000).

More recently, these notions associated with post-modernism, such as 'everyday forms of resistance', 'New Social Movements', 'identity politics', and so on, have come under increasing criticism.[10] Concerns such as famines,[11] food regimes,[12] the displacement of local food by capital,[13] the influence of agribusiness,[14] contract farming,[15] and commodity chains and their impact on poverty and food security are being increasingly written on.[16]

LITERATURE ON THE AGRARIAN QUESTION IN PAKISTAN

One of the difficulties of studying the development of agrarian relations in Pakistan is the paucity of data. Research on agriculture in Pakistan has been predominantly driven by a technocratic approach that focuses mainly on physical inputs and price incentives to stimulate growth. During the 1960s, research focused, almost exclusively, on the growth benefits of the Green Revolution (see for instance Dorfman et al., 1965; Falcon, 1964; Falcon and Gotsch, 1964; Gotsch, 1968a, 1968b; Mohammad, 1963, 1964a, 1964b, 1965; and Raquibuzzaman, 1966). Thus, the effect on crop yields and labour employment of the technology package of the Green Revolution dominated research during this period (see for instance Cownie et al., 1970; Johnston and Cownie, 1969; and Kaneda and Ghaffar, 1970). Where research focused on the question of inequality, it was mostly focused on inequality between East and West Pakistan (see for instance Griffin and Khan, 1972; McEwan, 1970; and McEwan, 1971). While there was much discussion of the impact of input subsidies and private incentives in relation to growth, there was little discussion of these policies in relation to class exploitation (see Bose and Clark, 1969; Kaneda, 1969).

Only after the end of the military regime of Ayub Khan did questions of distribution begin to receive more attention (see Kaneda, 1969; Gotsch, 1971, 1972). The 1970s saw the emergence of studies that incorporated questions of equity (see Gotsch, 1976; Khan, 1981, 1975; and Nulty, 1972). The literature on urban bias also influenced studies of the inter-sectoral transfer of resources as a result of agricultural taxation (see Afzal, 1974; Chaudhry, 1973; Hamid, 1970, 1973; Lewis, 1969; and Qureshi, 1973). Also to emerge, in this period, were studies on the nature of poverty, income distribution, and the conditions of agricultural workers and tenants (see Alauddin, 1975; Chaudhary, 1976; Chaudhary and Kamal, 1974; Gotsch, 1974; Guisinger and Hicks, 1978; Hirashima, 1978; Naseem, 1973; Salam, 1977b). A number of studies reviewed the social-democratic agrarian policies of the 1970s relatively favourably (see Berringer, 1962; Herring, 1979; Takahashi, 1976; Qadeer, 1977; Yasin, 1972).

Despite the social-democratic inclination of the Pakistan Peoples Party (PPP) government of the 1970s, the subject and framework of research on agriculture remained largely dominated by the approach of the 1960s. The dominant subjects remained the overall and individual relationship between factor inputs of the Green Revolution and productivity (see Aslam, 1978; Salam, 1976, 1978). These included individual studies on the impact of tube-wells on productivity (see Chaudhry, 1978; Clark, 1972; Eckert, 1974); the impact of fertiliser use on productivity (see Hamdani and Haque, 1978; Salam, 1977a); the impact of mechanisation on productivity (see Ahmed, 1972); the impact of increasing use of high yield variety wheat seeds on productivity (see Azhar, 1973a; Lowdermilk, 1972; Rochin, 1971); the impact of land size on productivity (see Khan, 1977, 1979; Naseem, 1971); the estimation of agricultural prices (see Afzal, 1973; Azhar, 1973b; Hussain, 1970; Qureshi, 1974, 1971); and linear programming to evaluate agricultural policy in terms of increases in productivity (see Gotsch, 1975).

The 1980s saw a powerful shift against the social democratic policies of the PPP. Under the influence of an Islamic fundamentalist military dictatorship, research on agrarian relations shifted in a similar direction. Research priorities were redirected by the government towards what they called a 'pragmatic strategy of growth' (*The Report of the Indus Basin Research Assessment Group*, 1978: 1–2; *The State of Pakistan's Economy 1970–71 to 1979–80*, 1980: 90). Owing to extremely stringent censorship laws at the time, it was very difficult to question the military's policies of Islamisation in the newspapers or even in academic journals. The view that landlordism must be eradicated gave way to the notion that 'alternative employment for the rural poor' was all that was required to address the plight of marginalised owners, sharecroppers, and agricultural workers (*The Fifth Five Year Plan 1978–1983*, 1978). Since the 1980s, the *Pakistan Development Review*, a key journal published by the Pakistan Institute of Development Economics, has been dominated by a focus on growth. In summary, agricultural research in Pakistan has rarely focused on class relations (Khan, 1998: 30).

The task of this study is not only to determine the features of the development of capitalism in agriculture—which was central to the agrarian debate between Marxists and populists—but, instead, to examine the particular form of capitalism that is developing in Pakistan. Can the concept of Asiatic capitalism be verified from the available economic data? If Asiatic capitalism exists, the economic data should demonstrate the development of private property, commodity production, the growing economic differentiation of the peasantry, and the gradual elimination of traditional tenant farming, combined with the relative *lack* of development of wage labour.

ASIATIC CAPITALISM IN PAKISTAN

In what is today Pakistan, the colonial transition to capitalism did not begin until nearly a century after the conquest of Bengal by the British in 1757. Sindh was conquered by the British in 1843. The Punjab was annexed by the British after the second Anglo-Sikh war and the Treaty of Lahore of 1849. Balochistan was annexed by the British in three stages: a negotiated agreement with Robert Sandeman in 1876; further annexation in 1879; and the leasing of the Bolan Pass in 1883. The North-West Frontier Province (recently renamed Khyber-Pakhtunkhwa) was annexed after the second Anglo-Afghan war in 1893—when the British imposed the Durand line separating the NWFP from Afghanistan. In summary, what is today Pakistan was conquered by the British between 1843 and 1893.

In the hundred years between the Battle of Plassey and the conquest of the Punjab, British capitalism had progressed from the Spinning Jenny and the Crompton Mule to the age of steel-hull shipping and Empire. On the one hand, the rapid capitalist development of Britain created larger and more dynamic markets while, on the other hand, the British gained increasing experience of colonial administration in India.

The 1857 Mutiny, or War of Independence, was a key event that changed the administration of British India. Firstly, India was brought directly under the Crown. Secondly, the British created a strong alliance with those classes that had helped them win the war. Among others, the zamindar class of the Punjab was a vital ally; this was the main explanation for the theory that the Punjabis are a 'martial race'. The pattern of reliance on the Punjab, for recruitment to the British army, continued from then on. About half the British army in India, in the late nineteenth century, was recruited from Punjab (Ali, 1988: 4). In summary, social support from Punjab was crucial for British domination over the rest of India. Hence, the economic transformation of Punjab and Sindh was, among other imperial imperatives, also informed by securing Punjab as a basis for bolstering British rule in India.

PERMANENT SETTLEMENT: PRIVATE PROPERTY AND COMMODITY PRODUCTION

As in the rest of India, the development of private property and commodity production in the region that is today Pakistan—that is, the process of capitalist primitive accumulation—was through the British policy of Permanent Settlement. The registration of land, as private property, began in Punjab in 1846 and continued until 1863 (Hambly, 1964: 50). This process superimposed a new relationship on the AMP. After the 1857 rebellion, the British administration believed that the retention of princes, and the extension of landlords, would buttress British rule. However, in the Punjab, this point of view—termed the 'aristocratic reaction'—was greatly tempered by the ideas of the Punjab school of thought, influenced by John Lawrence (Hambly, 1964: 49). The 1868 Punjab Tenancy Act is arguably reflective of the thinking of this Punjab school of thought.

At first, the British Indian government in Punjab was less concerned with determining land revenue and more with establishing the Permanent Settlement Act. However, once this Act was firmly established, a more comprehensive Punjab Land Revenue Act was introduced in 1887 (Khan, 1981: 146). Before the 1860s, the land tax burden was one-sixth of gross produce. Under this new Act, land revenue was increased to one-half of the net revenue of the landlord (net revenue is the landlord's share in the gross produce less his expenses on cultivation). The Act also regulated landlord-tenant relations, providing a measure of security for tenants against eviction, levies, and perquisites (Khan, 1981: 254–258).

Zamindars were compelled to farm cash crops in order to pay money (taxes). Failure to pay taxes or debts resulted in alienation from the land via the Courts of Civil Justice. In order to pay the taxes, the zamindars began to borrow more heavily from local money lenders. As a result of this increased borrowing to meet the high tax burden, significant sections of the zamindars and peasantry fell into debt and began to sell or mortgage their land. Consequently, there was a steady rise in the sale of mortgaged land to non-agrarian castes from 1887 (Islam, 1995: 271–272). Land was bought or mortgaged to usurers, tradesmen, and merchants who mostly belonged to urban and non-agrarian Hindu castes. By 1890, approximately 42 per cent of the land in Sindh was in the possession of usurers (Belokrenitsky, 1991: 42). These usurers would lease the land to other cultivators, and the cycle would continue. In summary, during the decade from 1860 to 1870, a land market emerged largely as a result of the Permanent Settlement Act (Belokrenitsky, 1991: 37).

The increasing bankruptcy of the traditional agrarian castes undermined social support for British colonialism. In order to protect the agrarian castes and ease the burden on landowners, the British instituted a series of reforms. In Punjab, the British introduced the Land Alienation Act of 1900–1901 and the Punjab Pre-Emption Act 1913. These Acts prohibited the sale of land to non-agrarian castes and only permitted land transfers within the related agricultural caste group in each district. Similarly, in 1912, the British gave full proprietary rights to landlords in Punjab. However, the indebtedness of the landlords or the peasantry did not substantially improve. By 1928, the situation had become so severe that the Punjab Tenancy Act of 1928 lowered the revenue burden from one half to one quarter of the revenue from each estate, and increased the period of settlement to 40 years (except in irrigated areas where it was kept at 30 years) (Khan, 1981: 254–258). At the same time, the Permanent Settlement Act, which stipulated that land revenue would be collected in cash, rapidly developed commodity production for export and domestic consumption. The crisis of indebtedness, the sale and mortgage of land, and the legislation to protect the zamindars were all the effects of the rapid emergence of private property in land as a consequence of the Permanent Settlement Act (Belokrenitsky, 1991; Raulet and Uppal, 1970: 337).

The increasing commercialisation of production was also made possible by the bringing under cultivation vast new land through canal irrigation. 'Between 1885 and the end of British rule in 1947 the canal-irrigated area in the Punjab, excluding the princely states, increased from under 3,000,000 to around 14,000,000 acres' (Ali, 1988: 9). By 1900, more than half of the entire irrigated area of undivided Punjab was irrigated through canals (ibid.). By 1920, nearly 80 per cent of the irrigated area was canal-irrigated (Belokrenitsky, 1991: 134)—representing a seven-fold increase in the area irrigated by canals. Up to 1919–1920, 40 per cent of the total capital outlay by the British government in India was spent on irrigation canals in Punjab (Hirashima, 1978: 22–35). Consequently, the share of irrigated acreage in Punjab was 50 per cent of the total for irrigated agricultural acreage (ibid.).

By 1870–1880, the region specialised in the export of wheat and cotton (Belokrenitsky, 1991: 37). The export of cotton from Sindh grew from being negligible in the 1840s to over 4,000 tonnes by 1873 (ibid.).

Similarly, in undivided Punjab, cotton production increased seven-fold in a single decade, and thirty times more wheat was exported by the 1880s than in the 1860s (Belokrenitsky, 1991: 37). This trend continued into the next century. In the undivided Punjab, the output of wheat increased from 0.87 million tonnes in 1904–1905 to 1.17 million tonnes in 1944–1945, maize from 0.28 to 0.33 million tonnes, cotton from 70,000 bales to 196,000 bales, and sugarcane from 124,000 tonnes to 279,000 tonnes (*Report of National Commission on Agriculture*, 1976). However, as already discussed (in Chapter 2), this growth had no impact on the per capita GNP at the all-India level.

Furthermore, in Punjab, the increase in land used for the growing of food grain was much slower than in land used for the growing of cash crops. For instance, between 1870 and 1879, food grain acreage increased at an average annual growth of 2.5 per cent and, in the following decade (1880 to 1890), it increased by 1.1 per cent (Siddiqi, 1986: 43). However, annual growth rates in acreage planted for cash crops were 4.5 per cent from 1870–1880, 3.8 per cent from 1880–1890, and 11.7 per cent from 1890–1899 (ibid.). As a result, the proportion of land utilised for non-food grain cash crops rose from 14 per cent in 1870 to 20 per cent by 1890 (ibid.).

Thus, in much the same way as in the rest of India, the British continued to extract surplus in the form of land revenue on the one hand and, on the other, the Permanent Settlement Act introduced private property and commodity production into the social fabric of Punjab and Sindh. This combination of private property in land and commodity production on the basis of labour relations other than wage labour is, as this study has argued, the economic basis of Asiatic capitalism. Now, let us examine in more empirical detail the agrarian class and caste relations of contemporary Pakistan.

Castes and Classes in Pakistan

Agricultural Overview

The area that is today Pakistan can be divided into five different regions in accordance with the landscape (see Figure 3.1). These are: (1) Northern High Mountainous Region; (2) Western Low Mountainous Region; (3) Balochistan Plateau; (4) Potwar Plateau (Upland); and

(5) the Indus plain in Punjab and Sindh (Khan, 1998: 6–15). Land tenure systems—which can be taken as an approximation of relations of production—vary according to the regions. The first four, especially the Northern districts (Gilgit, Baltistan, Hunza, Diamer, Chilas, Darel, and Tanger), Balochistan, and some parts of NWFP are considered 'unsettled areas'.

Figure 3.1: Map of Pakistan Land Use, 1992

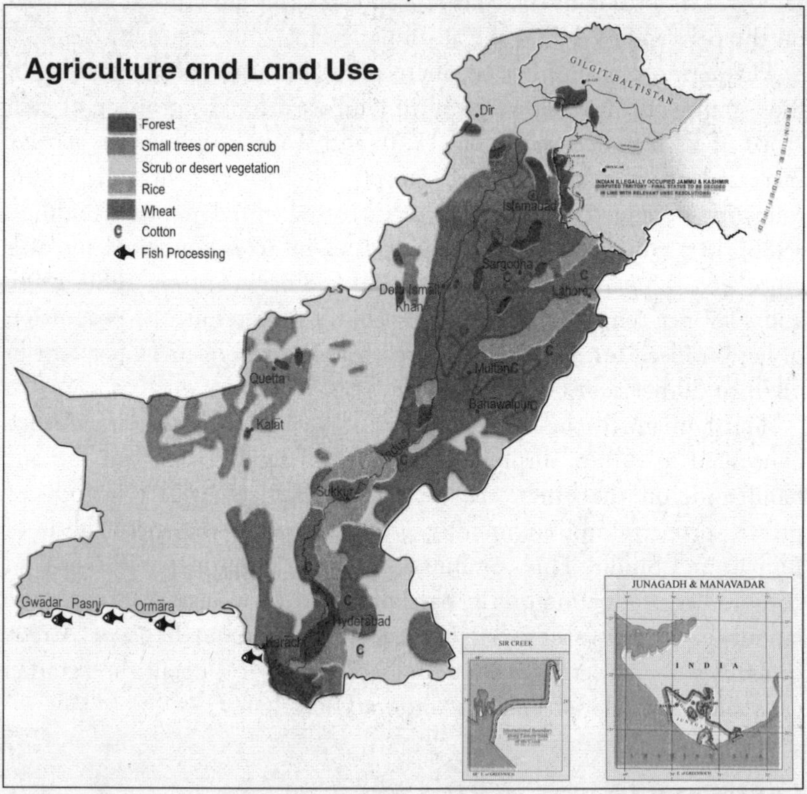

Source: Agriculture and Land Use (2009).

As Figure 3.1 shows, the Indus plain is the most important geographic region of Pakistan as far as agriculture is concerned. The provinces of Punjab and Sindh together (see Figure 3.2) contain about 80 per cent of the population of Pakistan, 85 per cent of the agricultural labour force, 85 per cent of the cultivated area, 92 per cent of the irrigated area,

88 per cent of the cropped area, 89 per cent of the major crops and food grains, 79 per cent of the owners, and 89 per cent of the area owned (Agriculture and Land Use, 2009; Khan, 1981: 10–11). Hence, it would not be incorrect to make certain generalisations about the dominant agrarian relations in contemporary Pakistan on the basis of Punjab and Sindh.

Figure 3.2: Political Map of Pakistan

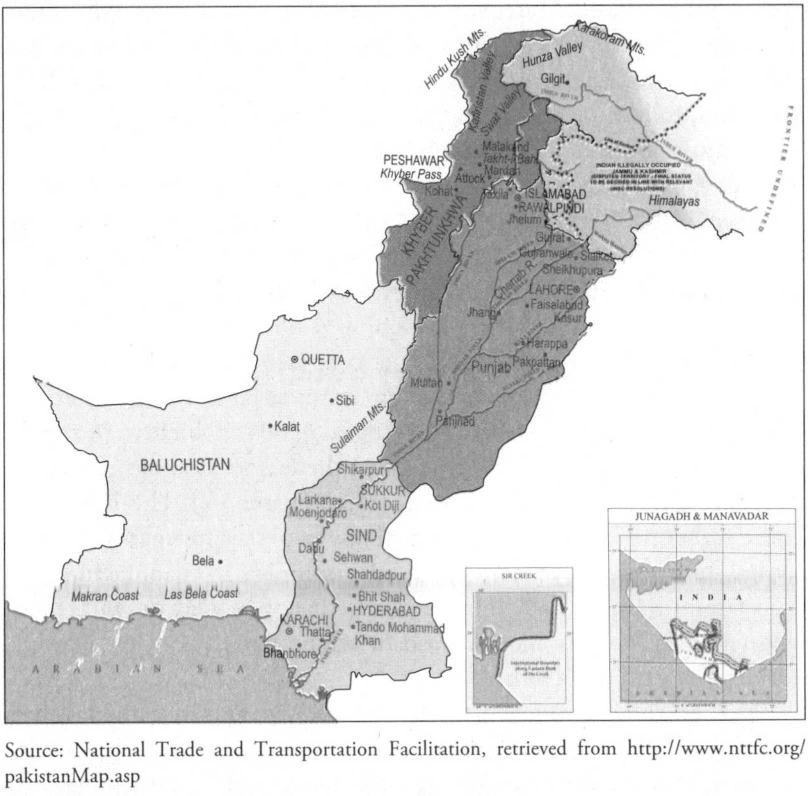

Source: National Trade and Transportation Facilitation, retrieved from http://www.nttfc.org/pakistanMap.asp

In the so-called unsettled areas, sardars, maliks, mirs, and rajahs dominate under a system of tribal ownership. While there is significant ambiguity with respect to property rights throughout Pakistan, there are simply no formal records pertaining to the use of land in these tribal regions (see Alam, 2006; Shah et al., 2007). Hence, property rights in these areas continue to be 'ill-defined' by capitalist standards, and these areas officially fall under the category of 'unreported areas' (Khan, 1998: 22).

Out of Pakistan's total geographic area of 197 million acres, the percentage of area reported rose from 58 per cent in 1947 to 75 per cent by 2002 (Zaidi, 2005: 56). The total cultivated area also rose from 36 million acres in 1947 (that is, 32 per cent of reported area in 1947) to 54 million acres in 2002 (37 per cent of reported area in 2002). Figure 3.3 demonstrates these trends, for roughly the same years.

Wheat, sugarcane, cotton, and rice account for more than 75 per cent of total crop output. Moreover, the percentage of area sown with these four crops has grown, over time, at the expense of all other crops (see Figure 3.4). Wheat is by far the largest food crop. In 2006–2007 Pakistan produced and consumed over 23 million tonnes of wheat (Agricultural Indicators: Federal Bureau of Statistics, 2007).

Over the last half century, one of the most dramatic transformations has been in the overall structure of the economy and the move away from agriculture. In 1949, agriculture contributed more than half of the GDP, but it contributed only a quarter in 2002 (see Figure 3.5).

Similarly, in 1949 agriculture employed 65 per cent of the labour force, but by 2002 it employed 48 per cent (see Figure 3.6).

Agriculture has also become less important as far as Pakistan's export earnings are concerned. In 1949, primary goods—which were mostly agricultural—contributed 99 per cent of the export earnings. By 2002, they were contributing only 11 per cent (see Figure 3.7). This is because, in the earlier period, Pakistan exported raw materials (primarily jute and cotton) but over the years it imported machinery to manufacture and export semi-finished and finished goods that were tied up with those raw materials. For instance, instead of selling raw cotton, textile mills now export yarn and cloth.

Based on these statistics, it is fair to conclude that over the last half century there has been a structural transformation away from agriculture in terms of contribution to GDP, employment, and export earnings. At a very broad level, this structural transformation is suggestive of a transition from one mode of production to another. The study returns to this transformation, from agriculture to industry, in the next chapter. For now, it is important to demonstrate the overall structural transformation to make one important point: such a transformation hardly seems possible without simultaneous changes within the agrarian class structure. What was the traditional agrarian structure, and how is it being transformed? To answer this question, let us begin by examining the caste system.

Figure 3.3: Land Utilisation, 1959 and 2002 (% use of reported area)

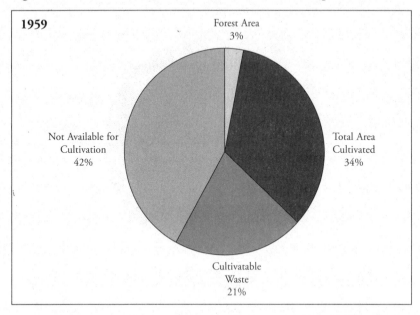

1959

Forest Area
3%

Not Available for
Cultivation
42%

Total Area
Cultivated
34%

Cultivatable
Waste
21%

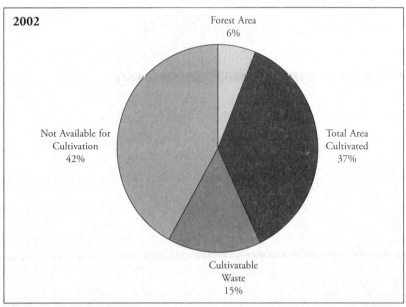

2002

Forest Area
6%

Not Available for
Cultivation
42%

Total Area
Cultivated
37%

Cultivatable
Waste
15%

Source: Zaidi (2005: 56).
Note: Cultivatable waste includes land available for cultivation that has not been cultivated for more than five years in succession.

Figure 3.4: Total Area Sown, 1960–1965 and 2002–2003 (%)

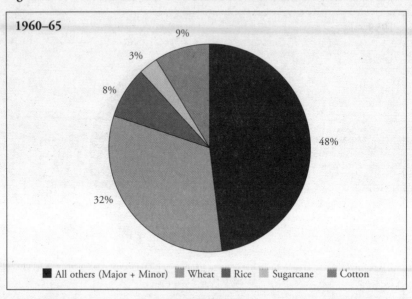

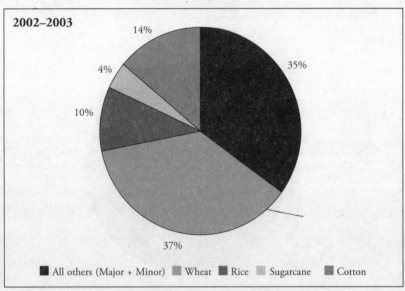

Source: Zaidi (2005: 60).
Note: Major crops are those that are harvested in the summer, including wheat, cotton, rice, sugarcane, gram, corn, sorghum, barley, rapeseed, mustard, and tobacco. Minor crops are harvested in the winter season and include pulses, potatoes, onion, chillies, and garlic.

Figure 3.5: Contribution to GDP, 1949 and 2002 (%)

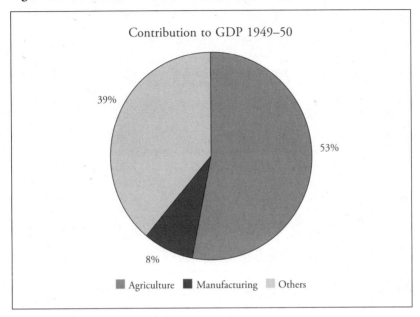

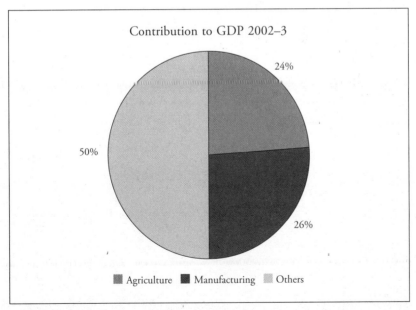

Source: Zaidi (2005: 4).
Note: Zaidi uses the category 'others' instead of 'services'.

Figure 3.6: Labour Force by Sector, 1950–1951 and 2002–2003 (%)

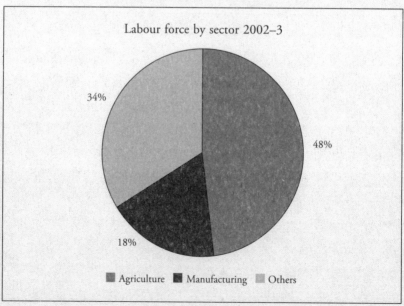

Source: Zaidi (2005: 4).

Figure 3.7: Composition of Exports, 1951–1952 and 2002–2003 (%)

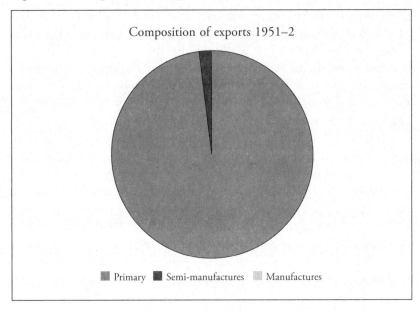

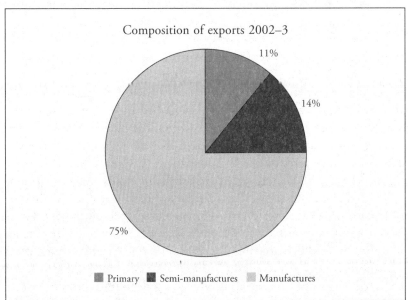

Source: Zaidi (2005: 4).

CASTES

Class analysis of agricultural relations in South Asia must be cognisant of the fact that, traditionally, caste played the dominant role in organising the division of labour of the rural economy. Chapter 2 touched upon the caste system. It stated that the caste system was a hereditary division of labour that was traditionally practiced throughout the subcontinent (Desai, 1976; Singh, 1977). What, then, is the relationship of caste to class?

Given the dearth of academic writing in Pakistan on this subject, theorising about the relation between caste and class must take recourse to the literature produced in India. There is some speculation about the historical origins of the caste system. Vevikananda Jha is of the view that the Harappan civilisation was not based on the caste system (Bhowmik, 1992: 1246); it evolved in the Vedic period (1000 BC) with the development of agricultural surplus and class exploitation. Emile Senart was perhaps one of the first scholars to point out that the four varnas—Brahmans (priests), Kshatryas (warriors), Vaisyas (commoners), and Sudras (untouchables)—were basically four classes. Paul Rosas has compared this to the system of estates found in medieval France: that is, the Brahmans are comparable to the first estate of priests, the Kshatryas to the second estate of knights and nobles, and Vaisyas to the third estate of commoners (Rosas, 1943: 157).

This simple schematic of varnas as classes tends to run into a serious issue. The reality of Indian society was somewhat more complex than the theoretical concept of varnas, as described in Brahmanical ancient texts such as the Puranas and Smritis. In fact, the system of 'jatis' formed the basis of Indian society, and these jatis were theoretically accorded various varna statuses by the Brahmans.

'Jaat' (or 'zaat' as it is called in Pakistan) means 'thus born', and delineated clans and tribes. Each jati had a specific role in the division of labour, which was hereditary. That hereditary role in the division of labour had a very specific social status that was maintained by detailed sets of rules, of which arguably the most important related to endogamy and the sharing and preparation of food. A caste-based village council enforced these rules of social, economic, and political status. In fact, many jatis, especially of a lower status, are still named after their traditional occupations.

This system of a hereditary division of labour, which coincides with clans and tribes, came about as the result of a long history of evolving induction, through conquest or agreement, of various independent and free tribes into a hierarchically-organised class society. As each tribe was inducted into Hindu class society, it accepted three conditions: the veneration of the cow, the caste system, and the dominance of the Brahmans. Aside from these changes, the tribe retained its religious practices. Over time, these various diverse tribes and their religions' narratives became, in various ways, part of the diverse narratives of Hinduism as a whole. Rosas, utilising the word 'caste' for 'jati', summed up this process quite succinctly (1943: 159):

> . . . caste is a caste only insofar as it is part of Hindu class society. If it is outside the pale of such a class society, it constitutes a tribe, as in the case of the aboriginal tribes still existing in India. And the transformation of a aboriginal tribe into a caste does not signify, as pointed out before, any internal changes; it merely signifies its being inducted as a unit member of Hindu *class* society, an induction which is symbolized by the acceptance of the leadership of the Brahmans, the great rationalizers and mystifiers of Hindu class society. The caste system as a system of castes is thus the expression of a class society, the classes of which in turn are composed of ingested but undigested tribal forms and whose position as members of the class society makes them castes.

However, one can note that although each jati had a traditional hereditary occupation (and many jatis were named directly after their occupation), even before the advent of colonial capitalism members of one jati did undertake different occupations. Conversely, one can also note that members of different jatis can be found in one occupation. How can this observation be reconciled with the above-stated view of the system of jatis being a system of the hereditary occupational division of labour?

To understand this apparent contradiction, one has to understand the historical conditions resulting in the subdivision of jatis. When a given jati prospered—either in terms of population, area, or wealth—the expansion also brought about a new division of labour. Sections of the jati would specialise in the new occupation. If that new occupation was of a higher status, they would create new rules of endogamy to protect their new social status. If the social status of the new occupation was lower than the status of their previous occupation, they would find themselves being excluded by the endogenous patterns of their own jati of a higher status. In many instances, they retained the name of their traditional jati and became a sub-jati with a different occupation.

Over long historical periods, jatis could gain or lose status, sub-divide or amalgamate with other jatis, and so on. Their jati name, however, would continue to denote their original traditional occupation. Moreover, while the component parts of the caste system were always in some degree of movement over the course of history, this movement did not necessarily mean that the caste system ceased to exist. However, it certainly demonstrates that the development of the division of labour in India had an impact on the form and evolution of the caste system.

In the caste system, every type of work undertaken by a jati was given an identifiable name and a very specific explicit social status in relation to all other forms of work. Hence, to understand castes in terms of class, one has to first grasp the specific relationship of a caste to the means of production. In other words, the specific economic relationship of a given caste to the means of production is the class of that caste. It can also be argued that struggles between subordinate and oppressing castes (which frequently assumed the form of religious struggles) were primarily struggles of pre-capitalist classes.

Therefore, to study the class structure of a particular pre-capitalist village or region, one must begin by examining the number, relative status, and proportion of caste households that existed in that area. The main difficulty is in finding, gathering, sifting, and mastering the enormous amount of information regarding castes. This difficulty in finding sources, in the context of an oral culture, is compounded by the fact that, over long historical periods, castes are still being created, destroyed, and sub-divided. Hence, there are thousands of castes that are divided further into sub-castes all over India and Pakistan.

In the Muslim regions of India the Arabic word 'quom' is used to describe castes as well as 'nation' (Gazdar, 2007: 5). In Pakistan, quoms are broadly divided into two distinct systems: land-owning quoms are known as zamindar quoms, and labouring class quoms are known as kammi quoms. Zamindar quoms include those that work their own land, as well as those who mainly live off the rent from their sharecropping tenants. The more powerful zamindar quoms tend to dominate village life. For instance, in Punjab, the zamindar quoms include Sayyed, Awan, Rajput, Gakhar, Gujjar, Jat, Arain, Rawn, Malik,

Shaikh, Bhatti, Gondal, and so on—these are all various names of different landowning castes.

Working quoms are known as kammi quoms. The word 'kammi' literally means worker (in Punjabi, 'kam' means 'to work').[17] There are numerous kammi quoms, such as chuhra/musali[18] (sweeper and scavenger), chammer (leather worker), nai (barber), chhimba and dhobi (washerman), mirasi (village bard and genealogist), kasai (butcher), kumhar (potter), tarkhan/badhai (carpenter), lohar (blacksmith), changar (reapers), mallah (fisherman), kewat (boatman), teli (oil presser), kahar (water carrier), gadadia (sheep herder), sonar (goldsmith), and darzi (tailor). In Sindh, they are called bheel, kolhi, toorkhail (literally 'black lineage'), kisabgar (menials), bagri, lachhi, lohri, and shahikhel. In Khyber-Pakhtunkhwa (NWFP), they are called neech zaat (low caste), badnasal (bad lineage) and, in Balochistan, they are simply called ghulams (slaves) (Gazdar, 2007: 2). According to Denzil Ibbetson, these working quoms, making up over a quarter of the population, were largely composed of 'the great mass of such aboriginal element [tribes] still to be found in the Panjab' (Ibbetson, 1986: 266).

The total number of zamindar and kammi quoms is far too great to describe in this chapter. For instance, in one of the landmark studies on the class structure of one Punjabi village in Sahiwal, Saghir Ahmed documented 23 zamindar quoms and 15 kammi quoms (Ahmed, 1977: 70–90). A detailed glossary of castes in the Punjab and NWFP (based on Ibbetson's Census Report of 1883 and compiled by H.A. Rose) called *A Glossary of the Tribes and Castes of the Punjab and North-West Frontier Provinces* documented thousands of castes and sub-castes (Rose, 1919). This massive study was essentially a study of the social division of labour in Punjab and NWFP, albeit coloured by the views of the colonial period (Rose, 1919).[19] Other similar comprehensive studies from the colonial period include Blunt (1931), Crooke (1974), Dutt (1968), Enthoven (1990), Nesfield (1885), O'Malley (1932), Risley (1981), Russell (1993), Senart (1977), Sherring (1872), Thurston (2001), and the annual Census Reports of India.

CLASSES

As a result of the development of colonial capitalism, the whole caste system was thrown into turmoil. At a very general level, relatively high castes metamorphosed into dominating capitalist classes while the low castes metamorphosed into wage labourers. However, certain castes were more suited to the new capitalist mode of production; in particular, trading castes rose in status above their former superiors. Trade and commerce in Pakistan, today, is dominated by five castes traditionally associated with trade: Memons, Khojas, Bohras, Chiniotis, and Saigols.[20]

Now, let us examine the agrarian classes that developed as a result of colonial capitalism. The categorisation of classes by Marxist researchers is mostly based on the methodology offered by Lenin's *Preliminary Draft Thesis* or Mao Zedong's *Analysis of the Classes in Chinese Society* (Lenin, 1920; Zedong, 1926). Generally, Marxists define class in terms of 'possession of the means of production and exploitation of labour' (Patnaik, 1990: 196). According to this analysis, those engaged in agriculture can be divided into five classes: landlords, rich peasants, middle peasants, poor peasants, and wageworkers. While this analysis is no doubt correct at the general level, it needs further qualification in the context of Pakistan. One of the more sophisticated analysis of the overall agrarian class structure of Pakistan is provided by Mahmood Hassan Khan (arguably one of the most prolific researchers on agrarian relations in Pakistan) (Khan, 1998).

Broadly speaking, agrarian relations can be divided into three land tenure systems—landlord-tenant, peasant proprietors, and a small and slowly emerging capitalist system (Khan, 1998: 59). The landlord-tenant system was concentrated in most areas of Sindh and several areas of Punjab, whereas the peasant proprietor relationship was concentrated in Punjab and NWFP (*Report of the Tenancy Legislation Committee*, 1945; *Report of the Government Hari Enquiry Committee 1947–48*, 1948; *Hari Enquiry Committee: Minute of Dissent by M. Masud*, 1949).

At the time of independence, about half the area of Punjab and NWFP, and over 70 per cent of the area in Sindh, was cultivated under the sharecropping system (*Report of the Agrarian Committee*, 1949). The peasant proprietor system was prominent in Punjab. Numerous peasant families owned about 55 per cent of the total farm area (ibid.). Certain estates, called jagirs, were completely exempt from payment of land revenue. Tillers of the land, whose right to cultivate was not recognised in law and whose tenure on land was entirely dependent on the whims of the landlord, were euphemistically called tenants-at-will in government reports. These were bonded sharecroppers known as 'haris' and 'muzareen'. The various classes that made up this complex agrarian structure were as follows:

Landlords: At the time of Independence, large landowners were a small percentage of the population but owned a large percentage of the land. For instance, landlords with holdings of over 500 acres constituted only 0.5 per cent of the rural population but owned 25 to 30 per cent of the agricultural area of Pakistan (Khan, 1981: 136). Today, sharecropping dominates the agrarian economy.

The landlord-tenant relation is what Pakistani writers generally refer to as 'feudalism'. Landlords earn their living from the surplus they extract from the tenant in the form of the share (in economic literature this share is referred to as 'rent'). This share-cropping system is known as 'batai', whereby half the produce is handed over to the landlord (Khan, 1981: 136). Landlords mostly extract labour from landless sharecroppers, but they may also utilise the labour of poor or middle peasants. In addition, they may also employ wage labour, especially during the harvesting and planting season when the need for labour is high. However, even though land is owned in large estates, it is actually cultivated in small parcels because landlords rent or lease land out to sharecroppers in parcels averaging about 15 acres (Khan, 1981: 204). As a result, few, if any, economies of scale come into operation and the system is extremely economically inefficient (Khan, 1981: 209–229).[21]

Traditionally, landlords belong to the higher quoms of the zamindar caste. For instance, landlords in the Punjab belong to the Syed, Rajput, or Jat castes. The Syeds claim Arab descent and trace their lineage back to the prophet Mohammad. Rajput literally means 'the king's son' (raj = king or kingdom; put = son). Some of the influential tribes of the Punjab that are part of the Rajput caste include the Bhattis, Punwars, Chauhans, Minhas, Tiwanas, Noons, Chibs, Ghebas, Jodhras, Janjuas, Sials, Wattus, and so on. Similarly, a large number of Punjabi zamindars belong to the Jat caste. The Jat caste includes tribes such as Bajwa, Chatta, Cheema, Randhawa, Ghammon, Buta, Kahlon, Gil, Sehota, Taror, Waraich, Summa, Wahla, Bhutta, Malhi, Sukhera, Alpial, Daha, Langah, Ranghar, Meo, Awan, Khokhar, Ghakkar, and so on.

During the pre-colonial period, the jagirdar was the representative of the state. Similarly, the landlords of contemporary Pakistan retain control not only over the village panchiat but also over the instruments of the modern state. Hence, to gain access to the organs of the state for social services, law and order, or other concerns, villagers have to mostly go through the landlords. Landlords are able to retain a despotic status in relation to the peasants by maintaining monopoly control over modern state institutions (Martin, 2008).

Peasant proprietors: The peasant proprietors are those that own their land but earn income through engaging in manual labour. The archetype of peasant proprietorship is the traditional self-sufficient farm based on family labour. Peasant proprietors may also hire out their labour to landlords in order to supplement their incomes. Hence, there is not a strict separation between the landlord-tenant and the peasant proprietor sectors of the economy. Nonetheless, there are also significant sections of the peasantry that are outside the ambit of the landlord-tenant relation.

According to the methodology that is dominant among Marxists, peasant proprietors can be further divided into rich, middle, and poor peasants (Lenin, 1920; Mao Zedong, 1926; Patnaik, 1990). This methodology can also be utilised in the context of Pakistan, where most peasant proprietorship is concentrated in the newly-settled and canal colonies of the Punjab (Khan, 1981: 136).

Rich peasants are owners that are distinguished from other peasant proprietors by the fact that they are rich enough to hire sharecroppers and wage labourers. They generally own most or a significant part of the land they cultivate and also rent and lease land from others. Generally, they do not rent or lease out their own land nor do they sell their own labour power to others. They organise production and supervise labour. Their income takes the form of rent, share, and profit (in money and in kind). Government and researchers have pinned their hopes of a capitalist transformation of agriculture on the rich peasant transforming into a capitalist farmer.

In the Punjab, rich peasants are mostly Jats and Rajputs. By virtue of belonging to the zamindar quom and being owners of land, rich peasant proprietors have a higher class status than the worker quoms. Thus, even if their income decreases, their social status as members of the zamindar caste remains higher than those belonging to the kammi castes. For instance, while zamindars marry each other, they are extremely opposed to marriage with someone from the kammi caste.

Middle peasants mostly rely on family labour. On average, they neither hire out nor hire in labour. If there is a Chayanovian peasant to be found anywhere, it is the middle peasant. Traditionally, middle peasants belong to the relatively lower status of zamindar quoms.

Poor peasants are those that are forced to supplement their earnings by working for others. Often, poor peasants will also rent out part, or the whole, of their land to rich peasants. Poor peasants are in constant danger of being reduced to landless sharecroppers and wageworkers. These small owners, known as ryots, form part of the peasant proprietor system called khud kasht (literally, self-cultivated).

These definitions of classes are represented schematically in Table 3.1.

Table 3.1: Agrarian Class Differentiation in Pakistan

Classes	Land	Labour
Landlords	Own land Rent out land Do not rent in land	Hire in labour Do not hire out labour
Rich Peasants	Own land Do not rent out land Rent in land	Hire in labour Do not hire out labour
Middle or Poor Peasants	Own land Rent out land Rent in land	Do not hire in labour Hire out labour
Sharecroppers	Do not own land Do not rent out land Rent in land	Do not hire in labour Hire out labour
Wageworkers	Do not own land Do not rent in land Do not rent out land	Do not hire in labour Hire out labour

Source: Khan (1985: 10–13).

The above definitions can also be approximated in terms of the area of land owned. However, it must be kept in mind that landownership can only be a proxy for class relations. For instance, the amount of land required to be able to live off the surplus of others varies with the productivity of the land—which varies across the regions of Pakistan. For instance, a person with 20 acres of land may be a rich or a middle peasant, depending on the productivity of the land as well as the availability of other resources.

The use of landownership as a proxy for class, however, allows us to roughly estimate the relative proportion of these classes to the total population of the landholding classes. Hence, this information gives us only an approximate, though somewhat outdated, picture of the class divisions among landowning households. Khan has made the following generalisation with respect to the landowning classes and ownership of land to percentage of population (see Table 3.2).

Table 3.2: Landowning Classes and Landholding Patterns

Class	Land Owned	Percentage of Population (1972)
Landlords	Generally own 50 acres or more	< 1 per cent of all landowning households.
Rich Peasants	Generally own anywhere between 25 and 50 acres	10% to 25% of all landowning households
Middle Peasants	Generally own anywhere between 12.5 to 25 acres	20% to 33% of all landowning households
Poor Peasants	Generally own between 5 and 12.5 acres	25% to 50% of all landowning households

Source: Khan, M. (1981: 70).
Note: those owning less than 5 acres of land are considered, effectively, to be landless.

Landless sharecroppers are bound by custom to share the output they produce with the landlord. This is generally one half of the output in the Indus plain. Landless sharecroppers may also sell their labour power to supplement their incomes. Since there is no economic security in agricultural wage labour, landless peasants generally prefer sharecropping to wage labour (Khan, 1981: 214). Traditionally, these were the kammi castes, such as the 'muzaras' or 'haris'. However, with the development of capitalism, poor peasants are constantly thrust into the category of landless sharecroppers. Hence, individuals of the zamindar castes may also be found among landless sharecroppers.

During the Mughal period, peasants traditionally working on non-revenue-paying jagirs were known as makhadims. Similarly, peasants working on revenue-paying lands were known as 'marusi muzareen'. Certain traditional rights of the makhadims and marusi muzareen were recognised by colonial law. Hence, they came to be categorised as 'occupancy tenants' in government reports. These occupancy tenants have a certain degree of legal protection.

Agricultural wageworkers are generally the poorest and lowest in terms of social status. They are poorer than sharecroppers—who often own some diminutive means of production such as animals, tools, and implements. Household surveys demonstrate that the highest incidence of poverty is to be found among agricultural wageworkers. In terms of caste, they have the lowest rank. They are mostly employed by rich peasant proprietors, and also by landlords. Their wage may partly be paid in cash and partly in kind. While they may work on a long-term basis, they mostly work on a seasonal basis—working in the non-agricultural sector during periods of low labour demand. Furthermore, not only are they employed in agriculture—where they perform the hardest tasks—but also as the personal servants of the landlord or other zamindar peasants. Because of the lower economic and social status of the agricultural wageworkers, landless tenants live under the constant threat of eviction. For instance, the main aim of the Anjuman Muzareen Punjab (landless tenant's movement) in 2000 was to prevent the state transforming the system of sharecropping (hissa batai) into a system of fixed land rent. The latter system would have meant that they would lose their status as tenants and would become agricultural wageworkers. Sharecroppers actually outnumber agricultural wageworkers.

Non-agricultural rural producers: About 30 to 40 per cent of the rural economy does not directly engage in cultivation—they are engaged in other professions, some of which may be indirectly related to agriculture. For instance, they may be artisans, mechanics, teachers, doctors, transporters, traders, shopkeepers, government employees, and so on.

Traditionally, non-agrarian rural work was mostly done by the members of the various kammi castes. More recently, the development of commodity production has given rise to a market-driven non-agricultural rural sector that is often dominated by small capitalist enterprises employing wage labour or petty commodity producers. The market-driven non-agricultural rural economy offers some opportunities for low caste people to escape their hereditary roles—although even in the non-agrarian economy, the lowest-paid jobs are occupied by the kammi castes while the best jobs go to those from higher castes (see Chapter 4).

The transformation from the pre-capitalist to the capitalist system occurs through a process of the differentiation of the peasantry. Marxists argue that the differentiation of the peasantry is symptomatic of the rise of capitalist relations in agriculture. What does the available data indicate about the differentiation of the peasantry in what is today Pakistan?

DIFFERENTIATION OF THE PEASANTRY

The most comprehensive data to examine the differentiation of the peasantry in contemporary Pakistan are provided by the five official Agricultural Censuses (1960, 1972, 1980, 1990, and 2000). However, it is pertinent to mention the criticism voiced by several scholars about the shortcomings of this data. Firstly, the quality and reliability of the statistics leave much to be desired. It is widely believed that the agricultural censuses after the first land reforms of 1959 have systematically under-reported land concentration (see Alavi, 1976; Gotsch, 1976; Naseem, 1977). Secondly, the agricultural censuses and the national surveys do not provide direct information on farm households on the basis of ownership and use of land. Landownership data has never been published by the government or made available to researchers. Thirdly, data on the tribal areas of NWFP and Balochistan is simply not available. Lastly, there are no satisfactory estimates of the number, or status, of landless agricultural workers. Despite these significant drawbacks, the government's Agricultural Censuses are the only available nationwide data. Hence, limited as they are, they are the only data that can help one understand the general class relations of Pakistan. The paucity of data implies that an analysis of class relations can only be a rough approximation.

Can landholding size and tenure relations be used as a proxy to understand class relations in the countryside? For this, we need to examine the relationship between landownership and agrarian classes.

Classes are defined in terms of 'possession of the means of production and exploitation of labour' (Lenin, 1920; Mao Zedong, 1926; Patnaik, 1990).[22] Hence, social relations, rather than the size of ownership of land, are the basis for class divisions. However, there are two shortcomings when utilising landownership as a benchmark for class differences. Firstly, it does not indicate the nature of the relations of production. For example, a landowner of 15 acres may be engaged in commercial farming (that is, selling the surplus on the market) or in self-sufficient family farming (consuming the surplus outside the market). Secondly, aside from other shortcomings such as poor data collection methodology and so on, landownership statistics do not account for the intensification of agricultural production. With respect to the latter, Lenin (1917) wrote:

> owing to the technical peculiarities of agriculture, the process of its intensification frequently leads to a reduction in the improved acreage on the farm, and at the same time expands it as an economic unit, increasing its output, and making it more and more of a capitalist enterprise.

Thus, a more accurate measure of the differentiation of the peasantry would be to group farms in terms of their value of output and wage employment. However, such statistics are simply not available in Pakistan. Hence, the use of landownership patterns as a proxy for class relations is necessary.

However, given that capitalist intensification of agriculture generally leads to the simultaneous reduction in the size of the farm as well as a higher output, it is safe to assume that landownership patterns under-estimate peasant differentiation over time. Moreover, it follows that the greater the intensification of agriculture, the greater the underestimation of differentiation. In this regard, Lenin (1917) wrote that categorisation by landownership:

> understates the displacement of small-scale by large-scale production, and that the understatement increases with the pace and scope of intensification of agriculture, and with the gap between the amounts of capital invested by the farms per unit of land.

Similarly, Utsa Patnaik, while analysing data on agrarian relations in Indian Punjab, argued that 'as capital intensification by particular groups of cultivators takes place, the identification of scale with size becomes more and more unsatisfactory' (Patnaik, 1990: 50–54).

Keeping in mind these qualifications, with respect to the use of landholding size and tenure relations as a proxy for class relations, let us look at the changes that have occurred over the last century in the region that is today Pakistan.

Overall, two major trends in ownership patterns and tenancy relations are observable from these Agricultural Censuses. First, the ownership and acreage of very small and medium sized farms has increased, whereas there has been a significant fall in the number and acreage of very large landholdings (Khan, 1998: 23–24). However, this is also attributable to bogus land transfers in anticipation of, and in response to, the Land Reform Acts of 1959 and 1972. Second, the number and acreage of owner-operated farms has increased, whereas the owner-cum-tenant and tenant farms have decreased in number and acreage (Khan, 1998: 23–24). Let us, now, turn to the individual Agricultural Censuses.

During the pre-colonial period, the Agricultural Censuses of Punjab and Sindh, conducted in 1924 and 1939, indicated a tendency towards the increasing concentration of land.

Table 3.3: Structure of Landownership in Punjab and Sindh, 1924, 1939 (%)

Plots (acres)	1924		1939	
	Owners	Area Owned	Owners	Area Owned
Up to 5	58.3	11.2	63.7	12.2
5–10	18.0	15.1	16.9	13.1
10–15	8.6	12.5	7.3	9.1
15–20	4.3	8.4	3.6	7.2
20–25	2.7	6.8	2.2	5.6
25–50	4.8	20.4	3.9	14.8
Over 50	3.3	25.7	2.4	38.0

Source: Belokrenitksy (1991: 99).
Note: The data is for undivided Punjab (East Punjab and West Punjab).

Table 3.3 indicates that between 1924 and 1939 a smaller number of owners possessed farms that were larger than 50 acres and controlled more total area. During the same period, both the area and the number of farms of 10 to 50 acres decreased. Moreover, the number of owners of farms that were smaller than 5 acres increased. One can simplify these trends by regrouping plots into three categories. The first category is those with less than 10 acres of land, the second is those with between 10 and 50 acres of land, and the third is those with more than 50 acres of land. If we graph these categories, the trends become much clearer.

Figure 3.8: Land Distribution, 1924–1939 (%)

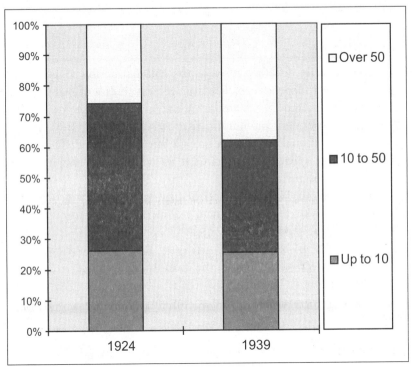

Source: Table 3.3.

Figure 3.8 shows that between 1924 and 1939 the percentage of land cultivated in farms larger than 50 acres increased, the percentage of farms between 10 and 50 acres decreased, and the percentage of farms below 10 acres remained stable.

A case can be made that since the colonial authorities invested heavily in the intensification of farms through the building of canals and canal colonies, especially in western Punjab (that is, part of present-day Pakistan), it follows that the actual differentiation of the peasantry was probably more advanced than suggested by these statistics on landownership.[23]

Finally, this data set is for undivided Punjab. After 1947, the eastern districts of Punjab became part of Pakistan while the western districts became part of India. Hence, any conclusions drawn from the above data set about western Punjab (which became part of Pakistan) must be tempered by this limitation.

INDEPENDENCE

The trend of class differentiation of the colonial period (Figure 3.8) continued after Independence. The average growth rate of real GDP of the region that became Pakistan during the late colonial period (1900–1947) was 1.3 per cent per annum (Kurosaki, 2000, 2002: 5). At the same time, the annual population growth rate was about 0.47 per cent (Thadani, 2002). Hence, per capita GDP in Pakistan probably increased but not by a substantial amount.

Moreover, about 71 per cent of this pre-Independence growth was due to the expansion of the area under cultivation (mainly through canal colonies). After Independence, from 1947 to 1990, the annual growth rate of real GDP increased to 3.7 per cent. Land productivity growth accounted for 65 per cent of the post-Independence growth in agricultural output (Thadani, 2002).

With respect to the differentiation, landownership statistics in 1955 demonstrated the following results.

Table 3.4: Distribution of Landownership in Punjab and Sindh, 1955 (%)

Farm Size (acres)	Pakistan		Punjab		Sindh	
	Owners	Area Owned	Owners	Area Owned	Owners	Area Owned
5 or less	64.4	15.3	66.3	15.7	29.8	3.6
5–25	28.7	31.7	28.9	39.0	46.0	18.8
25–100	5.7	24.8	4.1	21.9	16.2	23.2
100–500	1.1	15.8	0.6	13.6	7.1	25.3
500 and above	0.1	15.4	0.1	9.9	0.9	29.1

Source: Khan (1981: 68).

Table 3.4 shows that the poorest 64.4 per cent of the agrarian population owned approximately 15 per cent of all land in Pakistan. The richest 1 per cent owned nearly a third of the land in Pakistan. Belokrenitsky estimated that, from 1950 to 1955, approximately 6,000 landowning families—constituting about 0.1 per cent of all landowners—owned 15 per cent of all land in Pakistan (Belokrenitsky, 1991). In Punjab, fewer than 2,000 owners owned approximately 10 per cent of the land. In Sindh, a mere 3,000 people owned nearly 30 per cent of the land. The richest 8 per cent owned 54 per cent of all land in Sindh.

Large land-ownership was particularly widespread in Sindh, as demonstrated by Figure 3.9.

Figure 3.9: Land Distribution by Percentage Area in Pakistan, 1955

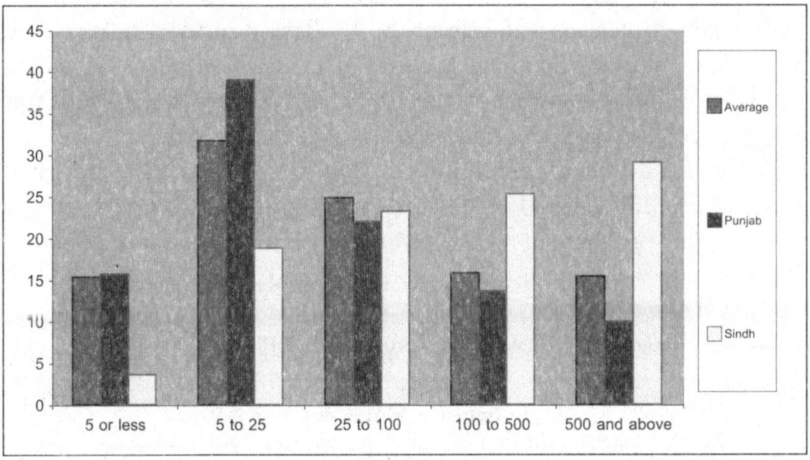

Source: from Table 3.4.

GREEN REVOLUTION AND THE ACCELERATION OF CAPITALIST DEVELOPMENT

By the late 1950s, agricultural output was not keeping pace with the annual population growth rate (Falcon and Gotsch, 1964). Between 1949 and 1958, the population grew at the rate of 3 per cent per annum, while agricultural output grew at an average annual rate of 1.43 per cent (Zaidi, 2005: 59). By the end of the decade, food deficits and lack of raw materials for industrial production convinced the government to reassess its agricultural policy.

The Planning Commission reasoned that although the 1950s saw substantial rates of growth in large-scale industry, agriculture stagnated and, as a result, per capita income did not rise significantly. At the same time, the Ford Foundation and the Harvard Advisory Group were developing and financing the so-called Green Revolution in Third World countries, in order to stem the growing influence of communism. The Green Revolution was also seen as a solution to Pakistan's slow rate of agricultural and economic growth.

The Green Revolution stimulated agricultural production and contributed to the rapid development and deepening of the internal market. To support the Green Revolution and develop capitalist farming, the Ayub government launched a land reform policy in 1958. Papanek wrote that 'the spurt in agricultural production was the main difference between the Pakistan of the 1950s and of the 1960s, as well as between Pakistan and other countries' (Papanek, 1967: 34). According to Lewis, unlike the growth of the 1950s, the growth in the 1960s was also driven by a developing domestic market (1969: 46).

In 1959, the government imposed a ceiling of 500 acres for irrigated land and 1,000 acres for non-irrigated land. Land taken by the government was compensated with interest-bearing government bonds. Table 3.5 shows the progress of the 1959 Land Reform.

Table 3.5: Progress of 1959 Land Reforms till 1981 (acres)

Area Resumed	Area Allotted	Area not Allotted	Households that Benefited
2,547,833	2,216,250	331,583	183,266

Note: area resumed = land taken up by the government in order to auction or grant.
Area allotted = land that the government auctioned or granted to peasants.
Source: Ahmed and Amjad (1984).

Mahmood Hasan Khan's detailed analysis, based on official statistics, shows that 15 per cent of the landowners were affected by the ceiling (Khan, 1981: 166–174). Most landlords were able to side-step the land reforms, and retained their holdings, through numerous provisions and loopholes in the law. For instance, many landlords transferred land to their dependants simply on paper (ibid.). Furthermore, the landlords often handed over the worst quality land at their disposal (ibid.). Khan estimated that approximately 57 per cent of the land appropriated by the government was uncultivated land (1981: 166–174). The market price set on some of this land was so high that it did not sell. Later, this unsold land was auctioned to military officials and rich farmers (Khan, 1981: 166–174). The result was that, even after a decade of the reform, only about 20 per cent of the resumed land was sold to landless workers (Khan, 1981: 166–174). No more than 2 per cent of the peasantry was able to purchase land in these land reforms (ibid.). Alavi (1976), Burki (1976), and Hussain (1980) have convincingly argued that the 1959 land reform did not undermine the power of the large landlords in Pakistan.

In the AMP, the state was a central economic feature that developed the preconditions for agriculture by undertaking large public works. Without these public works, agriculture in those environmental circumstances would be much harder, if at all possible (see Chapter 2). In some sense, the colonial state took over the role of the Asiatic state.

The colonial state extracted surplus in the form of land revenue, just as the Mughal state had done before it. The colonial state also took over the role of the Asiatic state, for the construction of canals and canal colonies. At the same time, the colonial state was one of the principal instruments through which capitalism was being introduced into India (see Chapter 2). With the help of foreign assistance, mainly from the USA, the post-colonial Pakistani state became an instrument of the Green Revolution.

After 1951, the Pakistani government came under the influence of the United States of America. Since then, the United States Agency for International Development (USAID) has provided nearly $7 billion to support Pakistan's various development efforts (USAID in Pakistan, 2007). During the first half of the 1960s, US assistance was so great that it made up more than half of all foreign aid to Pakistan, was one-third of Pakistan's development budget, and financed half of the country's import expenditures (ibid.). USAID worked with, and helped to finance, the Pakistan National Research Council, Pakistan Agricultural Research Council, Agricultural University in Peshawar, Arid Zone Research Institute in Quetta, Pakistan Forestry Institute in Peshawar, Agricultural Universities at Faisalabad in Punjab and Tando Jam in Sindh,

International Irrigation Management Institute in Lahore, Pakistan's Statistics Division, and the Economic Analysis Network. In addition, the US also facilitated development assistance through contributions from the World Bank, the Asian Development Bank, and United Nations programs.

Thus, on the one hand, the state continued as an organiser of large public works. For instance, the Pakistani state, together with the World Bank, organised the design, financing, and construction of some 100 projects in a period of 15 years under the aegis of the gigantic Indus Basin Development Project (IBDP) of 1960—including the Mangla Dam on the Jhelum River, link canals, five barrages, tube-wells, and drainage works, as well as the Tarbela Dam on the Indus (the largest earth and rock filled dam in the world) (Pochat, 2007). The largest donor to the IBDP project was USAID, providing $712 million; that is, 31 per cent of all contributions.

On the other hand, the state was an instrument for the development of capitalism. The Green Revolution, considered the greatest success story of the relationship between the US and Pakistan, introduced a new technology package in the countryside, including tube-wells, tractors, high yield variety seeds, pesticides, and fertilisers—leading to the mechanisation and commercialisation of agriculture. Let us, now, look at each of these developments briefly.

Tube-wells: Pakistan has the largest contiguous irrigation system in the world. Nearly 82 per cent of its agricultural area is covered by irrigation, which is the highest proportion in South Asia (Haq, 2007). Hence, irrigation patterns play an enormous role in the agrarian political economy of Pakistan. Before the Green Revolution, the canal system laid by the colonial state was the principal means of irrigation. In 1950, canals provided 81 per cent of all irrigation (see Table 3.6 and Figure 3.10).

The Green Revolution introduced tube-wells, on a mass scale, into the landscape of the countryside. From 1960 to 1964, approximately 25,000 tube-wells were installed (Sanderatne, 1986: 306). Between 1964 and 1969, the number of tube-wells increased from 34,000 to 79,000 (Zaidi, 2005: 29). By 1975, there were 156,000, and by 1992–93 a quarter of all irrigated land was irrigated with tube-wells (Zaidi, 2005: 30).

Tube-wells were also used to control the build-up of salt in the water table. For instance, the Salinity Control and Reclamation Program (SCARP) utilised tube-wells to pump out salty groundwater and to dilute the water table with canal water (Wheeler, 2007).

Much of this mechanisation was made possible because of the assistance provided by the US government. For instance, from 1982–1987, USAID provided $1.62 billion to improve 4,000 kilometres of canals and waterways and to upgrade irrigation workshops (USAID in Pakistan, 2007). 1,319 waterways were renovated and 75,000 acres of land were levelled. In addition, training centres and demonstration farms were established, for which more than $50 million was provided for vehicles, heavy machinery, computers, and other equipment (ibid.).

Table 3.6: Irrigated Area by Sources (thousand acres)

Year	Canals	Tube-Wells	Others	Total
1950–1955	7.8	0.0	1.8	9.4
1955–1960	8.6	0.1	1.5	10.3
1960–1965	9.0	0.4	1.6	11.1
1965–1970	8.9	1.0	2.3	12.3
1970–1975	9.2	2.3	1.2	12.7
1975–1980	10.3	2.3	1.1	14.2
1980–1985	11.4	3.1	1.0	15.5
1985–1990	11.5	3.9	0.8	16.2
1990–1993	12.1	4.3	0.6	16.9

Source: Pakistan Economic Survey (1994–95: 58).

Tractors: In 1960, there were 1,665 tractors in Pakistan; by 1984, there were 187,255 tractors (Gotsch, 1982). According to Gotsch, most of these tractors were very large—as recommended by the World Bank (Gotsch, 1982: 66). Gotsch estimated that 84 per cent of the tractors were of more than 35-horse power (ibid.). Unsurprisingly, ownership of tractors was mainly concentrated on holdings of over 25 acres. Numerous studies have shown that although tractors did not result in a significant increase in yield per acre, they allowed landowners to substitute capital for labour and to increase the size of their landholdings by increasing the amount of land leased from other peasants or by evicting sharecroppers and by substituting self-cultivation with hired

Figure 3.10: Percentage Irrigated Area by Source

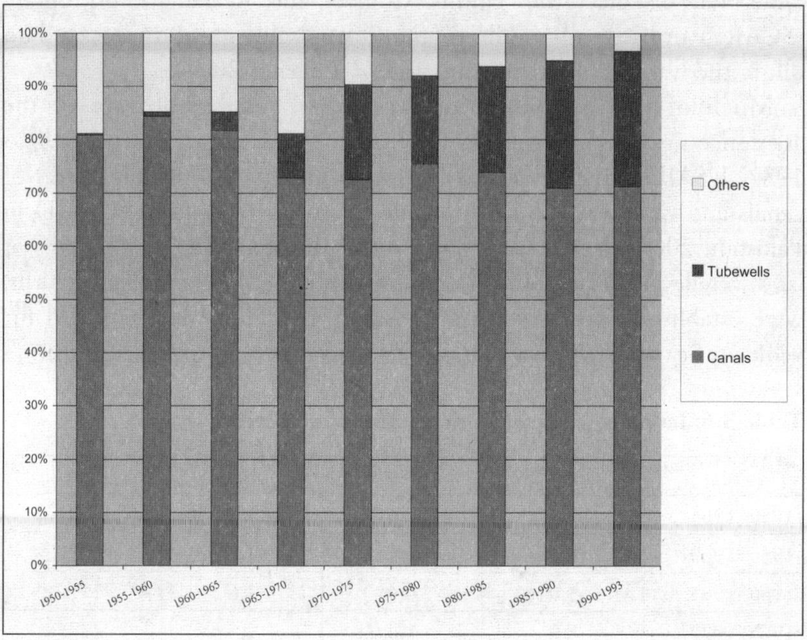

Source: Table 3.6.

labour (Ahmed, 1972; Bose and Clark, 1969; Gotsch, 1973; Naqvi, 1983; *Report of the Pakistan Agricultural Inquiry Committee 1951–52*, 1952; *Report of the Pakistan Food and Agricultural Commission 1960*, 1960; *The Consequences of Farm Tractors in Pakistan*, 1975; Salam, 1978, 1981). Tractor use is now a central feature of agriculture in Pakistan. The Agricultural Census of 2000 reported that 71 per cent of farms use only tractors for cultivation, while another 19 per cent use both tractors and draught animals (Agricultural Census 2000, 2003: Table 10). Thus, only 10 per cent of all farms today utilise draught animals alone (see Figure 3.11).

High Yield Variety Seeds (HYV), Pesticides, and Fertilisers: The yield per hectare increased rapidly in Pakistan owing to the introduction, in 1965, of the new technology package that included High Yield Variety seeds for wheat and rice, pesticides, and fertilisers. The wheat seeds had been developed by the International Wheat and Maize Research Institute in Mexico; the rice seeds had been developed by the International Rice

Figure 3.11: All Farms Reporting Use of Tractors, Draught Animals, or both for Cultivation by Size of Farm, 2000

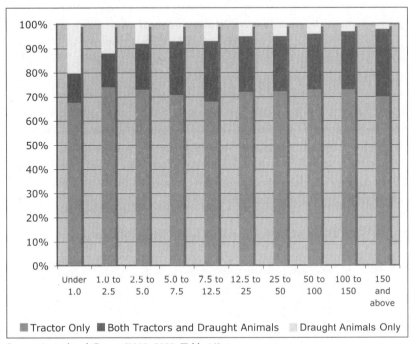

Source: Agricultural Census (2000, 2003: Table 10).

Research Institute (IRRI) in the Philippines based on the work of Norman Borlaug. For a detailed study on the impact of the increasing use of high yield variety wheat seeds on productivity and output, see Azhar (1973a), Lowdermilk (1972), and Rochin (1971).

By 1969, more than half the irrigated area of Pakistan—6 million acres—was cultivated with these new seeds (Zaidi, 2005: 29). Wheat yield increased from 776 kg/hectare in 1950 to 1,950 kg/hectare by 1990 (Cownie et al., 1982). Rice yield increased from 878 kg/hectare in 1950 to 1,622 kg/hectare by 1990 (ibid.). Wheat production rose from 4 million tonnes in 1967 to 20 million tonnes in 2007—a five-fold increase (Wheeler, 2007).[24]

HYV seeds respond rapidly to water and fertiliser. Hence, chemical fertilisers and pesticides were increasingly introduced in agriculture during the Green Revolution. Transnational pesticide and fertiliser companies were set up, during this period, to feed the growing market.

For instance, under USAID's agriculture chief Richard Newberg, Pakistan was granted $100 million worth of fertilisers (Wheeler, 2007). Funding was also given for the construction of the Fauji Fertiliser plant—which was built with the assistance of Haldor Topsoe of Denmark, and became operational in 1978. The use of fertilisers increased by 235 per cent between 1965 and 1971 (Zaidi, 2005: 29).

There can be no doubt that the Green Revolution produced unprecedented growth in agriculture in Pakistan (see Dorfman et al., 1965; Falcon, 1964; Falcon and Gotsch, 1964; Gotsch, 1968a, 1968b; Mohammad, 1963, 1964a, 1964b, 1965; Raquibuzzaman, 1966). Figure 3.12 illustrates the index of output from 1959 to 1995. The most impressive rates of growth were in the 1960s and 1980s, while in the 1950s and 1970s the agricultural growth rate fell below the growth rate of the population (Khan, 1998: 19).

Figure 3.12: Index of Agricultural Output, 1959–2002 (base year = 1959)

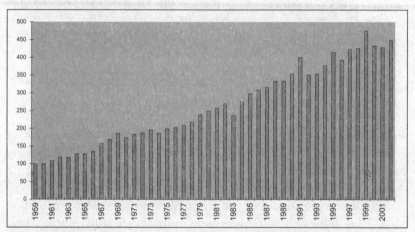

Source: Zaidi (2005: 58).

At the same time, following the general pattern of the introduction of modern industry in agriculture in other parts of the world, the Green Revolution technology package transformed social relations in Pakistani agriculture. About the transformation of agrarian social relations by capitalism, Marx (1887: 1071) wrote:

Modern industry alone, and finally, supplies in machinery the lasting basis of capitalistic agriculture, expropriates radically the enormous majority of the agricultural population, and completes the separation between agriculture and rural domestic industry, whose roots—spinning and weaving—it tears up.

However, while rapid advances in agriculture supplied the industrial sector with cheaper raw materials and labour-power, the Green Revolution also brought about greater regional and class inequities. Groundwater in Sindh was saline, and the ground was too hard and stony in Baluchistan and NWFP. Therefore, of the 76,000 tube-wells set up by 1968, approximately 91 per cent were set up in the Punjab (Sanderatne, 1982). Even within the Punjab, only a few districts received the bulk of the investment made possible by international aid. The agricultural output of Faisalabad, Sahiwal, and Multan grew at a rate of 8.9 per cent per annum from 1959 to 1964, owing to the far greater government resources flowing into these areas (Gotsch, 1982: 65). Most tractors also went to a handful of districts in the Punjab. For example, Carl Gotsch's study reported that 58 per cent of all tractors in the country, in 1970, were concentrated in the three districts of Lahore, Multan, and Bahawalpur (1982: 65).

At the same time, this influx of Green Revolution technology increased the imbalance of income and power within the peasantry (Dorosh et al., 2003; Falcon, 1970). For instance, tube-wells were not economically feasible in farms smaller than than 25 acres (that is, tube-wells were not scale neutral). Hence, approximately 75 per cent of tube-wells were installed by farmers who owned over 25 acres of land, and only 4 per cent were installed by farmers owning less than 13 acres of land (Sanderatne, 1982; see also *Pakistan Census of Agricultural Machinery*, 1977). While, on the one hand, there were few co-ops for tube-wells and tractors, on the other, 75 per cent of all tractors were in the hands of those who also owned tube-wells (Gotsch, 1982: 65).[25] Empirical evidence indicates that, from 1960 to 1980, there was substantial inequality in the distribution of irrigation facilities among agricultural households across farm size groups, both at the national and provincial levels, and that this trend was widening over time (Ahmed and Sampath, 1994; Gill and Sampath, 1992). Similarly, Rashida Haq's study also demonstrates the uneven distribution of Green Revolution-related irrigation facilities (2007). Punjab's share of tube-wells is far in excess of its percentage of cultivated area (see Tables 3.7 and 3.8). The

138   THE CLASS STRUCTURE OF PAKISTAN

data does, however, indicate that this inter-provincial inequality of tube-wells declined somewhat between 1990 and 2000.

Table 3.7: Distribution of Cultivated Area across Pakistan, 1990–1991 (%)

Area	Total Cultivated Area	Total Irrigated Area	Canal	Canal and Tube Well	Tube Well only	Other Sources
Punjab	63.30	67.60	41.60	96.30	87.74	21.90
Sindh	18.40	20.20	45.40	3.12	2.80	4.80
NWFP	10.90	7.10	8.60	0.58	4.21	39.90
Balochistan	7.40	5.10	4.40	–	6.05	33.50
Pakistan	100	100	100	100	100	100

Source: Haq (2007: 1015).
Note: Columns 6 and 7 add up to more than 100 per cent each. This error is present in the original report.

Table 3.8: Distribution of Cultivated Area across Pakistan, 2000–2001 (%)

Area	Total Cultivated Area	Total Irrigated Area	Canal	Canal and Tube Well	Tube Well only	Other Sources
Punjab	62.48	65.00	34.50	95.47	84.98	17.28
Sindh	19.75	23.20	52.10	3.40	1.82	9.00
NWFP	10.05	6.20	7.90	0.79	4.01	41.70
Balochistan	7.72	5.60	5.50	0.34	9.19	33.00
Pakistan	100	100	100	100	100	100

Source: Haq (2007: 1015).
Note: Column 7 adds up to more than 100 per cent. This error is present in the original report.

Further, Moazam Mahmood has shown that rich peasants and landlords had the cultural and financial collateral to negotiate for credit and to take advantage of this new technology package (Mahmood, 1982: 191). World Bank studies have shown that tail-enders on a given water course, who were usually middle and poor peasants, were at a significant disadvantage in procuring timely and adequate supplies of water and, hence, could not optimise the advantages of the Green Revolution technology package (*Farm Water Management Project*, 1981). This uneven distribution of water supplies counteracted the economic benefits of the increasing use of fertilisers (*Pakistan Fertilizer Demand Forecast Study*, 1978). The technology package was not scale neutral, but in fact resulted in larger gains for large farms. For all these reasons, the technology package of the Green Revolution reversed the oft-quoted inverse relationship between farm size and output per acre (Khan, 1975, 1979, 1981; Khan and Maki, 1979, 1980; Mahmood, 1977; Mahmood and Nadeem-ul-Haque, 1981; Salam, 1978). In summary, rich peasants and large landlords from the Punjab were the overwhelming beneficiaries of the Green Revolution, rather than the small-scale landowners.

Khan made the following analysis of the class structure of Pakistan at that time (see Table 3.9).

Table 3.9: Distribution of Rural Households in the Provinces* of Pakistan, 1971–1972 (%)

Class	Province	Less than 1.0 acres	1.0 to < 5.0 acres	5.0 to < 12.5 acres	12.5 to < 25.0 acres	25.0 to < 50 acres	50.0 to < 150.0 acres	150.0 acres and more	All Farm Sizes
Landlords	Punjab						0.2	0.0	0.2
	Sindh						0.6	0.1	0.7
	NWFP						0.2	0.0	0.3
Capitalist Farmers	Punjab				12.7	10.2	3.6	0.4	26.9
	Sindh				12.9	5.5	2.1	0.4	20.9
	NWFP				3.7	4.3	3.0	0.7	11.7
Family Farmers	Punjab	2.8	14.7	21.2	11.1				49.8
	Sindh	0.3	6.7	11.1	9.2				27.3
	NWFP	9.1	30.0	17.3	6.0				62.4
Share-croppers	Punjab	0.9	5.9	16.3					23.1
	Sindh	0.1	11.3	39.7					51.1
	NWFP	2.4	12.2	11.1					25.7
All Classes	Punjab	3.7	20.7	37.5	23.8	10.3	3.7	0.4	100
	Sindh	0.4	18.0	50.8	22.1	5.5	2.7	0.5	100
	NWFP	11.5	42.2	28.3	9.7	4.3	3.2	0.7	100

Source: Khan (1998: 84).
Note: The household data from the 1972 Agricultural Census has been combined with the landownership data provided by the provincial Land Commissions for the same year.
* Baluchistan excluded.

THE POPULIST LAND REFORMS OF 1972 AND 1977

A variety of political and economic factors led to the emergence of a popular upsurge, and the first democratic elections in the country were held in 1970. However, matters with East Pakistan had reached the point of no return; in 1971, after an extremely bloody civil war, East Pakistan seceded and became Bangladesh. In West Pakistan, the populist Pakistan Peoples Party (PPP) came to power.

In 1972, the PPP declared a ceiling of 150 acres of irrigated, and 300 acres of un-irrigated, land (Khan, 1981: 179–192). Two features distinguished this land reform from the previous land reform. Firstly, compensation was not given to the affected landlords. Secondly, this land was distributed for free to landless peasants. These reforms were undertaken amidst popular rhetoric about eliminating feudalism (Khan, 1981: 187). However, a closer examination reveals that the reforms were even smaller in size than the land reform of 1959. Table 3.10 shows the progress of land reforms, according to government sources. The estimated number of households that benefited from the 1972 land reform was 75,213. This figure was only about 1 per cent of all rural households in Pakistan at the time (Khan, 1981: 190). From 1972–1978, only about 308,390 acres were redistributed.

In 1977, the PPP instituted a second, and more radical, land reform program. The landholding ceiling was reduced to 100 acres for irrigated land and 200 acres for non-irrigated land. However, before the programme could be implemented, the government was overthrown by a military coup in July 1977, and General Ziaul Haq took the decision to permanently shelve the land reform.

Table 3.10: Progress of 1972 and 1977 Land Reforms, until 1981 (acres)

Year	Area Resumed	Area Allotted	Area not Allotted	Households benefited
1972	1,306,146	812,632	493,514	75,213
1977	166,836	47,823	119,013	3,834

Source: Ahmed and Amjad (1984).
Note: 'Area resumed' is the land taken up by the government in order to auction or grant it. 'Area allotted' is the land that the government auctioned or granted to peasants.

In summary, these political events did not significantly alter the basic structure of agrarian relations or the trends of development of capitalist relations in agriculture. Interestingly, despite vastly different overall political agendas, both the military and democratic governments remained committed to the basic strategy of the Green Revolution.

The overall impact of the Green Revolution and the development of capitalist agriculture can be traced through the four agricultural censuses taken in 1960, 1972, 1980, and 1990. The censuses categorise land holdings according to size. The figures in Table 3.11 and Figure 3.13, demonstrate the growing differentiation of the peasantry.

Table 3.11: Percentage Area by Size of Farm

Size of Farm (Acres)	1960	1972	1980	1990	2000
Under 5	9.0	5.0	7.0	11.0	16.0
5 – 12.5	22.0	25.0	27.0	27.0	28.0
12.5 – 25	26.0	27.0	25.0	21.0	19.0
25 – 50	19.0	19.0	18.0	16.0	16.0
50 – 150	13.0	15.0	15.0	14.0	13.0
Over 150	10.0	9.1	8.5	10.0	8.0

Source: Compiled from the 5 Agricultural Censuses of 1960, 1972, 1980, 1990, and 2000.

Figure 3.13: Percentage Area by Size of Farm

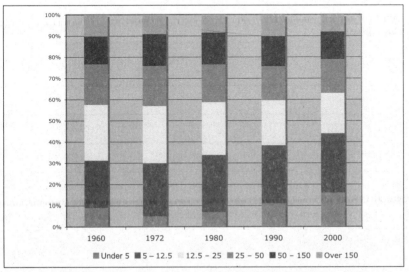

Source: Compiled from the Agricultural Censuses of 1960, 1972, 1980, 1990, and 2000.

The first striking result, from the above data, is the marked decline in the area (as a percentage) cultivated by owners of between 12.5 and 25 acres of land (see Figure 3.13). This decline in peasant-holdings of between 12.5 and 25 acres in land is so great that the average size of farms, all over Pakistan, fell from 13.04 acres in 1960 to 7.6 acres in 2000. Hence, the data from the Agricultural Census on landholding size (used as a proxy for classes) indicates the growing destruction of the middle strata of the peasantry (that is, between 12.5 and 25 acres).

A World Bank study estimated that the Gini coefficient[26] of landownership in Pakistan in 2000 was 0.66 (*Pakistan Promoting Rural Growth and Poverty Reduction*, 2007). Moreover, if rural landless households were included in the calculation, the landownership inequality Gini coefficient was 0.86 (ibid.).[27]

To quantify land inequality, Gill and Sampath used Theil's entropy measure to create an index of inequality that is similar to the Gini coefficient (see Gill and Sampath, 1992). This method was used by Qureshi and Qureshi (2004) to calculate the index of land inequality for the Agricultural Censuses of 1972, 1980, 1990, and 2000. Their research showed that while reported inequality dropped remarkably in 1972,[28] it continued to rise from that point onwards. Haq's (2007: 1018) more recent research has shown similar results (Table 3.12 and Figure 3.14).

Table 3.12: Index of Inequality in Land Distribution, 1960, 1972, 1980, 1990, 2000

Year	Inequality in Cultivated Area	Inequality in Irrigated Area
1960	0.5992	0.5926
1972	0.4215	0.3841
1980	0.4867	0.4433
1990	0.568	0.562
2000	0.609	0.599

Source: Haq (2007: 1018).

Figure 3.14: Index of Inequality in Land Distribution, 1960, 1972, 1980, 1990, 2000

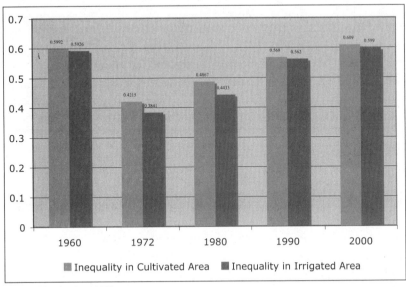

Source: Haq (2007: 1018).

Haq's (2007) research has also indicated that, from 1990 to 2000, land inequality has grown across Pakistan's cultivated and irrigated areas—whether canal irrigated or tube-well irrigated (see Table 3.13).

Table 3.13: Index of Land Inequality by Mode of Irrigation, 1990, 2000

Variables	1990	2000
Total Cultivated Area	0.568	0.609
Total Irrigated Area	0.562	0.599
Area Irrigated by Canal	0.549	0.618
Area Irrigated by Tube-well	0.545	0.586

Source: (Haq, 2007: 1017).

While more detailed evidence about income and output is required to strengthen these conclusions, the data certainly indicate that inequalities in landownership, and hence class differences across the agrarian political economy of Pakistan, are rising.

TENURE CLASSIFICATION TRENDS

The Agricultural Censuses also indicate a change in the relations of production. Government agricultural censuses divide land holdings into three categories: owner farms, owner-cum-tenant farms, and tenant farms (Khan, 1981: 110–121). Mahmood Hasan Khan has argued that owner farms are the closest approximation to capitalist agriculture, whereas tenant farming is the closest approximation to traditional agriculture (Khan, 1998: 316). While this categorisation is not entirely accurate—since capitalist farms would be ones that hire wage labour— these statistics can offer us an approximate understanding of the tendencies and trends in agrarian relations.

Table 3.14 is compiled from the information of the five agricultural censuses. It demonstrates that owner-farms—which are farther along the route of the transformation to capitalist farming—have grown, over the years, in terms of both acreage and numbers. Figure 3.15 graphs this transformation and shows the trends in terms of tenure classification. The white area represents the percentage area cultivated on the basis of traditional tenant farming. The black area represents the percentage area cultivated on the basis of owner-cum-tenant farming; the grey area represents the percentage area cultivated on the basis of owner farming. One can note, from Figure 3.15 that the area cultivated on the basis of traditional tenant farming or owner-cum-tenant farming is being displaced by the area cultivated on the basis of owner farms.

Table 3.14: Number and Acreage of Farms by Tenure Classification, 1960–2000 (%)

Year	Owner Farms		Owner-Cum Tenant Farms		Tenant Farms		Avg. size (acres)
	Farms	Acreage	Farms	Acreage	Farms	Acreage	
1960	41.0	36.0	17.0	23.0	42.0	39.0	10.1
1972	42.0	40.0	24.0	31.0	34.0	30.0	13.0
1980	55.0	52.0	19.0	26.0	26.0	22.0	11.6
1990	68.8	64.9	12.3	19.0	18.7	16.1	9.4
2000	77.6	73.3	8.4	14.5	14.0	12.1	7.6

Source: Agricultural Censuses of 1960, 1972, 1980, 1990, and 2000.

Figure 3.15: Tenure Classification of Farms

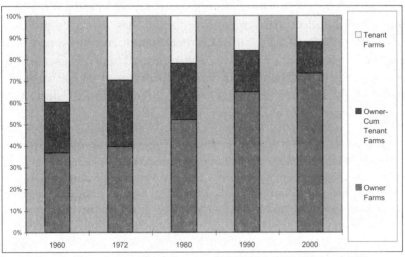

Source: Compiled from the Agricultural Censuses of 1960, 1972, 1980, 1990, and 2000.

Mahmood Hasan Khan has argued that the above transformation, in tenure relations, indicates the development of capitalist agriculture at the expense of traditional tenant farming (Khan, 1981: 66). Similarly, Akbar Zaidi has concluded, from the above information, that (1997: 44):

> The increase in owners and the decline in tenancy suggest that more and more landowners are acquiring land from tenants and are going in for self-cultivation, probably hiring in agricultural wage labour. It is unlikely that many of the tenants are in a position to become owners, so most of them will probably have been changed into agricultural or rural wage labourers or have migrated to urban areas and towns as they have been displaced by owner-cultivators.

However, this thesis has argued that, in the transitional form of Asiatic capitalism, one can expect to note certain capitalist features—private property, commodity production, differentiation of the peasantry—combined with the lack of development of wage labour. Let us turn to the data on wage labour to see if this can be substantiated.

WAGE LABOUR AND UNFREE LABOUR

Although there is a paucity of material on Pakistan, in India the debate on bonded, indentured, and unfree labour has invited significant scholarship. As in India, the use of extra-economic coercion is pervasive and well-documented in Pakistan. For instance, Human Rights Watch acknowledges that bonded labour is 'widespread in agriculture', particularly in those districts where large landlords dominate (*Contemporary Forms of Slavery in Pakistan*, 1995):

> Bondage in agrarian regions involves the purchase and sale of peasants among landlords, the maintenance of private jails to discipline and punish peasants, the forcible transference of teachers who train peasants to maintain proper financial accounts, and a pattern of rape of peasant women by landlords and the police. . . . Bonded labor in agriculture often emerges from historically hierarchical relationships between landlords and peasants. These relationships are reinforced by contemporary agricultural policies which give landlords privileged access to land, resources, and credit. In many cases peasant children inherit the debt, and thus the working conditions, of their parents.

Similarly, the International Labour Organisation has stated (*World Labour Report 1993*, 1993):

> [Pakistan] has some of the most serious problems of bonded labour. The ILO's Committee of Experts has noted reports which estimate that about 20 million people (of whom 7.5 million are children) are working as bonded labourers. Of these, the brick-kiln industry alone accounts for 2 million families. But there are reports of bonded labourers in many other industries, including fish cleaning and packing, shoe-making and quarrying and in the making of *bidis* (cigarettes). They are also common in agriculture where in certain districts they are called *gehna makhlooq* (mortgaged creatures). And there have been reports of the use of bonded labour by contractors known as *kharkars* in the construction of dams and irrigation tunnels. The carpet industry also has large numbers of bonded child workers: reports suggest around 500,000. The arrival of Afghan refugees has offered another exploitable group: an estimated half million Afghans, including children, have become bonded.

The Human Rights Commission of Pakistan has documented that, between 1992 and 2007, the number of registered cases of bonded labour stood at 16 million (*State of Human Rights 2007*, 2008: 172). The annual report of the Human Rights Commission of Pakistan, *State of Human Rights*, has reported scores of cases of bonded labourers (agricultural and others) who have been subjected to violence, beatings, rapes, incarceration in private jails, and even being kept bound in chains. For instance, in a much publicised case, Haji Ghulam Khokar of Sangar district of Sindh had over a dozen private jails, from which 295 labourers were released—only after a raid by the armed forces of Pakistan in 1991 (Mujtaba, 1992).

Thus, not only do landlords have the necessary gunmen to coerce labourers, but they also have a 'virtual monopoly over access to the state' (Martin, 2008: 15). Nicolas Martin's study of class formation within the Punjabi village of Bek Sagrana concluded that (2008: 4):

> The idea that rural labourers in the Pakistani Punjab have proletarian status in the first place is questionable given that they are often subject to forms of formal and informal political compulsion that restricts their ability to dispose of their labour freely and to thereby qualify as proletarians in the strict sense of the world.[29]

An accurate estimate of the relative proportion of wage labourers employed in agriculture would require information about the average outlay on wage labour in relation to other forms of labour over an entire production cycle. However, landlords are extremely reluctant to provide accurate information about their farms. After the 1972 land reforms, landlords have preferred to conceal such information as it may be employed to argue the case for land reforms.

The largest collection of data on agrarian relations remains the statistical publications of the Federal Bureau of Statistics (FBS). However, the data published by the FBS remains insufficient for the purposes of this study. Out of the seventeen statistical publications of the FBS, four are relevant to agrarian relations: *Agricultural Census, Household Integrated Economic Survey (HIES), Pakistan Social and Living Standards Measurement Survey*, and *Labour Force Survey (LFS)* (Federal Bureau of Statistics, 2008).

The HIES, which has a sample size of approximately 15,000 households, attempts to estimate income and consumption expenditure of households by consumption quintiles. However, the survey categories are, relatively, too broad to estimate wage labour within agriculture. For instance, the division by industry is based on the following categories:

1. Agriculture, forestry, fishing
2. Mining and quarrying, manufacturing
3. Electricity, gas, water, and construction
4. Wholesale and related trade
5. Transport and storage
6. Finance and real estate etc.
7. Social and personal services
8. Others (activities not defined)

Similarly, the division by occupation is based on the following categories:

1.   Legislators, senior officials, and managers
2.   Professionals
3.   Technicians and associate professionals
4.   Clerks
5.   Service, shop, and market sales workers
6.   Skilled agriculture and fishery workers
7.   Craft and related trade workers
8.   Plant and machine operators and assemblers
9.   Elementary occupations
10. Armed forces

The division by employment status is as follows:

1. Employer
2. Self-employed
3. Unpaid family helper
4. Employee
5. Not economically active

These categories are too broad to help estimate the percentage of wage labour that is utilised for cultivation. Moreover, the data on sources of income can easily be mistaken for data on wage labour in cultivation. Take, for instance, Table 3.15:

Table 3.15: Percentage Distribution of Rural Monthly Household Income by Source and Quintiles, 2005–2006

Source of Income	Total Monthly Income by Quintiles					
	Avg.	1st	2nd	3rd	4th	5th
Average monthly income Rs	10,929	6,768	8,339	9,670	11,924	19,277
Wages and Salaries	25.6	40.5	32.4	27.9	22.7	16.6
Crop Production	34.1	25.3	29.8	34.3	34.6	39.4
Livestock	10.6	14.3	10.7	12.2	11.2	7.4
Other Non-Agr. Activities	6.9	5.2	7.8	7.0	8.9	5.5
Property (Owner Occupied Houses Excluded)	3.3	0.5	1.4	1.3	2.1	7.6
Owner Occupied Houses	5.9	5.3	5.9	5.6	6.1	6.2
Social Insurance Benefits Including Pension	0.9	0.4	0.6	0.7	1.3	1.1
Gift Assistance	1.3	2.7	1.8	1.7	1.0	0.6
Foreign Remittances	5.1	1.1	1.8	3.1	5.1	9.6
Domestic Remittances	5.3	3.2	6.5	5.9	6.3	4.6
Other Sources	1.1	1.5	1.4	0.3	0.8	1.4
Total	100	100	100	100	100	100

Source: Household Integrated Economic Survey (2005–2006).

One is tempted to read the data on wages and salaries as the equivalent of wage labour in agriculture. However, it includes income from rural non-agricultural work. The aggregate income from crop production is in the following row. Thus, this data only estimates that about a quarter of the income in rural areas, from occupations other than cultivation, is from wages and salaries. What is required, to estimate wage labour in agrarian relations, is a further breakup of the category 'crop production' by source of income (that is, wage labour, rent, sharecropping, and so on).

The categories of the Labour Force Survey (LFS) are very similar to the HIES. The LFS has a sample size of about 30,000 and gathers data on the basis of age, gender, education, nature of activity, occupation, and employment status (Labour Force Survey, 2005–06). These categories are also too broad to estimate wage labour in agriculture.

For instance, the categories under 'industry divisions' are:

1. Agriculture, forestry, hunting, and fishing
2. Mining and quarrying
3. Manufacturing
4. Electricity, gas, and water
5. Construction
6. Wholesale and retail trade, and restaurants and hotels
7. Transport, storage, and communication
8. Financing, insurance, real estate, and business services
9. Community, social, and personal services
10. Activities not adequately defined

Under 'occupations', the categories are:

1. Legislators, senior officials, and managers
2. Professionals
3. Technicians and associate professionals
4. Clerks
5. Service workers, and shop and market sales workers
6. Skilled agricultural and fishery workers
7. Craft and related trades' workers
8. Plant and machine operators, and assemblers
9. Elementary (unskilled) occupations

Under 'employment status' the categories are:

1. Employer
2. Self-employed
3. Unpaid family helpers
4. Employees

And lastly, under sectors of employment the categories are:

1. Agriculture
2. Non-agriculture
3. Formal
4. Informal

The Pakistan Social and Living Standards Measurement Survey (PSLM) gathered data, from a sample of nearly 74,000 households, on education, health, housing, water supply, sanitation, and households' perceptions of their economic situation and satisfaction with facilities and services used (Pakistan Social and Living Standards Measurement Survey, 2006–7). Hence, it does not contain any information about source of income.

The Agricultural Census of Pakistan is the only publication that contains some data on wage labour in agriculture. Estimates about agricultural labour must, inevitably, take the seasonal nature of the work into account. Demand for labour during the planting and harvesting season rises substantially. This demand is often met with the employment of seasonal workers. Therefore, before examining the data, it is necessary to clarify the definition of permanent, casual, and family labour, as elaborated by the Agricultural Census Organisation.

Permanent hired labour is made up of those persons who 'work on the farm on whole time basis, employed for long periods, and get wages in cash and/or kind on a fixed period basis, that is, monthly, quarterly, yearly, etc.' (Agricultural Census 2000, 2003: XXIII).

Casual labour comprises of those 'employed occasionally on daily wage basis for a specific agricultural work' (ibid.).

All other forms of labour are put into a third category, called family workers, and are defined as 'household members of 10 years and above who do any kind of agricultural work on their holding' (ibid.).

As is clear from these definitions, family labour is too broad a term and potentially includes all forms of labour that are not wage labour. Be that as it may, let us first look at the overall trends of permanent wage labour from the first to the last Agricultural Census (1960 and 2000). See Tables 3.16, 3.17, and Figure 3.16.

Table 3.16: Holdings and Number of Permanent Hired Labour by Size of Farm, 1960

Type and Size (acres)	All Holdings	Holdings Reporting Permanent Hired Labour	Number of Permanent Hired Labourers
Total Agricultural Holdings	5,690,528	346,477	703,870
Livestock Holdings	830,545	24,355	61,850
Farms – Total	4,859,983	322,122	642,020
Under 1.0 ··	742,216	15,720	26,488
1.0 to 2.5	855,732	28,632	59,368
2.5 to 5.0	805,984	37,473	71,429
5.0 to 7.5	580,952	35,025	72,867
7.5 to 12.5	758,703	59,420	107,178
12.5 to 25	728,909	82,851	148,334
25 to 50	285,882	45,536	89,619
50 to 150	87,624	14,954	45,741
150 and Over	13,981	2,511	20,996

Source: Agricultural Census (1960 Vol. 1, 1963: 812).
Note: Permanent hired labour on large farms is low because these farms utilise tenant farming and family labour.

Table 3.17: Holdings and Number of Permanent Hired Labour by Size of Farm, 2000

Size of Farm (Acres)	All Farms Total	Holdings Reporting Permanent Hired Labour
Private Farms – Total	6,620,054	251,926
Under 1.0 Acres	735,771	5,628
1.0 to 2.5 Acres	1,653,656	17,122
2.5 to 5.0 Acres	1,425,579	25,795
5.0 to 7.5 Acres	966,320	29,871
7.5 to 12.5 Acres	891,451	46,415
12.5 to 25 Acres	579,738	53,455
25 to 50 Acres	260,523	43,993
50 to 150 Acres	77,886	19,569
150 Acres and Over	15,108	4,562

Source: Agricultural Census (2000, 2003: Table 8.4).
Note: The categories of 50 to 100 acres and 100 to 150 acres, in the Agricultural Census of 2000, were collapsed into the category of 50 to 150 acres, so that the figures could be compared to the 1960 statistics.

Figure 3.16: Percentage of Farms by Land Size Reporting Permanent Wage Labour, 1960 and 2000

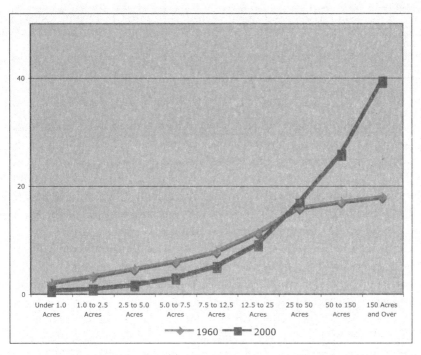

Source: Table 3.16 and Table 3.17.

Firstly, the data indicates that very few farms reported the hiring of permanent wage labour. The gross average was 6 per cent and 3.8 per cent for 1960 and 2000, respectively.

Secondly, a higher percentage of large farms reported the use of permanent waged labour. In the year 2000, nearly 40 per cent of farms above 150 acres reported the use of permanent waged labour, whereas the average for all farms was only 3.8 per cent.

Last but certainly not least, the data indicates that, in gross terms, there was a decline in the hiring of permanent wage labour in this period (from 6 per cent in 1960 to 3.8 per cent in 2000). The Agricultural Census of 1972, 1980, and 1990 also revealed the same overall results (see Table 3.18). The Agricultural Census Organisation attributed this decrease to the 'extensive use of tractors, tractor drawn implements and tube-wells' (Agricultural Workers, 2008).

**Table 3.18: Percentage of Farms Reporting Permanent Hired Labour,
1960–2000**

Type of Farms	1960	1972	1980	1990	2000
Per cent of farms reporting permanent hired labour	6	7	4	2	4

Source: Agricultural Workers (2008).

The small percentage of farms reporting permanent hired labour may
come as a surprise. However, non-governmental studies from various
samples have indicated the same overall pattern. The International Food
Policy Research Institute (IFPRI) conducted 12 rounds of household
surveys, in four districts of Pakistan, between July 1986 and September
1989. Although the data is now out of date, this was one of the most
thorough studies on the subject, and is hence worth revisiting. Close to
1,000 randomly selected households in 44 randomly selected villages
were interviewed 12 times, at roughly three to four-month intervals.
Fafchamps and Quisumbing analysed this data set and found that, on
average, a quarter of the income came from crops, 15 per cent from
livestock, 30 per cent from non-farm income (wages, self-employment,
crafts, trade, and services), and another 30 per cent came from rent and
remittances (Fafchamps and Quisumbing, 1998: 375–376). They
concluded that while wage labour in non-farm activities was 'common',
wage labour within agriculture was 'negligible' among the sample
households. Their results indicated that (ibid.):

> Hired labour—mostly male—accounts on average for as little at 2.6 per cent
> and 8.5 per cent of total labour devoted to cultivation in the kharif
> (summer) and rabi (winter) season respectively. Some 91 per cent of kharif
> farmers and 89 per cent of rabi farmers do not use any hired labour. . . .
> Surveyed households do not report employing any wage worker for either
> herding or nonfarm activities. Although surveyed households use some hired
> labour for crop production, they spent very little time hiring themselves out
> as labourers.

Another three-year survey by the IFPRI, during the same period (1986–
1989), of 727 households in three provinces of Pakistan indicated
similar results (Adamse, 1995). In this survey, the districts were not

selected at random. Instead, the poorest district was selected on the basis of a production and infrastructure index elaborated by H. Pasha and T. Hasan (Pasha and Hasan, 1982). These were Attock (Punjab), Badin (Sindh), Dir (NWFP), and Faisalabad (Punjab). With respect to wage labour, the study presented the data in Table 3.19.

Table 3.19: Summary of Agricultural Real Income Data, 1986–1989 (Rs '000)

Income	1986–87		1987–88		1988–89	
Source of Agricultural Income	Mean Annual Per Capita Income	Standard Deviation	Mean Annual Per Capita Income	Standard Deviation	Mean Annual Per Capita Income	Standard Deviation
Agricultural Wages	32.3	132.2	46.3	209.7	35.1	100.4
Total Income	791.9	2,223.1	896.9	2,242.5	896.0	2,102.5

Source: Adamse (1995: 476).
Note: Calculations are based on 680 households, representing the original 727 households, with zero or positive agricultural incomes in any of the three survey years. Mean income figures include negative source incomes recorded for some households in various years. In 1986, 1 Pakistani rupee = US$0.062. All rupee figures are in constant 1986 terms.

This study indicated that income earned from agricultural wages was an extremely small percentage of overall agricultural income—only 4 per cent. Hence, Adamse (1995: 475) concluded,

It is interesting to note the relative unimportance of agricultural wages. Income from agricultural wages is low in the sample because the widespread sharing of labour between families apparently serves as a substitute for the hiring of wage labour.

Now, let us examine the development of casual labour. The Agricultural Census Organisation reported the statistics in Table 3.20.

Table 3.20: Pattern of Agricultural Workers by Type of Labour

Type of Labour	1960	1972	1980	1990
% family workers per family (above age 10)	N.A	55	60	29
% of all farms reporting casual labour	N.A	30	45	50
% of farms reporting permanent hired labour	6	7	4	2

Source: Agricultural Workers (2008).
Note: Data on family and casual labour was not collected by the Agricultural Census of 1960.

The 'percentage of family workers per family (above age 10)' means the percentage of family members above the age of 10 that are working on their own farms on a whole or part-time basis.

The data shows that, in 1972, more than 50 per cent of family members above 10 years of age worked on their own farms on a whole or part-time basis. This number rose to 60 per cent in 1980, and then decreased dramatically to 29 per cent by 1990. The Agricultural Census Organisation argued that this may have, mainly, occurred as a result of the substitution of family labour for agricultural implements—which almost doubled between 1980 and 1990. Simultaneously, the use of casual labour shows a dramatic rise. The percentage of permanent and casual wage labourers is graphically represented in Figure 3.17).

The graph in Figure 3.17 shows a marked rise in casual labour from 1972 to 1990. Whereas only 30 per cent of farms reported the use of casual labour in 1972, this figure went up to 45 per cent in 1980, and to 50 per cent by 1990. The Agricultural Census Organisation estimated that this was because of the increased intensity of cropping, which raised the demand for seasonal labour especially at the time of sowing, harvesting, and threshing by machine operators. The data seems to indicate that both permanent hired labour and family labour were replaced by casual wage labour. However, these trends were somewhat tempered in the following decade. Data on the use of casual labour, from the Agricultural Census of 2000, is presented in Table 3.21.

The percentage of farms reporting the use of permanent or casual labour can be calculated from data in Table 3.22. These results are represented graphically in Figure 3.18.

Figure 3.17: Percentage of Farms Reporting Permanent and Casual Hired Labour, 1972, 1980, and 1990.

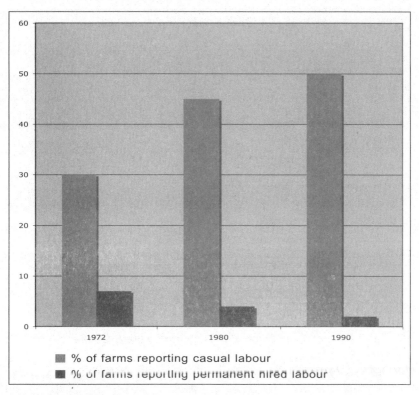

Source: Agricultural Workers (2008).

At the national level, nearly 42 per cent of farms reported the use of casual labour in 2000. Although this is an unexplained drop from 1990—when the figure had reached 50 per cent—nonetheless, the long-term trend shows a rise in the reported use of casual labour.

CONCLUSION

The objective of this chapter was to examine the available empirical data in relation to the concept of Asiatic capitalism in Pakistan. Asiatic capitalism has been defined as a system of commodity production based on private property with the use of Asiatic labour relations. The peculiar features, trajectories, and historical results of the metamorphosis, and

158   THE CLASS STRUCTURE OF PAKISTAN

Figure 3.18: Percentage of Farms Reporting the Use of Permanent or Casual Labour by Type of Tenure and Farm Size

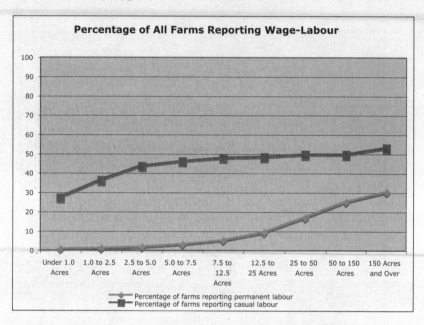

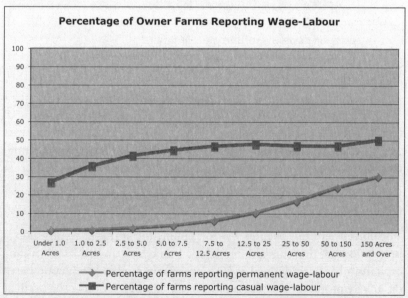

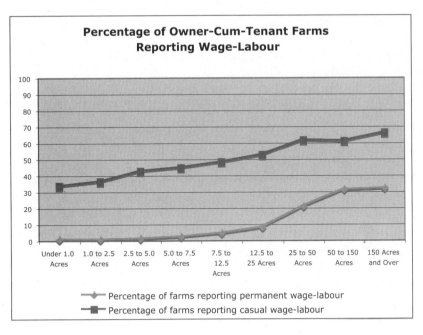

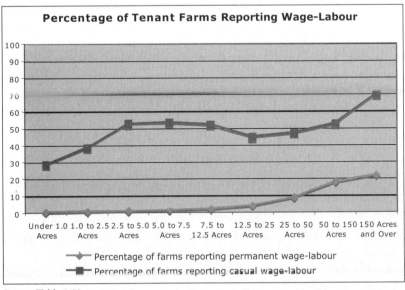

Source: Table 3.22.

the connections between the nature of this transition and the form of the Pakistani state are complex problems beyond the scope of this chapter. However, given the current availability of data, the study arrives at the four following observations.

First, the British conquered the region that is present-day Pakistan between 1843 and 1893; that is, nearly a century after the conquest of Bengal in 1757. Private property in land began with the colonial policy of permanent settlement. In the Punjab, the registration of land, as private property, began in 1846 and continued right through to 1863. In the decade from 1860–1870, a land market emerged; the production of cash crops was greatly accelerated with the heavy investment in canal irrigation in Punjab and Sindh. Between 1885 and 1947, there was a seven-fold increase in the area irrigated by canals. At the same time, the traditional system of state extraction of land revenue continued under the British colonial state. Hence, on the one hand, the Permanent Settlement Act led to the establishment of private property and commodity production and, on the other, the traditional system of land revenue extraction by the state continued side by side.

Second, the introduction of private property in land and commodity production led to a dramatic historical transformation in the overall structure of the economy. In overall terms of proportionate employment or output, agriculture has been declining in relation to manufacture and services. Also, the transformation of classes within agriculture is underway. The division of labour within agriculture, before the advent of colonial capitalism, was encoded as the caste system. The caste system was a hereditary division of labour based on kinship groups known as zaats or quoms. Hence, the specific economic relationship of a given caste to the means of production is the class of that caste.

Marxists contend, in opposition to populists, that the introduction of private property into such a pre-capitalist mode of production should result in growing class differentiation of the peasantry. To empirically verify peasant differentiation, the study utilises landownership as a proxy for class relations. However, the use of landownership as a proxy for class relations has two glaring limitations. Firstly, landownership does not indicate the nature of the relations of production; and secondly, landownership statistics do not account for the intensification of agricultural production. Nonetheless, land is one of the key means of production that determines class relations. Hence, an empirical analysis

Table 3.21: Farms Reporting Use of Casual Labour by Tenure and Size of Farm, 2000

Size of Farms (Acres)		Private Farms- Total	Under 1.0	1.0 to 2.5	2.5 to 5.0	5.0 to 7.5	7.5 to 12.5	12.5 to 25	25 to 50	50 to 150	150 and Over
All Farms	Total	6,620,054	735,771	1,653,656	1,425,579	966,320	891,451	579,738	260,523	77,886	15,108
	Perm.	251,926	5,628	17,122	25,795	29,871	46,415	53,455	43,993	19,569	4,562
	Casual	2,764,768	200,720	600,535	623,027	447,460	428,208	281,000	129,695	38,793	8,055
Owner Farms	Total	5,134,504	691,063	1,405,915	1,068,958	693,059	608,893	391,725	190,715	60,280	12,329
	Perm.	201,060	5,379	15,379	21,682	24,664	37,421	41,440	32,187	14,737	3,743
	Casual	2,053,368	187,508	506,308	445,262	310,314	285,457	188,201	89,963	28,448	6,195
Owner-cum-Tenant Farms	Total	558,991	8,961	42,568	105,566	105,110	125,408	108,043	46,755	12,493	2,104
	Perm.	34,486	92	353	1,476	2,655	5,812	8,780	9,831	3,908	674
	Casual	268,170	3,031	15,526	45,247	47,257	60,828	57,058	28,895	7,660	1,397
Tenant Farms	Total	926,562	35,741	205,093	251,065	168,159	157,159	79,974	23,061	5,119	669
	Perm.	16,381	157	1,410	2,631	2,556	3,185	3,235	1,978	914	146
	Casual	443,232	10,181	78,702	132,533	89,877	81,917	35,746	10,840	2,691	466

Source: Agricultural Census (2000, 2003). Table 8.4.

Table 3.22: Percentage of Private Farms Reporting the Use of Permanent or Casual Labour by Type of Tenure, 2000

Size of Farm (Acres)	All Farms		Owner Farms		Owner-cum-Tenant Farms		Tenant Farms	
	% of Farms Reporting Permanent Labour	% of Farms Reporting Casual Labour	% of Farms Reporting Permanent Labour	% of Farms Reporting Casual Labour	% of Farms Reporting Permanent Labour	% of Farms Reporting Casual Labour	% of Farms Reporting Permanent Labour	% of Farms Reporting Casual Labour
Private Farms—Total	3.8	41.8	3.9	40.0	6.2	48.0	1.8	47.8
Under 1.0 Acres	0.8	27.3	0.8	27.1	1.0	33.8	0.4	28.5
1.0 to 2.5 Acres	1.0	36.3	1.1	36.0	0.8	36.4	0.7	38.4
2.5 to 5.0 Acres	1.8	43.7	2.0	41.7	1.4	42.9	1.0	52.8
5.0 to 7.5 Acres	3.1	46.3	3.6	44.8	2.5	45.0	1.5	53.4
7.5 to 12.5 Acres	5.2	48.0	6.1	46.9	4.6	48.5	2.0	52.1
12.5 to 25 Acres	9.2	48.5	10.6	48.0	8.1	52.8	4.0	44.7
25 to 50 Acres	16.9	49.8	16.9	47.2	21.0	61.8	8.6	47.0
50 to 150 Acres	25.1	49.8	24.4	47.2	31.3	61.3	17.9	52.6
150 Acres and Over	30.2	53.3	30.4	50.2	32.0	66.4	21.8	69.7

Source: Table 3.21.

of landownership, nonetheless, provides a broad picture of the class structure in agriculture.

An empirical analysis of landownership reveals two broad patterns. Firstly, it demonstrates that there is a growing differentiation of the peasantry in terms of landownership. This is leading to a differentiation between landlords, peasant proprietors, landless sharecroppers, and agricultural workers. From 1924 to 1939, the number and area of farms between 10 and 50 acres showed a marked decline. The same trend could be seen after Independence. According to the Agricultural Census, by far the largest decline has been in the strata of peasantry owning between 12.5 and 25 acres. The aggregate results can also be gauged in terms of the rising land inequality index. In fact, there was only one period in which the land inequality index declined—mainly as a result of the announcement of the 1972 land reforms. When landlords transferred ownership titles to dependents to avoid land reforms, the land inequality index dropped from 0.5992 in 1960, to 0.4215 in 1972. From 1972 to 2000, the land inequality index showed a steady rise to 0.609. Hence, with the exception of the 1972 period when an uncompensated land reform threatened large landlords, land inequality has shown a steady rise. Secondly, agricultural statistics demonstrate the gradual erosion of traditional tenant farming. This process was accelerated by the Green Revolution, which introduced tube-wells, tractors, high yield variety seeds, pesticides, fertilisers, and the overall mechanisation and commercialisation of agriculture. Government surveys divide tenancy into three broad categories: owner farms, tenant farms, and owner-cum-tenant farms. In this division, owner farms are considered to be the closest to capitalist relations, whereas tenant farms are considered closer to traditional relations of production. According to the Agricultural Census, the percentage of area covered by owner farms has increased from 36 to 73 per cent from 1960 to 2000, respectively. During the same period, the percentage area of owner-cum-tenant farms and tenant farms has decreased from 23 to 14.5 per cent, and from 39 to 12.1 per cent, respectively. Academic literature produced in Pakistan has argued that this change in tenancy relations is an indication of a transformation towards capitalist relations (see for instance Khan, 1981; Zaidi, 1997, 2000).

Third, at no point in this agrarian transition was the power of large landlords broken through a mass peasant uprising or revolt, or even through institutional reforms promoted by central government. The three mild land reforms (1959, 1972, and 1977) were not organised on a scale that could result in the transformation of class relations in agriculture. It follows that the transition to capitalist relations did not occur through the revolutionary breakup of Asiatic relations, but rather through the slow metamorphosis of Asiatic relations into capitalist relations, guided and influenced by state and market forces.

Last, classical Marxism defines capitalism in terms of wage labour. Capital and wage labour are two sides of the same social relation. Capitalism is said to begin where surplus value is extracted systematically from wage labour, to the extent that this process plays a determinant role in the reproduction of society as a whole. Hence, the development of wage labour points to the gradual emergence of capitalist relations in agriculture. Empirical evidence from the agrarian political economy of Pakistan suggests that wage labour has developed relatively slowly. In fact, non-wage-based labour relations—loosely termed by government statisticians as 'family labour'—dominates agriculture in Pakistan. According to the Agricultural Census of 2000, permanent wage labour in agriculture was only around 3.8 per cent of the total agricultural labour force. However, casual wage labour figures are much higher. Whereas only 30 per cent of farms reported the use of casual wage labour in 1972, this figure rose to 45 per cent in 1980, 50 per cent by 1990, and then declined to 40 per cent by 2000. Despite the overall rise in casual wage labour, it is apparent from these statistics that agriculture continues to be dominated by non-wage based relations. An argument can also be made that wage labour is not essential to capitalism, or that family labour is also a form of disguised wage labour. However, as stated in the Introduction, for this study the defining feature of a mode of production is the mode of surplus extraction. Wage labour and capital, which are two names for the same social relation, is the mode of surplus extraction of the capitalist system. If this definition is accepted, then it follows that the existence of non-waged relations—whether pre-capitalist and/or non-capitalist—within the agrarian political economy of Pakistan implies the combination of capitalist and these other economic relations. In this instance, the evidence shows that capitalism is combined with the economic relations of muzarat, which is euphemistically called 'tenancy'. Muzarat is the continuation of the Asiatic mode of production of the Mughal period (see Chapter 2). Given the absence of more detailed and disaggregated data on muzarat in contemporary Pakistan, it seems reasonable to restrict the conclusion of this chapter to the view that the available evidence does not contradict the hypothesis of Asiatic capitalism. More data is necessary in order to prove this hypothesis definitively.

NOTES

1. That pre-capitalist relations of production continue to subject the working population is captured eloquently in Marx's phrase, 'We suffer not only from the living, but from the dead' (Marx, 1887: 22).
2. See for instance Aguilar Jr. (1994), Bhalla (1999), Ewert and Hamman (1996), Foeken and Tellegen (1997), Gaido (2000; 2002), London (1997), Majid (1998), Worby (1995).
3. See for instance Angelo (1995), Assies (2002), Byres (1998b; 2000), Chandrasekhar (1997), Corta and Venkateshwarlu (1999), Duncan (1997), Gordon (1999), Kannan (1999), Kapadia (1995a), Karshenas (1994; 1996/1997; 2000), Lerche (1999), Mann (2001), Milonakis (1995), Patnaik (1996/1997), Rao (1999b; 1999c), Rogaly (1996), Sahu, Madheswaran, and Rajasekhar (2004), Sivakumar (2001), Venkateshwarlu and Corta (2001).
4. The concept of peasant essentialism is re-examined and critiqued, among others, by Banaji (1976), Cox (1979), Ennew, Hirst and Tribe (1977), and Harrison (1975; 1977a; 1977b; 1979).
5. See for instance Baruah (2001), Byres (1998a), Cousins (1996), Desmarais (2002), Eyrferth, Ho, and Vermeer (2003), Garrabou, Planas, and Saguer (2001), Ho (2003), Hoefle (2003), Ito (2002), Jewitt (2000), Kaiwar (2000), Mawdsley (1998), Merkle (2003), Morvaridi (1995), Sinha, Gururani, and Greenberg (1997), Tauger (2003), Martinez-Alier (1995), Sinha (2000).
6. See for instance Agarwal (1994; 1998), Allina-Pisano (2004), Baumann (1998), Hardiman (1995), Indra and Buchignani (1997), Kapadia (1995b; 1996), O'Laughlin (1998), Tanner (1995), Vermeer (2003), Wilson (1999), Zhang (2003).
7. See for instance Assadi (1994), Banaji (1994), Dhanagare (1994), Gill (1994), Hasan (1994), Lindberg (1994), Martins (2002), Omvedt (1994), Petras and Veltmeyer (2002), and Veltmeyer (1997).
8. See for instance Brass (1994), Duncan (1999), Fletcher (2001), Gupta (2001), Jansen and Roquas (2002), Korovkin (2000), Lerche (1999), Srivastava (1999), Overton (2001), and Reed (2003).
9. Scott's views of everyday forms of resistance are criticised by Hart (1991), Korovkin (2000), and White (1986), among others.
10. See for instance Jassal (2003), Tocancipá-Falla (2001), McNeish (2002), Jansen and Roquas (2002), and Kumar (2000).
11. See for instance Nolan (1993), Sen (1993), Tauger (2003; 2004).
12. See for instance Araghi (2003).
13. See for instance Barkin (2002).
14. See for instance Banaji (1996/1997), Crabtree (2002), Goodman and Watts (1994), McClelland (1997), Mooij (1998), Raikes and Gibbon (2000), Swaminathan (2000), Wuyts (1994), Zhang (2003).

15. See for instance Konings (1998), Morvaridi (1995), Murray (2002), and White (1997).
16. See for instance Bernstein (1996), Gibbon (1997), Mendelson, Cowlishaw, and Rowcliffe (2003) Raikes and Gibbon (2000).
17. Many of these caste names are considered derogatory or used as an abuse. For instance, the abuse 'kameena' (dishonest person) is derived from the word 'kammi'. Similarly, the words 'chuhra' and 'chammar' (scavengers/cleaners and tanners) are used as an abuse.
18. Musali are chuhras that have converted to Islam.
19. Other similarly useful colonial studies on Punjab and Sindh include Calvert (1936), Darling (1930; 1934; 1947), Griffin(1940), Ross (1883), Thorburn (1886; 1904), Trevaskis (1928; 1931), and Wikely (1915).
20. Memons and Chiniotis were a merchant community. Saigols are a family within the Khatri caste (Khatri is the Punjabi term for Kshatriya, the warrior caste). Khojas and Bohras were Shia communities with some claiming Sayyed lineage.
21. There is a vast literature on the superior efficiency of large landholdings. See for instance Akram-Lodhi (1995), Bernstein (2004), Beverely (2004), Biswas (2001), Byres (2004), Eapen (2001), Edin (2003), Eyferth (2003), Griffin (2002; 2004), Guo (2001), Hart (1996), Lu (1997), Mukherjee (1995), Nanda (2001), Petras (2001), Singh (2002), Sinha (1997), Saith (1995), Veltmeyer (1997), and Xiande (2003).
22. Patnaik also offers a very precise discussion of the differences between the categorisation by Lenin and Mao, but that is not relevant to our discussion (Patnaik, 1990: 198–206).
23. Aeysha Jalal has argued that it was precisely the growing polarisation that fuelled Hindu Muslim tensions in Punjab in the 1940s. On the one hand, the predominantly Muslim landowners feared the power of the traders, merchants, and moneylenders who were largely Hindus. On the other hand, they feared that the Congress Party would introduce land reforms after Independence. Therefore, in Punjab and Sindh the landlords joined the Muslim League in order to safeguard their class interests (Jalal, 1985). By 1942, very large landlords accounted for 163 out of the 503 Muslim League parliamentary members (Khan, 1981: 147). According to Alavi, the demand for Pakistan, in part, was their demand to safeguard their class interests (1988).
24. For detailed studies on crop yields' growth due to the technology package of the Green Revolution. see Cownie, Johnston & Duff (1970), Johnston & Cownie (1969), Kaneda & Ghaffar (1970).
25. For an alternative view, see Kaneda (1969) or Chaudhry (1980; 1989).
26. Gini coefficient measures statistical dispersion (0 expresses total equality, 1 expresses maximal inequality).
27. For reference, Gini coefficients for landownership of India, Bangladesh, and Brazil were 0.71, 0.42, and 0.85, respectively (*Pakistan Promoting Rural Growth and Poverty Reduction*, 2007).
28. Land inequality probably drops because of under-reporting of large landholdings out of fear of land reforms enacted by the populist Bhutto government.
29. See Banaji and Brass on unfree labour (Banaji, 2003; Brass, 1999).

4

Industrial Relations

Modern industry, resulting from the railway system, will dissolve the hereditary divisions of labour, upon which rest the Indian castes, those decisive impediments to Indian progress and Indian power.

Karl Marx,
The Future Results of British Rule in India (1853)

The previous chapter examined the agrarian class relations of Pakistan. It concluded that while the differentiation of the peasantry, the erosion of traditional tenant farming, and the evolution towards wage labour pointed towards the capitalist transformation of agrarian relations, wage labour developed at a much slower pace. Hence, significant features of pre-capitalist and non-capitalist relations remained part of the social formation of agrarian Pakistan.

This chapter examines the empirical evidence of the combination of capitalist and Asiatic features, termed Asiatic capitalism, with respect to manufacturing and industrial production. Firstly, the chapter examines the large demographic changes in industrial relations in Pakistan since 1947; namely, population growth, urbanisation, and the structure of employment. Secondly, it retraces the history of industrial development and argues that manufacturing is largely dominated by the informal sector. The vast majority of the working people of Pakistan are employed in small enterprises. In summary, the class structure of industrial relations is dominated by petty commodity and petty bourgeois production.

POPULATION AND URBANISATION

In the last century, the region that is Pakistan today has transformed from a sparsely populated agricultural area of colonial India into one of the most densely populated and urbanised regions in South Asia (Arif and Hamid, 2007). At the turn of the twentieth century, the region that is Pakistan today had a population of 16.5 million; today, the population of Pakistan is estimated at 167 million (Population Association of Pakistan, 2009) (see Table 4.1).

Table 4.1: Population of West Pakistan, 1901–2009

Year	Population	Average Annual Growth Rate (%)
1901	16,576,000	
1911	19,382,000	1.69
1921	21,109,000	0.89
1931	23,542,000	1.15
1941	28,282,000	2.15
1951	33,780,000	2.35
1961	42,880,000	2.59
1972	65,309,000	2.99
1981	84,254,000	3.30
1998	132,352,000	2.47
2009(est)	167,514,500	2.04

Source: Population Association of Pakistan (2009) and United Nations Common Database: Annual Population Growth Rate of West Pakistan (2009).

Table 4.1 shows that the population growth rate was relatively low from 1901 to 1941, and only began to rise after Independence. Nearly 6.5 million refugees crossed the border after Partition and mostly settled in the urban areas (for details see Ali, 2002: 4554). The net balance of immigrants into Pakistan, following Partition, is believed to be around two million (Mahmood, 2009: 3). A detailed study of population growth in this early period was produced by the Pakistan Institute of Development Economics (PIDE), entitled *The Population of Pakistan* (Afzal and Hussain, 1974). Today, Pakistan is the sixth most populous country in the world (World Population Data Sheet, 2008: 4).[1]

Declining fertility rates since the 1980s are slowing the population growth rate and reducing the dependency ratio (see Table 4.2) (Arif and Ibrahim, 1998b: 509; Feeney and Alam, 2004: 509).[2] The main cause for these declining fertility rates, particularly in the urban areas, is, probably, increasing female education (Arif and Chaudhry, 2008: 38). As a result, between 1990 and 2004, declining fertility and mortality rates are expected to result in a 'demographic dividend' (Durr-e-Nayab, 2008). It is estimated that, by 2045, the increasing average age of the population will start raising the dependency ratio again, bringing this demographic dividend to a close (Durr-e-Nayab, 2008: 11).

Table 4.2: Dependency Ratio of Pakistan, 1992–2003

Year	1992	1995	1999	2000	2001	2003
Total Dependency Ratio	96.3	98.0	88.4	86.3	85.5	83.8

Source: Arif and Chaudhry (2008: 34).

Even more dramatic than the increase in the population growth rate is the rate of urbanisation. While the total population increased nearly five-fold from 1951–2009 (from 33 to 167 million), the urban population expanded over seven-fold in the same period. Table 4.3 shows that, in 1951, only about 17 per cent of the population was urban; whereas, by 1998, approximately 32.5 per cent of the population was urban (Population Census of Pakistan, 1951, 1998). By 2008, the urban population was 36 per cent of the total population (The World Fact Book: Pakistan, 2009). Table 4.3 shows the steady rise in the proportion of the urban to the total population of Pakistan. While overall urbanisation is low in comparison to industrially advanced nations, it is the highest in South Asia (Shirazi, 2006).

Table 4.3: Growth of Pakistan's Urban Population, 1951–1998 (in millions)

	1951	1961	1972	1981	1998
Total Population	33.78	42.88	65.31	84.25	132.35
Urban Population	6.02	9.65	16.59	23.83	42.46
Share of Urban to Total Population (%)	17.8	22.5	25.0	28.3	32.5

Source: Population Census of Pakistan (1951, 1961, 1972, 1981, 1998).

The number of urban centres[3] rose from 228 in 1981 to 468 in 1998. In 1981, there were only three cities with populations of more than one million people (Karachi, Lahore, and Faisalabad). According to Table 4.4, there were eight cities in Pakistan with a population of over a million people in 2009 (Pakistan: Largest Cities and Towns and Statistics of their Population, 2008). The share of these eight cities, in the overall urban population, was more than 50 per cent (Arif and Ibrahim, 1998b: 518).[4]

Table 4.4: Major Cities of Pakistan

	Name	Census 1981	Census 1998	2009 (estimate)	Annual Growth % between 1981 and 1998
1	Karachi	5,208,132	9,339,023	12,827,927	2.93
2	Lahore	2,952,689	5,143,495	6,936,563	2.76
3	Faisalabad	1,104,209	2,008,861	2,793,721	3.04
4	Rawalpindi	794,843	1,409,768	1,933,933	2.92
5	Multan	732,070	1,197,384	1,566,932	2.48
6	Hyderabad	751,529	1,166,894	1,536,398	2.53
7	Gujranwala	658,753	1,132,509	1,526,168	2.75
8	Peshawar	566,248	982,816	1,390,874	3.21
9	Quetta	285,719	565,137	859,973	3.89
10	Islamabad	204,364	529,180	673,766	2.22

Source: Pakistan: Largest Cities and Towns and Statistics of their Populations (2008).

Much like other third world countries, this rapid urbanisation has resulted in massive slums and squatter colonies called katchi abadis (temporary colonies) (see Davis, 2006). About 35 to 50 per cent of the urban population of Pakistan lives in such katchi abadis (Pakistan's Urban Population to Equal Rural by 2030: UNFPA 2007). In Karachi, there are more than 500 katchi abadis, more than 300 in Lahore, and at least 40 per cent of the population lives in katchi abadis in Faisalabad (ibid.).

What this data on population and urbanisation indicates is that however one categorises the process of transformation set in motion by British colonialism, the small and relatively isolated rural village communities that were the foundation of the AMP are being superseded by a burgeoning population and the development of massive cities. Do these demographic trends also indicate the transformation of the class structure of society? To answer this question, let us begin by examining the aggregate data on the composition of the labour force.

LABOUR FORCE AND CLASS COMPOSITION

According to the Federal Bureau of Statistics, the labour force consists of all persons aged 10 years and above who work either for pay or profit in cash or kind—including family helpers—for at least one hour during the week. The latest Labour Force Survey (LPS) (2006–2007) estimates that the labour force participation ratio is 31.8 per cent (Labour Force Survey, 2008: 2). This implies that the estimated total labour force is approximately 50.33 million (ibid., vii). The labour force participation ratio is relatively low mainly because, according to the Labour Force Survey methodology, those reporting housekeeping and other related activities are considered to be outside the labour force (Arif and Chaudhry, 2008: 31; Majid, 2000: 14). However, since 1991 housewives have also been identified as employed if they have spent time on certain specified agricultural and non-agricultural activities, regardless of whether they have received monetary compensation. This different methodology partially accounts for the increased adult female labour force participation rate, from 13 per cent in 1990 to 16 per cent in 2003 (Arif and Chaudhry, 2008: 41). All in all, while 39.92 million males are counted in the labour force, only about 10.41 million women are included (Labour Force Survey, 2008: vii).

Table 4.5: Labour Participation Rates by Urban/Rural and Gender, 1990–1991 to 2005–06

Year	1990–1991	1991–1992	1993–1994	1996–1997	1997–1998	1999–2000	2001–2002	2003–2004	2005–2006
All areas	43.2	42.9	42.0	43.0	43.3	42.8	43.3	43.7	46.3
Male	71.3	70.3	69.1	70.0	70.5	70.4	70.3	70.6	72.2
Female	12.8	14.0	13.3	13.6	13.9	13.7	14.4	15.9	19.3

Source: Arif and Chaudhry (2008: 41).

Owing to the abysmally low participation of women in activities other than housekeeping, Pakistan's labour force participation rate is among the lowest in Asia (see Table 4.6).[5]

**Table 4.6: Labour Force Participation Rates (Aged 15–64)
Male and Female, 2003**

Region/Countries	Male	Female	Gap
East Asia			
China, People's Rep. of	88.8	79.2	9.6
Hong Kong, China	85.6	57.7	27.9
Korea, Rep. of	79.9	59.7	20.0
Southeast Asia			
Indonesia	84.7	59.5	25.2
Malaysia	81.4	51.9	29.5
Philippines	82.6	52.0	30.6
Singapore	81.7	54.5	27.2
Thailand	89.7	77.7	12.0
Vietnam	83.5	77.3	6.2
South Asia			
Bangladesh	88.6	68.4	20.2
India	88.6	45.2	41.4
Nepal	86.5	58.4	28.1
Pakistan	85.6	39.3	46.3
Sri Lanka	82.6	47.8	34.8

Source: Arif and Chaudhry (2008: 44).

The overall trend in the labour force is a transition away from agriculture towards manufacturing and the service sector. In 1950–1951, the overall number of labourers in the manufacturing sector was only 9.5 per cent; by 2002, this had risen to 18 per cent (see Figure 4.1).

The latest figures available at the time of this study indicate that, by 2007, an estimated 21 per cent of the labour force was active in the manufacturing sector, 35.4 per cent in services, and 43.6 per cent in agriculture or agriculture related activities (see Figure 4.2).

These figures indicate a transformation in employment of the labour force, which is reflected in a more pronounced manner when one examines output. In 1949, manufacturing only contributed 7.8 per cent to the overall GDP of Pakistan. By 2002, it was contributing over 25 per cent (see Figure 4.3).

Figure 4.1: Labour Force by Sector, 1950 and 2002

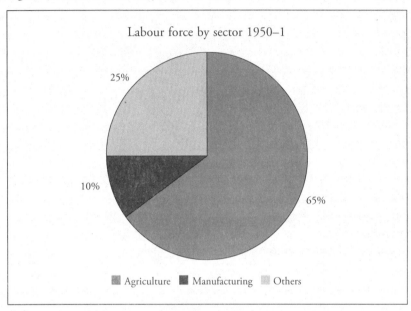

Labour force by sector 1950–1

25%

10%

65%

■ Agriculture ■ Manufacturing ■ Others

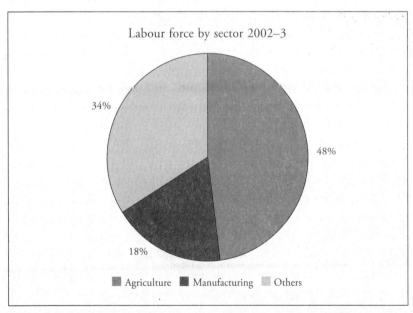

Labour force by sector 2002–3

34%

18%

48%

■ Agriculture ■ Manufacturing ■ Others

Source: Zaidi (2005: 4).
Note: Zaidi uses the category 'others' instead of 'services'.
Note: Values in charts are approximations to the nearest whole number.

Figure 4.2: Employment of Labour Force by Sector, 2006–2007

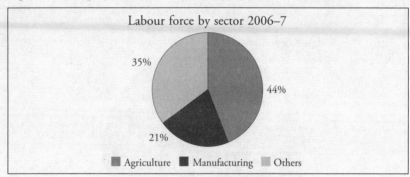

Source: Labour Force Survey (2008, vii).
Note: Values in charts are approximations to the nearest whole number.

Figure 4.3: Contribution to GDP, 1949 and 2002

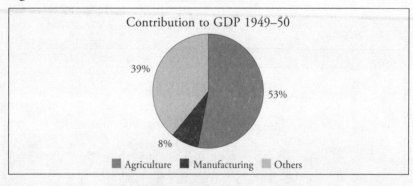

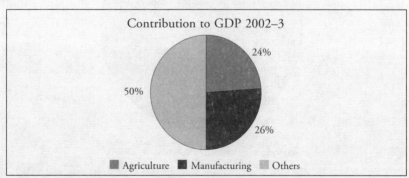

Source: Zaidi (2005: 4).
Note: The category 'others' is services.
Note: Values in charts are approximations to the nearest whole number.

In summary, this aggregate data shows that the manufacturing sector is expanding, both in terms of employment and output, in relation to the agricultural sector. Today, more than a fifth of the labour force is employed in various occupations related to manufacturing; this sector produces more than one-fourth of the overall income of society.

Further, disaggregated statistics on labour force employment in 2006–2007 indicate 42 per cent were employed in agriculture; 15 per cent in manufacturing; 15 per cent in construction; 11 per cent in community, social, and personal services; 9 per cent in wholesale and retail trade; and 8 per cent in transport, storage, and communication (see Figure 4.4).

Figure 4.4: Employment of Labour Force by Sector with Detail, 2006–2007

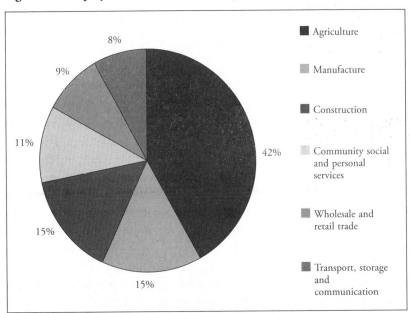

Source: Labour Force Survey 2006–2007 (2008: 2).
Note: Values in charts are approximations to the nearest whole number.

Time series data of employment of the labour force by industry and occupational divisions demonstrates a gradual, but clear, shift away from agriculture towards employment in services and manufacturing.

DATA FROM INDUSTRY DIVISIONS AND OCCUPATION DIVISIONS

Industry and occupation divisions do not tell us about classes in the strict sense. Class is the relationship of a stratum of society to the means of production, whereas industry divisions are determined by the type of product. For instance, the Federal Bureau of Statistics divides all industries in Pakistan in accordance with the International Standard Industrial Classification (Revision 2):

1. Agriculture, Forestry, Hunting, and Fishing
2. Mining and Quarrying
3. Manufacturing
4. Electricity, Gas, and Water
5. Construction
6. Wholesale and Retail Trade, and Restaurants and Hotels
7. Transport, Storage, and Communication
8. Financing, Insurance, Real-Estate, and Business Services
9. Community, Social, and Personal Services

The data on industry divisions indicates that there is a trend away from the agricultural sector and towards industry divisions that are more closely associated with urban professions. The data shows that the percentage of employed persons in agriculture, forestry, hunting, and fishing is steadily declining. On the other hand, those associated with mining, quarrying, manufacturing, electricity, gas and water, construction, wholesale and retail trade, restaurants and hotels, transport, storage and communication, finance, insurance, real estate, and business services are increasing (see Figure 4.5).

This decline in agriculture, forestry, and fishing is mainly due to the change in the composition of the labour force employed in rural areas. This is sharply illustrated by the data on the percentage distribution of employed persons by major industry division in rural areas. In 1968–1969, about a quarter of the work force in the rural areas was employed in non-agricultural work. By 2006–2007, about 40 per cent of the rural work force—which is 44 per cent of the overall workforce—was employed in non-agrarian categories (see Figure 4.6).

In contrast, the distribution of employed persons by major industry division has not changed as rapidly in the urban areas. In urban areas, a majority of the labour force is employed in manufacturing (about a quarter), wholesale and retail trade, restaurants, hotels, community services (another quarter), and social and personal services (another quarter) (see Figure 4.7).

Similarly, the occupation divisions do not tell us about class in the strict sense. Occupation divisions indicate the nature of work, not the nature of the relation of labour to the means of production. Hence, a sales worker and a clerical worker are in different occupations, but they may both be working for a salary or wage. The Federal Bureau of Statistics divides all occupations in Pakistan according to the International Standard Classification of Occupations 1968[6] devised by the ILO:

1. Professional, technical, and related workers
2. Administrative, executive, and managerial workers
3. Clerical workers
4. Sales workers
5. Farmers, fishermen, hunters, loggers, and related workers
6. Production and related workers, transport equipment operators, and labourers
7. Service, sports, and recreation workers

Figure 4.8 shows that the lion's share is taken up by agricultural occupations in the category of farmers, fishermen, hunters, loggers, and related workers. However, this occupation group is slowly declining. Manufacturing occupations have retained a quarter of employment during this entire period. Occupations such as sales workers, clerical workers, and to a lesser extent professional and technical occupations, are increasing.

In summary, in both instances, the proportion of labour closely related to agriculture is declining in favour of industry. However, do these aggregate changes in sectors, industry divisions, and occupational divisions indicate the rise of wage labour? A closer examination reveals that, as yet, large-scale industry is still a way away from having entirely replaced handicraft or manufacture.

Figure 4.5: Percentage Distribution of Employed Persons by Major Industry Division of Urban and Rural Pakistan, 1968–1969 to 2006–2007

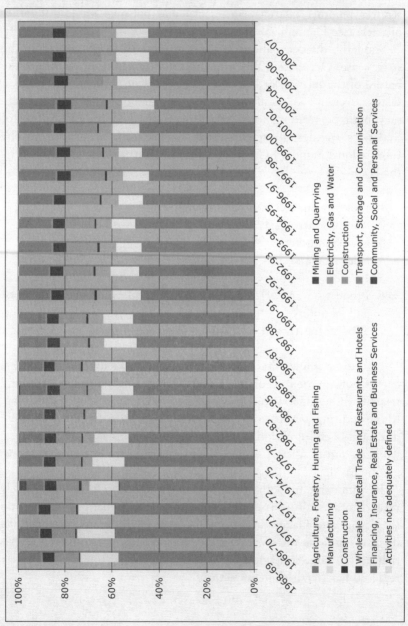

Source: Pakistan Statistical Yearbook (1968–69 to 2006–07). See Table 0.1 in the Appendix for data.

Figure 4.6: Percentage Distribution of Employed Persons by Major Industry Division in Rural Pakistan, 1968–1969 to 2006–2007

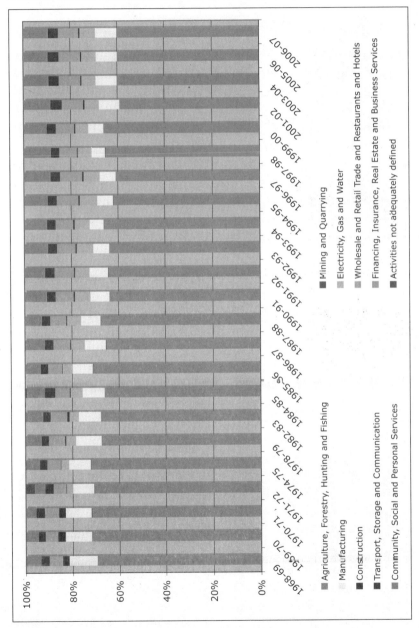

Source: Pakistan Statistical Yearbook (1968–69 to 2006–07). See Table 0.2 in the Appendix for data.

Figure 4.7: Percentage Distribution of Employed Persons by Major Industry Division in Urban Pakistan, 1968–1969 to 2006–2007

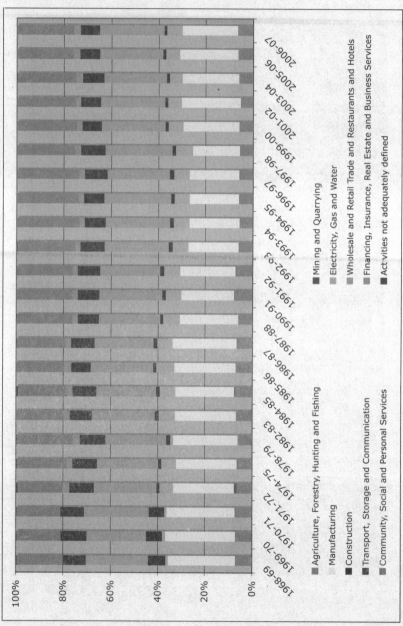

Source: Pakistan Statistical Yearbook (1968–69 to 2006–07). See Table 0.3 in the Appendix for data.

Figure 4.8: Percentage Employment by Occupation

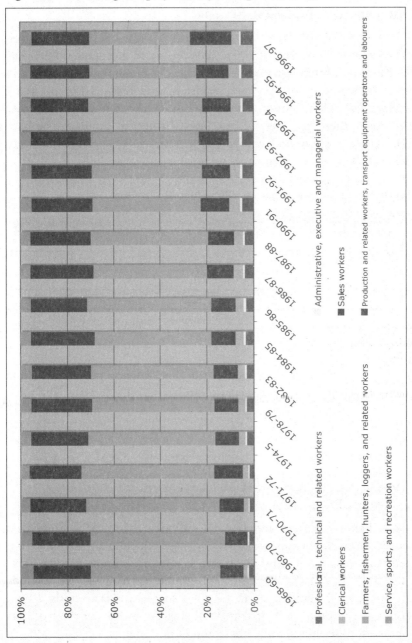

Source: Pakistan Statistical Yearbook (1968 - 1997). See Table 0.4 in the Appendix for data.

THE CHARACTER OF WAGE EMPLOYMENT
(FORMAL AND INFORMAL SECTOR)

The *Labour Force Survey* of 2005–2006 estimated that about 45 per cent of the labour force comes under the category of employees, and nearly half the working population of Pakistan is non-waged (53 per cent) (Table 4.7). The majority of the agricultural labour force works under relations other than wage labour (see Chapter 3). Similarly, Noman Majid's ILO study of employment patterns also estimates that only about half of all employment is wage labour (Majid, 2000: 1).

Table 4.7: Employment Status, 2005–2006

Employment Status	Approximate Numbers	Total Labour Force (%)
Employees	22.5 million	45.0
Own account workers	21.0 million	42.0
Unpaid family workers	5.5 million	11.0
Employers	0.8 million	1.5
Total Labour Force	50.0 million	100.0

Source: Labour Force Survey (2005–06: 2).

These studies imply that nearly half of all working people ostensibly come under the Marxian category of proletariat (that is, wage labourer). However, further disaggregated data demonstrate that this waged employment is overwhelmingly employed in enterprises of less than ten workers.

THE DISTINCTION BETWEEN HANDICRAFT, MANUFACTURING, AND INDUSTRIAL WAGE LABOUR

According to Marx, the development of industry and the working class occurs through three interpenetrating stages: handicraft, manufacture, and industry. Each of these stages is premised upon a progressive improvement of technique and a corresponding change in the relations of production. Handicraft, as the word suggests, is characterised by a technique of production that is dominated by the use of the hand (as opposed to machines) and is based on family labour.

The coming together of several handicraft workers under one roof constitutes the development from handicraft to manufacture. Responsibility for the purchase of raw materials, and ownership of the final product, now falls on the owner. However, the tools and implements continue to belong to the worker, and the technique of production is based on handicraft. This collection of workers under one roof represents an advance in the socialisation of production (for instance, economies of scale can accrue from manufacture). Nonetheless, manufacture does not bring about the complete separation of industry from agriculture, nor does it directly eliminate the handicraft small-producer. Hence, manufacture is still compatible with pre-capitalist forms of unfree labour. The truck system, the putting-out system, the holding system, and the cottage system are some of the forms of bondage peculiar to capitalist manufacture in Europe (Lenin, 1899: chapters 5, 6).

Large-scale capitalist industry, based on machine production, constitutes the final and complete divorce of the producer from the means of production. How does one distinguish machine production from manufacture or handicraft? In *Capital*, Marx drew the distinction between the motive force, transmission mechanism, and tool in every process of production. With the development of new techniques of production, each of these processes is eventually replaced by a mechanical mechanism. When the tool itself is replaced by a machine, and is therefore taken out of the hand of the handicraft worker, then machine production really begins. Hence, substitution of a tool for a machine brings about the complete and final development of industry, and the relationship of wage labour and capital.

At any given point, all three forms exist simultaneously and are interconnected through competition and/or integration. Where machine production has been introduced in a particular operation, handicraft and manufacture can normally compete only by accumulating greater absolute surplus value by increasing the intensity and length of the working day. Eventually, large-scale industry tends to render the tools of the handicraftsman economically obsolete. Moreover, even where the working of raw materials for large-scale industry is undertaken with a handicraft or manufacturing technique, industry subordinates the latter to the rhythms of industrial production. Hence, the completion of the transformation of pre-capitalist unfree labour into wage labour is only achieved as a consequence of large-scale industry. These distinctions between handicraft, manufacture, and industry are referred to in Marxian literature on labour relations as the 'technical mode of production' (see Baronian, 2009).

The Labour Force Survey of Pakistan divides the working class into two sectors; the formal and informal sectors. The informal sector is defined as (Labour Force Survey, 2008: 7):

- all household enterprises owned and operated by own-account workers, irrespective of the size of the enterprise (informal own-account enterprises),
- enterprises owned and operated by employers, with less than ten persons engaged. It includes the owner(s) of the enterprise, the contributing family workers and the employees, whether employed on an occasional or a continuous basis or as an apprentice,
- all enterprises engaged in agricultural activities or wholly engaged in non-market production are excluded

Hence, the informal sector is composed of all non-agrarian enterprises of less than ten workers. In Marx's terms, this is essentially small-scale capitalist enterprise at the handicraft and manufacture stage of production and/or petty commodity production. This distinction between the informal and formal sectors in the labour force survey can help to indicate the percentage of wageworkers who are employed in industry (that is, enterprises with more than ten workers).

Nearly all studies point to the fact that non-agricultural production in Pakistan is dominated by the informal sector in terms of employment, whereas output is dominated by the formal sector. For instance, an ILO study estimated that in 2000 the formal sector employed only 17 per cent of the approximately 4 million manufacturing workers (excluding services) but produced two-thirds of the value added in manufacturing (Majid, 2000: 4). A study by Candland has indicated that manufacturing in the formal sector contributed at least 16–17 per cent of GDP, but its share of employment was only about 3 per cent (Candland, 2007: 46).

Similarly, according to the Labour Force Survey of 2008, about 15 per cent (7.5 million) of the total labour force is engaged in the formal sector—comprised mainly of the spinning, weaving, cement, and sugar industries (see Table 4.8). The differences in numbers are a result of the fact that the Majid and Candland studies exclude the service sector.

Table 4.8: Allocation of Labour Force in Agricultural, Non-Agricultural, Formal and Informal Sectors, 2007

Category	Approximate Numbers (million)	Percentage of Total Labour Force
Agricultural	22	44
Non-Agricultural	28	56
Informal sector	20.5	41
Formal sector	7.5	15
Total Labour Force	50 million	100%

Source: Labour Force Survey (2008: 2).

On the other hand, small-scale manufacture employed 83 per cent of the approximately 4 million manufacturing workers (excluding services), and produced one-third of the value added in manufacturing (Majid, 2000: 4). The more recent Labour Force Survey of 2008 has estimated that about 73 per cent of all non-agricultural workers (including services) are part of the informal sector.

This proportion remains nearly the same in rural and urban areas. In rural areas, the informal sector accounts for 75 per cent of non-agricultural jobs; in urban areas, the informal sector accounts for 71 per cent of non-agricultural jobs (Labour Force Survey, 2005–2006: 2).

Overall, an estimated 41 per cent of the entire labour force—or more than 20 million out of 50 million people—is engaged in the non-agrarian informal sector (Labour Force Survey, 2008: 2). The vast majority of those in the informal sector are in the wholesale and retail trade, restaurants and hotels (36 per cent), followed by small-scale manufacturing (21 per cent), community, social, and personal services (18 per cent), construction (14 per cent), and transport (11 per cent) (see Figure 4.9).

The technique of production in the informal sector in Pakistan is extremely inefficient when compared with large-scale industry. It is also, mainly, in the informal sector that one sees capitalist enterprises using family labour, child labour, and other forms of unfree labour (*Contemporary Forms of Slavery in Pakistan*, 1995)—which is one of the explanations for why the output of this entire sector, which employs 41 per cent of the labour force of the country, is estimated at only 10 per cent of GDP (Ercelan et al., 2004).

Figure 4.9: Allocation of Labour in Informal Sector, 2007–2008

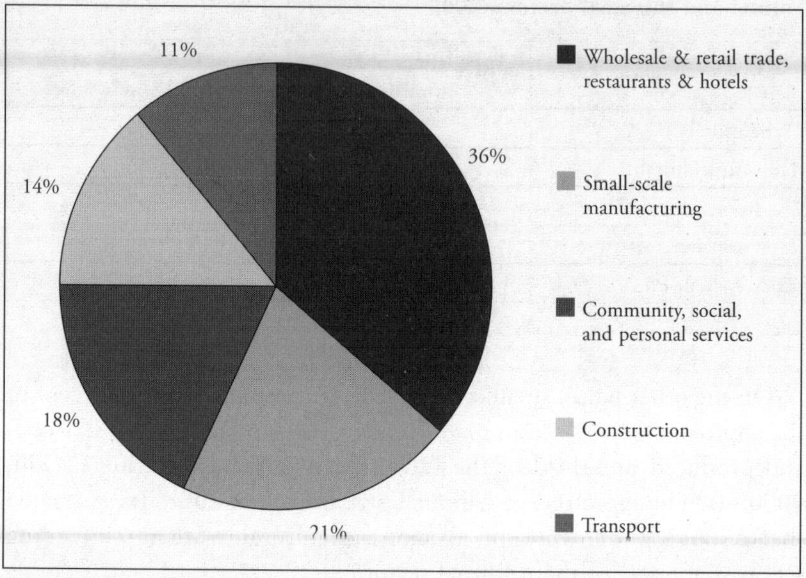

Source: Labour Force Survey (2007–08: 2).

In summary, nearly three quarters of the non-agricultural working population is employed in enterprises of less than ten workers. These figures are consistent with the claim that the majority of non-agricultural working people in Pakistan are connected to petty commodity and petty bourgeois production.

The term 'petty commodity production', or 'simple commodity production', was used by Marx and Engels to describe productive activities where independent producers trade their own products under the conditions of simple exchange of commodities. In *Capital Volume III*, Engels argued that petty commodity production was compatible with a range of relations of production including self-employment (where the producer owns his own means of production), family labour, slavery, peonage, indentured labour, serfdom, and Asiatic labour relations (see Marx, 1894: 1202).

Marx saw the development of industry as the inevitable product of capitalism. Public policy makers in Pakistan also view the development of large-scale industry as the essential economic foundation of modern society. While large-scale industry does not dominate employment, it nonetheless dominates output and consumption. The development of large-scale industry, therefore, is an important determinant of the development of capitalism in a given society.

How is it that in the last 60 years since Independence, large-scale industry remains smaller in terms of employment than petty commodity production and small-scale capitalism? To answer this question, let us turn to the history of the development of large-scale industry in Pakistan.

BRIEF HISTORICAL SKETCH OF INDUSTRIAL DEVELOPMENT

PRE-INDEPENDENCE INDUSTRIAL DEVELOPMENT

Prior to the creation of Pakistan, only a handful of Muslims had any experience of industry. According to Papenek, only 17 of the 100 leading industrialists in the 1960s had any experience of industry before 1947 (Papanek, 1967: 41). The rest were merchants, traders, and exporters.

Moreover, much like the caste system of pre-capitalist Indian agriculture, most leading business groups were also organised around castes and families. Among the leading pre-Independence Muslim families, there were the Dawoods (engineering), Adamjees (trading, match factory), Saigols (rubber shoes and Kohinoor textile mills), Bawanys (hosiery mill in Rangoon), Colony family (ginning factories, flour mills, Colony textile mills), Hashwanis (trading partners with Raleigh Brothers), Haroons (sugar traders, Moti sugar mills), Chinoys (chemical industry), Abdul Sattar Ahmad group (Sattar match factory, Karim jute mills, Dacca jute mills, and Karim commercial company), Khan Rahim Baksh Khan group (paint manufacturing and export), Aragwalas (grain and oil seed business), Rangoonwalas, Monnoos, Syed Maratib Ali family, and Tabanis (for details, see Rahman, 1998).

These names are familiar to most Pakistanis because these families went on to become the famous 22 richest families of Pakistan (Ghani et al., 2008). Dr Mahboob ul Haq, the chief economist of the Planning Commission, remarked that these leading families owned 66 per cent of the total industrial assets, 70 per cent of insurance, and 80 per cent of banking (Haq, 1968: 1). He listed Dawood, Saigol, Adamjee, Colony, Fancy, Valika, Jalil, Bawany, Crescent, Wazir Ali, Gandhara, Ispahani,

Habib, Khyber, Nishat, Beco, Gul Ahmed, Arag, Hafiz, Karim, Milwala and Dada as the leading industrial groups of Pakistan. As shown below, the dominating industrial families of Pakistan remain unchanged even today.

Pakistan inherited a very small industrial base. On the eve of independence, there were 14,569 manufacturing establishments, employing more than 20 workers each, in all of India. Of these, only 1,406 were located in the areas that became Pakistan (Industries in Pakistan, 1965: 2)—that is, Pakistan inherited about 9 per cent of the total industrial establishments of India (Ansari, 1999: 52). Moreover, most of these factories in Pakistan were smaller, in scale, than the ones located in India. If one excludes the food processing factories, there were less than 30 large-scale manufacturing establishments in Pakistan at the time of independence (Malaney, 1965). The large factories in Pakistan comprised of several cotton textile mills, a shoe factory, an electric steel-smelting furnace, a few cement and sugar factories, and railway workshops. The 900 small-scale enterprises were mostly exporters of raw materials. In addition, there were a few light engineering works and about 400 small mills for processing food crops (Richard, 1965: 590). Thus, while East and West Pakistan inherited a quarter of the population of India, it inherited less than 10 per cent of the existing manufacturing capacity and under 7 per cent of the manufacturing employment (Roth, 1971: 570).

According to another estimate, Pakistan had only 3.6 per cent of the factories, 2.6 per cent of the factory workers, and 7.3 per cent of the industrial employment of the major industries of British India (Akhtar, 1951: 263–264). Government sources estimate that the total number of workers in factories, mines, docks, and transport in 1950 was only 512,000 (Economy of Pakistan, 1951: 128). A more comprehensive survey of 5,000 factories estimated that there were some 646,000 manual workers, and another 208,000 contract workers, employed in the factories surveyed (Interim Manpower Survey Report, 1953: 28–35). The estimated industrial employment was 4 to 5 per cent of the overall labour force—that is, a little over a million persons; only about 5 per cent of this industrial workforce comprised of women (Keddie, 1957: 576–578).

Unsurprisingly, there was only a very small organised labour movement in Pakistan. Two unions—the communist-led All-India

Trade Union Congress (AITUC) and the anti-communist Indian Federation of Labour (IFL)—had strong support among the unionised workers of the region that became Pakistan. Nearly 90 per cent of these organised workers in West Pakistan belonged to the public railways. Unions were also strong in the Karachi Electric Supply Corporation, the Karachi Port Trust, and several cement plants in Karachi.

Table 4.9: Union Membership in Selected Areas on the Eve of Partition, 1946

Organisation	Bengal		Sindh and Punjab	
	Unions	Membership	Unions	Membership
AITUC	112	139,000	32	20,000
IFL	641	106,000	23	95,000
Total	753	245,000	55	115,000

Source: Shaheed (2007: 84).

After Partition, the AITUC renamed itself the Pakistan Trade Union Federation (PTUF), with Mirza Ibrahim as its president. Its main strength lay with the railway and textile workers in Punjab. In West Pakistan, the Indian Federation of Labour (IFL) changed its name to the Pakistan Federation of Labour (PFL), with M.A. Khan as its president. The PFL claimed a membership of 50,000 workers in 22 affiliated unions (Keddle, 1957: 380). At the same time, unions in East Pakistan united to form the East Pakistan Trade Union Federation (EPTUF), under the leadership of Dr M.A. Malik. In 1950, PFL and EPTUF merged to form the All-Pakistan Confederation of Labour (APCOL), with strong ties to the ruling Muslim League. APCOL was affiliated with the International Confederation of Free Trade Unions (ICFTU), and the government openly encouraged the dominance of this union. For instance, the labour policy of 1955 reads, 'It is the objective of the Government to encourage the affiliation of the trade unions with the All-Pakistan Confederation of Labour' (Pakistan Trade, Vi, 1955: 9–10). Dr M.A. Malik, the president of APCOL, became the Minister of Labour in 1950 and later an ambassador to Sweden.

British colonial laws influenced labour laws in the independent Pakistan. Labour legislation, under colonial rule, was mainly concerned with legitimising indentured and forced labour in the tea plantations and collieries. These included the Apprenticeship Act of 1850, the Merchant Shipping Act of 1859, the Workers Breach of Contract Act of 1859, the Dispute Act of 1860, the Indian Factories Act of 1881, and the Transport of Native Labourers Act of 1873 Amendment. The first recorded strike in colonial Britain was by the 'palki bearers' (transport workers) in Calcutta in 1827. But, it was only a century later that the labour movement was finally given legal recognition. Amendments to the Factory Act and the Workman's Compensation Act, during the 1920s, increasingly recognised protective legislation for labour. Trade unions were legalised in colonial India in 1926—a century after the palki bearers' strike of 1827.

Since labour unions in the region that became Pakistan were relatively weak, few changes were made to British law. An adjudicatory process to resolve labour disputes was set up by the state and served as a substitute for collective bargaining from 1947 to 1958. At this time there was no effective statutory determination of wages or terms of employment. Hence, the adjudicatory process became a substitute for collective bargaining and, as a result, industrial courts subordinated trade unionism (for details, see Amjad, 2001). According to Amjad, industrial legislation on the eve of Partition covered only about 480,000 workers in East and West Pakistan (2001: 67).

At Independence, it was not clear whether the country, among the poorest in the world, could grow more rapidly than its population (Papanek, 1967: 1). In April 1948, the government announced its industrial policy, emphasising that while Pakistan possessed considerable natural resources and raw materials, these remained untapped because of the under-development of industry. The Industrial Policy of April 1948 stated (Lewis, 1969: 67–68):

A country producing nearly 75 per cent of the world's production of jute does not possess a single jute mill. There is an annual production of over 15 lac [1.5 million] bales of good quality cotton, but very few textile mills to utilize it. There is an abundant production of hides and skins, wool, sugarcane and tobacco—to name a few of the important products—but Pakistan's considerable resources in mineral, petroleum and power remain as yet untapped.

In India, the Feldman-Mahalanobis model inspired the policy of prioritising heavy industry and substituting imports with domestic production. In Latin America, a similar strategy of economic development was known as import-substitution industrialisation (Baer, 1972; Bhagwati and Chakravarty, 1969). However, unlike other countries in which the import substitution industrialisation strategy was undertaken as an integral part of a broader commitment to anti-imperialism and anti-colonialism, Pakistan's government remained a strong ally of imperialist or former colonial powers. The government prioritised the development of 27 key industries, such as textiles, sugar, cement, electricity, heavy chemicals, heavy engineering, hydroelectric power, railway wagons, telephones, telegraphs, wireless apparatus, and arms and ammunition (Industrial Policy of the Government of Pakistan, 1961: 1–5).

At the very outset, the government made it very clear that labour would have to bite the bullet for the 'national interests' of growth (ibid.). At the very first tripartite labour conference in 1948, the Prime Minister stated (Shaheed, 2007: 85):

> Labour must remember that the interest and the welfare of Pakistan come before the interest of any individual or class of individuals and must not do anything which in any way weakens Pakistan.

Nonetheless, with the development of industry, the unionised labour force also began to develop. Official figures indicate that union membership tripled between 1950 and 1957, with 406 unions claiming a membership of 403,000 workers by 1957.[7] About a third of the labour force in large enterprises—employing over 20 individuals—was unionised (Keddie, 1957: 581). Most of these new unions were affiliated with APCOL, whose president Dr M.A. Malik encouraged the labour to be compliant. The view of the prime minister, that national interests should be put before class interests, was seconded by Dr Malik who stressed that demanding wage increases would be against the 'interests of the nation' (Shaheed, 2007: 86).

Employers' attitude towards trade unionism was also hostile. A study found that the majority of employers were inclined to identify trade union activity with communism (Keddie, 1957: 583). The communist-led PTUF, claiming a membership of some 410,755 workers representing 10 per cent of the organised workers of both East and West Pakistan in 1965, faced stiff state repression during that period (Pakistan Labour Gazette (July-August), 1965: 890). Leaders of the PTUF, such as Mirza

Ibrahim, Mohammed Afzal, and the poet Faiz Ahmed Faiz, were repeatedly incarcerated.[8] The introduction of the Essential Services Maintenance Act (ESMA), in 1949, denied large categories of workers the right to organise unions. According to this act, organising unions in any industry that was deemed 'essential' to the welfare of the nation became a criminal offence. The Industrial Disputes Act of 1947 and 1955 made it extremely difficult to organise strikes and led to the ILO protesting that the 'Act is really used to smash trade unionism' (Report of the ILO Labour Survey Mission on Labour Problems in Pakistan, 1953: 141).

FROM MERCHANT TO INDUSTRIAL CAPITAL

One of the most dramatic class transformations to occur during this early period was the conversion of the merchant capital of leading business families into industrial capital. This transformation began with what has been termed the 'devaluation controversy' during the Korean War boom.

In 1949, as part of the effort to reconstruct the war-torn British economy, the pound (sterling) was devalued by 30 per cent. The currencies of nine other countries—India, Australia, South Africa, New Zealand, Ireland, Denmark, Norway, Egypt, and Israel—were also devalued; the Pakistani government, however, took the controversial decision not to follow suit. Viqar Ahmed and Rashid Amjad argued (1984):

> The reason why the Pakistan government did not devalue its own currency at that moment is one of the most controversial questions of that period and the genesis of the pro-industrial bias in government policy in many ways can be traced back to this decision.

In September 1949, India suspended all trade with Pakistan. At the time (1948–1949), India absorbed 55.8 per cent of Pakistan's exports (Zaidi, 2005: 96). About 50 per cent of West Pakistan's trade, and 80 per cent of East Pakistan's trade, was with India (ibid.). Hence, this suspension of trade had the potential to cause severe economic disruption. However, the crisis did not materialise as the Korean War (June 1950) resulted in a massive increase in worldwide demand for jute. Pakistani merchants began to supply jute for the Korean War and, as a result, made windfall profits.

By 1952, demand for jute began to fall and Pakistan faced a balance of payments crisis. 'With the end of the Korean boom, international trade, and especially exporting, suddenly became unattractive' (Papanek, 1967: 34). Pakistan still did not devalue. Instead, the government placed exchange and import-export controls, such as tariffs and import licensing. While international prices came down as a result of the end of the Korean War, the prices of industrial goods and the profitability of industrial production for the domestic market was now much higher. The profits, made as a result of the Korean War boom, were now directed towards industry.

The government facilitated this transformation by building several public/private institutions in order to encourage investment in the manufacturing sector. One of the largest of these was the Pakistan Industrial Development Corporation (PIDC), established in 1952 with the aim of setting up industries and handing them over to the private sector. PIDC (later divided into West Pakistan IDIC and East Pakistan IDIC) invested in everything from jute, paperboard, heavy engineering, shipbuilding, chemicals, pharmaceuticals, fertilisers, sugar, cement, coal, exploitation of marine fisheries, industries based on forest products, development of cottage and small-scale industries, refractory products, and clay products. Other institutions to facilitate this industrial policy included the Pakistan Industrial Credit and Investment Corporation (PICIC), Industrial Development Bank (IDB), Investment Promotion Bureau (IPB), and Pakistan Industrial Finance Corporation (PIFCO).

In summary, government policy played a key role in catalysing investment into industry (*The Study on Japanese Cooperation in Industrial Policy for Developing Economies: Pakistan*, 1994; Lewis, 1969: 13). In terms of political economy, merchant capital was now being converted into industrial capital (Ahmed and Amjad, 1984: 66).

During the 1950s, the investment rate more than doubled. Between 1949 and 1954, large-scale manufacturing grew by 23.6 per cent. Between 1954 and 1960, it continued to grow at 9.3 per cent (Pakistan Economic Survey, 1984–5, 1985). In West Pakistan, between 1950 and 1958, the growth rate of large-scale manufacturing was 19.1 per cent (Zaidi, 2005: 91) (see Table 4.10).

Table 4.10: Annual Growth Rate of Large-scale Manufacturing and GDP, 1950–1958 (%)

Year	Large-scale Manufacturing	GDP
1950–1951	23.5	3.9
1951–1952	18.7	−1.8
1952–1953	23.6	1.7
1953–1954	28.7	9.4
1954–1955	24.1	2.7
1955–1956	17.5	3.4
1956–1957	8.1	3.0
1957–1958	4.9	2.6

Source: Pakistan Economic Survey (1985).

Although the manufacturing output recorded one of the most rapid increases in Asia from 1953 to 1962, this did not have an appreciable impact on the per capita GDP of Pakistan (Bukhari, 1965: 69). Between 1949 and 1954, per capita GNP increased by only 0.2 per cent, and by 0 per cent between 1954 and 1959 (Zaidi, 2005: 93).

Moreover, this growth in manufacturing was accompanied by the concentration of capital. The Credit Inquiry Committee of the State Bank of Pakistan revealed that 222 depositors controlled two-thirds of the total credit facilities offered by the banking system in 1959 (Rahman, 1998). Rehman Sobhan estimated, from the 1959–1960 Census of Manufacturing Industries, that merely 75 of the largest units—about 2.1 per cent of all industrial units—accounted for 43.8 per cent of all value added in the manufacturing industries (1965: 109). Similarly, Papanek's research showed that (1967: 67–68):

> While there were over 3,000 individual firms in Pakistan in 1959, only 7 individuals, families or foreign corporations controlled one-quarter of all private industrial assets and one-fifth of all industrial assets. Twenty-four units controlled nearly half of all private industrial assets. . . . It is also reported that approximately 15 families owned about three-quarters of all shares in banks and insurance companies.

According to the firms listed on the Karachi Stock Exchange in that year, 43 families or groups controlled 98 per cent of 197 non-financial companies, accounting for 53 per cent of the total assets (White, 1974: 58–59). White showed that the top four, namely Saigol, Dawood, Adamjee, and Amin, controlled one-fifth of the total assets, the top ten families controlled one-third, and the top thirty families controlled over half the listed assets (White, 1974: 58–59).

Throughout the 1950s and 1960s, private and public investment was disproportionately concentrated in West Pakistan. As a result, the disparities between East and West Pakistan grew further. The funds and facilities provided by organisations such as PIDC, PICIC, IDB, and PIFCO were mainly allocated to the relatively large industrial groups from West Pakistan.

For instance, the Investment Promotion Bureau was in charge of issuing licences for those industrial groups that utilised foreign private investment, foreign private loans, and foreign exchange. These licences were mainly issued to West Pakistani business families. Similarly, PICIC provided 'nearly half of all its loans' to a handful of leading industrialists in West Pakistan (Papanek, 1967: 88). About 66 per cent of PIDC investment, and 62 per cent of foreign loans, were directed towards industrialists in West Pakistan (Papanek, 1967: 101).

The export earnings from jute produced in East Pakistan were financing the industrialisation of West Pakistan; East Pakistan had a trade surplus while West Pakistan had a trade deficit (see Table 4.11).

Theoretically, the industrial and trade policies of Pakistan in the 1950s were influenced by the strategy of import substitution industrialisation based on: (i) the overvaluation of the rupee, (ii) the use of quantitative controls on imports to regulate the level and composition of imported goods, (iii) a highly differentiated structure of tariffs on imports, and export taxes on the two principal agricultural exports (jute and cotton) (Bruton and Bose, 1962; Lewis, 1969: 40). However, unlike India and some countries in Latin America, over time Pakistan became closely aligned with the USA. It can be argued that the Import Substitution Industrialisation policies in Pakistan were motivated by the imperative to develop an industrial capitalist class rapidly, through the accumulation and concentration of capital in the hands of the leading capitalist concerns. During the Ayub years, the policy of industrial concentration was termed 'functional inequality'.

Table 4.11: Trade Balance of East and West Pakistan, 1949–1958 (Rs millions)

Balance of trade (Rs million)	1949–50 to 1950–51	1950–51 to 1951–52	1951–52 to 1952–53	1952–53 to 1953–54	1953–54 to 1954–55	1954–55 to 1955–56	1955–56 to 1956–57	1956–57 to 1957–58
East Pakistan								
Exports	683	1,211	1,087	643	645	732	1,042	910
Imports	372	453	764	367	294	320	360	819
Balance of trade	311	758	323	276	351	412	682	91
West Pakistan								
Exports	535	1,343	922	867	641	491	742	698
Imports	912	1,167	1,473	1,017	824	783	965	1,516
Balance of trade	−377	176	−551	−150	−183	−292	−223	−818
Pakistan								
Exports	1,218	2,554	2,009	1,510	1,286	1,223	1,784	1,608
Imports	1,284	1,620	2,237	1,384	1,118	1,103	1,325	2,335
Balance of trade	−66	934	−228	126	168	120	459	−727

Source: Ahmed and Amjad (1984: 65).

THE PERIOD OF FUNCTIONAL INEQUALITY

Ayub Khan took power in a military coup in October 1958 and lashed out at the politically elected leaders as 'inefficient and rascally' (Mohiuddin, 2007: 164). About 7,000 elected representatives were convicted of 'misconduct' and banned from holding office under the Elective Bodies Disqualification Order (EBDO) and the Public and Representative Office Disqualification Order (PRODO) (Mohiuddin, 2007: 166). The main thrust of this persecution was against politicians from East Pakistan who were challenging the lopsided relationship between East and West Pakistan. At the same time, the Press and Publications Ordinance (1960) were used to muzzle the press and trade unions and student groups were closely monitored for subversive activity. Finally, a pliant assembly of 'basic democrats'[9] gave a legal veneer to the military regime, and the Constitution was redrafted to give greater power to the executive.[10]

On the economic front, Ayub strengthened the Planning Commission with the help of the Harvard Advisory Group funded by the Ford Foundation; by now, Pakistan was heavily dependent on foreign aid.

The Planning Commission's Industrial Policy of February 1959 was informed by the internationally dominant economic view at the time, described by Pakistani economists as the 'doctrine of functional inequality' (Cheema, 1995: 7). Omar Noman described this doctrine in the following terms (Noman, 1988: 40):

> The doctrine of functional inequality was based on the premise that the initial stages of capitalist development required a high degree of inequality. This was due to the necessity of channelling resources to those classes which have a high savings rate. These high savings would be converted into investment, which would raise the rate of economic growth.

Ayub's industrial policy allowed for 'tax holidays', of two to six years, for nascent industries under the pretext of giving them greater incentives to invest. Leading industrial groups were given special tax breaks, subsidies, and other incentives to lead an industrial revolution in the country; it was argued that high economic growth would eventually trickle down to the poor.

Trade policy continued as before, with the exception that the Ayub government shifted the emphasis on imports and domestic prices, from state control to market controls. For instance, the Export Bonus Scheme[11] and the Bonus Voucher Scheme[12] were policies that provided monetary incentives to exporters. In 1961, restrictions on imports[13] were eased by increasing the number of commodities that could be imported under the Open General Licence or the Free List.[14] Lastly, the tariff differentials were increased—tariffs on consumer goods were increased by a wider margin than other tariffs.

Pakistan also began to receive enormous amounts of foreign assistance in exchange for its role in supporting the West in the Cold War. Overall, foreign aid increased from 2.5 per cent of GNP in the mid-1950s to 7 per cent of GNP in the mid-1960s (Amjad, 1982: 5). This assistance was of such a large amount that Rashid Amjad and Viqar Ahmed referred to the Ayub regime as a 'foreign aid dependent regime' (Amjad, 1982: 166). An Asian Development Bank study concluded that important liberalisation during the first half of the 1960s would have been impossible without this large increase in aid (*Strategies for Economic*

Growth and Development: The Bank's Role in Pakistan, 1985: 359).
Similarly, Papanek wrote, 'foreign aid contributed significantly to
Pakistan's growth from the late 1950s; without it, the rapid increase in
development in the 1960s could not have been possible' (Papanek,
1967: 225). Up to 35 per cent of its first Five-Year Plan (1955–1960),
and 50 per cent of its second plan (1960–65), was supported by external
loans and grants (Jain, 2001: 147).

**Table 4.12: IMF Arrangements with Pakistan during the Ayub Era
(SDR millions)**

Date of Arrangement	Type of Arrangement	Date of Expiration or Cancellation	Amount Agreed (SDRm)	Amount Drawn (SDRm)	Undrawn Balance (SDRm)
8 Dec. 1958	Standby	22 Sep. 1969	25.0	-	25.0
16 Mar. 1965	Standby	16 Mar. 1966	37.5	37.5	-
17 Oct. 1968	Standby	16 Oct. 1969	75.0	75.0	-

Source: Zaman (1995: 81).
Note: Special Drawing Rights (SDRs) are allocated to nations by the International Monetary Fund
(IMF). SDR represents a claim to foreign currencies.

There can be no doubt, however, that these policies resulted in the
rapid growth of industry (see Table 4.13). Savings doubled between
1949 and 1965, and overall investment increased to over 18 per cent of
GNP in the first half of the 1960s (Zaidi, 2005: 98). Large-scale
manufacturing growth rates were on average 8 per cent per annum
between 1955 and 1960, 16.9 per cent from 1960 to 1965, and about
10 per cent from 1965 to 1968 (*Strategies for Economic Growth and
Development: The Bank's Role in Pakistan*, 1985: 359). Pakistan's
economy grew by an average of 6 per cent during the entire decade
(Noman, 1988: 120).

By 1965, Pakistan's manufactured exports were greater than those of
South Korea, Turkey, Thailand, and Indonesia combined (*The Study on
Japanese Cooperation in Industrial Policy for Developing Economies:
Pakistan*, 1994: 135–136). The export of raw jute fell from 60 per cent
of total exports in 1958 to 20 per cent in 1968–1969, while the export
of finished cotton and jute textiles increased from 8.3 to 35 per cent in
the same period. At the same time, the export of other manufactures
increased from 2 to 20 per cent. Table 4.13 shows that not only was

there growth in the output of consumer goods, but that it was being supplemented by growth in intermediate and capital goods. Typical of other developing countries during this period, there was relatively greater growth in investment goods earlier in the 1960s.

Table 4.13: Percentage Rate of Growth of Manufacturing Output, 1960–1970 (% per annum, average)

Industries	1960–1965	1965–1970	1960–1970
Consumer goods	10.6	9.0	10.0
Intermediate goods	12.0	8.0	9.0
Investment goods	20.0	8.0	13.0
Total manufacturing	**16.0**	**10.0**	**12.0**

Source: Zaidi (2005: 101).

By 1965, however, this high rate of growth had begun to decline (see Table 4.14). The slowdown in industrial growth can be attributed, in part, to the curtailment of foreign aid after the Pakistan-India war of 1965 (see Amjad, 1982: 166). One of the conditions of foreign assistance was that military hardware would only be used against the socialist bloc. As the Pakistan-India war of 1965 violated this agreement, foreign aid was curtailed.

According to Amjad, this slowdown in the economy, as a result of the curtailment of foreign aid, was indicative of the foreign aid-dependent character of capitalist development in Pakistan. He stated (1982: 166):

The explanation for the boom in private industrial investment in the first half of the sixties and its subsequent slowing down lies principally in the change in foreign aid inflows to the industrial sector in the sixties. . . . The system which operated in Pakistan came very close to being what we can term a 'Foreign Aid Dependent Regime' in which the mechanics of industrial growth were in one way or another made dependent on foreign aid inflows. Once these aid flows slowed down, the system, not being able to replace foreign aid with other forms of external finance like direct foreign investment, and without the peculiar boost to profitability associated with the local system for dispensing aid, found it difficult to sustain the earlier growth it had generated.

Table 4.14: Annual Growth Rate, 1958–1970 (%)

Year	Large-scale Manufacturing	GDP
1958–1959	5.6	5.5
1959–1960	2.7	0.9
1960–1961	20.3	4.9
1961–1962	19.9	6.0
1962–1963	15.7	7.2
1963–1964	15.5	6.5
1964–1965	13.0	9.4
1965–1966	10.8	7.6
1966–1967	6.7	3.1
1967–1968	7.6	6.8
1968–1969	10.6	6.5
1969–1970	13.9	9.8
1958–1964 (avg.)	**13.3**	**5.2**
1965–1970 (avg.)	**10.4**	**7.2**

Source: Pakistan Economic Survey, 1984–5 (1985).

In addition to foreign aid dependency, Lawrence White's detailed study entitled *Industrial Concentration and Economic Power in Pakistan* (1974) demonstrated that these policies fostered the concentration of capital. The 'managing agency system' played an important role in industrial concentration. This system appointed monopoly licences to importers and exporters of a particular product. For instance, the Rangoonwalas had complete monopoly control over cooking oil because their company (Liberty-American Tank Terminal Company) had a government-enforced monopoly on the import of cooking oil (Rahman, 1998). Similarly, the Steel Corporation of Pakistan (a company of the Fancy group), managed by Industrial Management Ltd. (a Fancy company), would buy from Pakistan Industries Ltd. (another Fancy company), and the products were marketed through Steel Sales Ltd. (another Fancy subsidiary) (Rahman, 1998). Allegedly, through this down-the-line monopoly control, the Fancy group was easily able to manipulate prices and earn monopoly profits (ibid.). Allegedly, this artificial monopoly was meant to guarantee profits leading to greater incentives for

Table 4.15: Leading Industrial Families of 1970 (Rs millions)

	Name	All Manufacturing Assets, Listed and Unlisted
1	Dawood	557.8
2	Saigol	556.5
3	Adamjee	473.2
4	Jalil (Amin)	418.8
5	Shaikh	342.7
6	Fancy	330.5
7	Valika	352.8
8	Bawany	237.4
9	Bashir (Crescent)	199.5
10	Wazir Ali	178.5
11	Ghandara	163.2
12	Ispahani	154.0
13	Habib	136.2
14	Khyber Textile	127.5
15	Nishat Group	126.9
16	BECO	113.6
17	Gul Ahmed	109.2
18	Arag (Haji Habib)	105.4
19	Hafiz	105.3
20	H.A. Karim	95.4
21	Millwala	95.0
22	Hyesons	94.3
23	Dada	90.6
24	Premier Group	89.3
25	Hussein Ebrahim	88.4
26	Monnoo	79.4
27	Maulabaksh	79.1
28	Adam	78.0
29	A.K. Khan	74.9
30	A.A. Ghani	71.2
31	Rangoonwala	68.2
32	Haroon	61.2
33	Hirjina	60.8
34	Shaffi	60.2
35	Fakir Chand	59.6
36	Haji Hashan	58.5
37	Dadabhoy	53.9
38	Shahnawaz	52.8
39	Fatch Textile	52.7
40	Noon	48.0
41	Hoti	45.8
42	Ghulam Faruque	36.7
43	Haji Dost Mohammad	31.6

Source: White (1974: 60–61).

investment. However, according to Rahman, it allowed entrepreneurs to hoodwink shareholders and evade income tax (Rahman, 1998).

White's study of industrial concentration concluded that about 44 industrial houses should be termed 'monopoly houses', since they controlled the lion's share of industrial and financial assets. For instance, by 1970, 77 per cent of the gross fixed assets of all the manufacturing companies listed on the Karachi Stock Exchange were controlled by those 44 monopoly houses (Amjad, 1982: 166). Similarly, the 44 monopoly houses controlled an estimated 35 per cent of all large-scale manufacturing (ibid.). Of the seventeen private Pakistani banks, seven were under the direct control of those monopoly houses; the seven banks controlled the lion's share of deposits and loans (Amjad, 1982: 166). Altogether, they accounted for 60 per cent of total deposits and 50 per cent of loans and advances (ibid.). The monopoly houses also had a close relationship with the government. Between 1958 and 1970, 37 monopoly houses received 65 per cent of all the loans disbursed by the PICIC (ibid.). Between 1961 to 1966, only 22 per cent of the PICIC loans went to East Pakistan (Talbot, 1998: 171). Table 4.15 lists the leading monopoly houses and their declared industrial assets in 1970.

In 1968, the 43 houses (see Table 4.15) controlled a staggering 73.7 per cent of all private Pakistani-controlled non-financial assets, and 58.2 per cent of all large-scale private Pakistani-controlled manufacturing assets listed on the Karachi Stock Exchange (White, 1974: 62–65).

Table 4.16: Economic Disparities: East and West Pakistan, 1949–1968

Year	GDP 1959–60 Prices (Millions of rupees)		Ratio of Per Capita GDP (West: East)
	East Wing	West Wing	
1949	13,130	11,830	1.10:1
1954	14,320	14,310	1.22:1
1959	15,550	16,790	1.32:1
1964	18.014	21,788	1.48:1
1968	20,670	27,744	1.64:1
Avg. annual growth rate	2.42%	4.59%	

Source: Papanek, Gustav (1967, 317).

Moreover, regional disparities between East and West Pakistan developed at an alarming rate. While per capita income in West Pakistan was 10 per cent higher than in East Pakistan in 1949–1950, this difference rose to 30 per cent by 1964–1965 (Lewis, 1969: 4). As Table 4.17 demonstrates, this disparity only grew worse by the end of the Ayub era.

Table 4.17: Per Capita GDP in East and West Pakistan at 1959–1960 Constant Prices

Year	Per capita GDP West	Per capita GDP East	West to East GDP Ratio
1959–1960	355	269	1.32
1964–1965	426	293	1.45
1969–1970	504	314	1.61

Source: Ahmed and Amjad (1984: 89).

Together with this industrial concentration, the head count ratio of poverty as a percentage of the total population rose from 40.24 in 1963 to 46.53 by 1969 (Kemal, 2001: 8). While industrialists enjoyed tax holidays, bonus schemes, and state guaranteed monopolies, workers found it harder to organise for their rights. For example, the Industrial Disputes Ordinance of 1959 'curtailed the rights in respect of collective bargaining and the formation of trade unions' (Amjad; 72).

The Development of the Industrial Proletariat

The capitalist development of the 1950s and 1960s created an industrial proletariat, on a large-scale, for the first time. Figure 4.10 demonstrates that, in 1948, the country had scarcely 1000 factories registered with the government. By the end of the Ayub era, this number had reached just under 6000 factories. It climbed slowly through the 1970s, 1980s, and 1990s, reaching over 10,000 factories by 2000.

The most glaring concern with respect to the figures in Figure 4.10 is the drop in the proportion of reporting factories to registered factories and working factories. In the first few years after independence, more than 90 per cent of registered and working factories were reporting factories. In the last few years, this figure dropped to less than

20 per cent. This means that information from 80 to 90 per cent of the working or registered factories is not included in labour statistics.

Figure 4.10: Number of Registered, Working and Reporting Factories in West Pakistan

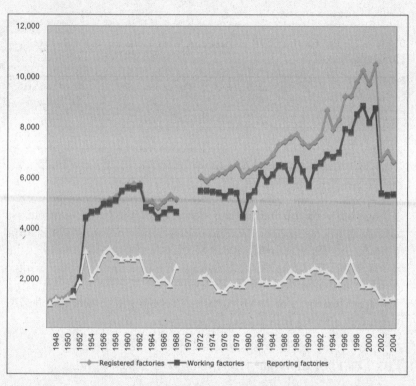

Source: Pakistan Statistical Yearbook (1948–2007). See Table 0.5 in the Appendix for data.
Note: 'Registered factories' are all the factories registered with the government. 'Working factories' are those factories that are known to be operational. 'Reporting factories' are those that have provided up-to-date information about labour conditions to the government.

Moreover, the absolute number of reporting factories has hardly risen at all. Over the entire period, their number has varied between 1200 and 2000 factories. This core group of reporting factories mostly consists of state-owned factories. Hence, the statistics published on employment, industrial disputes, trade unions, labour relations, and so on, by the Federal Bureau of Statistics simply do not take into account the remaining 80 per cent of working factories. The statistics are not exhaustive, nor can they be taken as a random sample of all factories since they are skewed towards government enterprises.

Roughly the same trends of industrial growth, as those mentioned above, can be gauged from the data on the average daily number of factory workers. In the early 1950s, there were approximately 120,000 workers in the reporting factories—the 1200 reporting factories accounted for over 90 per cent of all the working factories at that time. This figure rose to the high point of nearly 375,000 workers by the early 1970s—2000 reporting factories accounted for 30 to 40 per cent of the working factories at that time. This figure fell, in 2006, to 140,000 workers in the reporting factories—1295 factories that accounted for 20 per cent of the working factories at that time. A superficial glance at the table may lead to the conclusion that industrial labour reached its peak in the 1970s, and has been declining since then. However, such a conclusion cannot be drawn from the table because both the absolute number, and relative proportion, of reporting factories has decreased after the 1970s.

This growth of the working class and the global ideological changes of the late 1960s came together to form a popular left-wing working class movement in Pakistan. Spontaneous student and working class protests, in 1968, sparked a nationwide movement against the Ayub dictatorship. The high point, in the development of the working class movement, was during this period of the anti-Ayub movement. This is clearly visible when one examines the data on industrial disputes. Figure 4.12 demonstrates the rise of labour activity, which has not been seen before or since, in the brief history of Pakistan.

These industrial disputes accompanied the rise of the trade unions. Figure 4.13 shows the dramatic rise of trade unions after 1970. However, the problem with compiling figures related to the trade unions is that a number of larger unions represented workers in both East and West Pakistan. Figure 4.13, therefore, contains the total registered trade unions in East and West Pakistan before 1971 and the total registered trade unions in only West Pakistan after 1971. The vertical line in Figure 4.13 represents this division—its purpose is to illustrate the explosion in the number of trade unions after 1971. From approximately 1000–1500 unions before 1971, the figure climbed to nearly 8000 unions in a matter of a few years. Figure 4.13 shows that the number of unions remained at this level until the 1990s. Since the 1990s, the

Figure 4.11: Average Daily Number of Factory Workers in Reporting Factories

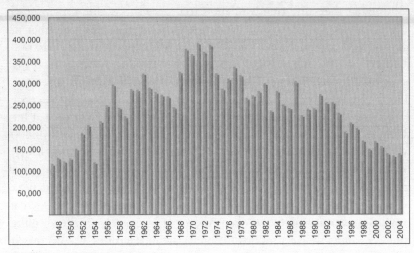

Source: Pakistan Statistical Yearbook (1948–2007). See Table 0.6 in the Appendix for data.

Figure 4.12: Number of Disputes, Workers Involved in Disputes, and Workdays Lost in Disputes, 1948–2003

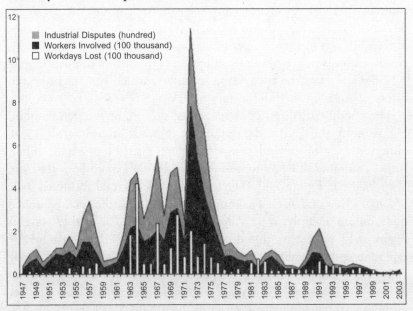

Source: Candland (2007: 43). See also Table 0.7 in the Appendix for data.

trade union movement has been losing its drive and members (also see Amjad, 2001; Kutty, 2004a, 2004b; Qadir, 2003).

Figure 4.13: Total Registered Trade Unions

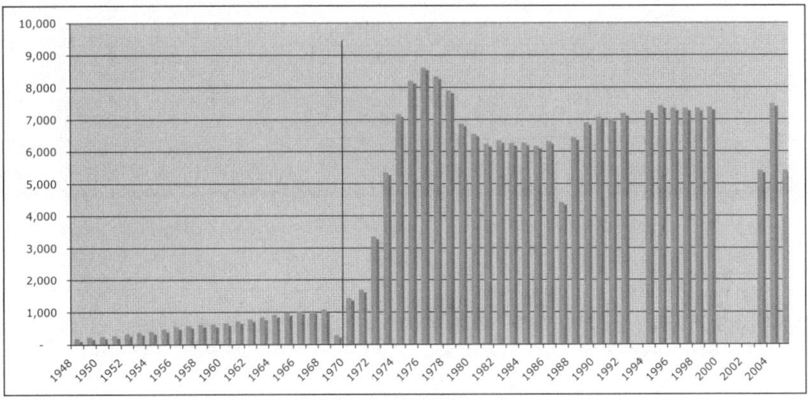

Source: Pakistan Statistical Yearbook (1948–2007). See Table 0.8 in the Appendix for data.
Note: The figures before the vertical line are for East and West Pakistan. The figures after the vertical line are only for West Pakistan. Data for 1993, 2000, 2001, and 2002 are not available.

Data on the total membership of registered unions shows that union membership rose steadily after 1962. The vast majority of organised workers were from East Pakistan (where the unions were stronger). Despite the enormous loss of numbers after the creation of Bangladesh, total membership of reporting unions in West Pakistan continued to rise, and remained at a relatively high level until 2001 (see Figure 4.14).

The main increase in numbers, after 1962, came about because of the explosion of unions among the textile workers.[15] The unionised labour movement, nonetheless, never represented more than a small percentage of the overall labour force in the country. At their high point, in terms of absolute numbers of members, the unions organised about 415,000 workers in 1992; that is, about 1.2 per cent of the overall labour force—of 35 million—of that year. By 2005, membership of unions had declined to about 120,000 workers. Given that the estimated labour force of Pakistan was about 50 million that year, the organised section of the labour force, consequently, was less than 0.24 per cent of the total (Labour Force Survey, 2005–06: 2).

Figure 4.14: Total Membership of Reporting Unions, 1948 to 2004

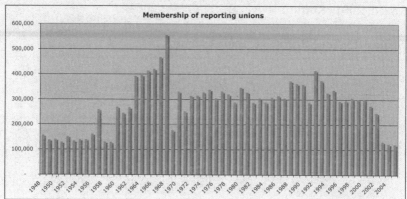

Source: Pakistan Statistical Yearbook (1948–2007). See Table 0.8 in the Appendix for data.
Note: The figures before 1971 are for East and West Pakistan. The figures after 1971 are only for West Pakistan.

If we exclude all agricultural workers from the equation—about 44 per cent of the labour force—then, the unions managed to organise just above 2 per cent of the non-agricultural labour force. By 2005, this proportion had fallen to 0.4 per cent of the non-agricultural labour force.

However, in the late 1960s when the unions were still growing, the labour movement secured greater protective legislation for labour. The Industrial Relations Ordinance of 1969 (IRO 1969) was promulgated under the influence of this rapidly developing, and increasingly militant, labour movement. This new legislation recognised workers' rights to form an elected Collective Bargaining Unit (CBU) under state supervision. CBUs had the right to raise industrial disputes and serve strike notices. Registered CBUs also enjoyed limited legal immunity against tort cases during strikes.

The legislation, however, contained several drawbacks for the labour movement too. It created a system of CBU dependence on management. Firstly, in practice the CBU could not strike without notice. When a strike notice was served, the dispute was taken over by the Labour Department conciliator. If the conciliator failed, the CBU was legally obliged to file a case for adjudication. In court, the case could proceed for years without resolution. Secondly, all enterprises related to civil administration and defence were declared 'essential services' and excluded from labour legislation. Thirdly, the IRO 1969 legislated that union dues from members were to be directly deducted from workers' salaries and transferred to CBU bank accounts. Fourthly, those unions that were not legally recognised CBUs could do nothing, legally, except challenge the CBU at the end of the tenure. Last but not least, the IRO 1969 prohibited the right of unions to set up political funds or nominate candidates in national or local elections.

In this way, IRO 1969 became a legal channel through which disputes were redirected into lengthy legal proceedings, primarily to prevent strike action and political activity (Siddique et al., 2006: 993).

NATIONALISATION

The political parties that captured the imagination of the labour movement in the late 1960s were the Awami League in East Pakistan and the Pakistan Peoples Party in West Pakistan. The Ayub dictatorship fell under pressure from popular protests—ironically, just as Samuel Huntington's famous book lauding Ayub Khan as a modern Rousseau was hitting the shelves. Ayub Khan resigned, and handed power over to General Yahya Khan in 1968. The latter, in 1970, decided to hold the first democratic elections in the history of Pakistan.

The anti-Ayub movement, and the first democratic elections, marked a watershed in the political history of the country. In East Pakistan, the Awami League was able to win an astounding 151 out of 153 National Assembly seats. In West Pakistan, the PPP was able to win 81 out of 131 National Assembly seats. In NWFP and Balochistan, the National Awami Party and Jamiat Ulema-e-Islam coalition won a clear majority in the Provincial Assembly (for detailed data on elections in Pakistan, see Wilder, 1999).

In accordance with the norms of democracy, the Awami League was entitled to form the central government. However, the ruling interests in West Pakistan—principally the army and the bureaucracy—prevented the Awami League from doing so because they did not want the latter to alter the unequal relationship between the eastern and western wings of Pakistan. In East Pakistan, the army attempted to quell the crisis through the use of force. The Indian army intervened in November 1971 and, after a few days of fighting, the Pakistani troops capitulated. East Pakistan separated and became Bangladesh.

In Bangladesh, the new government immediately nationalised the assets of nearly all the West Pakistani industrialists. Two hundred and sixty large units were nationalised, without compensation, and sixteen of the leading industrial families incurred heavy losses (Rahman, 1998). Dawood, Adamjee, Ispahani, Khaleeli, Bawany, and Amin were hit the hardest. Dawood lost Karnaphuli Paper Mills, Karnaphuli Rayon, Dawood Shipping, and warehouse facilities. Adamjee lost six tea gardens in Sylhet and six industrial units, including one of the biggest jute mills in Asia, while Jalil lost five units and was left with only one unit in West Pakistan. Bawany lost Latif Bawany Jute Mills. Habib Ahmad Haji (Aragwala) lost Arg Ltd Chittagong. A splinter Monnoo group lost Olympia Textile Mills at Tongi. Atlas group lost Honda Motorcycle Plant in East Pakistan (ibid.).

In West Pakistan, Zulfikar Ali Bhutto took power on 20 December 1971. The next month, the government passed the Nationalisation and Economic Reforms Order and took control of 31 large firms in 10 basic industries: iron and steel, basic metals, heavy engineering, motor vehicle assembly and manufacture, tractor assembly and manufacture, heavy and basic chemicals, petrochemicals, cement, public utilities, and power generation. Two months later an uncompensated land reform program was initiated (see Chapter 3 for details). At the same time, 32 life insurance companies were nationalised. The government banned the 'managing agency system' and restricted private monopolies in key economic fields relating to the manufacture of tractors, automobiles, and fertilisers. The State Bank of Pakistan reoriented credit policy towards small farmers and small industrial entrepreneurs. The rupee was devalued, the Export Bonus Scheme was closed down, and the government increased the procurement price for agricultural goods— thereby altering the pro-industry anti-agricultural bias of the previous growth strategy (Ahmed and Amjad, 1984: 94). In June of 1972, the government introduced one of the most progressive labour reforms seen in the country and, in August, a comprehensive public health program. From 1972 to 1974, all private educational institutions were nationalised.

Hence, in 1972 alone, the PPP nationalised 256 companies, including the principal assets of the 22 big families, and broke the power of monopoly capital in Pakistan (Burki, 1988; Noman, 1988; Rahman, 1998). To cope with rising prices as a result of the OPEC oil shocks, the PPP government nationalised trade in cotton and rice in June 1973, and vegetable oil, petroleum marketing, and shipping in September 1973. This lowered the prices of basic necessities. In January 1974, the government nationalised all private and domestically owned banks (see Haque and Kardar, 1993). Finally, to lower the prices of the basic necessities, the government nationalised 2815 cotton ginning, rice husking, and flour milling factories.

As Table 0.11 in the Appendix demonstrates, the Saigol, Dawood, Amin, and Fancy groups lost many companies. Industrialist C.M. Latif of BECO was completely bankrupted. Leading industrialists, such as Ahmad Dawood, Fakhar ud Din Valika, and Habib Ullah Khattak, were arrested. Many leading industrial families left, or attempted to leave, the country (Rahman, 1998). In response, the names of nearly all the major industrialists were placed on the Exit Control List.[16] Workers took over several factories; in one well-known incident, industrialist Habib Aragwala was gharoed (besieged) inside his office by workers.

Interestingly, while foreign policy was turning in the direction of non-alignment, the relationship with international financial institutions remained largely intact because, on the whole, foreign capital was not nationalised. During this period, the IMF and the World Bank continued to disburse credit and loans to the Pakistan government (see Table 4.18).

Table 4.18: IMF Agreements with Pakistan during the Bhutto Era

Date of Arrangement	Type of Arrangement	Date of Expiration or Cancellation	Amount Agreed (SDRm)	Amount Drawn (SDRm)	Undrawn Balance (SDRm)
18 May 1972	Standby	17 May 1973	100.00	84.00	16.00
11 Aug. 1973	Standby	10 Aug. 1974	75.00	75.00	-
11 Nov. 1974	Standby	10 Nov. 1975	75.00	75.00	-
9 Mar. 1977	Standby	8 Mar. 1978	80.00	80.00	-

Source: Zaman (1995: 81).

Nonetheless, as a whole, these economic policies represented a significant departure from the past. This departure can be clearly seen in the growth of public sector investment as a percentage of total investment. Private sector investment, which had been falling precipitously since 1965, fell to just 15 per cent of its 1969–1970 level by 1974–1975 (see Table 4.19). It then climbed from 5.3 per cent of total investment in 1970–1971 to 80 per cent in 1978–1979 (see Table 4.19). By any standard, this represented a re-orientation from the pattern of industrial development that Pakistan had experienced until that time.

Table 4.19: Investment in the Large-scale Manufacturing Sector, 1969–1980 (at Constant Prices of 1969–1970 Rs million)

Years	Private Sector	Public Sector	Total	Relative Share of Public Investment in Total (%)
1969–1970	1208.2	177.1	1385.3	12.8
1970–1971	1038.4	58.3	1096.7	5.3
1971–1972	699.9	63.8	763.7	8.4
1972–1973	313.1	45.1	358.2	12.6
1973–1974	230.8	113.7	344.5	33.0
1974–1975	182.8	276.8	459.6	60.0
1975–1976	344.5	831.5	1176.0	70.0
1976–1977	369.0	1085.3	1454.3	74.0
1977–1978	482.3	1922.1	2404.4	79.0
1978–1979	459.7	1944.9	2404.6	80.0
1979–1980	544.6	1644.0	2188.6	75.0

Source: Zaidi (2005: 106).

Many social scientists in Pakistan have argued that Bhutto's nationalisations undermined economic growth (see Burki, 1988; Gustafson, 1973). On the other hand, others have argued that the economic performance of the 1970s was influenced by certain exogenous factors that are not taken into account in the dominant narrative—(i) the loss of East Pakistan, (ii) the impact of the floods, and (iii) the impact of the oil shock (see Zaidi, 2005).

East Pakistanis constituted nearly 55 per cent of the population of Pakistan. 50 per cent of West Pakistan's products were sold in markets in East Pakistan in 1969–1970 (*The Study on Japanese Cooperation in Industrial Policy for Developing Economies: Pakistan*, 1994: 161). Similarly, 18 per cent of West Pakistan's imports came from East Pakistan (ibid.). The massive injection of investment, from jute sales, was lost. The secession of East Pakistan meant that the national market shrank to half its original size.

In August 1973, massive floods hit Pakistan and the country had to import food grains to meet basic needs. In 1974–1975, there was another massive crop failure and the total crop output declined by as much as 25 per cent compared to the previous year. Agriculture recorded a growth rate of –2.1 per cent (see Chapter 3). In 1976–1977, the country again experienced some of the worst floods in its history. Pakistan had to import food crops and spend heavily on the provision of public goods.

There was a four-fold increase in international petroleum prices after October 1973. This pushed up the prices of imports, including oil, fertilisers, and other essential inputs. The oil import bill rose from US$ 60 million in 1972–1973 to $225 million in 1973–1974. Import of fertiliser increased from US$40 million to US$150 million during the same period (Ahmed and Amjad, 1984: 94). This oil shock caused cost-push inflation within Pakistan. The global recession, caused by the oil shock, resulted in a steep drop in demand for Pakistani exports. The trade surplus was wiped out as a result of these higher import costs.

Moreover, the data on economic growth seems to indicate that the economy had already begun to slow down after 1965. By 1970, the economy had come to a grinding halt. Real GDP only grew by 0.3 per cent in 1970 and 1.2 per cent in 1971 (see Table 4.20). When the basic industries were nationalised, the GDP growth rate sprang up to 7.2 and 7.7 per cent—1972–1973 and 1973–1974, respectively. However, in the next year (1974–1975), the oil shock reduced the growth rate to 3.9 per cent. Despite the oil shock and the floods, the economy grew during this entire period—from 1971 to 1977—at an average rate of 4.4 per cent (see Table 4.20).

Table 4.20: Annual Growth Rate, 1971–1977 (at 1959–1960 factor cost %)

Year	Manufacturing Large-scale	GDP
1971–1972	–6.8	1.2
1972–1973	11.9	7.2
1973–1974	7.5	7.7
1974–1975	–1.7	3.9
1975–1976	–0.5	3.3
1976–1977	–0.2	2.9
1971–1977	1.7	4.4

Source: Pakistan Economic Survey (1984–85).

THE ZIA ERA

The 1970s represented a massive convulsion by various oppressed classes in society—not merely the industrial workers and various sections of the peasantry, but also the urban middle classes and oppressed nations within Pakistan. This upsurge challenged the traditional power of the bureaucracy, monopoly capitalists, and large landlords.

The response of the traditional ruling classes to this upsurge was the Islamic fundamentalist military dictatorship of General Ziaul Haq.[17] Since labour militancy and Bhutto's nationalisation and land reforms had made big capitalists and landlords insecure, labour militancy had to be stamped out to restore business confidence. The shift, by the military and a large section of the Pakistani capitalist elite, towards Islamic fundamentalism was a reaction to the class struggle of the 1970s (see Alavi, 1988). To achieve this, repression—justified by the ideology of Islamic fundamentalism—was the central focus of the Zia regime. If the Bhutto period can be considered a period when Pakistan was developing towards social democracy, the Zia period was one of a right-wing counter-revolution. In Pakistan, the rise of fundamentalist Islam cannot be understood without understanding the class struggle between the radicalism of the 1970s and the traditional ruling classes of Pakistan.

Leaving aside the repressive political and social policies of Zia, in terms of economic policy, the regime returned to the free market policies of the Ayub period. One of the first steps of the military regime was to permanently shelve the land reforms of 1977. In September 1977, a month after Zia assumed power, rice husking, flour milling, and cotton ginning mills, along with Ittefaq Foundry, Nowshera Engineering, and Hilal Vegetables, were privatised. In December 1977, Zia removed the state monopoly on the production of cement and fertilisers. Ayub's policy of tax holidays was revived in March 1978; export rebates returned in June 1978. Interest rates were reduced in June 1978, and controls and regulations on private investment were eased. The fifth Five-Year Plan was launched in 1978–1979.

Ironically, the Zia regime was careful not to privatise all industry immediately. Nonetheless, over the entire decade, public sector investment in large-scale industry declined—from above 70 per cent in 1978, to below 18 per cent by the end of the Zia regime in 1988 (see Table 4.21).

Table 4.21: Share of Public Industrial Enterprise in Total Large-scale Manufacturing, 1978–1988

Years	Employment Share (%)	Value Added (%)	Public Sector Share in Total Industrial Investment (%)
1978–1979	14.47	7.12	72.74
1979–1980	14.34	14.55	65.25
1980–1981	15.24	12.27	58.01
1981–1982	16.15	13.28	52.03
1982–1983	14.82	13.90	48.29
1983–1984	16.36	11.81	44.56
1984–1985	-	-	31.38
1985–1986	-	-	30.68
1986–1987	-	-	21.64
1987–1988	-	-	17.85

Source: Zaidi (2005: 117).

Foreign aid dependency returned in a new way. The foreign debt liabilities of the country doubled to US$15.5 billion during the Zia period (Gardezi, 2004: 430). The first of a series of loans under the Extended Fund Facility was negotiated with the IMF in November 1980 (see Table 4.22). According to Gardezi, 'by 1980 Pakistan had become the tenth largest recipient of the World Bank/IMF loans' (Gardezi, 2004: 430). However, the conditions attached to these EFF loans were relatively less stringent than similar agreements in Latin America at the time. The main goal of this agreement was fiscal adjustment.

Table 4.22: IMF Agreements with Pakistan during Zia Era

Date of arrangement	Type of Arrangement	Date of Expiration or Cancellation	Amount Agreed (SDRm)	Amount Drawn (SDRm)	Undrawn Balance (SDRm)
24 Nov. 1980	EFF	1 Dec. 1981	1,268.00	349.00	919.00
2 Dec. 1981	EFF	23 Nov. 1983	919.00	730.00	189.00
28 Dec. 1988	Standby	30 Nov. 1990	273.15	194.48	78.67
28 Dec. 1988	SAF	27 Dec. 1991	382.41	273.15	109.26

Source: Zaman (1995: 81).

In addition to these loans, there was a massive inflow of foreign exchange as a result of the Afghan Jihad. After the Saur revolution in 1978, the US administration provided billions of dollars in military and economic aid to fund the mujahideen in the so-called jihad against the Afghan communists and the Soviet Union. During the Zia period, Pakistan became the third largest recipient of US assistance (after Israel and Egypt). By 1986, US annual aid to Pakistan had reached US$4 billion. At the same time, aid for the jihad was also pouring in from Saudi Arabia. Some estimate that the total international aid to Pakistan from 1979 to 1988 was as much as US$40 billion (Hiro, 28 January 1999).

The oil boom in the Middle East resulted in a demand for labour. Hundreds of thousands of Pakistani workers left for the Middle East. These workers would send their earnings back to their families in Pakistan in the form of remittances. As Figure 4.15 demonstrates, although remittances began to enter the economy during the time of Z.A. Bhutto, they rose rapidly between 1977 and 1984.

Figure 4.15: Inflow of Remittances, 1973 to 1999 (US dollars millions)

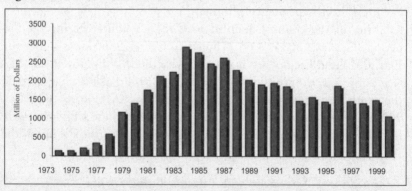

Source: Siddiqui and Kemal (2002: 389).

The contribution of these remittances to economic prosperity cannot be under-estimated. For instance, in 1983, they amounted to 10.1 per cent of GDP, and financed 96.6 per cent of the trade deficit, and 84.8 per cent of the current account deficit (see Table 4.23).

Table 4.23: Contribution of Remittances in Key Economic Indicators, 1980 to 2004 (%)

Year	Financing through Remittances of Current Account Balance	Financing through Remittances of Trade Deficit	Remittances/ GDP
1980–81	67.1	76.6	7.5
1982–83	84.8	96.6	10.1
1985–86	67.7	85.3	8.1
1990–91	46.0	74.4	4.1
1995–96	24.2	39.4	2.3
2000–01	53.6	71.4	1.5
2004–05	52.1	67.3	3.7

Source: Siddiqui and Kemal (2002: 390).

Moreover, since these remittances were going directly into working class homes in Pakistan, they also reduced poverty (Ahmad, 1993; Altaf et al., 1993; Ercelan, 1990). Although the remittances began to dry up by the late 1980s, nonetheless, they contributed enormously to economic growth during Zia's regime.[18]

As a result of these factors, growth rates were relatively high during this period. Between 1977 and 1986, manufacturing GDP grew at an annual average rate of 9.5 per cent, and industrial investment expanded at 15.6 per cent per annum (*Pakistan Growth through Adjustment*, 1988: 63). According to the World Development Report 1990, Pakistan's GDP grew at the rate of 6.5 per cent from 1980 to 1988 (*World Development Report*, 1990). From 1980 to 1988, real wages in Pakistani manufacturing grew at the rate of 6.2 per cent a year (*World Development Report*, 1990).

Bhutto's nationalisations, as well as the attempt to reinforce the rule of the traditional ruling classes, led to alterations in the social composition of the capitalist class. A comparison of the wealthiest families in 1970, 1990, and 1997 reveals some of these changes (see Table 4.25).

Table 4.25 lists the principal industrial families patronised by Ayub before the 1970s. Most of these families were based in Karachi—of the 43 groups ranked at the top in 1970, 25 were based in Karachi. An additional 12 were from the Punjab, and 5 from Khyber-Pukhtunkhwa (formerly NWFP). The Karachi-based groups belonged to the castes of Memons, Khojas, and Bhoras.

Table 4.24: GDP growth rate, 1980–1981 to 1990–1991 (% per annum)

Year	GDP Growth
1980–1981	6.4
1981–1982	7.6
1982–1983	6.8
1983–1984	4.0
1984–1985	8.7
1985–1986	6.4
1986–1987	5.8
1987–1988	6.4
1988–1989	4.8
1989–1990	4.6
1990–1991	5.6

Source: Anwar (1996: 911).

However, 29 of the original 42 had lost their positions as leading groups by 1997. Most of the 29 that fell-off the list were Karachi-based. Moreover, the Karachi-based groups that remained on the list dropped in ranking. For instance, Adamjee, Dawood, Habib, Bawany, and Gul Ahmed all dropped to the bottom of the list in 1997.

Instead, by 1997, 24 of the leading groups were from the Punjab; 15 of these Punjab-based groups were Chiniotis. Of the top 10 positions in 1997, Punjab-based business groups held 7 of them. An additional 18 were based in Karachi, and 3 were from Khyber-Pukhtunkhwa.

There is the peril of reading too much into the above lists. Firstly, after nationalisation, many business groups diversified their investments and kept only a part of their investments in Pakistan. Secondly, after the nationalisation drive, business groups have preferred not to declare their real manufacturing or financial assets. Given the corruption in the bureaucracy, many of these groups have the clout to evade taxes and hide assets. Thirdly, this list only takes the declared manufacturing assets into account. It does not take real estate, and other similar assets, into

Table 4.25: Leading Industrial Groups 1970, 1990, 1997 (Rs Millions Nominal)

Name	All Manufacturing Assets (listed and unlisted) 1970	Name	All Manufacturing Assets (listed and unlisted) 1990	Name	All Manufacturing Assets (listed and unlisted) 1997
Dawood	557	Habib	5,781	Nishat	27,792
Saigol	556	Crescent	4,237	Saigol	15,202
Adamjee	473	Dawood	3,265	Crescent	10,586
Jalil	418	Saigol	2,618	Dewan	10,113
Shaikh	342	Wazir Ali	2,279	Ittefaq	10,000
Fancy	330	Nishat	2,279	Chakwal	9,264
Valika	352	Sapphire	1,755	Habib	7,612
Bawany	237	Lakson	1,559	Sapphire/Gulistan	7,583
Crescent	199	Fazalsons	1,384	Gul Ahmad/Al-Karam	5,220
Wazir Ali	178	Gandhara	1,344	Packages	5,168
Ghandara	163	Dewan	1,344	Chakwal	4,592
Ispahani	154	Bawany	1,213	Atlas	4,359
Habib	136	Adamjee	1,141	Hashwani	4,251
Khyber	127	Al-Noor	1,124	Bibojee-Saifullah	3,806
Nishat Group	126	Ghulam Farooq	1,091	Dawood	3,780
BECO	113	Gul Ahmad	1,066	Monnoos	3,605
Gul Ahmed	109	Ghani	1,034	Fecto	3,542
Arag	105	Pakland	1,006	Lakson	2,876
Hafiz	105	Atlas	956	Gatron	2,870
H.A. Karim	95	Hashwani	808	Fateh	2,843
Millwala	95	Service	734	Sargodha	2,743
Hyesons	94	Colony	728	Al-Noor	2,573
Dada	90	Fazal	719	Ghulam Farooq	2,465
Premier	89	Fateh	458	Ibrahim	2,333
Hussein Ebrahim	88	Ittefaq	390	United	2,237
Monnoo	79			Bawany	2,189
Maulabaksh	79			Zahoor	2,178
Adam	78			Schon	2,038
A.K. Khan	74			Dadabhoy	2,016
A.A. Ghani	71			Jehangir Elahi	2,038
Rangoonwala	68			Fazalsons	2,000
Haroon	61			Rupali	1,910
Hirjina	60			Servis	1,707
Shaffi	60			Yunus Bros	1,689
Fakir Chand	59			Tawkkal	1,678
Haji Hashan	58			Sitara	1,619
Dadabhoy	53			Colony	1,620
Shahnawaz	52			Premier	1,501
Fateh Textile	52			Shahnawaz	1,299
Noon	48	Source: 1970 figures from		Sunshine/Sunrays	1,265
Hoti	45	White (1974). 1990 figures		Fazal/Fatima	1,263
Ghulam Faruque	36	from *Herald*, June 1990, in		Calico	1,235
Haji Dost Mohammad	31	Rahman (1998). 1997 figures from Rahman (1998).			

account. While the figures may not be entirely accurate, and may not take account of assets outside the country or un-declared assets, they do reveal that there was a change in the composition of the industrial elite of Pakistan after the nationalisation of the 1970s.

To put it succinctly, from the Ayub to the Zia era, the Karachi-based Memon groups fell in ranking while the Punjab-based Chinioti groups rose.[19] With the rise of the Punjabi Chinioti business community, during the Zia period, the locus of heavy industry shifted from Karachi to the Punjab. Anita Weiss also documented the rise of this new Punjabi capitalist class (Weiss, 1991). Similar observations were made by Asad Sayeed (Sayeed, 1990).

From the 1980s onwards, Pakistan's economic policy continued to move towards neo-liberal reforms. In spite of the return to democracy in 1988, as a result of the mysterious death of General Zia in a plane crash and the formation of a new PPP government led by Benazir Bhutto, government policy continued to implement IMF-negotiated Structural Adjustment Policies (SAP). Neither the ostensibly left-of-centre PPP, nor the conservative Muslim League, nor the military dictatorship of General Musharraf, altered this fundamental neo-liberal economic framework (see Table 4.26).

In the financial sector in the 1980s, the government liberalised the entry of private and foreign banks. Relatively small banks—such as Muslim Commercial Bank and Allied Bank of Pakistan—were the first to be part-privatised, larger state-owned banks were downsized, and the State Bank was granted autonomy. From 1997 to 2001, in the second phase of financial sector reforms, partially privatised banks were fully privatised, the cost structure of banks was restructured, national savings schemes were integrated with the financial markets, the mandatory placement of foreign currency deposits was eliminated, and the State Bank was strengthened (Khan and Qayyum, 2006). However, these reforms were only partially successful in increasing deposits and strengthening the financial sector (see Khan, 2003).

Trade policy was also liberalised during the 1990s. Tariff rates were reduced dramatically, from an average of 65 per cent in the 1990s to 11 per cent by 2000. Custom duties were reduced from 13 to 4 per cent after 1996. The maximum tariff rate on imports was reduced from 225 per cent in 1986 to 25 per cent by 2005. Quantitative import restrictions

Table 4.26: Transactions with the IMF from 1 May 1984 to 31 July 2010

Year	Total		Charges and Interest Paid
	Purchases and Loans		
	Disbursements	Repayments	
1984	0	61,311,993	74,456,432
1985	0	180,683,513	113,899,666
1986	0	315,278,124	83,447,385
1987	0	326,041,678	55,305,342
1988	0	235,761,678	38,935,837
1989	467,630,000	169,408,726	42,484,071
1990	0	122,400,226	38,543,238
1991	231,660,000	72,543,877	27,050,576
1992	189,550,000	116,060,837	25,012,528
1993	88,000,000	91,360,000	25,440,657
1994	295,400,000	45,068,500	24,598,304
1995	133,950,000	115,830,000	29,506,558
1996	107,160,000	221,605,000	28,725,930
1997	205,220,000	226,183,000	26,586,526
1998	132,680,000	116,194,500	25,568,697
1999	447,490,000	172,340,834	32,156,557
2000	150,000,000	217,472,834	37,934,420
2001	401,160,000	137,102,834	40,729,596
2002	258,420,000	201,830,835	29,912,124
2003	344,560,000	420,284,002	20,533,680
2004	172,280,000	382,977,998	13,961,896
2005	0	163,905,668	9,228,292
2006	0	72,030,668	7,131,850
2007	0	97,876,664	6,090,877
2008	2,067,400,000	116,158,163	4,604,599
2009	2,101,935,000	146,359,000	42,234,727
2010	766,700,000	111,984,000	32,560,312

Source: International Monetary Fund (2010).

were removed and import duties on over 4,000 items were eliminated (Khan and Qayyum, 2006).

However, trade liberalisation, ironically, resulted in a slowdown in the growth of exports—in the 1970s and 1980s, growth in exports averaged 14.97 and 8.5 per cent per annum, respectively. But in the 1990s, it slowed down to 5.6 per cent per annum (Khan and Qayyum, 2006: 719).

Table 4.27: Growth Rates of Exports and Imports and the Degree of Openness (%)

Year	1961–1970	1971–1980	1981–1990	1991–2000
Exports (X)	6.1	15.0	8.5	5.6
Imports (M)	8.4	18.8	4.5	3.2
(X+M)/GDP	18.3	26.3	29.9	32.9

Source: Khan and Qayyum (2006: 719).

In January 1991, the government set up the Privatisation Commission. The mandate of the Commission included the privatisation of nearly all large-scale industry, such as power, oil and gas, transport, aviation, railways, ports, shipping, telecommunications, banking, insurance, and so on (see Table 4.28). According to the figures provided by the Privatisation Commission, a total of 168 units were privatised between 1991 and 2007 (see Table 0.10 in the Appendix). Hence, more than half the units nationalised by the PPP in the 1970s were privatised. From 1991 to February 2009, privatisation earned a grand total of Rs 475,421.2 million.

These neo-liberal reforms are now the subject of increasing criticism in academic literature in Pakistan. Shah has shown that, far from improving efficiency, these neo-liberal reforms were accompanied by a decline in the rate of growth in certain key industries. For instance, the textile industry sustained a loss of an average of 3 per cent during the period 1995 to 1997 (Shah, 2007: 477). Bashir has shown that the impact of liberalisation on agricultural exports was 'relatively modest' (2003: 956). Financial sector liberalisation only produced gains in profit efficiency in the period immediately following privatisation. In subsequent years, only one private bank could be differentiated from the state-run banks in terms of profit efficiency (Bonaccorsi di Patti, Hardy

2005). Khan has shown that the impact of privatisation of industry was negative on both employment and output (Khan, 2003: 530). Siddique and Iqbal found that trade liberalisation had a long-running negative relationship to output (2005). Zafar and Butt noted that trade liberalisation is 'acting as a stimulator of external debt accumulation' (2008: 14). Anwar's detailed study demonstrated that, in the case of Pakistan, not only did liberalisation not improve growth but it contributed to increasing unemployment, poverty, decline in the growth rates of large-scale manufacturing, loss of government revenue, and increasing indebtedness (2002: 17–18). A number of poverty studies have indicated that poverty—which had declined, from an average of 40 per cent during the 1960s, to 20 per cent around the 1980s—increased to around 30 per cent during the 1990s (Chaudhry et al., 2006: 819).[20]

Table 4.28: Privatisations by Sectors, from 1991 to February 2009

Telecommunications	187,359.9
Capital Markets, Banking and Finance	156,827.4
Energy Sector	51,756.1
Fertiliser	38,941.1
Cement	16,176.9
Chemical	1,642.5
Industrial Units	1,101.9
Ghee	841.7
Textile	370.7
Rice	235.6
Engineering	182.5
Roti Plants	90.7
Mineral	6.1

Source: Table 0.10 in the Appendix.

Arguably the most dramatic change in the balance of class forces during the period of neo-liberal reforms was the decimation of workers' unions. During this period, both the number of unions and union membership continued to decline (see Table 4.29).

Table 4.29: Union Membership by Industry, 1995 and 2002 (top ten industries)

Industry	1995	2002
Textiles	63,658	46,710
Food	33,677	20,642
Banks	29,951	14,766
Municipalities	28,733	8,730
Transport	19,327	7,424
Irrigation	18,750	6,760
Docks	16,658	5,590
Mining	16,235	4,520
Electricity	11,202	4,503
Engineering	11,107	3,307
Total of Top Ten Industries	249,298	122,952
Participation in all Industries	340,569	138,456
Participation Rate of Top Ten Industries in Total Union Membership	73.20%	88.80%

Source: Siddique et al. (2006: 998).

In 1995, there were 1,635 unions with a membership of approximately 341,000. But by 2002, there were 1,201 registered unions with approximately 138,000 members. In other words, from 1995 to 2002 there was an overall decline of nearly 60 per cent in union membership and 25 per cent in the number of unions (see Table 4.30). In 2000, the unionised section of Pakistan's economically active population was only about 0.7 per cent (Candland, 2007: 46).[21] The union density rate—that is, the total union members to total employed minus self-employed and domestic employees—was only 0.76 per cent in 2002 (Siddique et al., 2006: 998).

At the same time, the decline in union militancy can be gauged by the fact that, despite the growth of employment, workdays lost because of strikes fell by over 80 per cent (from 63,626 in 1995 to 12,160 in 2002) (Siddique et al., 2006: 998).

Together with this decline in working class militancy, changes were made to the law that made it harder for workers to organise into unions. According to a 1997 Supreme Court judgement, the right to strike was no longer recognised as a fundamental right under Section 17(1) of the Constitution.

Table 4.30: Changes in Union Membership between 1995 and 2002 (%)

Industry	Percentage Decline
Textile	–26.6
Transport	+6.8
Docks	–11.4
Mining	–46.2
Banks	–75.2
Municipalities	–76.5
Electricity	–69.5
Tobacco	–1.0
Commerce	–10.2
Chemicals	–65.4
Food	–86.6
Total	–59.3

Source: Siddique et al. (2006: 998).

The Industrial Relations Ordinance of 2002 deprived workers of several rights that had been won in the 1970s (Ansari and Arshad, 2006: 207–222). For instance, the IRO 2002 reduced worker representation in plant-level management. The Management Committee and Joint Management Board, in which workers previously had 50 per cent representation, were altogether abolished. The new law reduced worker representation in the Joint Works Council[22] to 40 per cent. Moreover, it stipulated that the head of the Joint Works Council would be selected from the management. The authority of the Labour Courts was reduced. And, certain Export Processing Zones were carved out in which no labour laws applied at all.

CONCLUSION

This chapter set out to examine the development of industrial relations in Pakistan. However, owing to the dearth of research material and in-depth data on this subject, its conclusions can only remain very general.

Nonetheless, these general conclusions offer us a broad portrait of the overall class structure of industrial relations in Pakistan.

One of the most significant structural transformations is the rapid expansion of the population and its increasing urbanisation. In the last century, the population of the region that is now Pakistan expanded more than 10 times, from 16 million at the turn of the century to over 160 million at the century's close. This rapid expansion occurred mainly after independence from British colonial rule. Whether liberation from the structures of colonial rule was a factor in this sustained population growth requires further inquiry.

The significance of these broad transformations, with respect to the class structure of Pakistan, cannot be overstated. The entire edifice of the AMP in India was constructed on the foundation of the small and isolated village communities. Although cities were always the seat of power in Asiatic India, they were not the locus of economic production and surplus accumulation. Not only were India's ancient cities sustained by the surplus extracted from village communities but, in an economic sense, they played a predatory role in relation to the countryside. The small-scale production undertaken in the karkhanas was mainly for the ruling class of the cities and was rarely intended for trade with the countryside. The ruling class—including the jagirdars, mansabdars, and their retainers—lived in these often-walled and fortified cities, creating the impression that the cities resembled extended armed camps (see Chapter 3 for details).

Though this portrayal may not be entirely accurate and, indeed, has been challenged by many contemporary historians, nonetheless, it does underscore the fact that even though the centres of political power were ancient cities, the economic surplus necessary to sustain these cities came from the village communities. Hence, village communities were the economic foundation of the AMP in India.

In contrast, the last century of social and economic development, the rapid expansion of the overall population and, most importantly, of massive urban centres indicates that the ancient mode of production, based on the village communities, is being superseded by a new mode of production. Today, the principal locus of economic production and surplus extraction is no longer merely the agricultural production of the village community, but urban and semi-rural manufacturing and services. A half-century ago, manufacturing and services accounted for less than half the output and less than a third of the overall employment. Today, non-agricultural production accounts for more than three-fourths of output and more than half of overall employment (Zaidi, 2005: 4). Data from industry divisions and occupation divisions reveals the same trend—of a structural transformation away from agriculture and towards manufacturing and services.

Whether one considers this transformation more or less rapid in comparison to other societies during the twentieth century—as is the concern of most economic planners—is another matter. The point that this study wishes to underscore is that in relation to its own history— that is, the history of South Asia—this transformation is historically unprecedented and indicative of the destruction of the AMP and the rise of a new social formation.

The destruction of the AMP and the rise of capitalism is hardly a novel conclusion. However, the interesting insights from these very broad statistics are that, firstly, this process of transition to capitalism, though initiated by colonialism, actually appears to accelerate after liberation from colonialism. Anti-colonial writers, both nationalists and Marxists, have long emphasised that colonialism was a fetter on the modernisation of those societies. The rapid development of the population, urbanisation, and the structural transformation towards services and manufacturing in the late twentieth century seems to confirm this anti-colonial view.

Secondly, the mode of production that seems to be replacing the AMP at the mass level is not large-scale capitalism but petty commodity production and small-scale capitalism. This conclusion seems to be supported by the data on employment. Of the overall labour force—a significant portion of which is unaccounted for in official statistics because it is composed of women who work in their own homes as domestic workers—about half are characterised as wage labourers. Permanent wage employment in agriculture is very small (see Chapter 3). Of the non-agricultural labour force, about 70 to 80 per cent are employed in enterprises that employ less than 10 individuals—that is, about 21 million, out of 28 million non-agricultural workers, are involved in petty commodity production and small-scale capitalism.

Thus, even though large-scale industry dominates output—producing 17 per cent of the overall GDP, while employing only about 3 per cent of the overall employment—the everyday working experience, and hence the social formation of non-agricultural production, is numerically dominated by petty commodity production and small-scale capitalism.

Why is it, then, that in spite of half a century of post-colonial capitalist development, the industrial class structure of Pakistan remains dominated by petty commodity production and small-scale capitalism? On the one hand, there can be no doubt that the processes of destruction of petty commodity production and small-scale capitalism, at the hands of large-scale industry, can be nothing but a protracted historical process. On the other hand, the peculiar form of capitalist development, encouraged by the state and ruling class of Pakistan, must be examined.

During the early period of Pakistan's history, deliberate policies of industrial concentration were encouraged. These policies were justified by the argument that industrial concentration would encourage the rate of savings and investments to rise. Whether one examines the period of the transition of merchant to industrial capital or the state-led corporate industrial development under the PIDC and PICIC, the so-called functional inequality of the 1960s or the state-created trade monopolies through licensing, the final result of these policies was increasing class and national conflict.

By 1968, there was widespread unrest all over Pakistan and, by 1971, East Pakistan separated and became Bangladesh. The PPP government in Pakistan undertook some social democratic measures that may have led to a different model of capitalist development. However, these policies were brought to a quick end after only five years when the army overthrew the government in 1977. Under the cloak of Islamic fundamentalism, the state more or less returned to the framework of the pre-Bhutto period. Together with the return to democracy in 1988 came the shift towards neo-liberalism that more or less continues to this day.

What would have been the overall results had the Pakistani state adopted an alternative model of capitalist development? Would it have resulted in a more rapid structural transformation towards industrial development? Putting aside speculation, the comparative studies of other economies at similar stages of development may provide some insight into such questions. What one can say, with a certain degree of confidence, is that the current model of capitalist development adopted by the state of Pakistan has given rise to a small industrial sector and, by comparison, a gigantic sector of petty commodity production and small-scale capitalism.

The research implications of the numeric dominance of petty commodity production and of small-scale capitalism, with respect to class formation of the working class, are also interesting. In a society where about 80 per cent of the non-agricultural working class is involved in establishments that employ fewer than 10 individuals, can one expect an organised labour movement to rise up at the national level? We have seen in this chapter how unionised workers are a tiny fraction of the working population and are mainly restricted to large-scale industry. Workers involved in petty commodity production and small-scale capitalism are so few in number in any given enterprise, so scattered across enterprises, and so easily replaceable that they have little, if any, collective power.

Furthermore, one needs to investigate the extent to which petty commodity production and small-scale capitalism is conducive to the formation of class-consciousness. The identity of interest that emerges from collective work and collective struggles is absent in enterprises where ties of caste, blood, patronage, and so on tend to bond the working individual to their superiors. Asiatic forms of bondage can easily morph to become an integral part of petty commodity production and small-scale capitalism.

One also needs to examine the attitude of the owners of petty commodity production and small-scale capitalism towards the labour movement. As a petty bourgeois, the owners of these enterprises may, in fact, be hostile to the workers' movement and look to the big bourgeois for political and social leadership.

Last, but certainly not least, a line of further inquiry can be undertaken with respect to the cultural and ideological impact of the numeric dominance of petty commodity production and small-scale capitalism. If one accepts that cultural and ideological movements are influenced by and, in turn, influence the character of classes in any society, then the presence of petty commodity production and small-scale capitalism—where various remnants of pre-capitalist relations continue in new form—must also have an ideological impact. It is not merely the large-landed estates, but also the continuing existence of Asiatic remnants in the terrain of petty commodity production and small-scale capitalism, that may be fertile ground for the continuation of aspects of ideas that have their origin in the AMP. For instance, the continuing dominance of caste, even in urban areas, may find a solid economic foundation in petty commodity production and small-scale capitalism.

Unfortunately, these lines of research cannot be pursued within the context of this limited study. What one can conclude, however, is that although there has been a massive transformation away from the AMP towards capitalism, employment figures demonstrate that the numerically dominant form of capitalism is petty commodity production and small-scale capitalism. It is within this sphere of petty commodity production and small-scale capitalism that non-waged pre-capitalist labour relations are more likely to survive.

NOTES

1. For detailed contemporary studies of Pakistan's population, see Kemal et al. (2003) and Mahmood (2009).
2. From 1990 to 2004, the dependency ratio—that is the sum of the population under 15 and over 64 divided by the population in the intermediate range of 15–64—is expected to decline (Lee, 2003). For more detailed studies of declining fertility in Pakistan, see Afzal and Kiani (1993), Alam et al. (1983), Farooqi (1984), Feeney and Alam (2003), Sathar (1989; 1992; 1997), Sathar and Casterline (2001), Soomro (1986).
3. Till 1972, an area with more than 5000 inhabitants was considered urban. After 1981, the definition was changed. Areas were considered urban if they had a 'municipality, town committee, and cantonment board'. The result is an overall underestimation of urban growth after 1981. For a detailed discussion, see Reza Ali (2002: 4555).
4. For more detailed studies of urbanisation in Pakistan, see Abbasi (1987), Arif (2003), Arif and Hamid (2007), Arif and Ibrahim (1998a), Hashmi (1965), Hashmi and Sultan (1998), Helbock (1975b; 1975a), Irfan (1981).
5. For a detailed discussion of female labour force participation rates in Pakistan, see Afzal (1987) and Shah (1989).
6. Only the order of the categories of the FBS (Pakistan) is slightly different from the order of the ISCO–1968 categories.
7. These official statistics tend to overestimate the actual strength of the trade unions (see Keddie, 1957: 581–582).
8. In the mid-1950s, Pakistan moved into the United States' sphere of influence by becoming a formal member of the anti-communist military pacts of SEATO (the South East Asian Treaty Organisation which included the Philippines, Thailand, and Pakistan) and CENTO (the Central Treaty Organisation—Iraq, Turkey, Iran, Pakistan, and the UK). At the same time, the Communist Party of Pakistan was banned in 1954. Faiz Ahmed Faiz was imprisoned and charged with treason in the famous Rawalpindi Conspiracy Case. By 1958, the possession of communist literature was a punishable offence and all university libraries were purged of Marxist books (Candland, 2007: 47).

9. The Basic Democracy system divided the population into 80,000 geographical units, with an average electorate of 1000 each. These units were responsible for electing a 'basic democrat' who would then elect the country's President. On this basis, General Ayub Khan was elected President by a simple 'yes' or 'no' answer to the question: 'Have you confidence in President Ayub Khan?'

10. Arguably the only lasting positive contribution of the new laws brought in by Ayub was the relatively progressive Family Laws Ordinance (1962). The religious parties, especially the Jamaat-e Islami, opposed these laws as 'unIslamic', underscoring the reactionary nature of their opposition to Ayub Khan.

11. Under the Export Bonus Scheme (EBS), exporters became eligible to receive a voucher entitling the exporter to an import licence equivalent to a certain value of the exported commodity (Brutton and Bose, 1962; Zaidi, 2005: 98).

12. The Bonus Voucher Scheme enabled exporters of certain manufactured goods to receive bonus vouchers equivalent to a specified percentage of the foreign exchange earned.

13. To import any commodity in the 1950s, one had to obtain an import licence from the import trade controller and register it with the State Bank of Pakistan.

14. Commodities listed on the Open General Licence (OGL) could be imported without an import licence. The Free List was composed of items that did not require a licence of any sort for their import. The number of items on the Free List was increased from 4 items to 50 in 1964.

15. As Table 0.9 in the Appendix demonstrates, the railway workers were the largest proportion of organised labour in the 1950s. For instance, in 1952, railway workers made up half of the entire unionised working class. After the development of the textile industry, their share in the organised working class movement shrank and the role of the textile unions in private enterprises became more prominent.

16. Those on the Exit Control List were prohibited from travelling and asked to surrender their passports.

17. General Ziaul Haq put Bhutto on trial on allegations of murder and, on 4 April 1979, despite the split verdict of the Supreme Court and appeals of clemency from foreign heads of state, Bhutto was executed. In the same month, the Saur Revolution erupted in Afghanistan and Pakistan became a frontline state in the Cold War. General Zia indefinitely postponed elections and embarked on a plan of 'Islamisation'. This Islamisation program also provided the ideological justification for the CIA-funded Mujahideen 'jihad' against the Afghan communists and the reformist social democracy of the PPP.

18. For detailed studies on the impact on Pakistan's economy of migration to the Middle East, see Abbasi (1983), Amjad (1986), Arif (1999), Arif and Irfan (1997), Burney (1987), and Gilani (1981).

19. Of the 725 companies listed on the Karachi Stock Exchange, the Chiniotis and Memons together own 206 (Rahman).

20. Poverty studies include Naseem (1973; 1977), Alauddin (1975), Wasay (1977), Mujahid (1978), Ercelan (1990), Ahmad (1993), Altaf et al. (1993), Amjad and Kemal (1997), Zingel (1998), Ali and Tahir (1999), Jafri (1999), Qureshi and Arif (2001), Arif et al. (2001), Anwar and Qureshi (2003), Anwar et al. (2004), and Anwar (2006).

21. The comparative figure for India is 1.7 per cent.

22. Joint Works Council is the body that handles all industrial disputes.

Conclusion

Since civilisation is founded on the exploitation of one class by another class, its whole development proceeds in a constant contradiction. Every step forward in production is at the same time a step backwards in the position of the oppressed class, that is, of the great majority. Whatever benefits some necessarily injures the others; every fresh emancipation of one class is necessarily a new oppression for another class.

Engels (1891: 217)

This study has argued the case for a distinct path of historical development of South Asia. Chapter 1 reviewed orientalist writing and the literature on the AMP. It concluded that the AMP has four essential features. These are:

1) Natural economy
2) Absence of private property in land
3) Public works as the basis of the state
4) Surplus extraction by the state

Chapter 2 addressed the principal objections and critiques raised within the literature, with respect to each of the above-mentioned four features. It argued that the defining feature of any mode of production is the mode of surplus extraction. Given that the principal mode of surplus extraction in Mughal India was a system where land was not private property, and the form of surplus was land revenue extracted collectively from village communities, it seems untenable to accept Mughal India as feudal. Instead, the thesis of the AMP appears more convincing.

The chapter also investigated the specific path of the transition to capitalism in South Asia. It argued that this path of transition could not be put in the same category as the republican or Junkers path. Instead, it proposed the idea of a colonial path of capitalist transition, whose principal features are as follows:

1) Foreign domination
2) Siphoning the surplus
3) Capitalism planted upon the AMP

This path of transition gave rise to a transitory form that combined the features of the AMP with capitalism. More specifically, it gave rise to private property and commodity production without the development of wage labour. The study terms this phenomenon 'Asiatic capitalism'.

Chapter 3 examined the evidence in relation to the concept of Asiatic capitalism within the agrarian political economy of contemporary Pakistan. It showed that the British introduced private property in land, in the region that is today Pakistan, between 1846 and 1870 through the policy of Permanent Settlement. At the same time, the extraction of land revenue from village communities—a feature of the AMP—was the financial foundation of the colonial state. The introduction of private property and commodity production led to a dramatic transformation in class relations, which can be gauged by examining the statistics on peasant differentiation and the transformation of tenure relations. These trends indicate the development of capitalist relations. This transition to capitalism was not the product of the breakup of Asiatic relations at the hands of a peasant revolution, but occurred through the slow metamorphosis of Asiatic relations into capitalist relations. However, the statistics on wage labour demonstrate that permanent wage labour accounted for less than 4 per cent of the overall workforce. Casual wage labour was reported on about 40 per cent of the farms. Hence, it is quite clear that the dominant labour relations are not wage labour. The evidence does not contradict the view that Asiatic labour relations continue to exist on large landed estates, as well as on small farms engaged in petty commodity production and small-scale capitalism.

The last chapter examined the empirical evidence for the existence of Asiatic capitalism in the industrial sector. At the macro level, it identified the important changes in the class structure of Pakistan. The expansion of the population and urbanisation are two key changes that have transformed the country in the last half-century. This structural transformation undermined the AMP, which was based on small isolated village communities. However, the mode of production that has numerically dominated manufacturing is not large-scale capitalism but petty commodity production and small-scale capitalism. Of the non-agricultural work force, 70 to 80 per cent are employed in enterprises of less than 10 employees each. About 21 million, out of the 28 million, non-agricultural workers are involved in petty commodity production and small-scale capitalism. While large-scale manufacturing dominates output, it is petty commodity production and small-scale capitalism that is, by far, the economic relation that the vast majority of people encounter.

Petty commodity production and small-scale capitalism continue to dominate employment because of the industrial policies pursued by the State. With the exception of a brief populist period of five years in the 1970s, these policies have fostered industrial concentration under the pretext that they would increase savings and investment. While this model has not resulted in the development of a broad-based large-scale industrial sector, it has given rise to a small industrial sector that dominates output as well as a massive informal sector that dominates employment.

The conclusions of this study are limited by the nature of the questions addressed. To understand the class structure of Pakistan in its entirety, it is not enough to merely look at the economic relations of production but also to look at the terrain of politics, culture, and ideology. Secondly, even with respect to questions of political economy, the study has not looked at several questions of vital importance—for instance, the transformation of the Asiatic state into a colonial and neo-colonial state, the role of the military in Pakistan's economy, the tribal systems of class power in the North and West of the country, the economic position of women, the political economy of national, racial, and religious oppression, and many other questions.

In summary, this study advanced three hypotheses. First, pre-capitalist relations of South Asia were characteristic of the AMP and not feudalism. Second, the transition of South Asia to capitalism was distinct from the transition, through the republican or Junkers path, in Europe. South Asia's transition was through the colonial path. Third, this colonial path of transition gave rise to a transitory form that combined elements of capitalism and the AMP. This transitory form is termed Asiatic capitalism. Asiatic capitalism characterises contemporary class relations in the agrarian political economy of Pakistan, together with the existence of a small industrial sector and predominantly petty commodity production and small-scale capitalism in manufacture. These conclusions, whether accepted in their entirety or in part, have several implications for further study. Here are a few that follow on from the conclusions of the study.

AMP AND HISTORICAL MATERIALISM

The view that all societies follow the same stages of development enjoys wide currency across ideological schools. In the field of modernisation theory, one confronts Rostow's (1960) 'economic take-off', Huntington's (1966) 'expanded participation', Chalmers Johnson's (1966) 'multiple dysfunction', Jeffrey Sachs' (2005) 'ladder of development', and so on. Neo-classical economics is largely devoid of a theory of history. However, to the extent that it addresses questions pertaining to economic history, its central concern is economic growth as a linear progression (for instance, Arthur Lewis' Dual-Sector Model) (Lewis, 1955).

Moreover, unilinear evolutionism can be found in strains of Marxism. Despite the cautionary note by Marx that his sketch of the development of capitalism in Europe should not be utilised as a historico-philosophic theory of the general path that all societies were pre-destined to travel, many Marxists uphold that all societies develop through the same five modes of production—primitive communism, slavery, feudalism, capitalism, and socialism. For instance, Soviet writer S. Ol'denburg argued that 'The history of the Orient knows the same formations as those of the West' (Sawer, 1977: 76). Similarly, Soviet author Godes wrote that the 'Orient, in a very unique fashion, went through the same stages of social development as Europe' (Godes, 1981: 103). The same sort of unilinearism can be observed in Cohen's interpretation of Marxism that argues that all societies are destined to pass through the same stages of development as a functional necessity (Cohen, 1978).

However, Marx and Engels never held such a mechanical view of history. For instance, it can be shown that they were of the view that German tribes never passed through a period of slave society; the Greeks and Romans never passed through the AMP; Asia never evolved through slave or feudal society; and many African groups were forced directly into colonial capitalism. In summary, Marx and Engels recognised that history, in fact, develops in dialectical motion along multiple paths.

Moreover, Marx and Engels were just as open to the possibility of decay and the destruction of societies as they were to the historical or economic progress of societies. For instance, in the Communist Manifesto, Marx wrote that the class struggle could also result 'in the common ruin of the contending classes' (Marx and Engels, 1998). The concept of historical linearity, whether along a single-line or multiple-lines, is an attempt to substitute a mechanical developmentalism for historical materialism.

Categorising pre-colonial South Asia as feudal is essential for unilinear evolutionism. However, the inclusion of pre-colonial Asia in the category of feudalism can only be accomplished by broadening the definition of feudalism. This definitional broadening of feudalism undermines the clarity, definiteness, and explanatory power of the term. In the words of Frank Perlin (1985: 88), feudalism becomes:

> . . . a term with little analytical value, one that merely spreads confusion and prevents clear thought on the question at issue—a mask used to cover ignorance and intellectual uncertainty.

Arif Dirlik called this the 'universalisation of feudalism' brought about by a redefinition of feudalism so that it could 'accommodate disparate economic and social structures' (Dirlik, 1985: 212–215). Feudalism becomes, in the words of Harbans Mukhia, a 'catch-all category' (Mukhia, 1985: 229). Mukhia was quite right when he said that (ibid.):

> such a category can hardly serve as a rigorous definition capable of distinguishing one medieval society from another. We can speak of any pre-capitalist system as a world system only by reducing both the categories (of the world system and the pre-capitalist system) to considerable flabbiness.

Thus, the result of trying to fit the history of Asia, or in this case colonial India, into a European historical schema also results, firstly, in the broadening of the term 'feudalism' at the expense of clarity, definiteness, and explanatory power. Secondly, in a unilinear evolutionist view, that quite simply does not accord with the known facts of history.

The AMP helps to differentiate between, and highlight, the distinctive features of pre-colonial relations in India from Medieval Europe. By pinpointing these features, the AMP opens up new possibilities for comparative research with other pre-capitalist societies. Whether we talk of Asia as a whole, South Asia as a region, or Pakistan as a country, the one notion this thesis would like to impress upon the reader is that the attempt to fit the history of non-European societies into a schematic of European history is deeply problematic. It is, at best, a nationalist response that is the product of a period when struggles in India were centred on achieving political, social, and economic equality with the Europeans.

Take, for instance, the problem of the periodisation of Indian history. For Marx and Engels, the fall of the Roman Empire divided the history of pre-capitalist Western civilisation into two periods: ancient (Greco-Roman) and feudal (Medieval). That the fall of the Roman Empire was a period of qualitative transformation has long been accepted by Western thinkers and continues to invite vast scholarly interest even today. Therefore, it comes as no surprise that for Marx and Engels it also constituted a nodal point, or a point where society changed qualitatively from one mode of production to another.

Attempts to find such a nodal point in Asian history starkly demonstrate the futility of applying European stages of development to Asian history. Chattopadhyaya pointed out that leading historians of India have a spread of 1500 years for the beginning of feudalism (Chattopadhyaya, 1974: 203). For example, Kosambi argued that feudalism began as early as the second century (Kosambi, 1956), while Sharma claimed that it began around the fifth to eighth century and ended around AD 1200 (Sharma, 1965). Nurul Hasan applied the term only to the Mughal Empire, spanning the sixteenth to the nineteenth centuries (Hasan, 1973: 1–2). In other words, according to leading Indian historians, feudalism could have begun at any time from the second century to the sixteenth century. L.S. Vasil'ev stated that a very similar problem exists for those attempting to cram 3000 years of Chinese history into the European historical schema (Sawer, 1977: 100). This criticism is not meant to imply that Asian history does not have nodal points. But, it does indicate that the effort to fit Asian history into a European schema relies on very subjective criteria.

CASTE SYSTEM AND ASIATIC STAGNATION

Karl Marx wrote, 'Indian society has no history at all, at least no known history. What we call its history, is but the history of the successive intruders who founded their empires on the passive basis of that unresisting and unchanging society' (Marx, 1853). This view has caused great consternation, especially among the nationalist historians of India. However, there is an aspect of this statement that requires deeper analysis.

Marx and Engels defined history in terms of the development of the social division of labour and the class structure (Marx and Engels, 1998). Therefore, the phrase 'India has no history' means that India did not demonstrate any fundamental changes in the social division of labour or class structure.

The very existence of the caste system, dating back to some 3,500 years (if we estimate that the Hindu holy scriptures of the Vedas are from 1500 BC), is itself evidence of the relatively unchanging nature of the social division of labour of pre-colonial India. Caste is nothing but a division of labour that is hereditary. How can hereditary occupations exist in a non-stagnant society? Castes can only exist in societies in which the division of labour is relatively stagnant. In a word, the caste system is premised upon a relatively unchanging division of labour. The view that India was without history underscores the fact that the caste system of India was based on a relatively stagnant social division of labour. In a word, the very existence of the caste system is the best proof of Asiatic stagnation.

ASIATIC CAPITALISM AND CULTURE

By identifying the AMP as being central to the organisation of social division of labour in India, the thesis poses new questions for the re-examination of popular culture. Take, for instance, the relationship between the caste system, women's oppression, and folk culture.

Hereditary castes can only be maintained if there is no intermarriage of the castes; in other words, the caste system is based on endogamy (that is, marrying within your own caste or biraderi[1]). Hence, patriarchal traditions to ensure endogamy—such as arranged marriages within the biradari or cousin marriages—which are quite common among Pakistanis 'contribute to the strengthening of extended patriarchies' (Gazdar, 2007: 5). On the other hand, love affairs outside one's biradari inevitably go against the grain of the caste system. Till today, couples who marry for love rarely enjoy the support of their families. In fact,

Pakistani newspapers routinely contain stories about couples who are killed, kidnapped, or privately incarcerated to protect the 'honour' of their families.

Interestingly, while the caste system relegated love affairs to the lowest and most contemptible position, rebellions against the caste system raised the concept of love to the level of divinity. This relationship, in part, explains why the extremely popular Sufi tradition unites rebellion/ love with divinity. For instance, the four most revered epic poems, considered classics of Punjabi literature, are Heer Ranjha, Sassi Punhu, Sohni Mahiwal, and Mirza Sahiban. All these are about love affairs outside the biraderi that force the lovers into a rebellion against their families and end in tragedy. The opening line of the most famous of these poems, 'Heer', by Waris Shah (1706–1798), begins with the lines: 'Awal hamad khuda da vird karye, Ishq kita su jag da mool mian, Pehlan aap hi rabb ne ishq kita, Te mashooq he nabi rasool mian' (Shah, 1766).[2] To put it crudely, the essence of this rebellious Sufi poetry is that God is the first lover, God created the value of the world in terms of love, and hence, to deny love is a sin against God. Naturally, the dominant biraderis do not see it that way. Until today, the Siyals[3] rebuke Heer by saying that 'it never rains at the mazaar (grave) of Heer'.[4]

On another level, verbal abuse and discrimination against working castes are facts of everyday life in contemporary Pakistan. Discrimination in education, legal affairs, work, exclusion from social and religious gatherings under the ideology of ritual purity, and even rape and violence are part of the mechanisms through which the subordinate position of the lower castes is maintained (Gazdar, 2007: 5–9). In certain rare cases, some castes have been able to escape their fate of subjugation. Groups of individuals were, at times, able to change their status by running away and relocating to other areas—for instance, the Khaskhelis of Sindh were, until a few generations ago, the slaves of the Talpur Mirs. Similarly, the Darzadas of Makran have managed to change their social status since the 1980s by migrating to Muscat and through mass recruitment in the Royal Oman Army (Gazdar, 2007; 9; Hooper and Hamid, 2003: 10, 22–23). This history of caste struggle is the key to understanding the history of class struggle in South Asia. The ideological, cultural, and political manifestations of such struggles can be more deeply appreciated by putting the caste system, understood in class terms, at the centre of any analysis of culture and politics.

RESEARCH IMPLICATIONS OF ASIATIC CAPITALISM

The thesis had argued that the transition of agrarian relations in South Asia is occurring through the metamorphosis of Asiatic relations into capitalist relations. In a word, capitalist relations are not developing as a spatially distinct sector within agriculture. Instead, the whole agrarian economy is undergoing a slow metamorphosis from pre-capitalist to capitalist relations.

Hence, any research methodology that sets out to identify a purely capitalist sector, that can be compared with a pre-capitalist sector, will inevitably underestimate the development of capitalism as it would fail to note the metamorphosis of pre-capitalist relations. Moreover, there are some economic categories that make no sense outside capitalism—for example, profit rate—and can be systematically misreported or mis-represented in transitional holdings. It follows that any estimation of the development of capitalism should include the development of wage payments, utilisation of machines, market orientation, and so on for the whole of the agrarian economy over a period of time. This insight is also in keeping with the objections raised by various other authors regarding the study by Rudra et al. (see for instance Rao, 1990; Patnaik, 1990b, 1990a).

ASIATIC CAPITALISM AND THE SUPERSTRUCTURE

In contemporary Pakistan, one can observe the continuing existence of the caste system, honour killings, indentured labour, and other forms of extra-economic coercion of workers, peasants, women, and minorities. Is this superstructure of oppression merely a remnant of a pre-capitalist mode of production? For instance, Bandyopadhyaya argued that this pre-capitalist superstructure has 'over the centuries acquired a measure of autonomy, and in some ways behaves independently of the relations of production' (Bandyopadhyaya, 2002).

However, Chapters 3 and 4 demonstrate that, in agriculture, the prevalence of muzarat and 'family labour', and in industry the dominance of petty commodity production and small-scale capitalism, amply demonstrate that the working experience of the vast majority of the working people of Pakistan is based on non-wage based labour relations. The widespread prevalence of these non-waged labour relations supports the view that the pre-capitalist superstructure is not merely a remnant that is surviving in the context of an otherwise thoroughly capitalist era. On the contrary, this pre-capitalist superstructure is connected to the real economic relations of contemporarily existing Asiatic capitalism.

Furthermore, the political implications of the autonomy, or connection, of the pre-capitalist superstructure to the economic base are also not insignificant. The theory that the pre-capitalist superstructure is a mere ideological remnant, with little or no relation to the real economic foundations of society, inevitably leads to the conclusion that it can be overcome, purely or mainly, within the realm of ideas. However, Chapters 3 and 4 tend to point in the opposite direction, implying that this pre-capitalist superstructure is not merely a remnant of, but is very much rooted in the contemporary class structure of Pakistan in the form of Asiatic capitalism. Moreover, the slow metamorphosis of Asiatic relations to capitalist relations certainly amends this pre-capitalist superstructure, but poses no fundamental, antagonistic, radical, or revolutionary challenge to it.

It follows that this superstructure of oppression, which is embedded in the economic base, will not die out simply through the spread and further consolidation of economic growth. On the contrary, it is the economic base itself that supports, and is supported by, these ideas and social practices. These Asiatic relations can only be destroyed through a combination of a battle of ideas and a struggle against those real oppressive economic relations. In other words, the destruction of these oppressive relations requires a fundamental transformation in the very class structure of Asiatic capitalism.

WHERE DO WE GO FROM HERE?

In conclusion, recognising the distinct path of development also implies that the further transformation of Pakistan will be equally distinct from European historical paths. In other words, the schematic of pure categories of bourgeois-democratic and socialist revolutions in the context of Pakistan, and even South Asia, perhaps need to be re-examined. The bourgeois transformation of India and Pakistan is underway, but without the equivalent of the French Revolution or the Junkers transition—provided one accepts the interpretation of the French Revolution as a bourgeois-democratic revolution, and the Junkers transition as a metamorphosis from feudalism to capitalism.

There are, of course, class struggles over control of the neo-colonial state. For instance, the thesis mentions labour struggles from 1968. However, these struggles should not be considered the equivalents of the French Revolution, though there are always certain similarities between historical events. In other words, these were not bourgeois-democratic revolutions against a feudal monarchy, but were, arguably, struggles of a rising democratic, and even nascent, socialist movement. However, what makes these struggles distinct from European struggles is the specific configuration of class forces which are the product of Asiatic capitalism.

Lastly, recognising the distinct path of development also provides a new insight into the ambivalent relationship of various classes in Pakistan towards the capitalist West. These contradictions of the colonial path of capitalist modernisation of Asiatic society create their own unique contradictions in those societies. On the one hand, capitalist modernisation, secularism, democracy, and socialism originated in the West; on the other, this capitalist West is the cause of centuries of colonial rule that devastated the lives of millions of people. On the one hand, slavish worship of capitalist modernity; on the other, a search for a non-Western identity that inexorably leads to reactionary ideologies. On the one hand, sections of society that are completely westernised and more at home in London or New York than in Lahore or Karachi; on the other, sections of society opposed to westernisation and aspiring to re-create an Islamic Khilafat. On the one hand, a small bourgeois class linked to global capitalism; on the other, a reactionary form of anti-imperialism that aspires to the restoration of pre-capitalist relations. On the one hand, ideological submission to the economic and scientific superiority of the West; on the other, a hatred for modernity and an intense romance with even the most oppressive practices of the past. These contradictions were captured eloquently by Engels (1891: 217): 'every step forward is at the same time a step backwards.'

NOTES

1. Biraderi is tribal lineage.
2. Translation: First of all, let us acknowledge God; who has made love the worth of the world sir; it was God Himself that first loved; and the prophet is His beloved Sir.
3. The caste in which Heer was born
4. Leftist poetry of the late twentieth century, such as the Progressive Writers Movement, continued this tradition by utilising the ghazal (love song) as a form of protest poetry.

Appendix

TABLE 0.1: DISTRIBUTION OF EMPLOYED PERSONS BY MAJOR INDUSTRY DIVISION PAKISTAN RURAL AND URBAN (%)

Year	Agriculture, Forestry, Hunting and Fishing	Mining and Quarrying	Manufacturing	Electricity, Gas and Water	Construction	Wholesale and Rental Trade and Restaurants and Hotels	Transport, Storage and Communica-tion	Financing, Insurance, Real Estate and Business Services	Community, Social and Personal Services
1968–69	55.79	0.03	15.63	0.36	3.70	10.33	4.84		9.13
1969–70	57.03	0.12	15.45	0.41	3.93	9.89	4.73		8.20
1970–71	57.58	0.26	14.99	0.25	3.60	10.88	4.88		7.38
1971–72	57.32	0.45	12.47	3.41	0.37	9.89	4.84	0.86	7.27
1974–75	54.80	0.15	13.63	4.20	0.49	11.09	4.87	0.67	9.78
1978–79	52.65	0.14	14.52	4.92	0.74	11.08	4.73	0.86	10.10
1982–83	52.73	0.10	13.44	4.80	1.13	11.94	4.59	0.82	10.19
1984–85	50.56	0.17	13.67	5.60	0.69	11.54	5.20	0.88	11.07
1985–86	54.01	0.26	13.14	5.24	0.52	11.40	4.42	0.94	10.01
1986–87	49.24	0.20	14.00	6.01	0.73	12.05	5.25	0.77	11.48
1987–88	51.15	0.15	12.69	6.38	0.59	11.92	4.89	0.71	11.39
1990–91	47.45	0.15	12.23	6.62	0.83	13.24	5.24	0.89	13.27
1991–92	48.27	0.25	12.28	6.33	0.79	13.10	5.51	0.76	12.65
1992–93	47.55	0.10	10.90	6.93	0.84	13.32	5.52	0.82	13.83
1993–94	50.04	0.09	10.03	6.50	0.87	12.78	4.95	0.78	13.92
1994–95	46.79	0.12	10.38	7.21	0.82	14.50	5.07	0.77	14.28
1996–97	44.15	0.10	11.10	6.75	0.98	14.62	5.71	0.98	15.58
1997–98	47.25	0.19	9.96	6.26	0.70	13.87	5.48	0.87	15.36
1999–00	48.42	0.07	11.48	5.78	0.70	13.50	5.03	0.82	14.20
2001–02	42.09	0.07	13.84	6.05	0.81	14.85	5.90	0.89	15.50
2003–04	43.05	0.07	13.73	5.83	0.67	14.80	5.73	1.06	15.01
2005–06	43.37	0.09	13.84	6.13	0.66	14.67	5.74	1.10	14.35
2006–07	43.61	0.11	13.54	6.56	0.75	14.42	5.39	1.14	14.41

Source: Pakistan Statistical Yearbook 1948–2007.

TABLE 0.2: DISTRIBUTION OF EMPLOYED PERSONS BY MAJOR INDUSTRY DIVISION PAKISTAN RURAL (%)

Year	Agriculture, Forestry, Hunting and Fishing	Mining and Quarrying	Manufacturing	Electricity, Gas and Water	Construction	Wholesale and Rental Trade and Restaurants and Hotels	Transport, Storage and Communication	Financing, Insurance, Real Estate and Business Services	Community, Social and Personal Services	Activities not Adequately Defined
1968–69	69.54	0.10	12.00	0.13	2.69	5.82	3.48		6.18	0.15
1969–70	71.75	0.13	11.26	0.15	3.08	5.40	2.87		5.16	0.20
1970–71	71.76	0.29	11.07	0.05	2.78	6.24	3.47		4.22	0.12
1971–72	70.61	0.28	8.98	2.77	0.16	5.53	3.44	0.32	4.19	3.72
1974–75	72.08	0.13	9.32	3.41	0.23	5.81	2.94	0.09	5.70	0.29
1978–79	67.38	0.16	11.01	4.24	0.45	6.93	3.09	0.26	6.26	0.23
1982–83	67.69	0.11	9.38	4.12	0.96	7.14	3.09	0.26	6.94	0.31
1984–85	65.69	0.15	9.48	5.17	0.38	6.40	4.42	0.24	7.49	0.57
1985–86	70.94	0.29	8.52	4.36	0.23	6.00	3.07	0.22	6.30	0.06
1986–87	65.24	0.22	9.05	5.86	0.39	7.25	3.55	0.18	8.05	0.19
1987–88	67.49	0.18	8.34	6.08	0.39	6.85	3.45	0.20	6.91	0.10
1990–91	63.79	0.14	8.08	6.63	0.54	7.77	3.68	0.43	8.97	0.06
1991–92	64.15	0.25	7.97	6.16	0.43	8.37	4.03	0.28	8.34	0.04
1992–93	63.76	0.06	6.86	7.02	0.55	7.91	3.78	0.26	9.68	0.12
1993–94	65.00	0.10	6.00	6.44	0.60	7.60	3.58	0.26	9.39	0.03
1994–95	61.94	0.11	6.78	7.47	0.56	9.29	3.81	0.27	9.73	0.05
1996–97	60.83	0.09	6.79	6.80	0.64	9.51	4.11	0.31	10.9	0.02
1997–98	65.13	0.24	5.77	5.79	0.38	7.62	3.52	0.23	11.25	0.06
1999–00	65.85	0.07	6.46	5.57	0.45	7.98	3.85	0.19	9.57	
2001–02	59.01	0.07	8.68	6.23	0.56	9.20	4.82	0.30	11.13	?
2003–04	60.03	0.08	9.05	6.02	0.43	9.39	4.33	0.30	10.36	0.01
2005–06	59.87	0.12	9.00	6.23	0.39	9.30	4.64	0.35	10.06	0.03
2006–07	59.90	0.14	9.22	6.54	0.54	8.83	4.25	0.39	10.16	0.03

Source: Pakistan Statistical Yearbook, 1948–2007.

246

TABLE 0.3: DISTRIBUTION OF EMPLOYED PERSONS BY MAJOR INDUSTRY DIVISION PAKISTAN URBAN (%)

Year	Agriculture, Forestry, Hunting and Fishing	Mining and Quarrying	Manufacturing	Electricity, Gas and Water	Construction	Wholesale and Rental Trade and Restaurants and Hotels	Transport, Storage and Communication	Financing, Insurance, Real Estate and Business Services	Community, Social and Personal Services	Activities not adequately defined
1968–69	6.95	0.09	28.51	1.16	7.29	26.35	9.68		19.60	0.37
1969–70	6.98	0.13	29.70	1.30	6.82	25.19	11.06		18.55	0.36
1970–71	7.08	0.16	28.93	0.96	6.50	27.43	9.89		18.68	0.37
1971–72	6.54	1.07	25.79	5.85	1.16	26.56	10.20	2.92	19.05	0.86
1974–75	6.20	0.19	25.74	6.41	1.23	25.93	10.30	2.31	21.26	0.44
1978–79	5.65	0.08	25.69	1.11	1.66	24.30	9.97	2.77	22.35	0.40
1982–83	6.70	0.08	25.94	6.88	1.65	26.70	9.20	2.54	20.17	0.13
1984–85	7.39	0.21	24.89	6.74	1.50	25.29	9.95	2.58	20.63	0.81
1985–86	6.83	0.17	26.00	7.68	1.32	26.42	8.18	2.95	20.35	0.09
1986–87	6.37	0.24	27.25	6.40	1.63	24.91	9.81	2.32	20.66	0.41
1987–88	6.02	0.06	24.72	7.20	1.14	25.94	8.86	2.13	23.77	0.16
1990–91	7.63	0.17	22.35	6.59	1.55	26.57	9.07	2.25	23.75	0.07
1991–92	6.89	0.30	23.52	6.80	1.71	25.40	9.37	2.00	23.86	0.15
1992–93	5.80	0.20	21.31	6.72	1.59	27.26	10.00	2.23	24.53	0.37
1993–94	5.55	0.08	21.24	6.64	1.62	27.22	8.74	2.22	26.55	0.12
1994–95	5.80	0.14	21.10	6.49	1.53	28.63	8.47	2.13	26.58	0.13
1996–97	5.68	0.13	21.04	6.64	1.76	26.38	9.38	2.53	26.36	0.09
1997–98	5.57	0.08	19.74	7.37	1.44	28.43	10.04	2.35	24.95	0.03
1999–00	5.68	0.07	23.78	6.31	1.32	27.04	7.92	2.34	25.53	0.01
2001–02	5.19	0.07	25.08	5.67	1.33	27.19	8.26	2.18	25.03	
2003–04	5.94	0.04	23.97	5.41	1.20	26.62	8.80	2.71	25.17	.14
2005–06	6.32	0.02	24.71	5.91	1.25	26.71	8.22	2.79	24.00	0.06
2006–07	6.52	0.04	23.38	6.61	1.24	27.16	7.99	2.86	24.1	0.10

Source: Pakistan Statistical Yearbook, 1948–2007.

TABLE 0.4: DISTRIBUTION OF EMPLOYED PERSONS BY OCCUPATIONS URBAN AND RURAL (%)

Year	Professional, Technical and Related Workers	Administrative, Executive and Managerial Workers	Clerical Workers	Sales Workers	Farmers, Fishermen, Hunters, Loggers, and Related Workers	Production and Related Workers, Transport Equipment Operators and Labourers	Service, Sports, and Recreation Workers
1968–69	2.32	0.64	1.74	9.72	55.72	24.45	5.32
1969–70	2.08	0.64	0.19	9.28	56.95	24.46	4.71
1970–71	1.96	0.48	2.00	10.29	57.46	23.76	4.05
1971–72	2.00	0.51	2.30	12.05	57.22	22.12	3.71
1974–5	3.01	0.71	2.69	9.98	54.70	24.32	4.48
1978–79	3.05	0.73	2.92	10.11	52.64	25.94	4.61
1982–83	3.08	0.86	2.99	10.23	52.82	25.23	4.80
1984–85	3.49	0.88	3.45	10.19	50.07	27.15	4.50
1985–86	3.29	1.10	3.36	10.22	53.52	24.06	4.39
1986–87	3.84	0.69	4.01	11.33	48.83	26.89	4.33
1987–88	3.82	0.73	3.80	10.93	50.61	25.67	4.33
1990–91	4.85	0.97	4.53	12.15	46.64	25.97	4.90
1991–92	4.72	1.06	4.21	11.88	47.53	25.80	4.79
1992–93	4.83	1.19	4.55	12.56	46.63	25.65	4.59
1993–94	4.59	0.94	4.17	11.98	49.06	24.69	4.56
1994–95	5.04	0.91	4.59	13.63	46.01	25.38	4.44
1996–97	5.30	0.70	3.20	17.60	43.40	24.80	5.00

Source: Pakistan Statistical Yearbook, 1948–2007.

TABLE 0.5: REGISTERED, WORKING AND REPORTING FACTORIES AND OTHER FIGURES, 1948 TO 2005

Year	Registered Factories	Working Factories	Reporting Factories	Reporting Factories as % of Working Factories	Reporting Factories as % of Registered Factories	Avg. Daily Number of Factory Workers in Reporting Factories	Average Daily Employment in Mining
1948	1,126		1,045		93	117,355	
1949	1,277		1,214		95	131,515	9,400
1950	1,232		1,143		93	123,764	11,598
1951	1,368		1,254		92	130,742	14,301
1952	1,618	1,532	1,352	88	84	151,847	17,350
1953	2,137	2,066	1,929	93	90	186,901	17,656
1954	4,472	4,436	3,119	70	70	205,184	21,019
1955	4,664	4,664	2,058	44	44	120,977	21,944
1956	4,701	4,701	2,425	52	52	213,534	24,059
1957	5,056	4,979	2,990	60	59	250,896	25,495
1958	5,176	4,996	3,238	65	63	297,416	30,327
1959	5,283	5,128	2,922	57	55	244,922	25,611
1960	5,506	5,506	2,792	51	51	224,519	23,088
1961	5,732	5,631	2,837	50	49	286,605	27,511
1962	5,791	5,606	2,816	50	49	285,514	26,274
1963	5,797	5,698	2,907	51	50	322,000	30,644
1964	5,010	4,865	2,202	45	44	290,273	25,829
1965	5,107	4,755	2,192	46	43	280,300	26,303
1966	4,865	4,454	1,905	43	39	273,686	23,326
1967	5,109	4,646	2,038	44	40	270,634	25,729
1968	5,342	4,788	1,804	38	34	245,652	22,413
1969	5,183	4,677	2,530	54	49	325,698	42,711
1970	-	-	-	-	-	377,976	47,820
1971	-	-	-	-	-	365,838	245,235
1972	-	-	-	-	-	391,075	317,937
1973	6,087	5,514	2,096	38	34	371,156	447,379
1974	5,915	5,519	2,205	40	37	386,916	44,775
1975	6,095	5,478	1,924	35	32	322,608	35,355
1976	6,199	5,443	1,592	29	26	287,624	34,071

Year	Registered Factories	Working Factories	Reporting Factories	Reporting Factories as % of Working Factories	Reporting Factories as % of Registered Factories	Avg. Daily Number of Factory Workers in Reporting Factories	Average Daily Employment in Mining
1977	6,243	5,296	1,546	29	25	310,166	57,716
1978	6,436	5,488	1,829	33	28	337,141	48,991
1979	6,578	5,430	1,784	33	27	318,340	58,868
1980	6,117	4,483	1,776	40	29	266,127	74,490
1981	6,296	5,316	2,031	38	32	272,517	80,512
1982	6,426	5,500	4,840	88	75	282,168	100,557
1983	6,546	6,223	1,957	31	30	299,432	114,504
1984	6,679	5,899	1,885	32	28	237,297	106,155
1985	5,949	6,166	1,897	31	27	282,108	89,139
1986	7,345	6,516	1,808	28	25	251,421	89,378
1987	7,471	6,492	2,007	31	27	243,460	99,175
1988	7,643	5,955	2,343	39	31	303,743	96,618
1989	7,765	6,778	2,155	32	28	226,483	119,345
1990	7,412	6,284	2,189	35	30	241,881	119,206
1991	7,285	5,719	2,276	40	31	242,756	120,816
1992	7,453	6,454	2,487	39	33	274,689	140,833
1993	7,727	6,621	2,363	36	31	255,943	150,982
1994	8,720	6,946	2,306	33	26	256,620	138,156
1995	7,955	6,856	2,139	31	27	231,745	163,075
1996	8,360	7,025	1,866	27	22	188,791	119,701
1997	9,267	7,948	2,205	28	24	209,925	123,034
1998	9,283	7,832	2,780	35	30	196,933	103,312
1999	9,847	8,543	2,195	26	22	169,083	122,395
2000	10,282	8,875	1,781	20	17	150,255	131,975
2001	9,749	8,220	1,770	22	18	167,381	137,256
2002	10,518	8,785	1,680	19	16	156,416	140,111
2003	6,778	5,426	1,258	23	19	140,339	
2004	7,084	5,360	1,241	23	18	135,230	
2005	6,683	5,385	1,295	24	19	140,205	

Source: Pakistan Statistical Yearbook, 1948–2007.

TABLE 0.6: AVERAGE DAILY EMPLOYMENT AND TOTAL WAGES PAID IN FACTORIES IN WEST PAKISTAN UNDER THE PAYMENT OF WAGES ACT 1936, 1948 TO 2003

Year	Average Daily Number of Factory Workers	Total Wages Paid in Thousand Rupees	Year	Average Daily Number of Factory Workers	Total Wages Paid in Thousand Rupees
1948	95,344	55,408	1977	309,373	1,791,736
1949	109,378	72,102	1978	315,098	2,320,916
1950	102,269	71,286	1979	316,297	2,116,885
1951	107,235	79,597	1980	341,110	2,379,408
1952	123,726	93,511	1981	214,492	2,046,961
1953	159,526	128,691	1982	266,812	2,271,931
1954	168,450	141,954	1983	286,275	2,562,246
1955	76,494	81,098	1984	228,250	1,994,140
1956	140,011	153,086	1985	225,457	2,637,249
1957	175,111	182,278	1986	249,208	2,710,356
1958	151,966	166,665	1987	224,301	3,060,406
1959	196,244	204,843	1988	292,212	4,871,836
1960	195,448	236,800	1989	247,681	3,809,775
1961	215,438	246,125	1990	259,592	5,310,543
1962	207,101	336,725	1991	257,910	4,193,687
1963	276,011	354,180	1992	292,637	7,003,857
1964	243,034	372,234	1993	266,296	4,824,379
1965	292,124	421,853	1994	241,830	6,009,578
1966	253,660	397,882	1995	228,262	8,137,632
1967	291,420	422,700	1996	155,357	4,613,466
1968	231,727	379,704	1997	219,464	7,230,673
1969	974,652	1,836,610	1998	201,071	6,643,897
1970	244,257	—	1999	177,728	6,334,380
1971	254,224	462,864	2000	154,778	5,426,937
1972	272,612	532,929	2001	168,339	8,417,996
1973	359,939	1,061,479	2002	145,944	6,914,442
1974	260,565	919,685	2003	139,986	8,787,787
1975	321,977	1,359,546			
1976	270,932	1,257,515			

Source: Pakistan Statistical Yearbook, 1948–2007.

251

TABLE 0.7: INDUSTRIAL DISPUTES WEST PAKISTAN, 1949 TO 2005

Year	Number of Disputes	Number of Workers Involved	Number of Workdays Lost
1949	19	12,017	22,919
1950	11	8,605	47,830
1951	41	11,182	41,679
1952	42	15,784	76,147
1953	34	9,468	24,606
1954	70	49,795	213,909
1955	50	25,882	82,372
1956	94	41,908	195,064
1957	78	42,176	227,283
1958	42	14,566	169,420
1959	22	10,005	15,508
1960	30	19,663	60,818
1961	45	21,961	73,480
1962	87	49,855	268,386
1963	153	109,142	902,288
1964	107	79,889	405,255
1965	81	59,027	332,485
1966	98	63,873	253,671
1967	104	138,159	226,778
1968	107	60,037	324,804
1969	285	184,982	1,220,377
1970	304	193,807	2,447,959
1971	141	107,962	815,211
1972	779	361,149	2,018,308
1973	536	233,568	803,583
1974	191	141,150	736,174
1975	260	129,385	798,183
1976	171	77,502	514,891
1977	81	49,093	200,865
1978	85	58,565	299,865
1979	65	38,733	108,527
1980	59	24,710	247,867
1981	64	47,236	521,803
1982	26	22,409	690,872
1983	63	29,163	590,406
1984	81	30,702	157,748
1985	58	35,858	159,427
1986	26	12,929	189,025
1987	26	12,992	270,794
1988	18	8,231	197,351
1989	42	29,205	229,088
1990	99	65,918	186,726
1991	94	116,306	582,694
1992	40	73,257	398,128
1993	28	17,133	404,564
1994	25	15,434	341,196
1995	24	10,919	63,626
1996	30	18,566	203,323
1997	30	7,865	283,342
1998	20	6,097	122,519
1999	6	3,937	182,151
2000	4	225	667
2001	4	711	7,078
2002	4	516	12,160
2003	1	407	–
2004	4	373	1,036
2005	4	1,245	3,765

Source: Pakistan Statistical Yearbook, 1948–2007.

TABLE O.8: REGISTERED TRADE UNIONS EAST AND WEST PAKISTAN BEFORE 1971, ONLY WEST PAKISTAN AFTER 1971

Year	Registered Trade Unions	Registered Trade Unions Reporting	Membership of Reporting Unions	Membership of Reporting Unions Males	Membership of Reporting Unions Females
1948	181	134	157,246	156,058	1,188
1949	240	124	137,800	136,249	1,551
1950	255	126	140,373	139,351	1,022
1951	280	149	129,408	127,830	1,578
1952	340	180	151,804	149,943	1,861
1953	382	176	133,473	132,743	730
1954	404	203	139,922	139,922	2,409
1955	475	187	139,153	139,153	460
1956	549	201	161,970	160,649	1,321
1957	578	281	259,996	257,962	2,034
1958	620	241	129,913	128,830	1,083
1959	628	238	128,734	128,010	724
1960	666	395	269,334	264,873	4,461
1961	723	379	246,191	228,678	17,513
1962	789	377	267,879	216,611	51,268
1963	848	498	391,949	342,695	49,254
1964	920	490	396,370	346,260	50,110
1965	975	486	413,919	365,317	48,602
1966	1,022	612	420,416	370,225	50,191
1967	1,048	613	467,665	415,740	51,925
1968	1,082	698	556,294	503,021	53,273
1969	291	208	176,865	175,959	906
1970	1,436	794	330,255	325,672	4,583
1971	1,698	857	252,823	247,152	5,671
1972	3,350	1,802	314,300	308,644	5,656
1973	5,345	1,908	314,542	309,052	5,490
1974	7,172	1,825	327,818	323,143	4,684
1975	8,196	1,839	338,092	333,173	4,919
1976	8,611	1,551	304,739	300,501	4,238
1977	8,332	1,547	331,894	326,944	4,950
1978	7,894	1,381	320,446	313,156	7,290
1979	6,869	1,277	289,070	284,599	4,471
1980	6,551	1,465	346,511	340,942	5,569
1981	6,227	1,261	327,704	322,925	4,779
1982	6,344	1,204	287,445	284,085	3,360
1983	6,253	1,234	305,078	298,398	6,680
1984	6,271	1,233	289,501	285,502	3,999
1985	6,170	2,285	307,231	300,773	6,458
1986	6,322	1,476	314,710	307,894	6,816
1987	4,418	1,545	304,931	297,497	7,434
1988	6,428	1,631	373,193	363,694	9,499
1989	6,897	1,637	362,450	353,301	9,149
1990	7,080	1,763	359,633	352,270	7,363
1991	7,027	1,441	288,803	283,245	5,558
1992	7,185	1,834	415,768	406,419	9,349
1993	–	1,685	374,731	367,331	7,400
1994	7,273	1,718	325,677	317,617	8,060
1995	7,426	1,718	337,617	331,155	6,462
1996	7,349	1,594	293,530	288,327	5,203
1997	7,355	1,534	296,257	291,402	4,855
1998	7,356	1,478	305,340	298,815	6,525
1999	7,382	1,493	301,104	296,617	4,487
2000	–	1,356	301,332	296,737	4,595
2001	–	1,260	275,646	272,007	3,639
2002	–	1,201	247,539	245,405	2,134
2003	5,411	721	131,640	129,685	1,955
2004	7,486	724	123,775	121,629	2,146
2005	5,422	721	121,828	119,602	2,226

Source: Pakistan Statistical Yearbook, 1948–2007.

253

TABLE 0.9: TOTAL MEMBERS OF REPORTING UNIONS EAST AND WEST PAKISTAN BEFORE 1971, ONLY WEST PAKISTAN AFTER 1971

Year	Railways	Textiles	Printing Presses	Municipal	Docks and Port Trust	Engineering	Mines	Miscellaneous
1951	53,265	5,704	647	686	7,707	4,842	1,959	47,115
1952	86,392	8,327	460	1,251	7,921	4,794	2,859	31,451
1953	66,760	17,319	415	1,056	4,558	5,781	5,590	30,962
1954	50,216	18,628	1,487	1,291	6,035	6,810	6,455	36,804
1955	51,397	7,076	1,333	824	7,696	7,549	8,005	49,911
1956	58,224	23,057	2,531	2,705	13,895	13,895	3,370	36,129
1957	104,012	22,960	1,719	22,150	24,412	4,019	7,084	64,848
1958	22,590	15,963	894	23,926	15,059	4,503	4,311	39,562
1959	12,568	39,813	1,484	24,620	14,759	4,098	5,916	22,892
1960	75,380	77,061	4,180	28,022	12,307	5,950	5,336	6,604
1961	22,370	71,020	4,517	2,265	13,733	6,037	3,955	30,586
1962	27,087	48,614	1,405	3,418	1,132	5,213	3,472	13,207
1963	88,114	68,544	1,898	6,243	14,009	7,597	9,906	34,150
1964	68,932	75,634	4,294	7,219	28,450	6,611	8,676	37,370
1965	93,193	63,497	1,413	5,203	26,334	5,103	12,387	39,124
1966	64,507	79,323	5,520	28,685	32,778	9,660	12,346	14,190
1967	93,442	70,283	7,353	4,515	27,369	8,955	14,407	39,924
1968	105,041	80,840	3,911	6,079	32,823	12,144	12,818	44,631
1969	56,939	39,796	998	1,399	–	6,426	8,166	14,513
1970	80,454	74,517	5,800	11,792	7,719	9,452	8,598	14,684
1971	16,501	90,701	5,620	18,560	16,189	12,719	8,071	14,400
1972	20,956	99,387	8,675	15,448	6,793	22,716	13,609	28,586
1973	13,852	108,601	4,890	12,955	1,281	12,595	14,917	42,015
1974	15,684	118,121	7,820	16,249	9,333	13,192	12,888	17,393
1975	19,289	117,523	6,051	17,439	10,133	16,091	8,808	33,983
1976	14,051	96,426	4,350	11,033	798	18,504	12,286	28,059
1977	13,226	109,069	6,723	13,683	658	7,652	13,226	37,603
1978	13,630	101,009	4,770	27,415	935	9,682	13,578	29,548

Year	Railways	Textiles	Printing Presses	Municipal	Docks and Port Trust	Engineering	Mines	Miscellaneous
1979	15,172	95,555	4,243	11,419	885	10,528	14,977	22,195
1980	10,054	108,802	6,643	12,793	5,748	43,108	13,932	39,455
1981	18,866	78,158	2,520	14,520	3,895	9,528	18,653	79,404
1982	16,212	78,181	5,346	11,821	2,030	10,054	18,511	53,259
1983	17,982	80,609	4,408	18,517	2,215	20,435	4,674	26,512
1984	18,988	70,566	2,301	16,690	2,605	15,589	15,705	33,008
1985	10,331	60,055	3,132	13,478	5,796	13,545	16,723	62,141
1986	12,251	64,873	4,871	18,658	5,278	15,818	17,789	45,581
1987	11,552	65,307	5,959		4,253	17,459	11,933	46,820
1988	19,208	77,715	6,971	25,404	9,235	16,929	14,150	61,341
1989	18,141	86,342	7,344	25,283	1,221	20,243	10,744	56,445
1990	20,799	87,073	5,164	25,975	955	18,277	10,963	49,521
1991	20,371	83,287	8,761	16,427	1,664	11,870	4,893	35,379
1992	26,249	99,938	4,509	26,309	12,061	18,721	10,313	78,173
1993	21,715	84,150	6,955	21,701	19,964	16,659	31,792	43,094
1994	18,570	55,767	7,707	26,367	–	12,332	18,054	37,082
1995	19,322	63,658	7,589	28,733	16,658	11,107	16,235	37,082
1996	15,807	62,060	7,460	21,344	14,145	9,423	15,443	40,858
1997	19,794	68,494	7,354	23,478	17,481	7,270	12,306	44,684
1998	9,234	67,564	4,161	28,462	19,803	11,187	12,983	66,452
1999	21,253	74,635	4,209	22,419	18,646	17,720	10,132	48,199
2000	22,222	74,068	2,785	25,512	15,723	8,952	1,162	44,445
2001	348	15,122	2,484	12,784	369	5,477	7,246	134,970
2002	20,642	46,710	2,542	6,760	14,766	74	8,376	3,403
2003	25,348	10,751	3,022	8,286	8,264	3,346	100	25,214
2004	24,480	10,425	2,720	6,420	6,931	1,662	1,162	23,350
2005	16,118	9,570	3,397	9,760	4,059	14,068	8,569	27,140

Source: Pakistan Statistical Yearbook, 1948–2007.

TABLE 0.10: PRIVATISATIONS, 1991 TO JUNE 2007

No.	Unit Name	Sale Price Rs Million	Date of Transfer	Buyer Name / Controlling Interests
Banking and Finance				
	Bank			
1	Allied Bank Limited 51%	971.6	Feb–91	EMG
2	Muslim Commercial Bank 75%	2,420.0	Apr–91	National Group
3	Bankers Equity 51%	618.7	Jun–96	LTV Group
4	Habib Credit and Exchange 70% 52,500,000	1,633.9	Jul–97	Sh. Nahyan bin Mubarik Al-Nahyan
5	United Bank Ltd. 51% 1,549,465,680	12,350.0	Oct–02	Consortium of Bestway & Abu Dhabi Group
6	Bank Alfalah 30% 22,500,000	620.0	Dec–02	Abu Dhabi Group
7	Habib Bank 51%	22,409.0	Dec–03	Agha Khan Fund for Economic Development
	Total	41,023.2		
Capital Market Transaction				
8	Muslim Commercial Bank 6.8%	563.2	Jan–01	MCB Employees-PF & Pension Fund
9	Muslim Commercial Bank 4.4%	364.0	Nov–01	MCB Employees-PF & Pension Fund
10	NBP 10% shares IPO 37.3 million shares	373.0	Feb–02	General Public through Stock Exchange
11	Muslim Commercial Bank CDC24,024,560 shares	664.0	Oct–02	Sale through CDC
12	Pakistan Oil Fields Limited shares CDC28,546,810 shares	5,138.0	Oct–02	Sale through CDC
13	Attock Refinery Ltd. shares CDC 10,206,000 shares	1039.0	Jan–03	Sale through CDC
14	ICP Lot–A	175.0	Sep–02	ABAMCO
15	ICP Lot–B	303.0	Oct–02	PICIC
16	ICP–SEMF	787.0	Apr–03	PICIC
17	National Bank of Pakistan 10% SPO 37,303,932 shares	782.0	Nov–02	Sale Through CDC
18	DG Khan Cement shares CDC 3,601,126 shares	63.0	Dec–02	General Public through Stock Exchange
19	NBP 3.52% 3rd offer 13,131,000 shares	604.0	Nov–03	General Public through Stock Exchange
20	OGDCL 5%– IPO 215,046,420 shares	6,851.0	Nov–03	General Public through Stock Exchange
21	SSGC 10%–SPO 67,117,000 shares	1,734.0	Feb–04	General Public through Stock Exchange
22	PIA 5.8% shares SPO	1,215.1	Jul–04	General Public through Stock Exchange
23	PPL 15% IPO 102,875,000 shares	5,632.6	Jul–04	General Public through Stock Exchange
24	KAPCO 20% IPO 160,798,500 shares	4,814.8	Apr–05	General Public through Stock Exchange
25	UBL 4.2% IPO 21,867,000 shares	1,087.2	Aug–05	General Public through Stock Exchange

No.	Unit Name	Sale Price Rs Million	Date of Transfer	Buyer Name / Controlling Interests
26	OGDCL 9.5% GDR 408,588,000 Shares	46,963.0	Dec–06	GDR offering to international & domestic institutions
27	OGDCL 0.5% SPO 21,505,000 shares	2,359.6	Apr–07	General Public through Stock Exchange
28	UBL 21.74% GDR 175,951,092 shares	34,291.7	Jun–07	GDR offering to international & domestic institutions
	Total	115,804.2		
	Total Banking & Finance:	156,827.4		
Energy Sector				
29	Mari Gas 20%	102.4	Apr–94	Mari Gas Company Ltd.
30	Kot Addu Power Company 26%	7,105.0	Jun–96	National Power
31	Kot Addu Power Company 10%	3,046.0	Nov–96	National Power
32	Kot Addu Escrow A/c	900.7	Apr–02	National Power
33	SSGC LPG business	369.0	Aug–00	Caltex Oil Pak. Pvt Ltd.
34	SNGPL LPG business	142.0	Oct–01	Shell Gas LPG Pakistan
35	Badin II Revised	503.2	Jun–02	BP Pakistan & Occidental Pakistan
36	Adhi	618.9	May–02	Pakistan Oil Field
37	Dhurnal	161.0	May–02	Western Acquisition
38	Ratana	24.6	May–02	Western Acquisition
39	Badin I	6,433.0	Jun–02	BP Pakistan & Occidental Pakistan
40	Turkwal	75.6	Jun–02	Attock Oil Company
41	NRL 51% GOP shares	16,415.0	May–05	Consortium of Attock Refinery Ltd
42	KESC 73% GOP shares	15,859.7	Nov–05	Hassan Associates
	Total	51,756.1		
Telecommunications				
43	PTCL 2%	3,032.5	Aug–94	General Public through Stock Exchange
44	PTCL 10%	27,499.0	Sep–94	Through DR form
45	26% 1.326 billion B class of shares of PTCL	156,328.4	Jul–05	Etisalat UAE
46	Carrier Telephone Industries	500.0	Oct–05	Siemens-Pakistan Engineering Co. Ltd.
	Total	187,359.9		
Industrial Units				
Automobile				
47	Al-Ghazi Tractors Ltd.	105.6	Nov–91	Al-Futain Industries Pvt Ltd. UAE

No.	Unit Name	Sale Price Rs Million	Date of Transfer	Buyer Name / Controlling Interests
48	National Motors Ltd.	150.4	Jan–92	Biboojee Services
49	Millat Tractors Ltd.	306.0	Jan–92	EMG
50	Baluchistan Wheels Ltd.	276.4	May–92	Abdul Qadir & Saleem I. Kapoorwala
51	Pak Suzuki Co. Ltd.	172.0	Sep–92	Suzuki Motors Co. Japan
52	Naya Daur Motors Ltd.	22.3	Jan–93	Farid Tawakkal & Saleem I. Kapoorwala
53	Bolan Castings	69.2	Jun–93	EMG
	Total	**1,101.9**		
Cement				
54	Maple Leaf Cement	485.7	Jan–92	Nishat Mills Ltd.
55	Pak Cement	188.9	Jan–92	Mian Jahangir Ellahi & Ass
56	White Cement	137.5	Jan–92	Mian Jahangir Ellahi & Associates
57	D.G Khan Cement	1,960.5	May–92	Tariq Sehgal & Associates
58	Dandot Cement	636.7	May–92	EMG
59	Garibwal Cement	836.3	Sep–92	Haji Saifullah & Group
60	Zeal Pak Cement	239.9	Oct–92	Sardar M. Ashraf D. Baluch
61	Kohat Cement	527.9	Oct–92	Palace Enterprises
62	Dandot Works–National Cement	110.0	Jan–95	EMG
63	General Refractories Limited	18.9	Feb–96	Shah Rukh Engineering
64	Wah Cement	2,415.8	Feb–96	EMG
65	Associated Cement Rohri	255.0	Nov–03	National Transport Karachi
66	Thatta Cement	793.0	Jan–04	Al-Abbas Group
67	10% additional shares-Dandot Cement	8.3	Oct–04	EMG
68	10% additional shares-Kohat Cement	40.7	Oct–04	EMG
69	Mustehkam Cement Limited	3,204..9	Nov–05	Bestway Cement Limited
70	Javedan Cement Company Limited	4,315.9	Aug–06	Haji Ghani Usman & Group
	Total	**16,176.9**		
Chemical				
71	National Fibres Ltd	756.6	Feb–92	Schon Group
72	Kurram Chemicals	33.8	Feb–92	Upjohn Company USA
73	Pak PVC Ltc	63.6	Jun–92	Riaz Shaffi Reysheem

No.	Unit Name	Sale Price Rs Million	Date of Transfer	Buyer Name / Controlling Interests
74	Sind Alkalis Ltd	152.3	Oct–92	EMG
75	Antibiotics Pvt Ltd	24.0	Oct–92	Tesco Pvt Ltd.
76	Swat Elutriation	16.7	Dec–94	Sahib Sultan Enterprises
77	Nowshera PVC Co. Limited	20.9	Feb–95	Al Syed Enterprises
78	Swat Ceramics Pvt Limited	38.6	May–95	Imperial Group
79	Ittehad Chemicals	399.5	Jul–95	Chemi Group
80	Pak Hye Oils	53.6	Jul–95	Tariq Siddique Associates
81	Ravi Engineering Limited	5.4	Jan–96	Petrosin Products Pte
82	Nowshera Chemicals	21.2	Apr–96	Mehboob Ali Manjee
83	National Petrocarbon	21.9	Jul–96	Happy Trading
84	National Petrocarbon add'l 10% shares	2.3	Mar–02	Happy Trading
85	Khuram Chemicals additional 10%	6.0	Oct–03	Pfizer Pakistan
86	10% additional shares – Ittehad Chemicals	26.1	Oct–04	EMG
	Total	**1,642.5**		
Engineering				
87	Karachi Pipe Mills	18.9	Jan–92	Jamal Pipe Industries
88	Pioneer Steel	4.4	Feb–92	M. Usman
89	Metropolitan Steel Mills Limited	66.7	May–92	Sardar M. Ashraf D. Baluch
90	Pakistan Switchgear	8.9	Jun–92	EMG
91	Quality Steel	13.2	Apr–93	Marketing Enterprises
92	Textile Machinery Co	27.9	Oct–95	Mehran Industries
93	Indus Steel Pipe	42.5	Jul–97	Hussein Industries
	Total	**182.5**		
Fertilizer				
94	Pak China Fertilizers Company Limited	435.4	May–92	Schon Group
95	Pak Saudi Fertilizers Ltd.	7,335.9	May & Sep–02	Fauji Fertilizers
96	Pak Saudi Fertilizers Ltd. 10%	815.0	Sep–02	Fauji Fertilizers
97	Pak Arab Fertilizers Pvt Ltd. 94.8%	14,125.6	May–05	Export Reliance- Consortium
98	Pak American Fertilizers 100%	15,949.0	Jul–06	Azgard 9

No.	Unit Name	Sale Price Rs Million	Date of Transfer	Buyer Name / Controlling Interests
99	Lyallpur Chemical & Fertilizers	280.2	Dec-06	Al Hamd Chemical Pvt Limited
	Total	**38,941.1**		
Ghee				
100	Fazal Vegetable Ghee	21.2	Sep-91	Mian Mohammad Shah
101	Associated Industries	152.0	Feb-92	Mehmoob Abu-er-Rub
102	Sh Fazal Rehman	64.3	Apr-92	Rose Ghee Mills
103	Sh Fazal Rehmanaddl- 10% shares	2.3	May-05	Rose Ghee Mills
104	Kakakhel Industries	55.3	May-92	Mehmoob Abu-er-Rub
105	United Industries	15.5	May-92	A. Akbar Muggo
106	Haripur Vegetable Oil	30.1	Jul-92	Malik Naseer & Assoc.
107	Bara Ghee Mills	27.8	Jul-92	Dawood Khan
108	Hydari Industries	-	Aug-92	EMG
109	Chiltan Ghee Mills	42.5	Sep-92	Baluchistan Trading Co.
110	Wazir Ali Incustries	31.9	Dec-92	Treat Corporation
111	Asaf Industries Pvt Limited	11.4	Jan-93	Muzafar Ali Isani
112	Khyber Vegetable	8.0	Jan-93	Haji A. Majid & Co.
113	Surai Vegetable Ghee Industries	10.8	Jan-93	Trade Lines
114	Crescent Factories Vegetable Ghee Mills	46.0	Jan-93	S. J. Industries
115	Bengal Vegetable	19.1	Mar-93	EMG
116	A & B Oil Industries Limited	28.5	Mar-93	Al-Hashmi Brothers
117	Dargai Vegetable Ghee Industries	26.2	Nov-97	Gul Cooking Oil Industries
118	Punjab Veg. Ghee	18.7	May-99	Canal Associates
119	Burma Oil	20.1	Jan-00	Home Products Intl
120	E&M Oil Mills	94.0	Jul-02	Star Cotton Corp. Ltd.
121	Maqbool Oil Company Ltd.	27.6	Jul-02	Madina Enterprises
122	Kohinoor Oil Mills	80.7	May-04	Iqbal Khan
123	United Industries Limited	7.7	Sep-05	A. Akbar Muggo
	Total	**841.7**		
Mineral				
124	Makerwal Collieries	6.1	Jul-95	Ghani Group of Industries

No.	Unit Name	Sale Price Rs Million	Date of Transfer	Buyer Name / Controlling Interests
Rice				
125	Sheikhupura	28.0	May–92	Contrast Pvt Ltd.
126	Faizabad	21.2	May–92	Packages Ltd.
127	Siranwali	16.2	Jul–92	Enkay Enterprises
128	Hafizabad	20.0	Sep–92	Pak Pearl Rice Mills
129	Eminabad	24.1	Nov–92	Pak Arab Food Industries
130	Dhaunkel	79.2	Jun–93	Dhonda Pakistan Pvt Ltd.
131	Mabarikpur	14.4	Nov–93	Maktex Pvt Ltd.
132	Shikarpur	32.5	Mar–96	Afzaal Ahmad
	Total	**235.6**		
Roti Plants				
133	Gulberg, Lahore	8.7	Jan–92	Packages Ltd.
134	Peshawar	2.6	Jan–92	Saleem Group of Ind
135	Head Office, Lahore	10.2	Jan–92	Hajra Textile Mills
136	Hyderabad	2.6	Jan–92	Utility Stores Corp.
137	Faisalabad	11.5	Jan–92	Azad Ahmad
138	Bahawalpur	1.6	Feb–92	Utility Stores Corp.
139	Multan	2.5	Feb–92	Utility Stores Corp.
140	Quetta	4.8	Feb–92	Utility Stores Corp.
141	Islamabad	3.6	Mar–92	Utility Stores Corp.
142	Taimuria, Karachi	9.2	Jun–92	Spot Light Printers
143	SITE, Karachi	5.1	Sep–92	Specialty Printers
144	Multan Road, Lahore	3.5	Dec–92	Utility Stores Corp.
145	Korangi, Karachi	4.6	Apr–93	Utility Stores Corp.
146	Mughalpura, Lahore	-	Jun–96	Pakistan Railways
147	Gulshan-e-Iqbal, Karachi	20.2	Mar–98	Ambreen Industries
	Total	**90.7**		
Textile				
148	Quaidabad Woollen Mills	85.5	Jan–93	Jahangir Awan Associates
149	Cotton Ginning Factory	1.2	Jun–95	Hamid Mirza

No.	Unit Name	Sale Price Rs Million	Date of Transfer	Buyer Name / Controlling Interests
150	Bolan Textile Mills	128.0	Oct–05	Sadaf Enterprises
151	Lasbella Textile Mills	156.0	Nov–06	Raees Ahmed
	Total	**370.7**		
	Total all Industrial Units	**59,589.7**		
Miscellaneous				
152	National Tube-well Const Corp	18.6	Sep–99	Through Auction
153	Duty Free Shops	12.5	Sep–99	Weitnaur Holding Ltd.
154	Republic Motors Plot	6.3	Nov–99	Muhammad Mushtaq
155	Al Haroon Building Karachi	110.0	Sep–02	LG Group
156	International Advertising Pvt Ltd.	5.0	Apr–05	EMG
	Total	**152.4**		
Newspapers				
157	N.P.T. Building	185.0	Oct–93	Army Welfare Trust
158	Mashriq – Peshawar	26.6	Jun–95	Syed Tajmir Shah
159	Mashriq – Quetta	6.2	Jan–96	EMG
160	Progressive Papers Ltd.	46.1	May–96	Mian Saif-ur-Rahman
161	Mashriq – Karachi	6.7	Aug–96	EMG
	Total	**270.6**		
Tourism				
162	Cecil's Hotel	190.9	Jun–98	Imperial Builders
163	Federal Lodges-1-4	39.2	Jan–99	Hussain Global Assoc.
164	Dean's Hotel	364.0	Dec–99	Shahid Gul & Partners
165	Falleti's Hotel Lahore	1,211.0	Jul–04	4B Marketing
	Total	**1,805.1**		
	Total Misc.	**2,228.1**		
Capital Market Transaction from July 2007 to February 2009				
166	UBL 3.26% through GDR 26,392,660 shares	5,159.0	Jul–07	GDR offering to international & domestic institutions
167	HBL 7.5% through IPO 51,750,000 shares	12,161.0	Oct–07	General Public through Stock Exchange
168	Hazara Phosphate Fertilizers Limited	1,340.0	Nov–08	Pak American Fertilizers
	Grand Total 1991 to Feb. 2009	**475,421.2**		

Source: Privatisation Commission 2008.

TABLE 0.11: LARGE-SCALE INDUSTRIES NATIONALISED AND ITS OWNERSHIP, 1972

	Name of Company	Ownership		Name of Company	Ownership
	Units taken over in Karachi			**Nationalised Banks and their ownership**	
1	Steel Corporation of Pakistan	Fancy	1	Habib Bank Ltd.	Habib
2	Hyeson's Steel	Hyesons	2	United Bank Ltd	Saigol
3	Ali Automobiles	Jaffer Bros	3	Muslim Commercial Bank	Adamjee
4	Kandawala Industries	Kandawala	4	Australasia Bank	Colony
5	ROK Industries	ROK	5	Premier Bank	Arag
6	Haroon Industries	Haroon	6	Habib Bank Overseas	Habib
7	Wazir Ali Industries	Packages	7	Commerce Bank Ltd	Fancy
8	Gandhara Industries	Bibojee	8	Memon Cooperative Bank	Dawood
9	Indus Chemical and Industries	Indus	9	Lahore Commercial Bank	Dawood
10	Valika Cement	Valika	10	Punjab Cooperative Bank	Dawood
11	Karachi Gas	Fancy	11	Pakistan Bank Ltd	Dawood
12	Valika Chemicals	Valika	12	Bank of Bahawalpur	Dawood
13	Karachi Electric	Fancy-Jaffer Bros	13	Standards Bank	
14	National Refinery			**Nationalised Insurance Companies**	
15	Pakistan Fertilizer Corporation	Jaffer Bros	1	Eastern Federal Union EFU	Arag
	Units taken over in Punjab and NWFP		2	United Insurance	Valika
16	BECO	C.M.Latif	3	New Jubilee	Fancy
17	M.K. Foundry		4	Adamjee Insurance	Adamjee
18	Ittefaq Foundry	Ittefaq	5	Habib Insurance	Habib
19	Rana Tractors		6	Premier	Crescent
20	United Chemicals	Saigol	7	Central	Dawood
21	Pakistan Cement	Saigol	8	IGI	Packages
22	Ismaeel Cement	Colony	9	Union	Nishat
23	Central Iron and Steel Works			**Nationalised Shipping Companies**	
24	Valika Steel Works	Valika	1	Pan Islamic Shipping	Arag
25	Jaffer Steel Corporation	Jaffer Bros	2	United Oriental Shipping	Arag
26	Pakistan Progressive Cement Wah	Colony	3	Trans Ocean Shipping	
27	Pakistan Progressive Cement Dandot	Colony	4	Mohammadi Shipping	Arag
28	Rawalpindi Electrics		5	Pakistan Shipping	
29	Modern Steel Muredke		6	East and West Shipping	
30	Multan Electric Supply	Colony	7	Gulf Steam Shipping	
31	Karim Industries Nowshehra	Nishat	8	Chittagong Shipping	
			9	Crescent Shipping	Crescent

Source: Rahman 1998.

References

Abbasi, N. (1987). *Urbanisation in Pakistan: 1951–81*. Islamabad: Pakistan Institute of Development Economics: Report 177.

Abbasi, N. and Irfan, M. (1983). *Socio-Economic Effects of International Migration on the Families Left Behind*. Islamabad: Pakistan Institute of Development Economics: Report 7.

Adamse, R.H. (1995). 'Agricultural Income, Cash Crops, and Inequality in Rural Pakistan.' *Economic Development and Cultural Change*, Vol. 43, No. 3, pp. 467–91.

Afzal, M. (1973). 'Implications of the Green Revolution for Land Use Patterns and Relative Crop Profitability under Domestic and International Prices.' *Pakistan Development Review*, Vol. 12, No. 2, pp. 135–47.

Afzal, M. (1974). *The Pricing of Agricultural Capital Inputs in Pakistan*. Pakistan Institute of Development Economics Monograph No. 18.

Afzal, M. and Hussain, M. (1974). *The Population of Pakistan*. Committee for International Coordination of National Research in Demography.

Afzal, M. and Nasir, Z.M. (1987). 'Is Female Labour Force Participation Really Low and Declining in Pakistan: A Look at Alternative Data Sources?' *The Pakistan Development Review*, Vol. 26, No. 4, pp. 699–710.

Afzal, M., Kiani, K.K., and Muhammad, A. (1993). 'Indirect View of Fertility Change in Pakistan.' *The Pakistan Development Review*, Vol. 32, No. 4, pp. 1081–96.

Agarwal, B. (1994). 'Gender, Resistance and Land: Interlinked Struggles over Resources and Meanings in South Asia.' *Journal of Peasant Studies*, Vol. 22, No. 1, pp. 81–125.

Agarwal, B. (1998). 'Environmental Management, Equity and Eco-feminism: Debating India's Experience.' *Journal of Peasant Studies*, Vol. 25, No. 4, pp. 55–95.

Agarwala, N. (1989). 'The Unequal Exchange Thesis: A Critical Evaluation.' *Indian Economic Review*, Vol. 24, No. 1, pp. 67–81.

Agricultural Census 1960 Vol. 1. (1963). Agricultural Census Organisation, Government of Pakistan.

Agricultural Census 2000 (2003). Agricultural Census Organisation, Government of Pakistan. Retrieved from http://www.statpak.gov.pk/depts/aco/publications/agricultural_census2000/agricultural_census2000.pdf.

Agricultural Indicators: Federal Bureau of Statistics. (2007). Retrieved from http://www.statpak.gov.pk/depts/fbs/statistics/agri_indicators/agri_indicators.html

Agricultural Statistics of the Punjab (1937). Punjab Board of Economic Inquiry.

Agricultural Workers (2008). Retrieved from http://www.statpak.gov.pk/depts/aco/publications/agricultural_workers/Agri_work.html

Agriculture and Land Use (2009). Retrieved from http://images.nationmaster.com/images/motw/middle_east_and_asia/pakistan_ag_1973.jpg

Aguilar Jr., F.V. (1994). 'Sugar, Planter, State Relations and Labour Processes in Colonial Philippine Haciendas.' *Journal of Peasant Studies*, Vol. 22, No. 1, pp. 50–80.

Ahmad, A. (1992). *In Theory: Classes, Nations, Literatures*. Oxford University Press India.

Ahmad, M. (1993). 'Choice of Norm of Poverty Threshold and Extent of Poverty in Pakistan.' *The Journal of Development Studies*, No. 12.

Ahmed, A. (1995). 'Post-colonialism: What's in a Name?' In Campa, Kaplan and Sprinker (Eds.), *Late Imperial Culture*. Verso.

Ahmed, B. (1972). *Farm Mechanization and Agricultural Development: A Case Study of the Pakistan Punjab* (Unpublished doctoral dissertation). Michigan State University.

Ahmed, M. and Sampath, R.K. (1994). 'Irrigation Inequalities in Pakistan, 1960–1980.' *The Pakistan Development Review*, Vol. 33, No. 1, pp. 53–74.

Ahmed, S. (1977). *Class and Power in a Punjabi Village*. Monthly Review Press.

Ahmed, V. and Amjad, R. (1984). *The Management of Pakistan's Economy 1947–1982*. Oxford University Press.

Akhtar, S.M. (1951). *Economics of Pakistan*. Lahore.

Akram-Lodhi, A.H. (1993). 'Agrarian Classes in Pakistan: An Empirical Test of Patnaik's Labour-Exploitation Criterion' *Journal of Peasant Studies*, Vol. 20, No. 4, pp. 557–89.

Akram-Lodhi, A.H. (1995). 'M.H. Khan, A.V. Chayanov and the Family Farms of the North-West Frontier Province.' *Journal of Peasant Studies*, Vol. 22, No. 2, pp. 300–26.

Alam, A.R. (2006). 'Land Locked: An Examination of Some of the Inefficiencies Affecting Transactions Involving Immovable Property.' *The Pakistan Development Review*, Vol. 45, No. 4.

Alam, I. (1983). *Fertility Levels, Trends and Differentials in Pakistan: Evidence from Population, Labour Force and Migration Survey 1979–80*. Islamabad: Pakistan Institute of Development Economics: Report 1.

Alam, M. (1986). *The Crisis of Empire in Mughal North India: Awadh and the Punjab 1707–48*. Delhi.

Alauddin, T. (1975). 'Mass Poverty in Pakistan: A Further Study.' *Pakistan Development Review*, Vol. 14, No. 4, pp. 431–50.

Alavi, H. (1965). 'Peasant and Revolution.' In Kathleen Gough and Hari P. Sharma (eds.), *Imperialism and Revolution*. New York, pp. 293–334.

Alavi, H. (1975). 'India and the Colonial Mode of Production.' *Socialist Register*. London: Merlin Press. pp. 160–97.

Alavi, H. (1976). 'The Rural Elite and Agricultural Development in Pakistan.' In Stevens and Bertocci (Eds.) *Rural Development in Bangladesh and Pakistan*. University of Hawai Press.

Alavi, H. (1980). *Capitalism and Colonial Production*. London.

Alavi, H. (1981). 'Structure of Colonial Formation.' *Economic and Political Weekly*, Vol. XVI, No. 10, 11, 12.

Alavi, H. (1982). 'India: The Transition to Colonial Capitalism.' In Alavi, P.L. Burns, G.R. Knight, P.B. Mayer & D. McEachern (Eds.), *Capitalism and Colonial Production*. London: Croom Helm.

Alavi, H. (1988). 'Pakistan and Islam: Ethnicity and Ideology'. In F. Halliday & H. Alavi (Eds.), *State and Ideology in the Middle East and Pakistan*.Monthly Review Press.

Alavi, H., Burns, P.L., Knight, G.R., Mayer, P.B., & McEachern, D. (1982). *Capitalism and Colonial Production*. London: Croom Helm.

Albritton, R. (1993). 'Did Agrarian Capitalism Exist?' *Journal of Peasant Studies*, Vol. 20, No. 3, pp. 419–41.

Ali, I. (1988). *The Punjab under Imperialism, 1885–1947*. Princeton University Press.

Ali, K.A. (2005). 'The Strength of the Street Meets the Strength of the State: The 1972 Labor Struggle in Karachi.' *International Journal of Middle East Studies*, Vol. 37, No. 1, pp. 83–107.

Ali, M.A. (1993). 'The Mughal Polity: A Critique of Revisionist Approaches.' *Modern Asian Studies*, Vol. 27, No. 4, pp. 699–710.

Ali, R. (2002). 'Underestimating Urbanisation.' *Economic and Political Weekly*, Vol. 37, No. 44/45, pp. 4554–5.

Ali, S.S. and Tahir, S. (1999). 'Dynamics of Growth, Poverty and Inequality.' *The Pakistan Development Review*, Vol. 38, No. 1, pp. 837–57.

Allina-Pisano, J. (2004). 'Land Reform and the Social Origins of Private Farmers in Russia and the Ukraine.' *Journal of Peasant Studies*, Vol. 31, No. 3 & 4, pp. 489–514.

Almond, G.A. (1967). 'Review: Social Origins of Dictatorship and Democracy: Lord and Peasant in the Making of the Modern World by Barrington Moore, Jr.' *The American Political Science Review*, Vol. 61, No. 3, pp. 768–70.

Altaf, M.A., Ercelan, A., Bengali, K., and Rahim, A. (1993). 'Poverty in Karachi: Incidence, Location, Characteristics and Upward Mobility.' *The Pakistan Development Review*, Vol. 32, No. 2, pp. 159–78.

Amin, S. (1974). *Accumulation on a World Scale*. Pearce, B. (Trans.) Monthly Review Press.

Amin, S. (1976). *Unequal Development*. Hassocks.

Amjad, A. (2001). *Labor Legislation and Trade Unions in India and Pakistan*.Oxford University Press.

Amjad, R. (1982). *Private Industrial Investment in Pakistan, 1960–1970*. Cambridge University Press.

Amjad, R. (1986). 'Impact of Workers' Remittances from the Middle East on Pakistan's Economy: Some Selected Issues.' *The Pakistan Development Review*, Vol. 25, No. 4, pp. 757–85.

Amjad, R. and Kemal, A.R. (1997). 'Macroeconomic Policies and Their Impact on Poverty Alleviation in Pakistan.' *The Pakistan Development Review*, Vol. 36, No. 1, pp. 39–68.

Anderson, P. (1979). *Lineages of the Absolutist State*. Verso: London.

Anderson, K.B. (2010). *Marx at the Margins*. University of Chicago Press.

Angelo, L. (1995). 'Wage Labour Differed: The Recreation of Unfree Labour in the US South.' *Journal of Peasant Studies*, Vol. 22, No. 4, pp. 581–644.

Angotti, T. (1981). 'The Political Implications of Dependency Theory.' *Latin American Perspectives*, Vol. 8, No. 3/4, pp. 124–37.

Ansari, J. (1999). Macroeconomic Policy: An Alternative View. In S.R. Khan (Ed.), *Fifty Years of Pakistan's Economy*. Oxford University Press.

Ansari, J. and Arshad, Z. (2006). *Business Ethics in Pakistan*. Royal Book Company.

Anstey, V. (1952). *The Economic Development of India*. London: Longmans, Green & Co.

Anwar, T. (1996). 'Structural Adjustment and Poverty: The Case of Pakistan.' *Pakistan Development Review*, Vol. 35, No. 4, Part II, pp. 911–26.

Anwar, T. (2002). 'Impact of Globalization and Liberalization on Growth, Employment and Poverty.' World Institute of Development Economics Research (WIDER) Development Conference, 25–26 May 2001, Helsinki. Retrieved from http://www.wider.unu.edu/stc/repec/pdfs/rp2002/dp2002–17.pdf

Anwar, T. (2006). 'Trends in Absolute Poverty and Governance in Pakistan: 1998–99 and 2004–05.' *The Pakistan Development Review*, Vol. 45, No. 4 Part II, pp. 777–93.

Anwar, T. and Qureshi, S.K. (2003). 'Trends in Absolute Poverty in Pakistan: 1990–2001.' *The Pakistan Development Review*, Vol. 43, No. 4.

Anwar, T., Qureshi, S.K., and Ali, H. (2004). 'Landlessness and Rural Poverty in Pakistan.' *The Pakistan Development Review*, Vol. 43, No. 4.

Araghi, F. (2003). 'Food Regimes and the Production of Value: Some Methodological Issues.' *Journal of Peasant Studies*, Vol. 30, No. 2, pp. 41–70.

Arif, G.M. (1999). *Remittances and Investments at the Household Level in Pakistan*. The Pakistan Development Review: Report 166.

Arif, G.M. (2003). Urbanization in Pakistan: Trends, Growth and Evaluation of the 1998 Census. In I.A.M. Kemal (Ed.), *Population of Pakistan: An Analysis of 1998 Population and Housing Census*. Islamabad: Pakistan Institute of Development Economics.

Arif, G.M. and Chaudhry, N. (2008). 'Demographic Transition and Youth Employment in Pakistan.' *The Pakistan Development Review*, Vol. 47, No. 1, pp. 27–70.

Arif, G.M. and Hamid, S. (2007). *Life in a City: Pakistan in Focus*. United Nations Population Fund, Islamabad.

Arif, G.M. and Ibrahim, S. (1998a). 'Process of Urbanization in Pakistan.' *Pakistan Development Review*, Vol. 37, No. 4, pp. 507–22.

Arif, G.M. and Ibrahim, S. (1998b). 'The Process of Urbanisation in Pakistan, 1951–81.' *Pakistan Development Review*, Vol. 37, No. 4, Part II.

Arif, G.M. and Irfan, M. (1997). 'Return Migration and Occupational Change: The Case of Pakistani Migrants Returned from the Middle East.' *The Pakistan Development Review*, Vol. 36, No. 1, pp. 1–37.

Arif, G.M., Nazli, H., and Haq, R. (2001). 'Recent Rise in Poverty and Its Implications for Poor Households in Pakistan.' Paper presented at the 16th Annual General Meeting and Conference, Pakistan Society of Development Economists.

Aristotle. (1988). *The Politics*. Edited by Stephen Everson.

Arnold, D. (1994). *Colonizing the Body*. Berkeley.

Asiatic Mode of Production on *Marxist Internet Archive* (2009). Retrieved from http://marxists.org/glossary/terms/a/s.htm#asiatic-mode-production

Aslam, M.M. (1978). 'Some Comparative Aspects of Production and Profit Functions: Empirical Applications to a Punjab District.' *Pakistan Development Review*, Vol. 17, No. 2, pp. 191–211.

Assadi, M. (1994). ''Khadi Curtain', 'Weak Capitalism' and 'Operation Ryot': Some Ambiguities in Farmers' Discourse, Karnataka and Maharashtra 1980–93.' *Journal of Peasant Studies*, Vol. 21, No. 2 & 4, pp. 212–27.

Assies, W. (2002). 'From Rubber Estate to Simple Commodity Production: Agrarian Struggles in the Northern Bolivian Amazon.' *Journal of Peasant Studies*, Vol. 29, No. 3 & 4, pp. 83–130.

Aston, T.H. and Philpin, C.H.E. (Eds.), (1985). *The Brenner Debate: Agrarian Class Structure and Economic Development in Pre-Industrial Europe*. Cambridge University Press.

Avineri, S. (1968). *The Social and Political Thought of Karl Marx*. Cambridge University Press.

Azhar, B.A. (1973a). 'A Model for Forecasting Wheat Production in the Punjab.' *Pakistan Development Review*, Vol. 12, No. 4, pp. 407–15.

Azhar, B.A. (1973b). 'An Econometric Analysis of Price Behaviour in Pakistan.' *Pakistan Development Review*, Vol. 12, No. 4, pp. 375–86.

Baden-Powell, B.H. (1894). *A Short Account of the Land Revenue and Its Administration in British India*. Clarendon Press, Oxford.

Baden-Powell, B.H. (1895). 'The Permanent Settlement of Bengal.' *The English Historical Review*, Vol. 10, No. 38, p. 276.

Baden-Powell, B.H. (1896). 'The Origin of Zamindari Estates in Bengal.' *The Quarterly Journal of Economics*, Vol. 11, No. 1, pp. 36–69.

Baer, W. (1972). 'Import Substitution and Industrialization in Latin America: Experiences and Interpretations.' *Latin American Research Review*, Vol. 7, Spring, pp. 95–122.

Bagchi, A.K. (1982). *The Political Economy of Underdevelopment*. Cambridge University Press.

Bagchi, A.K. (1972). *Private Investment in India 1900–1939*. Cambridge University Press.

Bagchi, A.K. (1976). 'Deindustrialisation in Gangetic Bihar, 1809–1901.' In *Essays in Honour of Prof. S.C. Sarkar*. New Delhi.

Bagla, P. (2006). 'Controversial Rivers Project Aims to Turn India's Fierce Monsoon into a Friend.' *Science*, Vol. 313, No. 5790, pp. 1036–7.

Bailey, A.M. and Llobera, J.R. (Eds.), (1981). *The Asiatic Mode of Production: Science and Politics*. London: Routeledge & Kegan Paul.

Balibar, E. (1970). The Basic Concepts of Historical Materialism. In L. Althusser & E. Balibar (Eds.), *Reading Capital*. New Left Books, London.

Banaji, J. (1972). 'For a Theory of Colonial Modes of Production.' *Economic and Political Weekly*, Vol. VII, No. 52.

Banaji, J. (1976). 'The Peasantry in the Feudal Mode of Production: Towards an Economic Model.' *Journal of Peasant Studies*, Vol. 3, No. 3, pp. 299–320.

Banaji, J. (1977). 'Modes of Production in a Materialist Conception of History.' *Capital and Class*, Vol. 3, No., pp. 1–44.

Banaji, J. (1994). 'The Farmers' Movements: A Critique of Conservative Rural Coalitions.' *Journal of Peasant Studies*, Vol. 21, No. 3 & 4, pp. 228–45.

Banaji, J. (1996/1997). 'Globalisation and Restructuring in the Indian Food Industry.' *Journal of Peasant Studies*, Vol. 24, No. 1 & 2, pp. 191–210.

Banaji, J. (2003). 'The Fictions of Free Labour: Contract, Coercion, and So-Called Unfree Labour.' *Historical Materialism*, Vol. 11, No. 3, pp. 69–95.

Banaji, J. (2011) 'Mode of Production' in Fine, B. and Saad-Filho, A. (eds.) *The Elgar Companion to Marxian Economics*. Cheltenham: Edward Elgar.

Bandyopadhyaya, J. (2002). 'Class Struggle and Caste Oppression: Integral Strategy of the Left.' *The Marxist*, Vol. 18, July–December.

Banerjee, A. and Iyer, L. (2005). 'History, Institutions, and Economic Performance: The Legacy of Colonial Land Tenure Systems in India.' *The American Economic Review*, Vol. 95, No. 4, pp. 1190–213.

Banglapedia. (2009). Retrieved from http://banglapedia.search.com.bd/HT/B_0387.htm

Baran, P. (1957). *Political Economy of Growth*. Monthly Review Press.

Barkin, D. (2002). 'The Reconstruction of a Modern Mexican Peasantry.' *Journal of Peasant Studies*, Vol. 30, No. 1, pp. 73–90.

Baron, S.H. (1974). 'The Resurrection of Plekhanovism in Soviet Historiography.' *Russian Review*, Vol. 33, No. 4, pp. 386–404.

Baronian, L (2009). 'Abstract Labour and Modern Industry in Marx.' 36th Annual Conference of History of Economics Society, University of Denver, Colorado, 26–29 June, 2009.

Barrientos, S. (1991). 'The Classical Foundations of Unequal Exchange: A Critical Analysis.' *British Review of Economic Issues*, Vol. 13, No. 29, pp. 61–86.

Barrier, N.G. (1967). 'The Punjab Disturbances of 1907: The Response of the British Government in India to Agrarian Unrest.' *Modern Asian Studies*, Vol. 1, No. 4, pp. 353–83.

Baruah, S. (2001). 'Clash of Resource Use Regimes in Colonial Assam: A Nineteenth Century Puzzle Revisited.' *Journal of Peasant Studies*, Vol. 28, No. 3, pp. 109–24.

Bashir, Z. (2003). 'The Impacts of Reforms and Trade Liberalisation on Agricultural Export Performance in Pakistan.' *The Pakistan Development Review*, 42:4 Part II, pp. 941–60.

Basu, D. (2006). Benefits of the British Rule in India. Retrieved from http://www.ivarta.com/columns/OL_060610.htm

Baumann, P. (1998). 'The Persistence of Populism in Indian Forest Policy.' *Journal of Peasant Studies*, Vol. 25, No. 4, pp. 96–123.

Bayly, C.A. (1983). *Rulers, Townsmen and Bazaars: North Indian Society in the Age of British Expansion, 1770–1870*. Cambridge.

Bayly, C.A. (1985) 'State and Economy in India over Seven Hundred Years.' *The Economic History Review*, Vol. 38, No. 4, pp. 583–96.

Bayly, C.A. (1997). *Empire and Information: Intelligence Gathering and Social Communication in India, 1780–1870*. Cambridge University Press.

Beaglehole, T.H. (1977). 'From Rulers to Servants: The ICS and the British Demission of Power in India.' *Modern Asian Studies*, Vol. 11, No. 2, pp. 237–55.

Bellenoit, H.J.-A. (2007). *Missionary Education and Empire in Late Colonial India, 1860–1920*. Pickering & Chatto, London.

Belokrenitsky, V. (1991). *Capitalism in Pakistan: A History of Socioeconomic Development*. Patriot Publishers, New Delhi.

Bendix, R. (1967). 'Review: Social Origins of Dictatorship and Democracy: Lord and Peasant in the Making of the Modern World by Barrington Moore, Jr.' *Political Science Quarterly*, Vol. 82, No. 4, pp. 625–7.

Bernier, F. (1934). *Travels in the Mogul Empire: 1656–1668* (3rd ed.). Oxford University Press.

Bernstein, H. (1996). 'The Political Economy of the Maize Filie.' *Journal of Peasant Studies*, Vol. 23, No. 2 & 3, pp. 120–45.

Bernstein, H. (2004). "Changing before Our Very Eyes': Agrarian Questions and the Politics of Land in Capitalism Today.' *Journal of Agrarian Change*, Vol. 4.

Bernstein, H. and Brass, T. (Eds.) (1996). *Agrarian Questions: Essays in Appreciation of T.J. Byres*. Frank Cass.

Bernstein, H. and Byres, T.J. (2001). 'From Peasant Studies to Agrarian Change.' *Journal of Agrarian Change*, Vol. 1, No. 1, pp. 1–56.

Berringer, C. (1962). 'Welfare and Production Efficiency: Two Objectives of Land Reform in Pakistan.' *Pakistan Development Review*, Vol. 2, No. 2, pp. 173–88.

Beverley, J. (2004). 'Subaltern Resistance in Latin America: A Reply to Tom Brass.' *Journal of Peasant Studies*, Vol. 31, No. 2, pp. 261–75.

Bhagwati, J. and Chakravarty, S. (1969). 'Contributions to Indian Economic Analysis.' *American Economic Review*, Vol. 59, pp. 1–73.

Bhalla, S. (1999). 'Liberalisation, Rural Labour Markets and the Mobilisation of Farm Workers: The Haryana Story in an All-India Context.' *Journal of Peasant Studies*, Vol. 26, No. 2 & 3, pp. 25–70.

Bharadwaj, K. (1985). 'A View on Commercialisation in Indian Agriculture and the Development of Capitalism.' *Journal of Peasant Studies*, Vol. 12, No. 4, pp. 7–25.

Bhattacharyya, S. (2001). 'Capitalist Development, Peasant Differentiation and the State: Survey Findings from West Bengal.' *Journal of Peasant Studies*, Vol. 28, No. 4, pp. 95–126

Bhowmik, S.K. (1992). 'Caste and Class in India.' *Economic and Political Weekly*, Vol. 27, No. 24/25, pp. 1246–8.

Biswas, P.K. (2001). 'Surplus Yield and Production Structure: The Case of Small-Scale Rural Industries in West Bengal.' *Journal of Peasant Studies*, Vol. 28, No. 2, pp. 119–45.

Black, C.E. (1967). 'Review: Social Origins of Dictatorship and Democracy: Lord and Peasant in the Making of the Modern World by Barrington Moore, Jr.' *The American Historical Review*, Vol. 72, No. 4, p. 1338.

Blunt, E.A.H. (1931). *The Caste System of Northern India*. Oxford University Press.

Blyn, G. (1966). *Agricultural Trends in India, 1891–1947: Output, Availability, and Productivity*. University of Pennsylvania Press.

Bonaccorsi di Patti, E. and Hardy, D.C. (2005). 'Financial Sector Liberalization, Bank Privatization, and Efficiency: Evidence from Pakistan.' *Journal of Banking & Finance*, Vol. 29, No. 8–9, August–September 2005, pp. 2381–406.

Bose, S.R. and Clark, E.H. (1969). 'Some Basic Considerations on Agricultural Mechanization in Pakistan.' *Pakistan Development Review*, Vol. 9, No. 3, pp. 273–308.

Brass, T. (1994). 'The Politics of Gender, Nature and Nation in the Discourse of the New Farmers' Movements.' *Journal of Peasant Studies*, Vol. 21, No. 3 & 4, pp. 27–71.

Brass, T. (1999). *Towards a Comparative Political Economy of Unfree Labour*. Frank Cass, London and Portland.

Brass, T. and Van der Linden, M. (1997). *Free and Unfree Labour: The Debate Continues*. Peter Lang AG.

Breman, J. (1974). *Patronage and Exploitation: Changing Agrarian Relations in South Gujarat, India*. University of California Press, Berkeley.

Breman, J. (1993). *Beyond Patronage and Exploitation*. Oxford University Press, Delhi.

Breman, J. (2007). *Labour Bondage in Western India: From Past to Present*. Oxford University Press, New Delhi.

Brenner, R. (1976). 'Agrarian Class Structure and Economic Development in Pre-Industrial Europe.' *Past and Present*, Vol. 70, pp. 30–74.

Brenner, R. (1977). 'The Origins of Capitalist Development: A Critique of Neo-Smithian Marxism.' *New Left Review*, Vol. I, No. 104, pp. 25–92.

Brook, T. (Ed.). (1989). *The Asiatic Mode of Production in China*. M.E. Sharpe.

Brown, J.M. (1994). *Modern India: The Origins of an Asian Democracy*. Oxford University Press, Oxford and New York.

Brutton, H. and Bose, S.R. (1962). 'The Pakistan Export Bonus Scheme.' *Development Economics*, Vol. 11.

Bukhari, J. (1965). 'Balanced Industrial Growth.' *Trade Journal*, Vol. 5, No. 11–12.

Burki, S.J. (1976). 'The Development of Pakistan's Agriculture: An Interdisciplinary Explanation.' In R.D. Stevens & P.J. Bertocci (Eds.), *Rural Development in Bangladesh and Pakistan*. University of Hawai Press.

Burki, S.J. (1988). *Pakistan under Bhutto 1971–1977* (Second Edition). Macmillan.

Burney, N.A. (1987). 'Workers' Remittances from the Middle East and the Effect on Pakistan's Economy.' *The Pakistan Development Review*, Vol. 26, No. 4, pp. 745–64.

Byres, T. (1998a). 'Editorial Note–Chipko, the Environment, Eco-feminism and Populism/Neopopulism.' *Journal of Peasant Studies*, Vol. 25, No. 4, pp. 33–5.

Byres, T.J. (1983). *Sharecropping and Sharecroppers*. Frank Cass.

Byres, T.J. (1985). 'Modes of Production and Non-European, Pre-Colonial Societies: The Nature and Significance of the Debate.' In T.J. Byres & H. Mukhia (Eds.), *Feudalism and Non-European Societies*. Frank Cass, London.

Byres, T.J. (1996). *Capitalism from above and Capitalism from Below: An Essay in Comparative Political Economy*. Macmillan Press.

Byres, T.J. (1998b). 'Some Thoughts on a Heterodox View of the Causes of Low Agricultural Productivity.' *Journal of Peasant Studies*, Vol. 26, No. 1, pp. 159–69.

Byres, T.J. (2000). 'Perspectives on the Peasantries of Europe.' *Journal of Peasant Studies*, Vol. 27, No. 2, pp. 132–68.

Byres, T.J. (2004). 'Neo-Classical Neo-Populism 25 Years On: Déjá Vu and Déjá Passé. Towards a Critique.' *Journal of Agrarian Change*, Vol. 4, No. 1, 2, pp. 17–44.

Byres, T.J., & Mukhia, H. (Eds.), (1985). *Feudalism and Non-European Societies*. Frank Cass, London.

Cabral, A. (1969). *Revolution in Guinea: An African People's Struggle* (Handyside, R. Trans.). Stage 1, London.

Cabral, A. (1980). *Unity and Struggle: Speeches and Writings* (Wolfers, M. Trans.). Heinemann Educational, London.

Cahen, C. (1968). *Pre-Ottoman Turkey: A General Survey of the Material and Spiritual Culture and History c.1071–1330* (Jones-Williams, J. Trans.). Sidgwick and Jackson, London.

Calvert, H.C. (1936). *The Wealth and Welfare of the Punjab*. Lahore.

Candland, C. (2007). 'Workers' Organisations in Pakistan: Why No Role in Formal Politics.' *Critical Asian Studies*, Vol. 39, No. 1, pp. 35–57.

Cardoso, F.H. (1979). *Dependency and Development in Latin America/Fernando Henrique Cardoso and Enzo Faletto*. (Urquidi, M.M. Trans.).

Carnoy, M. (1974). *Education as Cultural Imperialism*. New York.

Carter, I. (1976). 'The Peasantry of Northern Scotland.' *Journal of Peasant Studies*, Vol. 3, No. 2, pp. 151–91.

Carter, I. (1977). 'Social Differentiation in the Aberdeenshire Peasantry, 1696–1870.' *Journal of Peasant Studies*, Vol. 5, No. 1, pp. 48–65.

Cassen, R.H. (1978). *India: Popularion, Economy, and Society*. Macmillan, London.

Centre for Global Development (2010). 'Aid to Pakistan by the Numbers' Retrieved from http://www.cgdev.org/section/initiatives/_active/pakistan/numbers

CERM. (1969). *Sur Le Mode De Production Asiatique*. Editions Sociales Paris.

Chakrabarty, D. (1989). *Rethinking Working-Class History: Bengal, 1890–1940*. Princeton University Press.

Chandra, B. (1979). *Colonialism in Modern India*. Delhi.

Chandra, S. (1959). *Parties and Politics at the Mughal Court, 1707–1740*. Aligarh.

Chandrasekhar, C.P. (1997). 'The Economic Consequences of the Abolition of Child Labour: An Indian Case Study.' *Journal of Peasant Studies*, Vol. 24, No. 3, pp. 137–79.

Chardin, J.S. (1996). *Travels: A Journey to Persia: Jean Chardin's Portrait of a Seventeenth-Century Empire*. I.B. Tauris, London.

Charlesworth, N. (1980). "The 'Middle Peasant Thesis' and the Roots of Rural Agitation in India, 1914–1947.' *Journal of Peasant Studies*, Vol. 7, No. 3, pp. 259–80.

Chatterjee, P. (1993). *The Nation and Its Fragments*. Princeton.

Chattopadhyaya, B.D. (1974). 'Trade and Urban Centres in Early Medieval North India.' The *Indian Historical Review*, Vol. I, No. 2, pp. 203–19.

Chaudhary, M.G. and Kamal, A.R. (1974). 'Wheat Production under Alternative Production Functions.' *Pakistan Development Review*, Vol. 13, No. 2, pp. 222–6.

Chaudhary, M.S. (1976). 'Impact of Optimal Cropping Patterns on Incomes in a Punjab District.' *Pakistan Development Review*, Vol. 15, No. 2, pp. 222–30.

Chaudhry, G.M. (1980). *The Green Revolution and Income Inequality: Some Empirical Evidence from Rural Pakistan, 1960–1975* (Unpublished doctoral dissertation). University of Wisconsin.

Chaudhry, G.M. (1989). 'Technological Change and Distribution of Agricultural Land: The Case of Pakistan.' *The Pakistan Development Review*, Vol. 28, No. 4, pp. 617–27.

Chaudhry, I.S., Malik, S., and Imran, A. (2006). 'Urban Poverty and Governance: The Case of Multan City.' *The Pakistan Development Review*, Vol. 45, No. 4 Part II, pp. 819–30.

Chaudhry, M.A. (1978). 'Determination of Cost of Tube Well Water and Estimation of Economic Rent in Canal Irrigation.' *Pakistan Development Review*, Vol. 18, No. 2, pp. 139–68.

Chaudhry, M.G. (1973). 'Problems of Agricultural Taxation in West Pakistan and an Alternative Solution.' *Pakistan Development Review*, Vol. 12, No. 2, pp. 93–122.

Chaudhuri, K.N. (1985). *Trade and Civilization in the Indian Ocean, an Economic History from the Rise of Islam to 1750*. Cambridge University Press.

Chayanov, A.V. (1966). 'The Theory of Peasant Economy.' In D. Thorner, B. Kerblay, and R.E.F. Smith, (eds.) (1986). *The Theory of Peasant Economy*. Second Edition, University of Wisconsin Press.

Cheema, A. (1995). *Pakistan's Textile Policy and Trade Performance: 1972–1990*. Sidney Sussex College, Cambridge.

Chibber, V. (1998). 'Breaching the Nadu: Lordship and Economic Development in Pre-Colonial South India.' *Journal of Peasant Studies*, Vol. 26, No. 1, pp. 1–42.

Chibber, V. (2006). 'On the Decline of Class Analysis in South Asian Studies.' *Critical Asian Studies*, Vol. 38, No. 4.

Chicherov, A.I. (1971). *Indian Economic Development in the Sixteenth-Eighteenth Centuries: Outline History of Crafts and Trade*. Moscow.

Childe, V.G. (1971). *Progress and Archaeology*. Greenwood Press.

Clark, E.H. (1972). *The Development of Tube Well Irrigation in the Punjab: An Investigation into Alternative Modes of Groundwater Development* (Unpublished doctoral dissertation). Princeton University.

Cohen, G. (1978). *Karl Marx's Theory of History: A Defence*. Princeton University Press.

Cohen, M. (1990). 'Peasant Differentiation and Proto-Industrialisation in the Ulster Countryside: Tullylish, 1680–1825.' *Journal of Peasant Studies*, Vol. 17, No. 3, pp. 413–32.

Cohn, B.S. (1960). 'The Initial British Impact on India: A Case Study of the Benares Region.' *Journal of Asian Studies*, Vol. 19, No. 4.

Cohn, B.S. (1961). 'From Indian Status to British Contract.' *The Journal of Economic History*, Vol. 21, No. 4, pp. 613–28.

Comninel, G.C. (2000). 'English Feudalism and the Origins of Capitalism.' *Journal of Peasant Studies*, Vol. 27, No. 4, pp. 1–53.

Condorcet. (1995). 'Condorcet on Human Progress.' *Population and Development Review*, Vol. 21, No. 1, pp. 153–61.

Contemporary Forms of Slavery in Pakistan. (1995). Human Rights Watch/Asia, London.

Coomaraswamy, A.K. and Lipsey, E.B.R. (1977). *Coomaraswamy*. Princeton University Press.

Cooper, A. (1983). 'Sharecroppers and Landlords in Bengal, 1930–50: The Dependency Web and Its Implications.' In T.J. Byres (Ed.), *Sharecropping and Sharecroppers*. Frank Cass, London.

Corta, L. and Venkateshwarlu, D. (1999). 'Unfree Relations and the Feminisation of Agricultural Labour in Andhra Pradesh, 1970–95.' *Journal of Peasant Studies*, Vol. 26, No. 2 & 3, pp. 71–139.

Cousins, B. (1996). 'Livestock Production and Common Property Struggles in South Africa's Agrarian Reform.' *Journal of Peasant Studies*, Vol. 23, No. 2 & 3, pp. 166–208.

Cowen, M.P. and Shenton, R.W. (1998a). 'Agrarian Doctrines of Development: Part I.' *Journal of Peasant Studies*, Vol. 25, No. 2, pp. 49–76.

Cowen, M.P. and Shenton, R.W. (1998b). 'Agrarian Doctrines of Development: Part II.' *Journal of Peasant Studies*, Vol. 25, No. 3, pp. 31–62.

Cownie, J., Johnston, B.F., and Duff, B. (1970). 'The Quantitative Impact of the Seed-Fertilizer Revolution in West Pakistan: An Exploratory Study.' *Food Research Institute Studies*, Vol. 9, No. 1, pp. 57–75.

Cownie, J., Johnston, B.F., and Duff, B. (1982). 'The Quantitative Impact of the Seed Fertiliser Revolution in West Pakistan.' In K. Ali (Ed.), *Pakistan: The Political Economy of Rural Development*. Vanguard Publications, Lahore.

Cox, T. (1979). 'Awkward Class or Awkward Classes? Class Relations in the Russian Peasantry before Collectivization.' *Journal of Peasant Studies*, Vol. 7, No. 1, pp. 70–85.

Crabtree, J. (2002). 'The Impact of Neo-Liberal Economics on Peruvian Peasant Agriculture in the 1990s.' *Journal of Peasant Studies*, Vol. 29, No. 3 & 4, pp. 131–61.

Crooke, W. (1974). *The Tribes and Castes of the North Western India*. Cosmo Publications, Delhi.

Currie, K. (1980). 'Problematic Modes and the Mughal Social Formation.' *Insurgent Sociologist*, Vol. IX, p. 4.

Currie, K. (1984). 'The Asiatic Mode of Production: Problems of Conceptualising State and Economy.' *Dialectical Anthropology*, Vol. 8, No. 4.

Dange, S.A. (1955). *India: From Primitive Communism to Slavery*. Peoples Publishing House, New Delhi.

Darling, M.L. (1930). *Rusticus Loquitor or the Old Light and the New in the Punjab Village*. Oxford University Press.

Darling, M.L. (1934). *Wisdom and Waste in the Punjab Village*. Oxford University Press.

Darling, M.L. (1947). *The Punjab Peasant in Prosperity and Debt* (4th Ed.). Oxford University Press.

Davis, M. (2001). *Late Victorian Holocausts: El Nino Famines and the Making of the Third World*. Verso.

Davis, M. (2006). *Planet of Slums: Urban Involution and the Informal Working Class*. Verso.

Desai, A.R. (1966). *Social Background of Indian Nationalism*. Popular Prakasan, Bombay.

Desai, A.R. (1964). *India's Path of Development: A Marxist Approach*. Popular Prakashan, Bombay.

Desai, A.R. (Ed.). (1971). *Essays on Modernization of Underdeveloped Societies*. Thacker, Bombay.

Desai, I.P. (1976). *Untouchability in Rural Gujarat*. Popular Prakashan, Bombay.

Desmarais, A.A. (2002). 'The Campesina: Consolidating an International Peasant and Farm Movement.' *Journal of Peasant Studies*, Vol. 29, No. 2, pp. 91–124.

Dhanagare, D.N. (1994). 'The Class Character and Politics of the Farmers' Movement in Maharashtra during the 1980s.' *Journal of Peasant Studies*, Vol. 21, No. 3 & 4, pp. 72–94.

Dieterich, H. (1982). 'Some Theoretical and Methodological Observations about the Inca Empire and the Asiatic Mode of Production.' *Latin American Perspectives*, Vol. 9, No. 4, pp. 111–32.

Digby, W. (1901). 'Prosperous British India.' Retrieved from http://www.guardian.co.uk/books/2001/jan/20/historybooks.famine

Dinerman, A. (2001). 'From 'Abaixo' To 'Chiefs of Production': Agrarian Change in Nampula Province, Mozambique, 1975–87.' *Journal of Peasant Studies*, Vol. 28, No. 2, pp. 1–82.

Dirlik, A. (1985). 'The Universalisation of a Concept: From 'Feudalism' to 'Feudalism' in Chinese Marxist Historiography.' *The Journal of Peasant Studies*, Vol. 12, No. 2, 3.

Dirlik, A. (1997). *The Postcolonial Aura*. Westview Press.

Dobb, M. (1954). *The Transition from Feudalism to Capitalism*. George Toutledge & Sons.

Dobb, M. (1958). *Capitalism Yesterday and Today*. Lawrence & Wishart.

Dobb, M. (1963). *Studies in the Development of Capitalism*. Routledge & Kegan Paul.

Dorfman, R., Revelle, R., and Thomas, H. (1965). 'Waterlogging and Salinity in the Indus Plain: Some Basic Considerations.' *Pakistan Development Review*, Vol. 3, No. 3, pp. 331–70.

Dorosh, P., Niazi, M.K., and Nazli, H. (2003). 'Distributional Impact of Agricultural Growth in Pakistan.' *The Pakistan Development Review*, Vol. 42, No. 3, pp. 249–76.

Duncan, I. (1997). 'Agricultural Innovation and Political Change in North India: The Lok Dal in Uttar Pradesh.' *Journal of Peasant Studies*, Vol. 24, No. 4, pp. 246–68.

Duncan, I. (1999). 'Dalits and Politics in Rural North India: The Bahujan Samaj Party in Uttar Pradesh.' *Journal of Peasant Studies*, Vol. 27, No. 1, pp. 35–60.

Dunn, S. (1982). *The Fall and Rise of the Asiatic Mode of Production*. Routledge.

Durr-e-Nayab. (2008). 'Demographic Dividend or Demographic Threat in Pakistan?' *The Pakistan Development Review*, Vol. 47, No. 1, pp. 1–26.

Dutt, N.K. (1968). *Origin and growth of caste in India*. Firma K.L. Mukhopadhyay, Calcutta.

Dutt, R.C. (1906). *The Economic History of India in the Victorian Age*. London.

Dutt, R.P. (1940). *India Today*. Lawrence and Wishart.

Dutt, R.P. (1957). *The Crisis of Britain and the British Empire*. Lawrence and Wishart.

E. San Juan, J. (2002). 'The Poverty of Post-colonialism.' *Literary and Cultural Studies*, Vol. 11, No. 1, pp. 57–74.

Eapen, M. (2001). 'Rural Non-Farm Employment: Agricultural Versus Urban Linkages–Some Evidence from Kerala State, India.' *Journal of Peasant Studies*, Vol. 28, No. 3, pp. 67–89.

Enthoven, R.E. (1990). *The Tribes and Castes of Bombay*. Asian Educational Services.

Eberhard, W. (1958). '"Oriental Despotism': Political Weapon or Sociological Concept.' In A.M. Bailey & J.R. Llobera (Eds.), *The Asiatic Mode of Production: Science and Politics*. Routeledge & Kegan Paul.

Eckert, J.B. (1974). 'Private Tubewell Numbers in Pakistan: A Synthesis.' *Pakistan Development Review*, Vol. 13, No. 1, pp. 94–105.

Economy of Pakistan. (1951). Pakistan Ministry of Economic Affairs, Karachi.

Edin, M. (2003). 'Local State Corporatism and Private Business.' *Journal of Peasant Studies*, Vol. 30, No. 3 & 4, pp. 278–95.

Edwardes, M. (1972). *Ralph Fitch, Elizabethan in the Indies*. Faber and Faber.

Efimov, A.V. (1930). 'Concepts of Economic Formations in the Work of Marx and Engels and Their Use in Clarifying the Structure of Eastern Societies.' *Istorik Marksist*, Vol. 16.

Elphinstone, M. (1841). *The History of India*. John Murray, London.

Emmaneul, A. (1972). *Unequal Exchange: A Study of the Imperialism of Trade*. Monthly Review Press.

Engels, F. (1850). *The Peasant War in Germany*.Retrieved from http:marxists.org/archive/marx/works/1850/peasant-war-germany/index.htm

Engels, F. (1853). 'Engels to Marx, 6 June 1853.' Retrieved from http:marxists.org/archive/marx/works/1853/letters/53_06_06.htm

Engels, F. (1874). 'On Social Relations in Russia.' Retrieved from http:marxists.org/archive/marx/works/1874/refugee-literature/ch05.htm

Engels, F. (1891). *Origins of the Family, Private Property and the State*. Retrieved from http://www.marxists.org/archive/marx/works/1884/origin-family/index.htm

Engels, F. (1881). 'Engels to Nikolai Danielson in St Petersburg.' Retrieved from http://www.marxists.org/archive/marx/works/1881/letters/81_02_19.htm

Engels, F. (1894). *Peasant Question in France and Germany*. Retrieved from http://www.marxists.org/archive/marx/works/download/Engles_The_Peasant_Question_in_France_and_Germany.pdf

Engels, F. (1894–95). 'On the History of Early Christianity.' Retrieved from http:marxists.org/archive/marx/works/1894/early-christianity/index.htm

Engels, F. (1934). *Anti-Duhring*. Lawrence & Wishart.

Ennew, J., Hirst, P., and Tribe, K. (1977). 'Peasantry as an Economic Category.' *Journal of Peasant Studies*, Vol. 4, No. 4, pp. 295–322.

Ercelan, A. (1990). 'Absolute Poverty in Pakistan, Poverty Lines, Incidence and Intensity.' Draft Paper, Applied Economics Research Centre University of Karachi.

Ercelan, A., Ali, K., and Abbas, U. (2004). 'Does Labour Regulation Hinder Small Enterprise Growth.' *APRNET*, Vol. 55, No. 11.

Ewert, J. and Hamman, J. (1996). 'Labour Organisation in Western Cape Agriculture: An Ethnic Corporatism?' *Journal of Peasant Studies*, Vol. 23, No. 2 & 3, pp. 146–65.

Eyferth, J. (2003). 'How Not to Industrialize: Observations from a Village in Sichuan.' *Journal of Peasant Studies*, Vol. 20, No. 3 & 4, pp. 75–92.

Eyferth, J., Ho, P., and Vermeer, E.B. (2003). 'Introduction: The Opening-up of China's Countryside.' *Journal of Peasant Studies*, Vol. 30, No. 3 & 4, pp. 1–17.

Fafchamps, M. and Quisumbing, A.R. (1998). 'Human Capital, Productivity, and Labour Allocation in Rural Pakistan.' *The Journal of Human Resources*, Vol. XXXIV, No. 2.

Falcon, W.P. (1964). 'Farmer Response to Price in a Subsistence Economy: The Case of West Pakistan.' *American Economic Review*, Vol. 54, No. 3, pp. 580–91.

Falcon, W.P. (1970). 'The Green Revolution: Second Generation Problems.' *American Journal of Agricultural Economics*, Vol. 52, No., pp. 698–710.

Falcon, W.P. and Gotsch, C.H. (1964). *Agriculture in West Pakistan: An Analysis of Past Progress and Future Prospects* (Mimeographed). Pakistan Institute of Development Economics.

Farm Water Management Project. (1981). World Bank.

Farooqui, M.N.I. (1984). 'Analysis of Fertility Changes in Pakistan.' *The Pakistan Development Review*, Vol. 23, No. 2, pp. 225–36.

Federal Bureau of Statistics. (2008). Retrieved from http://www.statpak.gov.pk/depts/fbs/statistics/statistics.html

Feeney, G. and Alam, I. (2003). 'Fertility, Population Growth, and Accuracy of Census Enumeration in Pakistan.' In I. Kemal, and Mahmood (Ed.), *Population of Pakistan: An Analysis of 1998 Population and Housing Census*. Pakistan Institute of Development Economics.

Feeney, G. and Alam, I. (2004). 'New Estimates and Projections of Population Growth in Pakistan.' *Population and Development Review*, Vol. 29, No. 3, pp. 483–92.

Ferguson, A. (1966). *An Essay on the History of Civil Society (1767)*. London.

Ferguson, N. (2004). *Empire: How Britain Made the Modern World*. Penguin.

Ferguson, N. (2005). *Colossus: The Rise and Fall of the American Empire*. Penguin.

Fernández, R. and Ocampo, J. (1974). 'The Latin American Revolution: A Theory of Imperialism, Not Dependence.' *Latin American Perspectives*, Vol. 1, Spring, pp. 30–61.

Fisher, M.H. (1984). 'Indirect Rule in the British Empire: The Foundations of the Residency System in India (1764–1858).' *Modern Asian Studies*, Vol. 18, No. 3, pp. 393–428.

Fletcher, R. (2001). 'What Are We Fighting For? Rethinking Resistance in a Pewenche Community in Chile.' *Journal of Peasant Studies*, Vol. 28, No. 3, pp. 37–66.

Floto, E. (1989). 'The Centre-Periphery System and Unequal Exchange.' *Cepal Review*, Vol. 39, pp. 135–54.

Foeken, D. and Tellegen, N. (1997). 'Proletarianisation, Land, Income and Living Conditions of Farm Labourers in Kenya.' *Journal of Peasant Studies*, Vol. 24, No. 4, pp. 296–313.

Fogel, J.A. (1984). *Politics and Sinology: The Case of Naitokonan (1866–1934)*. Harvard University Press.

Fogel, J.A. (1988). 'The Debates over the Asiatic Mode of Production in Soviet Russia, China, and Japan.' *The American Historical Review*, Vol. 93, No. 1, pp. 56–79.

Foran, J. (1988). 'The Modes of Production Approach to Seventeenth-Century Iran.' *International Journal of Middle East Studies*, Vol. 20, No. 3, pp. 345–63.

Foster-Carter, A. (1978). 'The Modes of Production Controversy.' *New Left Review*, Vol. I, No. 107, pp. 47–77.

Fox, R.G. (1984). 'Urban Class and Communal Consciousness in Colonial Punjab: The Genesis of India's Intermediate Regime.' *Modern Asian Studies*, Vol. 18, No. 3, pp. 459–89.

Frank, A.G. (1969). *Capitalism and Underdevelopment in Latin America: Historical Studies of Chile and Brazil.* Monthly Review Press.

Fussman, G. (1982). 'Central and Provincial Administration in Ancient India.' *Indian Historical Review*, Vol. XIV, No. 1–2.

Gaido, D. (2000). 'A Materialist Analysis of Slavery and Sharecropping in the Southern United States.' *Journal of Peasant Studies*, Vol. 28, No. 1, pp. 55–94.

Gaido, D. (2002). 'The American Path of Bourgeois Development.' *Journal of Peasant Studies*, Vol. 29, No. 2, pp. 1–23.

Gallagher, J. and Robinson, R. (1953). 'The Imperialism of Free Trade.' *The Economic History Review*, Vol. 6, No. 1, pp. 1–15.

Gardezi, H.N. (2004). 'Globalization and Pakistan's Dilemma of Development.' *The Pakistan Development Review*, Vol. 43, No. 4 Part I, pp. 423–40.

Garrabou, R., Planas, J., and Saguer, E. (2001). 'Sharecropping and the Management of Largerural Estatesin Catalonia, 1850–1950.' *Journal of Peasant Studies*, Vol. 28, No. 3, pp. 89–108.

Gazdar, H. (2007). 'Class, Caste, or Race: Veils over Social Oppression' *Economic and Political Weekly*, Vol. 42, No. 2, pp. 86–9

Gellner, E. (1964). *Thought and Change.* Weidenfeld and Nicolson.

Gellner, E. (Ed.). (1980). *Soviet and Western Anthropology.* Duckworth, London.

Gerschenkron, A. (1952). 'Economic Backwardness in Historical Perspective.' In B.F. Hoselitz (Ed.), *Progress of under-developed areas.* University of Chicago Press.

Ghani, W.I., Haroon, O., and Ashraf, J. (2008). 'Business Groups, Corporate Governance, and Financial Performance: Evidence from Pakistan' Retrieved from http://ravi.lums.edu.pk/cmer/conference2008/images/Waqar_G_Business_Groups.pdf.

Gibbon, P. (1997). 'Prawns and Piranhas: The Political Economy of a Tanzanian Private Sector Marketing Chain.' *Journal of Peasant Studies*, Vol. 25, No. 1, pp. 1–86.

Gilani, E. (1981). 'Labour Migration from Pakistan to the Middle East and Its Impact on the Domestic Economy.' Report 126, 127, 128, Pakistan Institute of Development Economics.

Gill, S.S. (1994). 'The Farmers' Movement and Agrarian Change in the Green Revolution Belt of North-West India.' *Journal of Peasant Studies*, Vol. 21, No. 3 & 4, pp. 195–211.

Gill, Z.A. and Sampath, R.K. (1992). 'Inequality in Irrigation Distribution in Pakistan.' *The Pakistan Development Review*, Vol. 31, No. 1, pp. 75–100.

Gilmartin, D. (1994). 'Scientific Empire and Imperial Science: Colonialism and Irrigation Technology in the Indus Basin.' *The Journal of Asian Studies*, Vol. 53, No. 4, pp. 1127–49.

Godes, M.S. (1981). The Reaffirmation of Unilinearism. In A.M. Bailey & J.R. Llobera (Eds.), *The Asiatic Mode of Production: Science and Politics.* Routledge & Kegan Paul.

Goodman, D. and Watts, M. (1994). 'Reconfiguring the Rural or Fording the Divide Capitalist Restructuring and the Global Agro-Food System.' *Journal of Peasant Studies*, Vol. 22, No. 1, pp. 1–49.

Gopal, S. (1949). *The Permanent Settlement in Bengal and Its Results.* Allen and Unwin.

Gordon, A. (1999). 'The Agrarian Question in Colonial Java: Coercion and Colonial Capitalist Sugar Plantations, 1870–1941.' *Journal of Peasant Studies*, Vol. 27, No. 1, pp. 1–35.

Gotsch, C.H. (1968a). 'A Programming Approach to Agriculture Policy Planning in West Pakistan.' *Pakistan Development Review*, Vol. 8, No. 2, pp. 192–225.

Gotsch, C.H. (1968b). 'Regional Agricultural Growth: The Case of West Pakistan.' *Asian Survey*, Vol. 8, No. 3, pp. 188–205.

Gotsch, C.H. (1971). 'Technology, Prices and Incomes in West Pakistan Agriculture: Some Observations on the Green Revolution.' Harvard University Development Advisory Service: Report 199.

Gotsch, C.H. (1972). 'Notes on the Current Status and Future Development of Pakistan Agriculture.' Harvard University Development Advisory Service: Report 218.

Gotsch, C.H. (1973). 'Tractor Mechanization and Rural Development in Pakistan.' *International Labour Review*, Vol. 107, No. 2.

Gotsch, C.H. (1974). Economics, Institutions and Employment Generation in Rural Areas. In E.O. Edwards (Ed.), *Employment in Developing Nations*. Columbia University Press.

Gotsch, C.H. (1975). 'Linear Programming and Agricultural Policy: Micro Studies of the Pakistan Punjab.' *Food Research Institute Studies*, Special Issue 15, No. 1, pp. 1–106.

Gotsch, C.H. (1976). 'The Green Revolution and Future Development in Pakistan.' In R.D. Stevens, H. Alavi & P.J. Bertocci (Eds.), *Rural Development in Bangladesh and Pakistan*. University of Hawai Press.

Gotsch, C.H. (1982). 'Tractor Mechanization and Rural Development in Pakistan.' In K. Ali (Ed.). *Pakistan: The Political Economy of Rural Development*. Vanguard Publications.

Gough, K. (1969). 'Class and Agrarian Change: Some Comments on Peasant Resistance and Revolution in India.' *Pacific Affairs*, Vol. 42, No. 3, pp. 360–68.

Gray, J. (1993). 'Rural Industry and Uneven Development: The Significance of Gender in the Irish Linen Industry.' *Journal of Peasant Studies*, Vol. 20, No. 4, pp. 590–611.

Griffin, K. (1974). *The Political Economy of Agrarian Change*. Macmillan.

Griffin, K. and Khan, A.R. (Eds.), (1972). *Growth and Inequality in Pakistan*. St. Martin's Press.

Griffin, K., Khan, A.R., and Ickowitz, A. (2002). 'Poverty and Distribution of Land.' *Journal of Agrarian Change*, Vol. 2, No. 3, pp. 279–330.

Griffin, K., Khan, A.R., and Ickowitz, A. (2004). 'In Defence of Neo-Classical Neo-Populism.' *Journal of Agrarian Change*, Vol. 4, No. 3, pp. 361–86.

Griffin, L.H. and Massy, C.F. (1940). *Chiefs and Families of Note in the Punjab*. Lahore.

Guha, R. (1974). 'Neel-Darpan: The Image of a Peasant Revolt in a Liberal Mirror.' *Journal of Peasant Studies*, Vol. 2, No. 1, pp. 1–46.

Guha, R. (1983). *Elementary Aspects of Peasant Insurgency in Colonial India*. Oxford University Press.

Guha, R. (1988). *An Indian Historiography of India*. K.P. Bagchi & Company.

Guha, R. (1997). *Dominance without Hegemony: History and Power in Colonial India*. Harvard University Press.

Guha, R. (Ed.). (2000). *A Subaltern Studies Reader, 1986–1995*. Oxford University Press.

Guisinger, S. and Hicks, N.L. (1978). 'Long-Term Trends in Income Distribution in Pakistan.' *World Development*, Vol. 6, No. 11–12, pp. 1271–80.

Guo, X. (2001). ''It's All a Matter of Hats': Rural Urbanization in South-West China.' *Journal of Peasant Studies*, Vol. 29, No. 1, pp. 109–28.

Gupta, D. (2001). 'Everyday Resistance or Routine Repression! Exaggeration as Stratagem in Agrarian Conflict.' *Journal of Peasant Studies*, Vol. 29, No. 1, pp. 89–108.

Gupta, P.S. and Deshpande, A. (Eds.), (2002). *The British Raj and Its Indian Armed Forces, 1857–1939*. Oxford University Press.

Gusfield, J. (1967). 'Review: Social Origins of Dictatorship and Democracy: Lord and Peasant in the Making of the Modern World by Barrington Moore, Jr.' *Social Forces*, Vol. 46, No. 1, pp. 114–15.

Gustafson, E. (1973). 'Economic Reforms under the Bhutto Regime.' *Journal of Asian and African Studies*, Vol. 3, No. 3–4, pp. 242–58.

Habermas, J. (2006). 'The European Nation State—Its Achievements and Its Limits. On the Past and Future Sovereignty and Citizenship.' In G. Balakrishan (Ed.), *Mapping the Nation*. Vernon.

Habib, I. (1963). *The Agrarian System of Mughal India*. Asia Publishing House, Bombay.

Habib, I. (1969). 'Potentialities of Capitalistic Development in the Economy of Mughal India.' *The Journal of Economic History*, Vol. 29, No. 1, pp. 32–78.

Habib, I. (1985). 'Studying a Colonial Economy—without Perceiving Colonialism.' *Modern Asian Studies*, Vol. 19, No. 3.

Habib, I. (1985). 'Classifying Pre-Colonial India.' In T.J. Byres & H. Mukhia (Eds.), *Feudalism and Non-European Societies*. Frank Cass.

Habib, I. (1995). *Essays in Indian History*. Tulika.

Habib, I. (2002). *Essay in Indian History: Towards a Marxist Perspective*. Tulika.

Haggerty, W. (1969). *Higher and Professional Education in India.* United States Government Printing Office, Washington DC.

Haj, S. (1994). 'Land, Power and Commercialization in Lower Iraq, 1850–1958: A Case of 'Blocked Transition'. *Journal of Peasant Studies,* Vol. 22, No. 1, pp. 126–63.

Haldon, J. (1993). *The State and the Tributary Mode of Production.* Verso.

Hambly, G.R.G. (1964). 'Richard Temple and the Punjab Tenancy Act of 1868.' *The English Historical Review,* Vol. 79, No. 310, pp. 47–66.

Hamdani, K. and Haque, N.U. (1978). 'The Demand for Fertilizer: A Critical Review.' *Pakistan Development Review,* Vol. 17, No. 4, pp. 451–67.

Hamid, J. (1970). 'Suggested Approach to Agricultural Taxation Policy in West Pakistan.' *Pakistan Development Review,* Vol. 17, No. 4, pp. 422–47.

Hamid, J. (1973). 'The Problem of Agricultural Taxation in West Pakistan and an Alternative Solution: A Comment.' *Pakistan Development Review,* Vol. 12, No. 3, pp. 311–14.

Haq, M. (1968). *Business Recorder,* 25 April.

Haq, R. (2007). 'Land Inequality by Mode of Irrigation in Pakistan, 1990–2000.' *The Pakistan Development Review,* Vol. 46, No. 4, pp. 1011–22.

Haque, N. and Kardar, S. (1993). 'Constraints to the Development of Financial Markets in Pakistan' International Monetary Fund (Mimiographed).

Hardiman, D. (1995). 'Community, Patriarchy, Honour: Raghu Bhanagre's Revolt.' *Journal of Peasant Studies,* Vol. 23, No. 1, pp. 88–130.

Masud, M. (1949) 'Minute of Dissent.' Sindh Hari Enquiry Committee, Karachi.

Harootunian, H.D. (1968). 'Review: Social Origins of Dictatorship and Democracy: Lord and Peasant in the Making of the Modern World by Barrington Moore, Jr.' *The Journal of Asian Studies,* Vol. 27, No. 2, pp. 372–4.

Harrison, M. (1975). 'Chayanov and the Economics of the Russian Peasantry.' *Journal of Peasant Studies,* Vol. 2, No. 4, pp. 389–417.

Harrison, M. (1977a). 'Resource Allocation and Agrarian Class Formation: The Problems of Social Mobility among Russian Peasant Households, 1880–1930.' *Journal of Peasant Studies,* Vol. 4, No. 2, pp. 127–61.

Harrison, M. (1977b). 'The Peasant Mode of Production in the Work of A.V. Chayanov.' *Journal of Peasant Studies,* Vol. 4, No. 4, pp. 323–36.

Harrison, M. (1979). 'Chayanov and the Marxists.' *Journal of Peasant Studies,* Vol. 7, No. 1, pp. 86–100.

Hart, G. (1991). 'Engendering Everyday Resistance: Gender, Patronage and Production Politics in Rural Malaysia.' *Journal of Peasant Studies,* Vol. 19, No. 1, pp. 93–121.

Hart, G. (1996). 'The Agrarian Question and Industrial Dispersal in South Africa: Agro-Industrial Linkages through Asian Lenses.' *Journal of Peasant Studies,* Vol. 23, No. 2 & 3, pp. 245–77.

Hasan, I. (1970). *Central Structure of the Mughal Empire.* New Delhi.

Hasan, S.N. (1973). *Thoughts on Agrarian Relations in Mughal India.* New Delhi.

Hasan, Z. (1994). 'Shifting Ground: Hindutva Politics and the Farmers' Movement in Uttar Pradesh.' *Journal of Peasant Studies,* Vol. 21, No. 3 & 4, pp. 165–94.

Hashmi, S.S. (1965). 'People of Karachi: Demographic Characteristics.' Pakistan Institute of Development Economics.

Hashmi, S.S. and Sultan, M. (1998). 'Population Trends and Rates of Population Growth in Pakistan: Assessment of Preliminary Results of the 1998 Census.' *The Pakistan Development Review,* Vol. 37, No. 4, pp. 495–506.

Hegel, G.W.F. (1837). 'Hegel's Philosophy of History.' Retrieved from http://www.marxists.org/reference/archive/hegel/works/hi/history5.htm

Helbock, R.W. (1975a). 'Differential Urban Growth Distance Consideration in Domestic Migration Flows in Pakistan.' *The Pakistan Development Review,* Vol. 14, No. 1, pp. 53–84.

Helbock, R.W. (1975b). 'Urban Population Growth in Pakistan: 1961–62.' *The Pakistan Development Review,* Vol. 14, No. 3, pp. 315–33.

Herodotus, B.B.C. (1942). *Histories: The Persian Wars*. Translated by George Rawlinson.

Herring, R.J. (1979). 'Zulfiqar Ali Bhutto and the Eradication of Feudalism in Pakistan.' *Comparative Studies in Society and History*, Vol. 21, No. 4, pp. 519–57.

Hilton, R. (1974). 'Medieval Peasants: Any Lessons?' *Journal of Peasant Studies*, Vol. 1, No. 2, pp. 509–19.

Hilton, R. (1978). 'Reasons for Inequality among Medieval Peasants.' *Journal of Peasant Studies*, Vol. 5, No. 3, pp. 271–84.

Hilton, R. (1990). 'Why Was There So Little Champart Rent in Medieval England?' *Journal of Peasant Studies*, Vol. 17, No. 4, pp. 509–19.

Hilton, R. (Ed.). (1976). *The Transition from Feudalism to Capitalism*. New Left Books.

Hindess, B., & Hirst, P.Q. (1975). *Pre-Capitalist Modes of Production*. Routledge & Kegan Paul.

Hirashima, S. (1978). *The Structure of Disparity in Developing Agriculture*. Institute of Developing Economies.

Hiro, D. 'The Cost of an Afghan 'Victory'.' *The Nation*, 28 January 1999.

Ho, P. (2003). 'Wasteland Auction Policy in Northwest China: Solving Environmental Degradation and Rural Poverty?' *Journal of Peasant Studies*, Vol. 30, No. 3 & 4, pp. 121–59.

Hobsbawm, E. (1964). 'Introduction.' In *Pre-Capitalist Economic Formations: Karl Marx*. Lawrence & Wishart.

Hobsbawm, E.J. (1967). 'Review: Social Origins of Dictatorship and Democracy: Lord and Peasant in the Making of the Modern World by Barrington Moore, Jr.' *American Sociological Review*, Vol. 32, No. 5, pp. 821–2.

Hoefle, S.W. (2003). 'Beyond Cold War Pipe Dreams: What the West Was Not.' *Journal of Peasant Studies*, Vol. 30, No. 2, pp. 95–123.

Hooper, E., & Hamid, A.I. (2003). 'Scoping Study on Social Exclusion in Pakistan: A Summary of Findings' Department of International Development (DFID).

Household Integrated Economic Survey. (2005–6). Retrieved from http://www.statpak.gov.pk/depts/fbs/statistics/hies05_06/table11.pdf

Hunter, W.W.S. (1882). *The Indian Empire: Its History, People, and Products*. Trübner, London.

Huntington, S.P. (1966). *Political Order in Changing Societies*. New Haven.

Hussain, S.A. (1980). 'The Impact of Agricultural Growth on the Agrarian Structure of Pakistan, with Special Reference to the Punjab Province: 1960 to 1978.' Unpublished Ph.D. Thesis. University of Sussex.

Hussain, S.M. (1970). 'Price Incentives for the Production of High-Yielding Mexican Varieties of Wheat.' *Pakistan Development Review*, Vol. 10, No. 4, pp. 448–67.

Ibbetson, D. (1986). *Panjab Castes*. Government Printing Press, Lahore.

Indra, D.M. and Buchignani, N. (1997). 'Rural Landlessness, Extended Entitlements and Inter-Household Relations in South Asia: A Bangladesh Case.' *Journal of Peasant Studies*, Vol. 24, No. 3, pp. 25–64.

Industrial Policy of the Government of Pakistan. (1961). Government of Pakistan Planning Commission.

Industries in Pakistan. (1965). Department of Films and Publications, Government of Pakistan.

Interim Manpower Survey Report. (1953). Pakistan Ministry of Economic Affairs.

International Monetary Fund (2010). 'Transactions with the Fund from May 01, 1984 to July 31, 2010.' Retrieved from http://www.imf.org/external/np/fin/tad/extrans1.aspx?memberKey1=760&endDate=2010%2D09%2D05&finposition_flag=YES

Iolk, E.S. (1931). 'The Amp and the Class Struggle.' In A.M. Bailey & J.R. Llobera (Eds.), *The Asiatic Mode of Production: Science and Politics*. Routledge & Kegan Paul.

Irfan, M. (1981). 'The Population, Labour Force and Migration.' Pakistan Institute of Development Economics, International Labour Organisation, United Nations Population Fund: Report 118.

Islam, M.M. (1995). 'The Punjab Land Alienation Act and the Professional Moneylenders.' *Modern Asian Studies*, Vol. 29, No. 2, pp. 271–91.

Islam, S. (1979). *The Permanent Settlement in Bengal: A Study of Its Operation*. Bangla Academy, Dacca.

Ito, S. (2002). 'From Rice to Prawns: Economic Transformation and Agrarian Structure in Rural Bangladesh.' *Journal of Peasant Studies*, Vol. 29, No. 2, pp. 47–70.

Jafri, S.M.Y. (1999). 'Assessing Poverty in Pakistan: In a Profile of Poverty in Pakistan.' Mahbub ul Haq Center for Human Development, Islamabad.

Jain, A.K. (Ed.). (2001). *The Political Economy of Corruption*. Routledge.

Jalal, A. (1985). *The Sole Spokesman: Jinnah, the Muslim League and the Demand for Pakistan*. Cambridge University Press.

Jassal, S. (2003). 'Bhojpuri Songs, Women's Work and Social Control in Northern India.' *Journal of Peasant Studies*, Vol. 30, No. 2, pp. 159–206.

Jayasval, K.P. (1988). *Hindu Polity: A Constitutional History of India in Hindu Times*. Eastern Book House.

Jewitt, S. (2000). 'Mothering Earth? Gender and Environmental Protection in the Jharkhand, India.' *Journal of Peasant Studies*, Vol. 27, No. 2, pp. 94–131.

Jha, H. (1980). 'Permanent Settlement in Bihar.' *Social Scientist*, Vol. 9, No. 1, pp. 53–7.

Jha, S.C. (1963). *Studies in the Development of Capitalism in India*. Firma K.L. Mukhopadhyay, Calcutta.

Jodhka, S.S. (2002). 'Caste and Untouchability in Rural Punjab.' *Economic and Political Weekly*, Vol. 37, No. 19, pp. 1813–23.

Johnson, C. (1966). *Revolutionary Change*. Boston.

Johnston, F. and Cownie, J. (1969). 'The Seed-Fertilizer Revolution and Labour Force Absorption.' *American Economic Review*, Vol. 59, No. 4, pp. 569–82.

Jones, R. (1956). *Essay on the Distribution of Wealth*. Kelley & Millman.

Joseph, G.G. and Tomlinson, M. (1991). 'Testing the Existence and Measuring the Magnitude of Unequal Exchange Resulting from International Trade: A Marxian Approach.' *Indian Economic Review*, Vol. 26, No, 2, pp. 124–48.

Kaiwar, V. (2000). 'Nature, Property and Polity in Colonial Bombay.' *Journal of Peasant Studies*, Vol. 27, No. 2, pp. 1–49.

Kalyvas, A. and Katznelson, I. (1998). 'Adam Ferguson Returns: Liberalism through a Glass, Darkly.' *Political Theory*, Vol. 26, No. 2, pp. 173–97.

Kaminsky, A.P. (1979). 'Morality Legislation and British Troops in Late Nineteenth-Century India.' *Military Affairs*, Vol. 43, No. 2, pp. 78–84.

Kaneda, H. (1969). 'Economic Implications of the 'Green Revolution' and the Strategy of Agricultural Development in West Pakistan.' *Pakistan Development Review*, Vol. 9, No. 2, pp. 111–43.

Kaneda, H. and Ghaffar, M. (1970). 'Output Effects of Tubewells on the Agriculture of the Punjab.' *Pakistan Development Review*, Vol. 10, No. 1, pp. 68–87.

Kannan, K.P. (1999). 'Rural Labour Relations and Development Dilemmas in Kerala: Reflections on the Dilemmas of a Socially Transforming Labour Force in a Slowly Growing Economy.' *Journal of Peasant Studies*, Vol. 26, No. 2 & 3, pp. 140–81.

Kant, I. (1983). *Perpetual Peace: A Philosophical Sketch*. Hackett.

Kapadia, K. (1995a). 'The Profitability of Bonded Labour: The Gem-Cutting Industry in Rural South India.' *Journal of Peasant Studies*, Vol. 22, No. 3, pp. 446–83.

Kapadia, K. (1995b). 'Where Angels Fear to Tread? Third World Women' and 'Development'.' *Journal of Peasant Studies*, Vol. 22, No. 2, pp. 356–68.

Kapadia, K. (1996). 'Property and Proper Chastity: Women's Land Rights in South Asia Today.' *Journal of Peasant Studies*, Vol. 23, No. 4, pp. 166–73.

Karshenas, M. (1994). 'Concepts and Measurement of Agricultural Surplus: A New Accounting Framework with Application to Iran.' *Journal of Peasant Studies*, Vol. 21, No. 2, pp. 235–61.

Karshenas, M. (1996/1997). 'Dynamic Economies and the Critique of Urban Bias.' *Journal of Peasant Studies*, Vol. 24, No. 1 & 2, pp. 60–102.

Karshenas, M. (2000). 'Relative Prices and the International Comparison of Real Agricultural Output and Productivity.' *Journal of Peasant Studies*, Vol. 27, No. 4, pp. 112–37.

Kautsky, K. (1988). *The Agrarian Question*. Zwan Publications.

Kay, C. (1974). 'Comparative Development of the European Manorial System and the Latin American Hacienda System.' *Journal of Peasant Studies*, Vol. 2, No. 4, pp. 418–45.

Kay, G. (1975). *Development and Underdevelopment: A Marxist Analysis*. Macmillan.

Keddie, N.R. (1957). 'Labor Problems of Pakistan.' *The Journal of Asian Studies*, Vol. 16, No. 4, pp. 575–89.

Kedia, K.L. and Sinha, A. (1987). *Roots of Underdevelopment: A Peep into India's Colonial Past*. Varanasi: Self Published.

Kelly, K.D. (1984). 'Review of '*the Fall and Rise of the Asiatic Mode of Production*'.' *Contemporary Sociology*, Vol. 13, No. 2, p. 198.

Kemal, A.R. (2001) 'Structural Adjustment, Macroeconomic Policies, and Poverty Trends in Pakistan' paper presented at the Asia and Pacific Forum on Poverty: Reforming Policies and Institutions for Poverty Reduction at the Asian Development Bank, Manila, 5–9 February 2001. Retrieved from http://www.adb.org/poverty/forum/pdf/Kemal.pdf

Kemal, A.R., Irfan, M., and Mahmood, N. (2003). *Population of Pakistan: An Analysis of 1998 Population and Housing Census*. Pakistan Institute of Development Economics.

Khan, I.A. (1976). 'The Middle Classes in the Mughal Empire.' *Social Scientist*, Vol. 49.

Khan, I.A. (2003). 'Impact of Privatisation on Employment and Output in Pakistan.' *The Pakistan Development Review*, Vol. 42, No. 4, Part II, pp. 513–36.

Khan, M.A. (2003). 'Restructuring of Financial Sector in Pakistan.' *Journal of the Institute of Bankers Pakistan*, No. 70, pp. 49–68.

Khan, M.A. and Qayyum, A. (2006). 'Trade Liberalisation, Financial Sector Reforms, and Growth.' *The Pakistan Development Review*, Vol. 45, No. 4, pp. 711–31.

Khan, M.H. (1975). *The Economics of the Green Revolution in Pakistan*. Praeger.

Khan, M.H. (1977). 'Land Productivity, Farm Size and Returns to Scale in Pakistan Agriculture.' *World Development*, Vol. 5, No. 4, pp. 317–23.

Khan, M.H. (1979). 'Farm Size and Land Productivity Relationships in Pakistan.' *Pakistan Development Review*, Vol. 18, No. 1, pp. 69–76.

Khan, M.H. (1981). *Underdevelopment and Agrarian Structure in Pakistan*. Westview Press.

Khan, M.H. (1985). *Lectures on Agrarian Transformation in Pakistan*. Pakistan Institute of Development Economics.

Khan, M.H. (1998). *Public Policy and the Rural Economy of Pakistan*. Vanguard.

Khan, M.H. and Maki, D.R. (1979). 'Effects of Farm Size and Economic Efficiency: The Case of Pakistan.' *American Journal of Agricultural Economics*, Vol. 61, No. 1, pp. 64–9.

Khan, M.H. and Maki, D.R. (1980). 'Relative Efficiency by Farm Size and the Green Revolution in Pakistan.' *Pakistan Development Review*, Vol. 19, No. 1, pp. 51–64.

Kiernan, V.G. (1967). 'Marx and India.' *Socialist Register*, pp. 159–89.

Kiernan, V.G. (1974). *Marxism and Imperialism*. Edward Arnold.

Kiernan, V.G. (1981). *Development, Imperialism, and Some Misconceptions*: Norwich. Geo Books.

Kiernan, V.G. (1995). *Imperialism and Its Contradictions*. Routledge.

Kitching, G. (1985). 'Suggestions for a Fresh Start on an Exhausted Debate.' *Canadian Journal of African Studies*, Vol. 19, No. 1, pp. 116–26.

Klein, I. (2000). 'Materialism, Mutiny and Modernization in British India.' *Modern Asian Studies*, Vol. 34, No. 3, pp. 545–80.

Koebner, R. (1951). 'Despot and Despotism. Vicissitudes of a Political Term.' *Journal of the Warburg and Courtauld Institutes*, Vol. 14, No. 3/4, pp. 275–302.

Kokin, M.D. (1931). 'The Asian Bureaucracy as a Class.' In A.M. Bailey & J.R. Llobera (Eds.), *The Asiatic Mode of Production*. Routeledge & Kegan Paul.

Kolakowski, L. (1978). *Main Currents of Marxism*. Oxford.

Konings, P. (1998). 'Unilever, Contract Farmers and Co-Operatives in Cameroon: Crisis and Response.' *Journal of Peasant Studies*, Vol. 26, No. 1, pp. 112–38.

Korovkin, T. (2000). 'Weak Weapons, Strong Weapons? Hidden Resistance and Political Protest in Rural Ecuador.' *Journal of Peasant Studies*, Vol. 27, No. 3, pp. 1–29.

Kosambi, D.D. (1956). An Introduction to the Study of Indian History. Retrieved from http://www.vidyaonline.net/arvindgupta/introhisddk.pdf

Kosambi, M. and Brush, J.E. (1988). 'Three Colonial Port Cities in India.' *Geographical Review*, Vol. 78, No. 1, pp. 32–47.

Krader, L. (1975). *The Asiatic Mode of Production: Sources, Development and Critique in the Writings of Karl Marx*. Van Gorcum & Comp.

Krader, L. (1981). Principles and Critique of the Asiatic Mode of Production. In A.M. Bailey & J.R. Llobera (Eds.), *The Asiatic Mode of Production: Science and Politics*. Routledge & Kegan Paul.

Krishnaji, N. (1995). 'Family Size and Wealth—Standing Chayanovon His Head in the Indian Context.' *Journal of Peasant Studies*, Vol. 22, No. 2, pp. 261–78.

Kumar, A. (2000). 'Beyond Muffled Murmurs of Dissent? Kisan Rumour in Colonial Bihar.' *Journal of Peasant Studies*, Vol. 28, No. 1, pp. 95–125.

Kumar, D. (1965). *Land and Caste in South India*. Cambridge.

Kumar, D. (1985). 'Private Property in Asia? The Case of Medieval South India.' *Comparative Studies in Society and History*, Vol. 27, No. 2, pp. 340–66.

Kurosaki, T. (2000). 'Compilation of Agricultural Production Data for India and Pakistan Areas, c.1900–1990.' Paper presented at the Asian Historical Statistics Project, Hitotsubashi University.

Kurosaki, T. (2002). 'Agriculture in India and Pakistan, 1900–95: A Further Note.' *Economic and Political Weekly*, Vol. 37, No. 30, pp. 3149–52.

Kutty, B.M. (2004a). 'Political Parties of Pakistan and the Labor Movement.' www.thesouthasian.org/archives/000172.html

Kutty, B.M. (2004b). 'The Pakistani Labor Movement: Bhutto and Zia Years.' Retrieved from http://www.thesouthasian.org/archives/000181.html

Labour Force Survey. (2005–06). Retrieved from http://www.statpak.gov.pk/depts/fbs/publications/lfs2005_06/lfs2005_06.html

Labour Force Survey. (2008). Retrieved from http://www.statpak.gov.pk/depts/fbs/publications/lfs2006_07/lfs2006_07.html

Laclau, E. (1977). *Politics and Ideology in Marxist Theory*. New Left Books.

Lal, D. (1984). *The Hindu Equilibrium: Cultural Stability and Economic Stagnation in India 1500 BC–AD 1980, Volume 1*. Oxford.

Lazarus, N. (1999). *Nationalism and Cultural Practice in the Postcolonial World*. Cambridge University Press.

Leach, E. (1959). 'Hydraulic Society in Ceylon.' *Past and Present*, Vol. 15, April, pp. 2–26

Leach, E. (1981). 'Hydraulic Society in Ceylon.' In A.M. Bailey & J.R. Llobera (Eds.), *The Asiatic Mode of Production: Science and Politics*. Routledge & Kegan Paul.

Lee, R. (2003). 'The Demographic Transition: Three Centuries of Fundamental Change.' *Journal of Economic Perspectives*, Vol. 17, No. 4, pp. 167–90.

LeFebvre, G. (2001). *The French Revolution: From Its Origins to 1793*. Routledge.

Lefebvre, G., Palmer, R.R., and Tackett, T. (2005). *The Coming of the French Revolution*. Princeton University Press.

Lenin, V.I. (1894a). 'The Economic Content of Narodism and the Criticism of It in Mr Struve's Book.' Retrieved from http:marxists.org/archive/lenin/by-date.htm

Lenin, V.I. (1894b). 'What the 'Friends of the People' Are and How They Fight the Social-Democrats.' Retrieved from http:marxists.org/archive/lenin/works/1894/friends/index.htm

Lenin, V.I. (1897a). 'The Heritage We Renounce.' Retrieved from http:marxists.org/archive/lenin/works/1897/dec/31c.htm

Lenin, V.I. (1897b). 'The Tasks of the Russian Social-Democrats.' Retrieved from http:marxists. org/archive/lenin/works/1897/dec/31b.htm

Lenin, V.I. (1899). *The Development of Capitalism in Russia.* Institute of Marxism Leninism.

Lenin, V.I. (1900). 'The War in China.' Retrieved from http:marxists.org/archive/lenin/ works/1900/dec/china.htm

Lenin, V.I. (1901a). 'Review of Home Affairs.' Retrieved from http:marxists.org/archive/lenin/ works/1901/home/index.htm

Lenin, V.I. (1901b). 'The Drafting of 183 Students into the Army.' Retrieved from http:marxists. org/archive/lenin/works/1901/jan/drafting.htm

Lenin, V.I. (1901c). 'The Workers' Party and the Peasantry.' Retrieved from http:marxists.org// archive/lenin/works/1901/feb/peasantry.htm

Lenin, V.I. (1902a). 'Draft Programme of the Russian Social-Democratic Labour Party' Retrieved from http:marxists.org/archive/lenin/works/1902/draft/02feb07.htm

Lenin, V.I. (1902b). 'Notes on Plekhanov's Second Draft Programme.' Retrieved from http:marxists.org/archive/lenin/works/1902/draft/04mar07.htm

Lenin, V.I. (1902c). 'The Draft of a New Law on Strikes.' Retrieved from http:marxists.org/archive/ lenin/works/1902/sep/01b.htm

Lenin, V.I. (1903a). 'The Autocracy Is Wavering . . .' Retrieved from http:marxists.org/archive/ lenin/works/1903/mar/01.htm

Lenin, V.I. (1903b). 'The Tasks of the Revolutionary Youth.' Retrieved from http:marxists.org/ archive/lenin/works/1903/sep/30b.htm

Lenin, V.I. (1904). 'One Step Forward, Two Steps Back.' Retrieved from http:marxists.org/archive/ lenin/works/1904/onestep/index.htm

Lenin, V.I. (1905a). 'A Revolution of the 1789 or the 1848 Type?' Retrieved from http:marxists. org/archive/lenin/works/1905/apr/00.htm

Lenin, V.I. (1905b). 'Between Two Battles.' Retrieved from http:marxists.org/archive/lenin/ works/1905/nov/15.htm

Lenin, V.I. (1905c). 'Oneness of the Tsar and the People, and of the People and the Tsar.Retrieved from http:marxists.org/archive/lenin/works/1905/aug/29.htm

Lenin, V.I. (1905d). 'Party Organisation and Party Literature.' Retrieved from http:marxists.org/ archive/lenin/works/1905/nov/13.htm

Lenin, V.I. (1905e). 'The First Results of the Political Alignment.' Retrieved from http:marxists. org/archive/lenin/works/1905/oct/31.htm

Lenin, V.I. (1905f). 'The Socialist Party and Non-Party Revolutionism.' Retrieved from http:marxists.org/archive/lenin/works/1905/dec/02.htm

Lenin, V.I. (1905g). 'The Third Congress of the R.S.D.L.P.' Retrieved from http:marxists.org/ archive/lenin/works/1905/3rdcong/index.htm

Lenin, V.I. (1905h). 'Two Tactics of Social-Democracy in the Democratic Revolution.' Retrieved from http:marxists.org/archive/lenin/works/1905/tactics/index.htm

Lenin, V.I. (1906a). 'An Attempt at a Classification of the Political Parties of Russia.' Retrieved from http:marxists.org/archive/lenin/works/1906/sep/30d.htm

Lenin, V.I. (1906b). 'Before the Storm.' Retrieved from http:marxists.org/archive/lenin/ works/1906/aug/21.htm

Lenin, V.I. (1906c). 'Report on the Unity Congress of the R.S.D.L.P.' Retrieved from http:marxists. org/archive/lenin/works/1906/rucong/iii.htm#v10pp65–328

Lenin, V.I. (1906d). 'The Declaration of Our Group in the Duma.' Retrieved from http:marxists. org/archive/lenin/works/1906/jun/22.htm

Lenin, V.I. (1906e). 'The Dissolution of the Duma and the Tasks of the Proletariat.' Retrieved from http:marxists.org/archive/lenin/works/1906/dissolut/index.htm

Lenin, V.I. (1907a). 'Notes of a Publicist.' Retrieved from http:marxists.org/archive/lenin/ works/1907/aug/22.htm

Lenin, V.I. (1907b). 'The Agrarian Programme of Social-Democracy in the First Russian Revolution, 1905–1907.' Retrieved from http:marxists.org/archive/lenin/works/1907/agrprogr/index.htm

Lenin, V.I. (1907c). 'The Menshevik Tactical Platform.' Retrieved from http:marxists.org/archive/lenin/works/1907/mar/00.htm

Lenin, V.I. (1908). 'The Agrarian Question in Russia Towards the Close of the Nineteenth Century.' Retrieved from http:marxists.org/archive/lenin/works/1908/agrquest/index.htm

Lenin, V.I. (1910a). 'The Campaign against Finland.' Retrieved from http:marxists.org/archive/lenin/works/1910/apr/26.htm

Lenin, V.I. (1910b). 'The Lessons of the Revolution.' Retrieved from http:marxists.org/archive/lenin/works/1910/oct/30.htm

Lenin, V.I. (1911a). 'Lev Tolstoi and His Epoch.' Retrieved from http:marxists.org/archive/lenin/works/1911/jan/22.htm

Lenin, V.I. (1911b). 'Speech Delivered in the Name of the R.S.D.L.P. At the Funeral of Paul and Laura Lafargue, November 20 (December 3), 1911.' Retrieved from http:marxists.org/archive/lenin/works/1911/nov/20.htm

Lenin, V.I. (1911c). 'Stolypin and the Revolution.' Retrieved from http:marxists.org/archive/lenin/works/1911/oct/18.htm

Lenin, V.I. (1911d). 'The Social Structure of State Power, the Prospects and Liquidationism.' Retrieved from http:marxists.org/archive/lenin/works/1911/mar/00.htm

Lenin, V.I. (1911e). 'The Social-Democratic Group in the Second Duma.' Retrieved from http:marxists.org/archive/lenin/works/1911/nov/00.htm

Lenin, V.I. (1913a). 'Backward Europe and Advanced Asia.' Retrieved from httpimarxists.org/archive/lenin/works/1913/may/18.htm

Lenin, V.I. (1913b). 'Critical Remarks on the National Question.' Retrieved from http:marxists.org/archive/lenin/works/1913/crnq/index.htm

Lenin, V.I. (1913c). 'Russian Government and Russian Reforms.' Retrieved from http:marxists.org/archive/lenin/works/1913/sep/26b.htm

Lenin, V.I. (1913d). 'The Development of Revolutionary Strikes and Street Demonstrations.' Retrieved from http:marxists.org/archive/lenin/works/1913/jan/12.htm

Lenin, V.I. (1914a). 'Karl Marx.' Retrieved from http:marxists.org/archive/lenin/works/1914/granat/index.htm

Lenin, V.I. (1914b). 'Serf Economy in the Rural Areas.' Retrieved from http:marxists.org/archive/lenin/works/1914/apr/20.htm

Lenin, V.I. (1914c). 'Socialism Demolished Again.' Retrieved from http:marxists.org/archive/lenin/works/1914/mar/00.htm

Lenin, V.I. (1914d). 'The Right of Nations to Self-Determination.' Retrieved from http:marxists.org/archive/lenin/works/1914/self-det/index.htm

Lenin, V.I. (1917). 'New Data on the Laws Governing the Development of Capitalism in Agriculture.' Retrieved from http:marxists.org/archive/lenin/works/1915/newdev/index.htm

Lenin, V.I. (1917). 'Imperialism: The Highest Stage of Capitalism.' Selected Works, Volume 1, Moscow.

Lenin, V.I. (1919). 'A Great Beginning: Heroism of the Workers in the Rear 'Communist Subbotniks'.' Retrieved from http://marxists.org/archive/lenin/works/1919/jun/28.htm

Lenin, V.I. (1920). 'Draft Theses on National and Colonial Questions for the Second Congress of the Communist International.' Retrieved from http:marxists.org/archive/lenin/works/1920/jun/05.htm

Lenin, V.I. (1920). 'Preliminary Draft Theses on the Agrarian Question for the Second Congress of the Communist International.' Retrieved from http:marxists.org/archive/lenin/works/1920/jun/x01.htm

Lenin, V.I. (1922). 'Pages from a Diary.' Retrieved from http:marxists.org/archive/lenin/works/1923/jan/02.htm

Lenin, V.I. (1923). 'On Cooperation.' Retrieved from http:marxists.org/archive/lenin/works/1923/jan/06.htm

Lerche, J. (1999). 'Politics of the Poor: Agricultural Labourers and Political Transformations in Uttar Pradesh.' *Journal of Peasant Studies*, Vol. 26, No. 2 & 3, pp. 182–241.

Lerche, J. (2007). 'Book Review: Labour Bondage in Western India.' *Journal of Agrarian Change*, Vol. 7, No. 3, pp. 405–23.

Levada, I.A. (1962). 'Wittfogel's 'Oriental Despotism': A Soviet Review.' In A.M. Bailey & J.R. Llobera (Eds.), *The Asiatic Mode of Production: Science and Politics*. Routledge & Kegan Paul.

Lewin, G. (1963). 'Wittfogel on the Asiatic Mode of Production.' In A.M. Bailey & J.R. Llobera (Eds.), *The Asiatic Mode of Production: Science and Politics*. Routledge & Kegan Paul.

Lewin, M. (1968). *Russian Peasants and Soviet Power. A Study of Collectivization*. George Allen and Unwin.

Lewis, A. (1955). *Theory of Economic Growth London*. Allen & Unwin.

Lewis, M.W. and Wigen, K. (1999). 'A Maritime Response to the Crisis in Area Studies.' *Geographical Review*, Vol. 89, No. 2, pp. 161–8.

Lewis, S.R. (1969). *Economic Policy and Industrial Growth in Pakistan*. Allen and Unwin.

Lindberg, S. (1994). 'New Farmers' Movements in India as Structural Response and Collective Identity Formation: The Cases of the Shetkari Sanghatana and the Bku.' *Journal of Peasant Studies*, Vol. 21, No. 3 & 4, pp. 95–125.

Link, E.M. (1967). 'Review: Social Origins of Dictatorship and Democracy: Lord and Peasant in the Making of the Modern World by Barrington Moore, Jr.' *The Journal of Economic History*, Vol. 27, No. 2, pp. 261–2.

Lipton, M. (1977). *Why Poor People Stay Poor. A Study of Urban Bias in World Development*. Temple Smith.

London, C.E. (1997). 'Class Relations and Capitalist Development: Subsumption in the Colombian Coffee Industry, 1928–92.' *Journal of Peasant Studies*, Vol. 24, No. 4, pp. 269–95.

Lowdermilk, M.K. (1972). *Diffusion of Dwarf Wheat Technology in Pakistan's Punjab* (Unpublished doctoral dissertation). Cornell University.

Lowenthal, D. (1968). 'Review: Social Origins of Dictatorship and Democracy: Lord and Peasant in the Making of the Modern World by Barrington Moore, Jr.' *History and Theory*, Vol. 7, No. 2, pp. 257–78.

Lu, X. (1997). 'The Politics of Peasant Burden in Reform China.' *Journal of Peasant Studies*, Vol. 25, No. 1, pp. 113–38.

Ludden, D. (Ed.). (1995). *Agricultural Production and Indian History*. Oxford University Press.

Lukacs, G. (1967). 'What Is Orthodox Marxism?' Retrieved from http://www.marxists.org/archive/lukacs/works/history/orthodox.htm

Luxemburg, R. (1973). *Accumulation of Capital*. Monthly Review Press.

M. Barratt-Brown. (1974). *The Economics of Imperialism*. Penguin.

Macaulay, T.B. (1835). 'Minute by the Honourable T.B. Macaulay, Dated the 2nd February 1835.' Retrieved from http://www.columbia.edu/itc/mealac/pritchett/00generallinks/macaulay/txt_minute_education_1835.html

MacFarquhar, R. (1995). 'The Founding of the China Quarterly.' *The China Quarterly*, No. 143, pp. 692–6.

Maddison, A. (2001). *The World Economy: A Millennial Perspective*. OECD.

Mahmood, M. (1977). 'The Pattern of Adoption of Green Revolution Technology and Its Effects on Land Holdings in the Punjab.' *Pakistan Economic and Social Review*, Vol. 15, No. 2.

Mahmood, M. (1992). 'The Pattern of Adoption of Green Revolution Technology and Its Effect on Landholdings in the Punjab.' In K. Ali (Ed.), *Pakistan: The Political Economy of Rural Development*. Vanguard.

Mahmood, M. and Nadeem-ul-Haque. (1981). 'Farm Size and Productivity Revisited.' *Pakistan Development Review*, Vol. 20, No. 2.

Mahmood, N. (2009). *Population and Development: Demographic Research at PIDE.* Pakistan Institute of Development Economics: Report 4.

Maine, H. (1880). *Village Communities in the East and West.* Henry Holt.

Maine, H. (1907). *Lectures on the Early History of Institutions.* J. Murray.

Majid, N. (1998). 'The Joint System of Share Tenancy and Self-Cultivation: Evidence from Sind, Pakistan.' *Journal of Peasant Studies*, Vol. 25, No. 3, pp. 63–85.

Majid, N. (2000). 'Pakistan: Employment, Output and Productivity.' International Labour Office, Geneva.

Major, A.J. (1999). 'State and Criminal Tribes in Colonial Punjab: Surveillance, Control and Reclamation of the 'Dangerous Classes'.' *Modern Asian Studies*, Vol. 33, No. 3, pp. 657–88.

Majumdar R.C., H.C. Paychaudhuri, and Datta, K. (1967). *An Advanced History of India.* Macmillan; St. Martin's Press.

Malaney, K.U. (1965). *A Portrait of S.I.T.E.* Publicity Society of Pakistan.

Mandle, J.R. (1983). 'Sharecropping and the Plantation Economy in the United States South.' *Journal of Peasant Studies*, Vol. 10, No. 2–3, pp. 120–9.

Mann, G. (2001). 'The State, Race, and 'Wage Slavery' In the Forest Sector of the Pacific North-West United States.' *Journal of Peasant Studies*, Vol. 29, No. 1, pp. 61–88.

Mann, S.A. (1987). 'The Rise of Wage Labour in the Cotton South: A Global Analysis.' *Journal of Peasant Studies*, Vol. 14, No. 2, pp. 226–42.

Manning, B. (1975). 'The Peasantry and the English Revolution.' *Journal of Peasant Studies*, Vol. 2, No. 2, pp. 133–58.

Manucci, N. (1996). *Storia Do Mogor.* Low Price Publications.

Mao Tse-Tung. (1926). 'Analysis of the Classes In Chinese Society.' Retrieved from http:marxists. org/reference/archive/mao/selected-works/volume–1/mswv1_1.htm

Mao Tse-Tung. (1927). 'Report on an Investigation of the Peasants Movement in Hunan.' Retrieved from http:marxists.org/reference/archive/mao/selected-works/volume–1/mswv1_2. htm

Mao Tse-Tung. (1933). 'How to Differentiate the Classes in the Rural Areas.' Retrieved from http:marxists.org/reference/archive/mao/selected-works/volume–1/mswv1_8.htm

Marshall, P.J. (1976). *East India Fortunes: The British in Bengal in the Eighteenth Century.* Clarendon Press.

Marshall, P.J. (1997). 'British Society in India under the East India Company.' *Modern Asian Studies*, Vol. 31, No. 1, pp. 89–108.

Martin, N.E. (1999). 'The Political Economy of Bonded Labour in the Pakistani Punjab.' *Contributions to Indian Sociology*, Vol. 43, No. 1, pp. 35–59.

Martinez-Alier, J. (1995). 'In Praise of Smallholders.' *Journal of Peasant Studies*, Vol. 23, No. 1, pp. 140–8.

Martins, J.d.S. (2002). 'Representing the Peasantry? Struggles for/About Land in Brazil.' *Journal of Peasant Studies*, Vol. 29, No. 3 & 4, pp. 300–35.

Marx, K. (1843a). 'Critique of Hegel's Philosophy of Right.' Retrieved from http:marxists.org/ archive/marx/works/1843/critique-hpr/ch02.htm#003

Marx, K. (1843b). 'Marx to Arnold Ruge, May 1843.' Retrieved from http:marxists.org/archive/ marx/works/1843/letters/43_05.htm

Marx, K. (1844). *Economic & Philosophical Manuscripts of 1844.* Retrieved from http: marxists.org/ archive/marx/works/1859/critique-pol-economy/preface.htm

Marx, K. (1846). 'Letter from Marx to Pavel Vasilyevich Annenkov.' Retrieved from http:marxists. org/archive/marx/works/1846/letters/46_12_28.htm

Marx, K. (1847). 'The Poverty of Philosophy.' Retrieved from http:marxists.org/archive/marx/ works/1847/poverty-philosophy/index.htm

Marx, K. (1853). 'The Future Results of the British Rule in India.' Retrieved from http: marxists. org/archive/marx/works/1853/07/22.htm

Marx, K. (1853a). 'Marx to Engels, 2 June 1853.' Retrieved from http:marxists.org/archive/marx/
works/1853/letters/53_06_02.htm

Marx, K. (1853b). 'The British Rule in India.' Retrieved from http:marxists.org/archive/marx/
works/1853/06/25.htm

Marx, K. (1853c). 'Marx to Engels, 14 June 1853.' Retrieved from http:marxists.org/archive/marx/
works/1853/letters/53_06_14.htm

Marx, K. (1857). 'Revelations of the Diplomatic History of the 18th Century.' Retrieved from
http:marxists.org/archive/marx/works/1857/rince/index.htm

Marx, K. (1857a). 'Indian News in the New-York Daily Tribune, August 14.' Retrieved from
http:marxists.org/archive/marx/works/1857/08/14a.htm

Marx, K. (1857b). 'The Indian Revolt.' Retrieved from http:marxists.org/archive/marx/
works/1857/09/16.htm

Marx, K. (1858a). *Grundrisse*. Retrieved from http:marxists.org/archive/marx/works/1857/
grundrisse/ch09.htm#p471

Marx, K. (1858b). 'Lord Canning's Proclamation and Land Tenure in India.' Retrieved from
http:marxists.org/archive/marx/works/1858/06/07.htm

Marx, K. (1859). *A Contribution to the Critique of Political Economy*. Retrieved from http:marxists.
org/archive/marx/works/1859/critique-pol-economy/preface.htm

Marx, K. (1861). *Theories of Surplus Value*. Retrieved from http:marxists.org/archive/marx/works/
date/index.htm

Marx, K. (1867). 'Poland and the Russian Menace.' Retrieved from http:marxists.org/archive/marx/
works/1867/01/22.htm

Marx, K. (1877). 'Marx to Editor of the Otyecestvenniye Zapisky.' Retrieved from http:marxists.
org/archive/marx/works/1877/11/rince.htm

Marx, K. (1881). 'Letter to Vera Zasulich.' Retrieved from http:marxists.org/archive/marx/
works/1881/03/zasulich1.htm

Marx, K. (1998a). *Capital Volume I*. In K. Marx and F. Engels, *Classics in Politics* (CD-Rom).
London: The Electric Book Company.

Marx, K. (1998b). *Capital Volume II*. In K. Marx and F. Engels, *Classics in Politics* (CD-Rom).
London: The Electric Book Company.

Marx, K. (1998c). *Capital Volume III*. In K. Marx and F. Engels, *Classics in Politics* (CD-Rom).
London: The Electric Book Company.

Marx, K. (1973). *Grundrisse*. Penguin.

Marx, K. (1982). *Herr Vogt*. New Park

Marx, K. and Engels, F. (1960). *On Colonialism*. Moscow Foreign Languages Press.

Marx, K. and Engels, F. (1968). *German Ideology*. Progress Publishers.

Marx, K. and Engels, F. (1979). *Pre-Capitalist Socio-Economic Formations*. Progress Publishers.

Marx, K. (1998d). *Preface to the Contribution to the Critique of Political Economy*. In K. Marx and
F. Engels, *Classics in Politics* (CD-Rom). London: The Electric Book Company.

Marx, K. and Engels, F. (1998). *The Communist Manifesto*. In K. Marx and F. Engels, *Classics in
Politics* (CD-Rom). London: The Electric Book Company.

Mason, P. (1973). 'Delusions and Discoveries About the British in India.' *Pacific Affairs*, Vol. 46,
No. 3, pp. 430–4.

Mawdsley, E. (1998). 'After Chipko: From Environment to Region in Uttaranchal.' *Journal of
Peasant Studies*, Vol. 25, No. 4, pp. 36–54.

McClelland, G.M. (1997). 'Social Origins of Industrial Agriculture: Farm Dynamics in California's
Period of Agricultural Nascence.' *Journal of Peasant Studies*, Vol. 24, No. 3, pp. 1–24.

McClelland, G.M. (1997). 'Social Origins of Industrial Agriculture: Farm Dynamics in California's
Period of Agricultural Nascence.' *Journal of Peasant Studies*, Vol. 24, No. 3, pp. 1–24.

McEwan, A. (1970). 'Problems of Interregional and Inter Sectoral Allocation: The Case of
Pakistan.' *Pakistan Development Review*, Vol. 10, No. 1, pp. 1–23.

McEwan, A. (1971). *Development Alternatives in Pakistan*. Harvard University Press.

McFarlane, B., Cooper, S., and Jaksic, M. (2005). 'The Asiatic Mode of Production: A New Phoenix.' *Journal of Contemporary Asia*, Vol. 35, No. 3.

McNeish, J. (2002). 'Globalization and the Reinvention of Andean Tradition: The Politics of Community and Ethnicity in Highland Bolivia.' *Journal of Peasant Studies*, Vol. 29, No. 3 & 4, pp. 228–69.

Memmi, A. (1991). *The Colonizer and the Colonized*. Beacon Press.

Mendelson, S., Cowlishaw, G., and Rowcliffe, J.M. (2003). 'Anatomy of a Bushmeat Commodity Chain in Takoradi, Ghana.' *Journal of Peasant Studies*, Vol. 31, No. 1, pp. 73–100.

Menzel, J.M. (1956). 'The Sinophilism of J.H.G. Justi.' *Journal of the History of Ideas*, Vol. 17, No. 3, pp. 300–10.

Merkle, R. (2003). 'Ningxia's Third Road to Rural Development: Resettlement Schemes as a Last Means to Poverty Reduction?' *Journal of Peasant Studies*, Vol. 30, No. 3 & 4, pp. 160–91.

Methold, W. (1931). *Relations of Golconda in the Early Seventeenth Century*. London: printed for the Hakluyt Society.

Mill, J. (1821). *The History of British India*. London: Baldwin, Cradock and Joy.

Mill, J.S. (1848). *Principles of Political Economy*. London: Longmans, Green and Co.

Milonakis, D. (1995). 'Commodity Production and Price Formation before Capitalism: A Value Theoretic Approach.' *Journal of Peasant Studies*, Vol. 22, No. 2, pp. 327–55.

Misra, A.M. (2000). ''Business Culture' and Entrepreneurship in British India, 1860–1950.' *Modern Asian Studies*, Vol. 34, No. 2, pp. 333–48.

Misra, B.B. (1961). *The Indian Middle Classes*. Oxford University Press.

Mitrany, D. (1961). *Marx against the Peasant. A Study in Social Dogmatism*. University of North Carolina Press.

Mlynář, Z. (1990). *Can Gorbachev Change the Soviet Union? The International Dimensions of Political Reform*. Westview Press.

Mody, A. (1982). 'Population Growth and the Commercialization of Agriculture: India 1890–1940.' *IESHR*, Vol. 19, No. 3 & 4.

Mohammad, G. (1963). 'Some Physical and Economic Determinants of Cotton Production in West Pakistan.' *Pakistan Development Review*, Vol. 3, No. 4, pp. 491–526.

Mohammad, G. (1964a). 'Some Strategic Problems in Agriculture in Pakistan.' *Pakistan Development Review*, Vol. 4, No. 2, pp. 223–60.

Mohammad, G. (1964b). 'Water Logging and Salinity in the Indus Plain: A Critical Analysis of Some of the Major Conclusions of the Revelle Report.' *Pakistan Development Review*, Vol. 4, No. 3, pp. 357–403.

Mohammad, G. (1965). 'Private Tubewell Development and Cropping Patterns in West Pakistan.' *Pakistan Development Review*, Vol. 5, No. 1, pp. 1–53.

Mohiuddin, Y.N. (2007). *Pakistan: A Global Studies Handbook*. ABC-CLIO.

Montesquieu. (1977). *The Spirit of the Laws*. University of California Press.

Mooij, J. (1998). 'Food Policy and Politics: The Political Economy of the Public Distribution System in India.' *Journal of Peasant Studies*, Vol. 25, No. 2, pp. 77–101.

Mookerjee, R. (1919). *Occupancy Right: Its History and Incidents*. University of Calcutta.

Moore, B. (1966). *Social Origins of Dictatorship and Democracy: Lord and Peasant in the Making of the Modern World*. Beacon Press.

Moreland, W.H. (1929). *Agrarian Systems of Moslem India*. Cambridge: Heffer.

Morison, S.T. (1911). *The Economics Transition in India*. London: Murray.

Morris, M.D. (1960). 'The Recruitment of an Industrial Labour Force in India, with British and American Comparisons.' *Comparative Studies in Society and History*, Vol. 2, No. 3, pp. 305–28.

Morvaridi, B. (1995). 'Contract Farming and Environmental Risk: The Case of Cyprus.' *Journal of Peasant Studies*, Vol. 23, No. 1, pp. 30–45.

Mujahid. (1978). 'A Note of Measurement of Poverty and Income Inequalities in Pakistan: Some Observations Are Methodology.' *The Pakistan Development Review*, Vol. 17, No. 3, pp. 365–77.

Mujtaba, H. (1992, December). 'The Living Dead.' *Newsline*, p. 49.

Mukherjee, A. (2004). 'Some Thoughts on the Drain of Wealth: Colonial India and Imperial Britain.' *World History Bulletin*, Vol. XX, No. 1.

Mukherjee, C. And Krishnaji, N. (1995). 'Dynamics of Family Size and Composition: A Computer Simulation Study with Reference to Rural India.' *Journal of Peasant Studies*, Vol. 22, No. 2, pp. 279–99

Mukherjee, R. (1933). *Land Problems of India*. London: Longmans, Green & Co.

Mukherjee, R. (1985). 'Early British Imperialism in India: A Rejoinder.' *Past and Present*, Vol. 106, Feb., pp. 169–73.

Mukherjee, S.N. (1970). 'Class, Caste and Politics in Calcutta, 1815–50.' In E.R. Leach & S.N. Mukherjee (Eds.), *Elites in South Asia*. Cambridge University Press.

Mukhia, H. (1981). 'Was There Feudalism in Indian History.' *Journal of Peasant Studies*, Vol. VIII, No. 19.

Mukhia, H. (1985). 'Peasant Production and Medieval Indian Society.' In T.J. Byres & H. Mukhia (Eds.), *Feudalism and Non-European Societies*. Frank Cass.

Mukhia, H. (1985b). 'Was There Feudalism in Indian History?' In T.J. Byres & H. Mukhia (Eds.), *Feudalism and Non-European Societies*. Frank Cass.

Murray, W.E. (2002). 'From Dependency to Reform and Back Again: The Chilean Peasantry During the Twentieth Century.' *Journal of Peasant Studies*, Vol. 29, No. 3 & 4, pp. 190–227.

Myrdal, G. (1968). *Asian Drama: An Inquiry into the Poverty of Nations*. Penguin Books.

Nakajima, A. and Izumi, H. (1995). 'Economic Development and Unequal Exchange among Nations: Analysis of the U.S., Japan, and South Korea.' *Review of Radical Political Economics*, Vol. 27, No. 3, pp. 86–94.

Nanavati, M.B. and Anjaria, J.J. (1944). *The Indian Rural Problem*. Bombay: Indian Society of Agricultural Economics.

Nanda, M. (2001). 'We Are All Hybrids Now: The Dangerous Epistemology of Post-Colonial Populism.' *Journal of Peasant Studies*, Vol. 28, No. 2, pp. 162–86.

Nandy, A. (1983). *The Intimate Enemy*. Oxford University Press.

Naoroji, D. (1901). *Poverty and Un-British Rule*. London S. Sonnenschein Publication

Naqvi, S.N.H. (1983). 'The P.I.D.E. Macro-Econometric Model of Pakistan's Economy.' Pakistan Institute of Development Economics.

Naseem, M. (1971). *Small Farmer and Agricultural Transformation in Pakistan Punjab* (Unpublished doctoral dissertation). University of California.

Naseem, M. (1973). 'Mass Poverty in Pakistan: Some Preliminary Findings.' *Pakistan Development Review*, Vol. 12, No. 4, pp. 317–60.

Naseem, M. (1977). 'Rural Poverty and Landlessness in Pakistan.' In *Poverty and Landlessness in Rural Asia*. International Labour Organisation, Geneva.

Needham, J. (1959). 'Review of 'Oriental Despotism'.' *Science and Society*, Vol. XXIII, No. 23, pp. 58–65.

Needham, J. (1969). *The Grand Titration: Science and Society in East and West*. Allen & Unwin.

Nesfield, J.C. (1885). *Brief View of the Caste System of the North-Western Provinces and Oudh-Allahabad*. Government of the North-Western Provinces.

Ness, G.D. (1967). 'Review: Social Origins of Dictatorship and Democracy: Lord and Peasant in the Making of the Modern World by Barrington Moore, Jr.' *American Sociological Review*, Vol. 32, No. 5, pp. 818–20.

Newman, R.P. (1992). *Owen Lattimore and The 'Loss' of China*. University of California Press.

Nolan, P. (1993). 'The Causation and Prevention of Famines: A Critique of A.K. Sen.' *Journal of Peasant Studies*, Vol. 21, No. 1, pp. 1–28.

Noman, O. (1988). *The Political Economy of Pakistan 1947–85*. London and New York: KPI.

Nove, A. (1979). 'Review of 'the Alternative in Eastern Europe'.' *Soviet Studies*, Vol. 31, No. 4, pp. 595–600.

Nugent, S. (2002). 'Whither Campesinato? Historical Peasantries of Brazilian Amazonia.' *Journal of Peasant Studies*, Vol. 29, No. 3 & 4, pp. 162–89.

Nulty, L. (1972). *The Green Revolution in West Pakistan: Implications of Technological Change.* Praeger Publishers.

Nureev, R. (1990). 'The Asiatic Mode of Production and Socialism.' *Pravda and Voprosy ekonomiki*, No. 3, pp. 47–58.

O'Laughlin, B. (1998). 'Missing Men? The Debate over Rural Poverty and Women-Headed Households in Southern Africa.' *Journal of Peasant Studies*, Vol. 25, No. 2, pp. 1–48.

O'Leary, B. (1989). *The Asiatic Mode of Production: Oriental Despotism, Historical Materialism, and Indian History.* Basil Blackwell.

O'Malley, L.S.S. (1932). *Indian Caste Customs.* The University Press.

Omvedt, G. (1994). '"We Want the Return of Our Sweat": The New Peasant Movement in India and the Formation of a National Agricultural Policy.' *Journal of Peasant Studies*, Vol. 21, No. 3–4, pp. 126–64.

Orenstein, H. (1954). 'The Evolutionary Theory of V. Gordon Childe'. *Southwestern Journal of Anthropology*, Vol. 10, No. 2, pp. 200–14.

Overton, J. (2001). 'Peasants on the Internet? Informalization in a Global Economy.' *Journal of Peasant Studies*, Vol. 28, No. 4, pp. 149–70.

Pakistan Census of Agricultural Machinery (1977). Pakistan Ministry of Food and Agriculture, Agricultural Census Organisation.

Pakistan Economic Survey, 1984–85 (1985). Federal Bureau of Statistics, Government of Pakistan.

Pakistan Economic Survey, 1994–95 (1995). Federal Bureau of Statistics, Government of Pakistan.

Pakistan Fertilizer Demand Forecast Study (1978). ESSO Pakistan Fertilizer, Karachi.

Pakistan Growth through Adjustment (1988). Report 7118-Pak, World Bank.

Pakistan Labour Gazette (July August) (1965). Government of Pakistan.

Pakistan Promoting Rural Growth and Poverty Reduction (2007). Sustainable Development Unit, South Asia Region, World Bank.

Pakistan Social and Living Standards Measurement Survey (2006–7). Retrieved from http://www.statpak.gov.pk/rince/fbs/statistics/pslm2006_07/pslm2006_07.html

Pakistan Statistical Yearbook (1948–2007). Federal Bureau of Statistics, Government of Pakistan.

Pakistan Trade, VI (1955). Government of Pakistan.

Pakistan: Largest Cities and Towns and Statistics of Their Population (2008). Retrieved from http://world-gazetteer.com/wg.php?x=&men=gcis&lng=en&des=wg&geo=-172&srt=npan&col=abcdefghinoq&msz=1500&pt=c&va=&srt=pnan

Papanek, G. (1967). *Pakistan's Development: Social Goals and Private Incentives.* Harvard University Press.

Pasha, H. And Hasan, T. (1982). 'Development Ranking of Districts of Pakistan.' *Pakistan Journal of Applied Economics*, Vol. 1 Winter, pp. 157–92.

Patnaik, P. (1996/1997). 'Trade as a Mechanism of Economic Retrogression.' *Journal of Peasant Studies*, Vol. 24, No. 1 & 2, pp. 211–25.

Patnaik, P. (2006). 'Appreciation: The Other Marx.' In I. Husain (Ed.), *Karl Marx on India.* Tulika Books.

Patnaik, U. (1990a). 'Capitalist Development in Agriculture Further Comment.' In U. Patnaik (Ed.), *Agrarian Relations and Accumulation: The 'Mode of Production Debate in India'.* Oxford University Press

Patnaik, U. (1990b). 'Capitalist Development in Agriculture: Note.' In U. Patnaik (Ed.), *Agrarian Relations and Accumulation: The 'Mode of Production Debate in India'.* Oxford University Press

Patnaik, U. (Ed.). (1990). *Agrarian Relations and Accumulation: The 'Mode of Production Debate in India'.* Oxford University Press

Patnaik, U. and Dingawey, M. (Eds.), (1985). *Chains of Servitude: Bondage and Slavery in India.* Sangam Books.

Peabody, N. (2001). 'Cents, Sense, Census: Human Inventories in Late Precolonial and Early Colonial India '*Comparative Studies in Society and History*, Vol. 43, No. 4, pp. 819–50.

Peers, D.M. (2006). *India under Colonial Rule 1700–1885*. Harlow and London: Pearson Longmans.

Perlin, F. (1983). 'Proto-Industrialization and Pre-Colonial South Asia.' *Past and Present*, Vol. 98.

Perlin, F. (1985). 'State Formation Reconsidered.' *Modern Asian Studies*, Vol. 19, No. 3, pp. 415–80.

Perlin, F. (1985). 'Concepts of Order and Comparison, with a Diversion on Counter Ideologies and Corporate Institutions in Late Pre-Colonial India.' In T.J. Byres & H. Mukhia (Eds.), *Feudalism and Non-European Societies*. Frank Cass.

Pernau, M. (Ed.). (2006). *The Delhi College: Traditional Elites, the Colonial State, and Education before 1857*. Oxford University Press.

Persky, J. (1992). 'Unequal Exchange and Dependency Theory in George Fitzhugh.' *History of Political Economy*, Vol. 24, No. 1, pp. 117–28.

Petras, J. (1978). *Critical Perspectives on Imperialism and Social Class in the Third World*. Monthly Review Press.

Petras, J. and Veltmeyer, H. (2001). 'Are Latin American Peasant Movements Still a Force for Change? Some New Paradigms Revisited.' *Journal of Peasant Studies*, Vol. 28, No. 2, pp. 83–118.

Petras, J. and Veltmeyer, H. (2002). 'The Peasantry and the State in Latin America: A Troubled Past, an Uncertain Future.' *Journal of Peasant Studies*, Vol. 29, No. 3 & 4, pp. 41–82.

Phear, S.J.B. (1880). *The Aryan Village*. Macmillan.

Platje, S.T. (1975). *Mhudi*. Quagga Press.

Plekhanov, G. (1883). 'Socialism and the Political Struggle.' Retrieved from http:marxists.org/archive/rinceton/1883/struggle/chap1.htm

Plekhanov, G. (1889). 'A New Champion of Autocracy.' Retrieved from http:marxists.org/archive/rinceton/1889/champ/pt04.htm

Plekhanov, G. (1897). 'Belinski and Rational Reality.' Retrieved from http:rinceto.org/archive/rinceton/1897/belinski/part3.htm

Plekhanov, G. (1969). *Fundamental Problems of Marxism*. Lawrence and Wishart.

Pochat, V. (2007). *Dams and Development Project: DDP*. International Policy in Shared River Basins.

Poggi, G. (1968). 'Review: Social Origins of Dictatorship and Democracy: Lord and Peasant in the Making of the Modern World by Barrington Moore, Jr.' *The British Journal of Sociology*, Vol. 19, No. 2, pp. 215–17.

Polo, M (1959). *The Travels of Marco Polo*. Penguin Books.

Population Association of Pakistan (2009). Retrieved from http://www.pap.org.pk/statistics/population.htm

Population Census of Pakistan (1951). Government of Pakistan.

Post, C. (1995). 'The Agrarian Origins of Us Capitalism: The Transformation of the Northern Countryside before the Civil War.' *Journal of Peasant Studies*, Vol. 22, No. 3, pp. 389–445.

Post, C. (2003). 'Plantation Slavery and Economic Development in the Antebellum Southern United States.' *Journal of Agrarian Change*, Vol. 3, No. 3, pp. 289–332.

Poulantzas, N. (1973). *Political Power and Social Classes*. New Left Books.

Prakash, G. (1990). *Bonded Histories: Genealogies of Labor Servitude in Colonial India*. Cambridge University Press.

Privatisation Commission (2008). Retrieved from http://www.privatisation.gov.pk/about/Completed%20Transactions%20(new).htm

Programme of Communist Party of India (Marxist-Leninist) (2005). Retrieved from http://www.cpiml.in/programme.htm

Programme of the Communist Party of India (Marxist) (2000). Retrieved from http://www.cpim.org/documents/programme.htm

Qadeer, M.A. (1977). *An Evaluation of the Integrated Rural Development Programme*. Pakistan Institute of Development Economics, Monograph No. 19.

Qadir, A. (2003). 'Unions and Challenges: An Analysis of the Pakistani Situation.' Retrieved from http://fesportal.fes.de/pls/portal30/docs/FOLDER/WORLDWIDE/GEWERKSCHAFTEN/BERICHTE/PAKISTAN.HTML

Qureshi, S.K. (1971). 'Price Incentives for the Production of High Yielding Varieties of Wheat: A Comment.' *Pakistan Development Review*, Vol. 11, No. 1, pp. 54–62.

Qureshi, S.K. (1973). 'The Problem of Agricultural Taxation in Pakistan and Alternative Solution: A Comment.' *Pakistan Development Review*, Vol. 12, No. 4, pp. 433–7.

Qureshi, S.K. (1974). 'The Performance of Village Markets for Agricultural Produce: A Case Study of Pakistan.' *Pakistan Development Review*, Vol. 13, No. 3, pp. 280–307.

Qureshi, S.K. (1974). 'Price Responsiveness of Marketed Surplus of Wheat in Pakistan.' *Pakistan Development Review*, Vol. 13, No. 2, pp. 115–28.

Qureshi, S.K. and Arif, G.M. (2001). *Profile of Poverty in Pakistan, 1998–99*. Pakistan Institute of Development Economics (MIMAP Technical Report No. 2).

Qureshi, S.K. and Qureshi, M. (2004). 'Impact of Changing Profile of Rural Land Market in Pakistan.' *The Pakistan Development Review*, Vol. 43, No. 4, pp. 471–92.

Rahman, S. (1998). *Who Owns Pakistan*. Retrieved from http://richpaki.tripod.com/

Raikes, P. and Gibbon, P. (2000). "Globalisation' and African Export Crop Agriculture.' *Journal of Peasant Studies*, Vol. 27, No. 2, pp. 50–93.

Raj, K. (2000). 'Colonial Encounters and the Forging of New Knowledge and National Identities: Great Britain and India, 1760–1850.' *Osiris* 2nd Series, Vol. 15, *Nature and Empire: Science and the Colonial Enterprise* (2000), pp. 119–34. University of Chicago Press.

Raj, K.N., Bhattacharya, Guha, and Padhi (Eds.), (1985). *Essays on the Commercialization of Indian Agriculture*. Oxford University Press.

Rajan, M.S. (1969). 'The Impact of British Rule in India.' *Journal of Contemporary History*, Vol. 4, No. 1, pp. 89–102.

Ram, N. (1972). 'Impact of Early Colonisation on Economy of South India '*Social Scientist*, Vol. 1, No. 4, pp. 47–65.

Rao, J.M. (1999). 'Agrarian Power and Unfree Labour.' *Journal of Peasant Studies*, Vol. 26, No. 2 & 3, pp. 242–62.

Rao, J.M. (1999b). 'Freedom, Equality, Property and Bentham: The Debate over Unfree Labour.' *Journal of Peasant Studies*, Vol. 27, No. 1, pp. 97–121.

Rao, R.S. (1990). 'In Search of the Capitalist Farmer.' In U. Patnaik (Ed.), *Agrarian Relations and Accumulation: The 'Mode of Production Debate in India'*. Oxford University Press

Raquibuzzaman, M. (1966). 'Marketed Surplus Function of Major Agricultural Commodities in Pakistan.' *Pakistan Development Review*, Vol. 6, No. 3, pp. 376–94.

Raulet, H.M. and Uppal, J.S. (1970). 'The Social Dynamics of Economic Development in Rural Punjab.' *Asian Survey*, Vol. 10, No. 4, pp. 336–47.

Raychaudhuri, H. (1953). *Political History of Ancient India: From the Accession of Parikshit to the Extinction of the Gupta Dynasty*. University of Calcutta.

Raychaudhuri, T. And Habib, I. (Eds.), (1982). *The Cambridge Economic History of India 1200–1750*. Cambridge University Press.

Reed, J.-P. (2003). 'Indigenous Land Policies, Culture and Resistance in Latin America.' *Journal of Peasant Studies*, Vol. 31, No. 1, pp. 137–56.

Rehman, S. (1965). 'Strategy for Industrialization in Pakistan.' In A.I. Qureshi (Ed.), *Third Five-Year Plan and Other Papers*. Rawalpindi.

Report of National Commission on Agriculture (1976). India Ministry of Agriculture, New Delhi: Controller of Publication.

Report of the Agrarian Committee (1949). Karachi: Pakistan Muslim League.

Report of the Government Hari Enquiry Committee 1947–48 (1948). Karachi: Sind, Hari Enquiry Committee.

Report of the Pakistan Agricultural Inquiry Committee 1951–52 (1952). Karachi: Pakistan Ministry of Food and Agriculture.

Report of the Pakistan Food and Agricultural Commission 1960 (1960). Karachi: Pakistan Ministry of Food and Agriculture.

Report of the Tenancy Legislation Committee (1945). Karachi: Sind, Tenancy Legislation Committee.

Riazanov, D. (1925a). 'Karl Marx on China and India.' *Under the Banner of Marxism*, Vol. 1, No. 2.

Riazanov, D. (1925b). 'Revolution in China and in Europe.' *Pravda*, 14 January 1925.

Richard, S. (1965). 'A View of Pakistan's Industrial Development.' *Asian Survey*, Vol. 5, No. 12, pp. 590–5.

Risley, H.H. (1981). *The Tribes and Castes of Bengal.* 2 Vol., Calcutta.

Roberts, R. (1975). *The Classic Slum.* Penguin.

Rochin, R.I. (1971). *A Micro-Economic Analysis of Smallholder Response to High-Yielding Varieties of Wheat in West Pakistan* (Unpublished doctoral dissertation). Michigan State University.

Rodinson, M. (1977). *Islam and Capitalism.* Middlesex: Harmondsworth.

Roe, S.T. (1926). *The Embassy of Sir Thomas Roe to India 1615–19.* Oxford University Press.

Rogaly, B. (1996). 'Agricultural Growth and the Structure of 'Casual' Labour-Hiring in Rural West Bengal.' *Journal of Peasant Studies*, Vol. 23, No. 4, pp. 141–65.

Rosas, P. (1943). 'Caste and Class in India.' *Science & Society*, Vol. 7, No. 2, pp. 141–67.

Rose, E. (1951). 'China as a Symbol of Reaction in Germany, 1830–1880.' *Comparative Literature*, Vol. 3, No. 1, pp. 57–76.

Rose, H.A. (1919). *A Glossary of the Tribes and Castes of the Punjab and North-West Frontier Provinces.* Government Printing Press, Lahore.

Ross, D. (1883). *The Land of the Five Rivers and Sindh.* London. Retrieved from http://www.scribd.com/doc/19964326/The-Land-of-the-Five-Rivers-and-Sindh

Rostow, W.W. (1960). *The Stages of Economic Growth: A Non-Communist Manifesto.* Cambridge University Press.

Roth, I.J. (1971). 'Government and the Development of Industry in Pakistan: 1947–1967.' *Asian Survey*, Vol. 11, No. 6, pp. 570–81.

Rothman, S. (1970). 'Barrington Moore and the Dialectics of Revolution: An Essay Review.' *American Political Science Review*, Vol. 64.

Roy, M.N. (1987). 'Indian in Transition.' In S. Ray (Ed.), *Selected Works of M.N. Roy Volume 1 1917–1922.* Oxford University Press.

Rudra, A. (2000). 'Unfree Labour and Indian Agriculture.' In K. Basu (Ed.), *Agrarian Questions.* Oxford University Press.

Rudra, A., Majid, A., and Talib, B.D. (1990). 'Big Farmers of Punjab.' In U. Patnaik (Ed.), *Agrarian Relations and Accumulation: The 'Mode of Production Debate in India'.* Oxford University Press.

Russell, R.C. (2000). 'Parliamentary Enclosures, Common Rights and Social Change: Evidence from the Parts of Lindsey in Lincolnshire.' *Journal of Peasant Studies*, Vol. 27, No. 4, pp. 54–111.

Russell, R.V. (1993). *The Tribes and Castes of the Central Provinces of India.* Asian Educational Services.

Sabir, M. and Aftab, Z. (2006). 'Province-Wise Growth Patterns in Human Capital Accumulation.' *The Pakistan Development Review*, Vol. 45, No. 4 Part II, pp. 873–90.

Sachs, J. (2005). *The End of Poverty: Economic Possibilities for Our Time.* Penguin Press.

Sahu, G.B., Madheswaran, S., and Rajasekhar, D. (2004). 'Credit Constraints and Distress Sales in Rural India: Evidence from Kalahandi District, Orissa.' *Journal of Peasant Studies*, Vol. 31, No. 2, pp. 210–41.

Said, E. (1978). *Orientalism.* Routledge & Kegan Paul.

Saith, A. (1995). 'From Collectives to Markets: Restructured Agriculture-Industry Linkages Inrural China–Some Micro-Level Evidence.' *Journal of Peasant Studies*, Vol. 22, No. 2, pp. 201–60.

Salam, A. (1976). 'Resource Productivity in Punjab Agriculture.' *Pakistan Development Review*, Vol. 15, No. 2, pp. 115–33.

Salam, A. (1977a). 'Economic Analysis of Fertilizer Demand in the Punjab.' *Pakistan Development Review*, Vol. 15, No. 2, pp. 181–91.

Salam, A. (1977b). 'Technical Change, Tenant Displacement and Adjustment in Pakistan.' *Pakistan Development Review*, Vol. 16, No. 4, pp. 435–48.

Salam, A. (1978). 'Factor Inputs Use and Factor Productivity on Different Farm Categories in the Punjab.' *Pakistan Development Review*, Vol. 17, No. 3, pp. 316–32.

Salam, A. (1981). 'Farm Tractorization, Fertilizer Use and Productivity of Western Wheat in Pakistan.' *Pakistan Development Review*, Vol. 20, No. 3.

Sanderatne, N. (1986). 'Landowners and Land Reforms in Pakistan.' In K. Ali (Ed.), *Pakistan: The Political Economy of Rural Development*. Vanguard Publications, Lahore.

Sangwan, S. (1995). 'The Sinking Ships: Colonial Policy and the Decline of Indian Shipping 1735–1835.' In R.M. MacLeod & D. Kumar (Eds.), *Technology and the Raj: Western Technology and Technical Transfers to India, 1700–1947*. Sage Publications.

Santos, T.D. (1970). 'The Structure of Dependence.' *The American Economic Review*, Vol. 60, May.

Saran, P. (1941). *The Provincial Government of the Mughals 1526–1658*. Allahabad, Kitabistan.

Sarkar, S. (1983). *Modern India 1885–1947*. Macmillan, India.

Sathar, Z.A. (1989). 'Possible Reasons for Retardation in Fertility Change in South Asia.' *The Pakistan Development Review*, Vol. 28, No. 4, pp. 655–60.

Sathar, Z.A. (1992). 'Child Survival and Changing Fertility Patterns in Pakistan.' *The Pakistan Development Review*, Vol. 31, No. 4, pp. 699–713.

Sathar, Z.A. (1997). *Women's Autonomy, Livelihood and Fertility: Study of Rural Punjab*. Pakistan Institution of Development Economics.

Sathar, Z.A. and Casterline, J.B. (2001). 'Onset of Fertility Transition in Pakistan.' *The Pakistan Development Review*, Vol. 40, No. 3, pp. 237–8.

Saul, S.B. (1960). *Studies in British Overseas Trade 1870–1914*. Liverpool.

Sawer, M. (1977). *Marxism and the Question of the Asiatic Mode of Production*. Martinus Nijhoff, The Hague.

Sayeed, A. (June 1990). 'The Emergence of a New Breed of Entrepreneurs under Zia'. *Herald*.

Senart, E. (1977). *Caste in India*. (Trans. Sir E. Denison Ross), Datta Book Centre, Delhi.

Schweickart, D. (1991). 'The Politics and Morality of Unequal Exchange.' *Economics & Philosophy*, Vol. 7, No. 1, pp. 13–36.

Scott, C.D. (1977). 'Review of Griffin 1974.' *Journal of Peasant Studies*, Vol. 4, No. 2, pp. 244–8.

Scott, J. (1976). *The Moral Economy of the Peasant*. Yale University Press.

Scott, J.C. (1990). *Weapons of the Weak: Everyday Forms of Peasant Resistance*. Oxford University Press.

Seal, A. (1968). *The Emergence of Indian Nationalism*. Cambridge University Press.

Sen, A. (1982). *The State, Industrialization, and Class Formation in India: A Neo-Marxist Perspective on Colonialism Underdevelopment and Development*. Routledge and Kegan Paul.

Sen, A. (1982). *The State, Industrialization, and Class Formation in India: A Neo-Marxist Perspective on Colonialism Underdevelopment and Development*. Routledge and Kegan Paul.

Sen, A. (1993). 'The Causation and Prevention of Famines: A Reply.' *Journal of Peasant Studies*, Vol. 21, No. 1, pp. 29–40.

Sen, N. (1992). *India in the International Economy 1858–1913: Some Aspects of Trade and Finance*. Calcutta: Orient Longman.

Sen, S. (1998). *An Empire of Free Trade: The East India Company and the Making of the Colonial Marketplace*. University of Pennsylvania Press.

Shabad, T. (1959). 'Non-Western Views of The 'Hydraulic Society'.' *Annals of the Association of American Geographers*, Vol. 49, No. 3, pp. 324–5.

Shah, N.M. (1989). 'Female Labour Force Participation and Fertility Desire in Pakistan: An Empirical Investigation.' *The Pakistan Development Review*, Vol. 14, No. 2, pp. 185–206.

Shah, S.A.H., and Khalid, M. (2007). 'Incompatibility of Laws and Natural Resources: A Case Study of Land Revenue Laws and Their Implications in Federal Areas of Pakistan.' *The Pakistan Development Review*, Vol. 46, No. 4 Part II, pp. 1105–17.

Shah, S.M.A. (2007). 'Corporate Debt Policy—Pre- and Post-Financial Market Reforms: The Case of the Textile Industry of Pakistan.' *The Pakistan Development Review*, Vol. 46, No. 4, Part II, pp. 465–78.

Shah, W. (1766). *Heer*. Retrieved from http://www.apnaorg.com/poetry/heercomp/

Shaheed, Z. (2007). *The Labour Movement in Pakistan: Organisation and Leadership in Karachi in the 1970s*. Oxford University Press.

Shanin, T. (1971). *Peasants and Peasant Societies*. Basil Blackwell.

Shanin, T. (1972). *The Awkward Class: Political Sociology of Peasantry in a Developing Society, Russia 1910–1925*. Oxford: Clarendon Press.

Shanin, T. (1973). 'The Nature and Logic of Peasant Economy Part I.' *Journal of Peasant Studies*, Vol. 1, No. 1, pp. 63–80.

Shanin, T. (1974). 'The Nature and Logic of the Peasant Economy Part II.' *Journal of Peasant Studies*, Vol. 1, No. 2, pp. 186–206.

Shanin, T. (1985). *The Roots of Otherness: Russia's Turn of Century. Vol. I, Russia as a 'Developing Society'*. Macmillan.

Shanin, T. (1986). *The Roots of Otherness: Russia's Turn of Century. Vol. II, Russia, 1905–07, Revolution as Moment of Truth*. Macmillan.

Shanin, T. (Ed.). (1983). *Late Marx and the Russian Road: Marx and the 'Peripheries of Capitalism'*. Routledge & Kegan Paul.

Shapiro, G. (1967). 'Review: Social Origins of Dictatorship and Democracy: Lord and Peasant in the Making of the Modern World by Barrington Moore, Jr.' *American Sociological Review*, Vol. 32, No. 5, pp. 820–1.

Sharma, R.S. (1965). *Indian Feudalism*. Calcutta University Press.

Sharma, R.S. (1985). 'How Feudal Was Indian Feudalism?' In T.J. Byres & H. Mukhia (Eds.), *Feudalism and Non-European Societies*. Frank Cass.

Shelvankar, K.S. (1943). *The Problem of India*. Harmondsworth: Penguin.

Sherring, M.A. (1872). *Hindu Tribes and Castes*. Thacker, Spink & Co.

Shirazi, S.A. (2006). 'Patterns of Urbanization in Pakistan: A Demographic Appraisal.' Retrieved from http://paa2006.princeton.edu/download.aspx?submissionId=61209

Siddiqi, A. (Ed.). (1995). *Trade and Finance in Colonial India, 1750–1860*. Oxford University Press.

Siddiqi, A.H. (1986). 'Agricultural Changes in Punjab in Nineteenth Century: 1850–1900.' *GeoJournal*, Vol. 12, No. 1, pp. 43–56.

Siddiqi, N.A. (1970). *Land Revenue Administration under the Mughals 1700–1750*. Bombay: Asia Publishing House.

Siddique, M.Z., Ansari, J.A., and Salman, Q.M. (2006). 'Governing the Labour Market: The Impossibility of Corporatist Reforms.' *The Pakistan Development Review*, Vol. 45, No. 4 Part II, pp. 981–1000.

Siddiqui, A.H. and Iqbal, J. (2005). 'Impact of Trade Openness on Output Growth for Pakistan: An Empirical Investigation.' MPRA Paper No. 23757, posted on 9 July 2010. University Library of Munich, Germany. Retrieved from http://mpra.ub.uni-muenchen.de/23757/1/MPRA_paper_23757.pdf

Siddiqui, R. And Kemal, A.R. (2002). *Remittances, Trade Liberalisation, and Poverty in Pakistan: The Role of Excluded Variables in Poverty Change Analysis*. Pakistan Institute of Development Economics.

Singh, C. (1988). 'Centre and Periphery in the Mughal State: The Case of Seventeenth Century Punjab.' *Modern Asian Studies*, Vol. 22, No. 2, pp. 299–318.

Singh, H. (1983). *The Asiatic Mode of Production: A Critical Analysis*. University of Toronto.

Singh, H. (2002). 'Caste, Class and Peasant Agency in Subaltern Studies Discourse: Revisionist Historiography, Elite Ideology.' *Journal of Peasant Studies*, Vol. 30, No. 1, pp. 91–134.

Singh, H. (Ed.). (1977). *Caste among Non-Hindus in India*. New Delhi: National.

Sinha, S. (2000). 'The 'Other' Agrarian Transition? Structure, Institutions and Agency in Sustainable Rural Development.' *Journal of Peasant Studies*, Vol. 27, No. 2, pp. 169–204.

Sinha, S., Gururani, S., and Greenberg, B. (1997). 'The 'New Traditionalist' Discourse of Indian Environmentalism.' *Journal of Peasant Studies*, Vol. 24, No. 3, pp. 65–99.

Sivakumar, S.S. (2001). 'The Unfinished Norödnik Agenda: Chayanov, Marxism and Marginalism Revisited.' *Journal of Peasant Studies*, Vol. 29, No. 1.

Smith, A. (1976). *Wealth of Nations*. University of Chicago Press.

Smith, E. (1979). 'Comment on M. Dove's Review of the Asiatic Mode of Production.' *American Anthropologist*, Vol. 81, No. 2, pp. 370–2.

Soboul, A. (1975). *The French Revolution, 1787–1799: From the Storming of the Bastille to Napoleon*. Random House.

Soomro, G.Y. (1986). 'Determinants of Aggregate Fertility in Pakistan.' *The Pakistan Development Review*, Vol. 25, No. 4, pp. 553–70.

Southwood, J. (1924). 'Thomas Stephens, S.J., the First Englishman in India.' *Bulletin of the School of Oriental Studies, University of London*, Vol. 3, No. 2, pp. 231–40.

Spear, P. (1958). 'From Colonial to Sovereign Status: Some Problems of Transition with Special Reference to India.' *The Journal of Asian Studies*, Vol. 17, No. 4, pp. 567–77.

Spivak, G.C. (1988). *In Other Worlds: Essays in Cultural Politics*. Routledge.

Srivastava, R.S. (1999). 'Rural Labour in Uttar Pradesh: Emerging Features of Subsistence, Contradiction and Resistance.' *Journal of Peasant Studies*, Vol. 26, No. 2 & 3, pp. 263–315.

State of Human Rights 2007 (2008). Human Rights Commission of Pakistan.

Stein, B. (1980). *Peasant, State and Society of Medieval South India*. Oxford University Press.

Stein, B. (1985). 'Politics, Peasants and the Deconstruction of Feudalism in Medieval India.' In T.J. Byres & H. Mukhia (Eds.), *Feudalism and Non-European Societies*. Frank Cass.

Stevenson, H.N.C. (1954). 'Status Evaluation in the Hindu Caste System.' *The Journal of the Royal Anthropological Institute of Great Britain and Ireland*, Vol. 84, No. ½, pp. 45–65.

Stillman, L. (1984). 'Review of 'the Rise and Fall of the Asiatic Mode of Production'.' *Journal of American Oriental Society*, Vol. 104, No. 4, p. 767.

Stojanovi'c, S. (1973). *Between Ideals and Reality: A Critique of Socialism and Its Future* (Translated by Gerson S. Sher). Oxford University Press.

Stokes, E. (1973). 'The First Century of British Colonial Rule in India: Social Revolution or Social Stagnation?' *Past and Present*, Vol. 58, pp. 136–60.

Stokes, E. (1978). *The Peasant and the Raj: Studies in Agrarian Society and Peasant Rebellion in Colonial India*. Cambridge University Press.

Strategies for Economic Growth and Development: The Bank's Role in Pakistan (1985). Asian Development Bank.

Swaminathan, M. (2000). 'Consumer Food Subsidies in India: Proposals for Reform.' *Journal of Peasant Studies*, Vol. 27, No. 3, pp. 92–114.

Sweezy, P. (1946). *The Theory of Capitalist Development*. Dobson.

Szymanski, A. (1977). 'Capital Accumulation on a World Scale and the Necessity of Imperialism.' *Critical Sociology*, Vol. 7, No. 35.

Takahashi, A. (1976). 'Pakistan: Land Reforms from Above.' In Z.M. Ahmed (Ed.), *Land Reforms in Asia, with Particular Reference to Pakistan*. International Labour Office.

Talbot, I. (1998). *Pakistan: A Modern History*. Hurst & Company.

Tanner, C.L. (1995). 'Class, Caste and Gender in Collective Action: Agricultural Labour Unions in Two Indian Villages.' *Journal of Peasant Studies*, Vol. 22, No. 4, pp. 672–98.

Tauger, M.B. (2003). 'Entitlement, Shortage and the Bengal Famine of 1943: Another Look.' *Journal of Peasant Studies*, Vol. 31, No. 1, pp. 45–72.

Tauger, M.B. (2004). 'Soviet Peasants and Collectivization, 1930–1939: Resistance and Adaptation.' *Journal of Peasant Studies*, Vol. 31, No. 3 & 4, pp. 427–56.

Tavernier, J.B.b.d.A. (1925). *Six Voyages: Travels in India*. Oxford University Press.

Terry, E. (1655). *A Voyage to East-India*. London: T.W.

Thadani, S. (2002). 'The Colonial Legacy—Myths and Popular Beliefs.' Retrieved from http://india_resource.tripod.com/colonial.html

Thanh, K.L. (1973). 'A Contribution to the Study of the Asiatic Mode of Production: The Case of Ancient Vietnam.' *La Pensée*, Vol. 171, No. 1.

The Consequences of Farm Tractors in Pakistan (1975). Staff Working Paper No. 210, World Bank.

The Fifth Five Year Plan 1978–1983 (1978). Planning Commission, Ministry of Food and Agriculture Pakistan.

The Report of the Indus Basin Research Assessment Group (1978). Pakistan Ministry of Food and Agriculture.

The State of Pakistan's Economy 1970–71 to 1979–80. (1980). Pakistan Institute of Development Economics.

The Study on Japanese Cooperation in Industrial Policy for Developing Economies: Pakistan. (1994). Institute of Developing Economies.

'The World Fact Book: Pakistan.' (2009). Retrieved from https://www.cia.gov/library/publications/the-world-factbook/geos/pk.html

Thorburn, S.S. (1886). *Mussalmans and Moneylender in the Punjab*. Blakewoods and Sons.

Thorburn, S.S. (1904). *The Punjab in Peace and War*. Blakewoods and Sons.

Thorner, A. (1982). 'Semi-Feudalism or Capitalism? Contemporary Debate on Classes and Modes of Production in India.' *Economic and Political Weekly*, Vol. XVII, December 4, 11, 18.

Thorner, D. (1947). 'Industrial Capital in India.' *Far Eastern Survey*, Vol. 16, No. 7, pp. 82–3.

Thorner, D. (1955). 'The Pattern of Railway Development in India.' *The Far Eastern Quarterly*, Vol. 14, No. 2, pp. 201–16.

Thurston, E. (2001). *Castes and Tribes of South India Asian*. Educational Services, New Delhi.

Tichelman, F. (1980). *The Social Evolution of Indonesia: The Asiatic Mode of Production and Its Legacy* (Translated by J. Sanders). Martinus Nijhoff, Hague, Boston, London.

Tocancipá-Falla, J. (2001). 'Women, Social Memory and Violence in Rural Colombia.' *Journal of Peasant Studies*, Vol. 28, No. 3, pp. 125–42.

Tomilson, B.R. (1982). 'Review: Congress and the Raj: Political Mobilization in Late Colonial India.' *Modern Asian Studies*, Vol. 16, No. 2, pp. 334–49.

Tomlinson, B.R. (1979). *The Political Economy of the Raj 1914–1947*. Cambridge University Press.

Tomlinson, B.R. (1982). 'The Political Economy of the Raj: The Decline of Colonialism.' *The Journal of Economic History*, Vol. 42, No. 1, pp. 133–7.

Toynbee, A.J. (1958). 'Review of 'Oriental Despotism: A Comparative Study of Total Power'.' *The American Political Science Review*, Vol. 52, No. 1, pp. 195–8.

Trevaskis, H.K. (1928). *The Land of the Five Rivers*. Oxford University Press.

Trevaskis, H.K. (1931). *The Punjab of Today*. Lahore.

Tripathi, R.P. (1956). *Some Aspects of Muslim Administration*. Central Book Depot.

Turner, G. (1990). *British Cultural Studies: An Introduction*. Allen & Unwin.

Ulmen, G.L. (1972). 'Review of Sur Le Mode Production Asiatique.' *Slavic Review*, Vol. 31, No. 2, pp. 438–41.

Varga, E. (1925). 'Economic Problems of the Revolution in China.' *Planned Economy*, Vol. 12.

Veltmeyer, H. (1997). 'New Social Movements in Latin America: The Dynamics of Class and Identity.' *Journal of Peasant Studies*, Vol. 25, p. 1.

Venkateshwarlu, D. and Corta, L. (2001). 'Transforma- Tions Intheageandgender of Unfreeworkers Onhybridcotton Seed Farms in Andhra Pradesh.' *Journal of Peasant Studies*, Vol. 28, No. 3, pp. 1–36.

Vermeer, E.B. (2003). 'Determinants of Income from Wages in Rural Wuxi and Baoding: A Survey of 22 Villages.' *Journal of Peasant Studies*, Vol. 30, No. 3 & 4, pp. 93–120.

'Visualizing Economics' (2008). Retrieved from http://www.visualizingeconomics.com/2008/01/20/ share-of-world-gdp/

Voltaire (2001). 'Customs.' *The Philosophical Dictionary*, Retrieved from http://history.hanover. edu/texts/voltaire/volcusto.html

Wallerstein, I.M. (1974). *The Modern World-System*. New York, London: Academic Press.

Ward & Trent, E.A. (Ed.). (1907–21). *The Cambridge History of English and American Literature*. New York: G.P. Putnam's Sons.

Warren, B. (1973). 'Imperialism and Capitalist Industrialization.' *New Left Review*, Vol. I, No. 81.

Warren, B. (1980). *Imperialism: Pioneer of Capitalism*. Verso.

Wasay, A. (1977). 'Urban Poverty Line Estimates.' *The Pakistan Development Review*, Vol. 16.

Washbook, D.A. (1988). 'Progress and Problems: South Asian Economic and Social History, 1720–1860.' *Modern Asian Studies*, Vol. XXII, pp. 57–96.

Washbrook, D. (1994). 'The Commercialization of Agriculture in Colonial India: Production, Subsistence and Reproduction in the 'Dry South', c. 1870–1930' *Modern Asian Studies*, Vol. 28, No. 1, pp. 129–64.

Weeks, J. and Dore, E. (1977). 'International Exchange and the Causes of Backwardness.' *Latin American Perspectives*, Vol. 6.

Weiss, A.M. (1991). *Culture, Class, and Development in Pakistan: The Emergence of an Industrial Bourgeoisie in Punjab*. Westview Press.

Well, R. (1979). 'The Development of the English Rural Proletariat and Social Protest, 1700–1850.' *Journal of Peasant Studies*, Vol. 6, No. 2, pp. 115–39.

Wheeler, J.C. (2007). 'Pakistan's Green Revolution.' Retrieved from http://www.oecd.org/docum ent/57/0,3343,en_2649_93721_39575353_1_1_1_1,00.html

White, B. (1997). 'Agro-Industry and Contract Farmers in Upland West Java.' *Journal of Peasant Studies*, Vol. 24, No. 3, pp. 100–36.

White, C.P. (1986). 'Everyday Resistance, Socialist Revolution and Rural Development: The Vietnamese Case.' *Journal of Peasant Studies*, Vol. 13, No. 2, pp. 49–63.

White, L. (1974). *Industrial Concentration and Economic Power in Pakistan*. Princeton University Press.

Whitehead, C. (2003). *Colonial Educators: The British Indian and Colonial Education Service 1858–1983*. London: I.B. Tauris.

Wickham, C. (1985). 'The Uniqueness of the East.' In T.J. Byres & H. Mukhia (Eds.), *Feudalism and Non-European Societies* (pp. 166–96). Frank Cass.

Wickham, C. (2005). *Framing the Early Middle Ages: Europe and the Mediterranean, 400–800*. Oxford University Press.

Wiener, J.M. (1976). 'Review: Social Origins of Dictatorship and Democracy: Lord and Peasant in the Making of the Modern World by Barrington Moore, Jr.' *History and Theory*, Vol. 15, No. 2, pp. 146–75.

Wikely, J.M. (1915). *Punjabi Mussalmans*. New Delhi: Manohar Publications.

Wilder, A. (1999). *The Pakistani Voter: Electoral Behaviour in the Punjab*. Oxford University Press.

Wilks, M. (1930). *Historical Sketches of the South of India, in an Attempt to Trace the History of Mysoor, from the Origin of the Hindoo Government of That State, to the Extinction of the Mohammedan Dynasty in 1799*. Printed at the Government Branch Press, Mysore.

Wilson, K. (1999). 'Patterns of Accumulation and Struggles of Rural Labour: Some Aspects of Agrarian Change in Central Bihar.' *Journal of Peasant Studies*, Vol. 26, No. 2 & 3, pp. 316–54.

Wink, A. (1986). *Land and Sovereignty in India. Agrarian Society and Politics under the Eighteenth Century Maratha Svarajya*. Cambridge University Press.

Wink, A. (1990). *Al-Hind: The Making of the Indo-Islamic World*. Leiden: E.J. Brill.

Wittfogel, K.A. (1935). 'The Stages of Development in Chinese Economic and Social History.' In A.M. Bailey & J.R. Llobera (Eds.), *The Asiatic Mode of Production: Science and Politics*. Routledge & Kegan Paul.

Wittfogel, K.A. (1938). 'The Theory of Oriental Society.' In A.M. Bailey & J.R. Llobera (Eds.), *The Asiatic Mode of Production: Science and Politics*. Routledge & Kegan Paul.

Wittfogel, K.A. (1963). *Oriental Despotism: A Comparative Study of Total Power*. Yale University Press.

Wolf, E. (1966). *Peasants*. Englewood Cliffs, New Jersey: Prentice Hall.

Wolf, E. (1969). *Peasant Wars in the Twentieth Century*. Harper and Row.

Wolpe, H. (1980). *The Articulation of Modes of Production: Essays from Economy and Society*. Routledge and Kegan Paul.

Worby, E. (1995). 'What Does Agrarian Wage-Labour Signify? Cotton, Commoditisation and Social Form in Gokwe, Zimbabwe.' *Journal of Peasant Studies*, Vol. 23, No. 1, pp. 1–29.

World Development Report (1990). The World Bank.

World Labour Report (1993). Geneva: International Labour Organisation.

World Population Data Sheet (2008). Retrieved from http://whip-round/pdf08/08WPDS_Eng.pdf

Wright, H.R.C. (1954). 'Some Aspects of the Permanent Settlement in Bengal.' Economic History Review, Vol. 7, No. 2, pp. 204–15.

Wrightson, K. (1977). 'Aspects of Social Differentiation in Rural England, c. 1580–1660.' *Journal of Peasant Studies*, Vol. 5, No. 1, pp. 33–47.

Wuyts, M. (1994). 'Accumulation, Industrialisation and the Peasantry: A Reinterpretation of the Tanzanian Experience.' *Journal of Peasant Studies*, Vol. 21, No. 2, pp. 159–93.

Xiande, L. (2003). 'Rethinking the Peasant Burden: Evidence from a Chinese Village.' *Journal of Peasant Studies*, Vol. 30, No. 3 & 4, pp. 45–74.

Yadav, B.N.S. (1973). *Society and Culture in North India in the Twelfth Century*. Allahabad University Press.

Yasin, C.G. (1972). *Socio-Economic Effects of Land Reforms of 1959* (Vol. 151). Punjab Board of Economic Inquiry.

Zafar, S. and Butt M.S. (2008). 'Impact of Trade Liberalization on External Debt Burden: Econometric Evidence from Pakistan' MPRA Paper no. 9548, posted 12 July 2008. University Library of Munich. Retrieved from http://mpra.ub.uni-muenchen.de/9548/1/MPRA_paper_9548.pdf

Zagorin, P. (1973). 'Theories of Revolution in Contemporary Historiography.' *Political Science Quarterly*, Vol. 88.

Zaidi, S.A. (1997). *Issues in Pakistan's Economy*. Oxford University Press.

Zaidi, S.A. (2005). *Issues in Pakistan's Economy*. Oxford University Press.

Zaman, A. (1995). 'The Government's Present Agreement with the IMF: Misgovernment or Folly?' *Pakistan Journal of Applied Economics*, Vol. 11, No. 1 & 2.

Zedong, M. (1926). 'Analysis of the Classes in Chinese Society.' Retrieved from http:marxists.org/reference/archive/mao/selected-works/volume–1/mswv1_1.htm

Zhang, H.X. (2003). 'Gender Difference in Inheritance Rights: Observations from a Chinese Village.' *Journal of Peasant Studies*, Vol. 30, No. 3 & 4, pp. 252–77.

Zingel, W.-P. (1998). 'Alleviating Urban Poverty: The Pakistan Way.' *Manpower Journal*, Vol. 34, No. 3, pp. 127–47.

Zmolek, M. (2000). 'The Case for Agrarian Capitalism: A Response to Albritton.' *Journal of Peasant Studies*, Vol. 27, No. 4, pp. 138–59.

Index